Directory of World Futures and Options

A guide to international futures and
options exchanges and products

MALCOLM J. ROBERTSON

Director of Derivative Products at Société Générale
Strauss Turnbull Equities Ltd

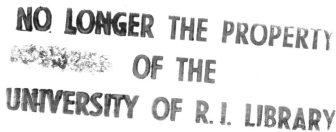

Prentice Hall
NEW YORK LONDON TORONTO
SYDNEY TOKYO SINGAPORE

First published in the United States of America by
Prentice Hall Inc.
440 Sylvan Avenue
Englewood Cliffs, NJ 07632, USA
A division of Simon & Schuster International Group

Published in Great Britain by
Woodhead-Faulkner Limited
Simon & Schuster International Group
Fitzwilliam House, 32 Trumpington Street
Cambridge CB2 1QY, England

First published 1990

Library of Congress Cataloging in Publication Data

Robertson, M. J. M. (Malcolm J. M.)
  Directory of world futures and options: a guide to
  international futures and options exchanges and
  products / Malcolm Robertson.
    p. cm.
  ISBN 0–13–217878–8: $125.00
  1. Futures market–Directories.   2. Commodity
    exchanges – Directories.   I. Title.
  HG6024.A3R63 1990
  332.6′45–dc20   90–35661
                                                       CIP

Designed by Geoff Green
Typeset by SB Datagraphics Ltd., Colchester
Printed in Great Britain by Page Bros, Norwich

1 2 3 4 5   94 93 92 91 90

Contents

Preface

There are over 80 specialist futures and options exchanges worldwide, and that figure does not include all the other exchanges that trade literally thousands of options on individual equities. It refers instead to exchanges that trade futures and options 'products', e.g. stock indices, wheat, treasury bonds, gold, etc. On these exchanges there are nearly 500 available products. Which is the right one to suit your investment, hedging or other requirements?

I was prompted to begin compiling this directory when, a couple of years ago, I was actively studying charts and as a technical analyst, was not particular about the instrument that I traded. If the charts said soyabean oil was going up, I wanted to know what was the best way to trade the instrument profitably, taking into account my risk/reward profile. What options and/or futures were available? At which exchanges were they traded? What were the contract sizes? What expiry months were available? The trading hours? Where could I obtain quotation information?, etc. Some products and in particular the futures and options available on these products were extremely volatile and the prices fast moving. How could I obtain the latest accurate contract specifications before prices moved against me?

All these and many other questions needed answering before I could take advantage of my view on the product. In addition, the information was never easily forthcoming. It seemed that there was no one place or publication that listed all currently available futures and options products, and thus my task commenced.

Of course, to the contract user, the first avenue of exploration is the futures broker. However, a futures broker is often a specialist in a particular area of futures and options, e.g. stock indices, precious metals or some other relatively narrow field. Perhaps your regular broker would not be fully aware of the particular instrument that you are interested in. And what if you are the specialist broker and although you are not regularly involved in, say, base metal futures you do not wish to lose this potential business? By the time you have obtained all the relevant information, prices have moved or the client has taken his business elsewhere.

The second course of action for the user or broker alike is to obtain the contract specifications from individual exchanges. But you do not know what you are looking for and you certainly are not aware that there are over 80 exchanges and 500 products available amongst them (an average of over six per exchange and a range over the exchanges from one to over 30). In the case of most major exchanges contract information is relatively easily obtainable within a short space of time. This is not necessarily the case for some smaller exchanges. What are their addresses to start with? Most users and potential users are aware of the Chicago Board of Trade, but what is widely known about the Maebashi Dried Cocoon Exchange? Additionally, new exchanges are materialising all the time, new products are being listed, defunct products delisted and existing contract specifications regularly changing to keep up to date with investment requirements. How do you keep track of them?

A fully cross-referenced directory of all these exchanges and products was needed. Not an easy task – first, to pinpoint those exchanges, I had to extract the appropriate contract information, then collate it into a standardised format and, over the period of compilation of the directory, it was vital to keep abreast of new developments.

This is the finished product. It is, I hope, the most extensive directory of its type, covering all the most widely traded futures and options products worldwide and a lot of the less widely followed ones as well.

To make the directory as useful and accessible as possible, four indexes are included, so that a particular product may be approached from several different starting points. There are, of course, other publications available in the field, but these either concentrate on particular areas of the futures and options product range, or are more narrative in their approach. I believe this to be the most comprehensive standardised reference on the subject, and I hope it will soon prove its worth.

Who will benefit from use of this directory?

I believe that the following categories of user, and probably many others as well, can be identified as those who would find this reference manual of futures and options exchanges and products invaluable:

1. *Brokers*, need to have the most up-to-date contract information with which to service their client base most effectively. This group is likely to be the first call from a potential investor and it is vital for them to be well informed.

2. *Producers*, the manufacturers of raw materials, the miners, the farmers and other producers will wish to establish in advance a price that they are able to obtain in the future for their supplies of materials.

3. *Consumers* – the converse of the case of the producers, but along the same principles, consumers of raw materials, etc. for secondary stages of production will also need to budget in advance for their raw material costs.

4. *Speculators*, want to know what products are available to suit different time frames, risk/reward profiles, etc.

5. *Hedgers*, need to be aware of the different products available for risk management and to be assured that they are using the optimum method of hedging.

6. *Institutional investment managers*, will need to be aware of any useful products to perform their role in the most efficient manner and to achieve higher performance figures.

7. *Corporate treasurers*, need to know what tools are available in their corporate risk management, purchasing, hedging and other activities.

8. *Arbitrageurs*, are always looking for new markets and products to tap for additional opportunities.

9. *Exchanges* – what new instruments are being introduced by competing exchanges and are our contract specifications still meeting investor requirements?

Malcolm J. Robertson

Introduction: a brief history of the development of the futures and options markets

Early origins

Futures and options are by no means a new instrument of this century. The history of options can be traced back to Holland and the tulip bulb industry of the late 1500s where suppliers wished to guarantee in advance the future price they would receive for their crops. In turn, consumers also wished to know what price they were going to have to pay so they could budget accordingly.

However, this early market was not one of the success stories of the industry as, in the early seventeenth century, many speculative writers of put options suffered severe losses as prices plummeted. The market closed for around 100 years. The Dutch were not deterred however and after only a brief time, options trading was recorded on certain Dutch stocks.

Futures trading started soon afterwards in Osaka, in rice futures and many of the initial products traded in Japan are still evident today. In fact, many of the current Japanese exchanges can trace their history back to these early rice markets.

The agricultural markets

Due to the vagaries of pestilence and weather, agricultural producers and consumers, particularly in the United States of America in the late nineteenth century, also wished to budget in advance for the prices paid and received for crops, and therefore once again the futures and options markets flourished, although this time in a more organised and regulated fashion. By fixing the price of a trade in advance, both producers and consumers alike could protect themselves against future adverse price movements. Throughout the text on individual exchanges, the date the exchange started trading is shown and often this dates back to the mid-1800s. Many of these exchanges have either continued to specialise in agricultural-based products or have diversified into financial futures and options.

Financial products

The movement off the Gold Standard and the breakdown of the Bretton Woods Agreement of fixed exchange rates in 1971 led to a new era of fully adjustable, and then floating, exchange rates through the Smithsonian Agreement. Sharp moves in oil prices and various systems of international foreign exchange and interest-rate policy led to high levels of volatility in the financial markets. Therefore, participants in the financial market-place became subject to the same types of volatility that the agriculture industry had experienced a century before.

It was only natural, therefore, for futures and options products to expand swiftly into this arena, led by the Chicago Mercantile Exchange and its newly created International Monetary Market and six currency contracts in 1972. In 1975 the Chicago Board of Trade created the world's first interest-rate contract on the Government National Mortgage Association (GNMA).

The current situation

There are now over 80 exchanges worldwide and this number is forever increasing with a continual innovation of new product types. There are now three clear generations of exchanges: first-generation agricultural exchanges, second generation financial exchanges and the third generation of electronic exchanges. The current major movements forward by the exchanges can be summarised under the following headings:

1. New product innovation – for example, the innovative interest-rate differential contracts at the CME.
2. Automation of trading and clearing functions – the main leaders in this field being the OM stable of exchanges.
3. Domestic and international trading links – the current inter-exchange link-ups are summarised in Appendix B. The main fungible trading link is the IOCC precious metal options link between the EOE, the VSE, the ME and the AOM.
4. Extended trading hours – some exchanges now have both early morning and late evening dealing sessions opening these exchanges to participants from other time zones, with the movement to 24-hour trading.

Where possible every exchange that is currently trading has been included in this directory. Some exchanges are in the process of opening and where the information is available, it has been included, even if trading has not yet started.

Contracts are now available on forwards, futures, options on futures, options on cash and options on physicals covering a range of products from Brazilian cruzados to Japanese yen, from interest-rate differentials to government bonds and from gold bullion to dried cocoons. There are nearly 500 different contracts included in this directory.

In addition, forwards, futures and call and put options are available on thousands of individual stock issues and there are a wealth of over-the-counter ('OTC') derivative products available. These products are not covered by this directory.

Specialities

Various exchanges have become renowned for their specialism in particular products and this is where their major strengths lie.

For example, the Philadelphia Stock Exchange leads the way in foreign currency options and although its sister exchange, the Philadelphia Board of Trade, lists a wide range of currency futures, the main market in currency options lies with the Chicago Mercantile Exchange. For a complete range, the PHLX lists currency futures for both American-style and European-style exercise procedures.

The Chicago Board Options Exchange is the specialist in US stock and stock index options, the New York Mercantile Exchange in energy-related products and the London Metal Exchange in base metal futures and options but there is no clear leader in agricultural products, with a whole host of exchanges offering both exclusive and similar products.

The Chicago Board of Trade is a major exchange in every sense of the word, leading the way in interest-rate futures and options.

In addition, many exchanges specialise primarily in 'local' products, for example the Swiss Options and Financial Futures Exchange, the OM stable of exchanges, the New Zealand Futures Exchange and the Deutsche Terminboerse, to name but a few.

In contrast, few exchanges offer a truly international range of products, the London International Financial

Futures Exchange and the Singapore International Monetary Exchange being the main examples.

Too many products chasing too few traders?

In addition to the comments above, many exchanges list individual products that have no clearly definable differences from products listed on other exchanges.

For example, there are US Government Treasury Bond futures contracts listed on the Chicago Board of Trade, the Tokyo Stock Exchange, the Mid-American Commodity Exchange and the London International Financial Futures Exchange.

There is of course the argument in favour of these competing products where there are clearly definable time zone boundaries, allowing trading 24 hours a day. This would be more satisfactory if more exchanges would liase in terms of contract fungibility. However, in the case of the three-month Euro-Deutschmark interest rate futures contract that trades in the same zone on two different exchanges, LIFFE and MATIF, there is clearly a waste of scarce resources and one must question the individual exchanges' long-term liquidities. This is even more true for the range of exchange-rate products worldwide and the range of agricultural products competed between the various domestic exchanges of Japan.

How to use the directory

An explanation of the full options and futures contract specifications as found throughout the text

Shown below is a descriptive explanation of the structure of an entry of an individual options and futures product traded on a specific exchange. In some cases not all these contract specifications are listed due to non-publication by the exchange, or, for a new contract, because the terms have not yet been formalised.

The contract specifications have been collated from sources believed to be reliable and every effort has been made to ensure the accuracy of these details, but it will be appreciated that contract specifications, in particular margin requirements, are subject to possible frequent change. It is advised that the most recent contract details should be clarified with the relevant exchange or your broker before executing any transactions in any product.

Contract name

Contract size

The underlying value of the contract, for example £25.00 multiplied by the FT-SE 100 Stock Index (representing a value of £40,000 when the Index stands at 1,600).

Standard delivery method

The method of delivery of the contract: (a) into a futures contract; (b) by settlement of cash value differentials; or (c) by delivery of a particular instrument or basket of instruments. In the case of physical deliveries of a commodity, the grade quality of the instrument deliverable is also shown. In the case of delivery of a futures contract through an options contract, the long holder of a call option or the short writer of a put option would both receive a long futures position in the relevant delivery month, whilst the long holder of a put option or the short writer of a call option would receive a short futures position, in all cases at the strike price.

Trading months	The range of calendar contract months normally available for the contract and where available the number of expiry months available for trading at any one time.
Trading hours	The formal exchange trading period for the contract, shown in local time, and alternative trading times on other exchanges for fungible products.
Price quotation method	The basis for displaying and calculating the price of a contract, i.e. in which currency the quote is made, and whether it is in index points, in tons, etc.
Minimum price move (value)	The smallest increment by which the future or option quote may move (one tick) and its value, calculated by multiplying the tick size by the contract size.
Daily price limits	The maximum price movement in the contract from the previous official closing level before trading is suspended for a period. All or some delivery months may be affected. Often price limits stay in force for a brief period, and are then expanded or lifted later in the day or on subsequent days.
Position limits	The maximum number of contracts (net) that may be held by one party. Sometimes this is only limited to those contract users classed as speculators, and may also apply to the largest number of option contracts that may be exercised on any one day.
Last trading day	The final permissible day (and where this differs from normal trading hours, the latest time) for trading a contract for each contract month.
Delivery day	The day for settlement of positions following the end of trading of the contract month either by cash settlement, futures or physical delivery. The first notice day (or notice period) is also shown where applicable. This is the first day (or period) that notices of intent to deliver the underlying security of a contract may be lodged, often at the seller's choice. In the case of options, the expiry timing of the option may be shown.
Initial (Variation) margin	The initial exchange (or clearing house) deposit required as a 'measure of good faith' when entering into a futures or options contract. This may be a specified cash amount or a percentage of the underlying value of the contract. 'Variation margin' is required on adverse movements in the option or

future, as a form of 'top-up' deposit. Some exchanges
will differentiate between speculators and hedgers for
margining purposes, and generally the quoted figures
are minimum requirements (individual brokers may
require a higher figure). For options, there are often a
series of margin requirements and therefore only those
margins relating to uncovered (or naked) short position
in puts or calls are shown. This data is subject to
frequent alteration according to market conditions,
and should be checked before dealing.

Spread margin

The allowable level of reduced margins (if applicable)
for spread transactions between one delivery month
and another, or in the case of traded options between
different strike prices. Sometimes, inter- or intra-
commodity spreads may be allowed. These are
generally not shown as the list may be extensive but
are often referred to.

Reuters Monitor (Quote)

The full monitor page on the Reuters quotation system
to obtain price information on the options or futures
contract and, where available, the quote symbol for
quick quotes.

Telerate page

The Telerate page for full options or futures contract
quotation information.

For exchange traded options only

Strike price intervals

The normal differential between the quoted strike
prices for the option (e.g. at 5-point intervals: i.e.
175.00, 180.00, 185.00, etc.).

Option type

Whether 'American style' i.e. the option is
continuously exercisable on any business day during its
life into the underlying instrument, or 'European style',
i.e. the option may only be exercised into the
underlying instrument on the last trading day or the
expiry of the contract.

*Method of introduction of
new series/strikes*

The basis upon which the exchange will introduce
higher or lower strike (exercise) prices to maintain in-
the-money and out-of-the-money series through the life
of the option, and where there is a standard policy,
when new delivery (expiry) months are added. Often
no new series are added shortly before an option series
is due to expire.

List of exchanges by abbreviation

AMEX American Stock Exchange
AOM Australian Options Market
APPTM Amsterdam Pork & Potato Terminal Market
ASX ASX Futures Market

BFE Baltic Futures Exchange
BIFFEX Baltic International Freight Futures Exchange
BM&F Bolsa Mercantil y de Futuros
BMSP Bolsa de Mercadorias de São Paulo

CBOE Chicago Board Options Exchange
CBOT Chicago Board of Trade
CME Chicago Mercantile Exchange
CME (IMM) International Monetary Market (CME)
CME (IOM) Index and Options Market (CME)
COMEX Commodity Exchange Inc.
CRCE Chicago Rice & Cotton Exchange
CSCE Coffee Sugar & Cocoa Exchange
CSE Copenhagen Stock Exchange

DTB Deutsche Terminboerse GmbH

EOE European Options Exchange (Optiebeurs) NV

FINEX Financial Instrument Exchange
FOB Finnish Options Brokers Ltd
FOX London FOX (The Futures & Options Exchange)
FTA Financiele Termijnmarkt Amsterdam NV

HGE Hokkaido Grain Exchange
HKFE Hong Kong Futures Exchange Ltd

ICEB Indonesian Commodity Exchange Board
IFOX Irish Futures & Options Exchange
INTEX International Futures Exchange (Bermuda)
IPE International Petroleum Exchange

JFCE Japan Federation of Commodity Exchanges Ltd

KBOT Kansas City Board of Trade
KCE Kanmon Commodity Exchange
KGE Kobe Grain Exchange

KLCE	Kuala Lumpur Commodity Exchange
KRE	Kobe Rubber Exchange
KRSE	Kobe Raw Silk Exchange
LGFM	London Grain Futures Market
LIFFE	London International Financial Futures Exchange
LME	London Metal Exchange
LMFM	London Meat Futures Market
LPFM	London Potato Futures Market
LPM	Marché à Terme de la Pomme de Terre de Lille
LTOM	London Traded Options Market
MACE	Mid-American Commodity Exchange
MATIF	Marché à Terme International de France
MDCE	Maebashi Dried Cocoon Exchange
ME	The Montreal Exchange
MEFF	Mercado Español de Futuros Financiero
MGE	Minneapolis Grain Exchange
MIFEX	Manila International Futures Exchange
MONEP	Marché des Options Négociables de la Bourse de Paris
NGSE	Nagoya Grain & Sugar Exchange
NOM	Norwegian Options Market
NSX	Nagoya Stock Exchange
NTE	Nagoya Textile Exchange
NYCE	New York Cotton Exchange
NYCE(CA)	Citrus Associates of the New York Cotton Exchange
NYFE	New York Futures Exchange
NYMEX	New York Mercantile Exchange
NYSE	New York Stock Exchange
NZFX	New Zealand Futures Exchange Ltd
OGE	Osaka Grain Exchange
OM-F	OM France
OM-I	OM Iberica
OM-L	OM London
OM-S	OM Sweden
OSE	Osaka Sugar Exchange
OSX	Osaka Securities Exchange
OTE	Osaka Textile Exchange
PBOT	Philadelphia Board of Trade
PHLX	Philadelphia Stock Exchange
PSE	Pacific Stock Exchange
ROEFEX	Rotterdam Energy Futures Exchange
SFX	Sydney Futures Exchange Ltd
SIMEX	Singapore International Monetary Exchange

SMFM	Soyabean Meal Futures Market
SOFFEX	Swiss Options and Financial Futures Exchange
TCBOT	Twin Cities Board of Trade
TDCE	Toyohashi Dried Cocoon Exchange
TFE	Toronto Futures Exchange
TGE	Tokyo Grain Exchange
TIFFE	Tokyo International Financial Futures Exchange
TOCOM	Tokyo Commodity Exchange for Industry
TSE	Toronto Stock Exchange
TSUG	Tokyo Sugar Exchange
TSX	Tokyo Stock Exchange
VSE	Vancouver Stock Exchange
WCE	Winnipeg Commodity Exchange
YRSE	Yokohama Raw Silk Exchange

Exchange rate abbreviations used in this directory

Currency	Abbreviation
Asia and Australasia	
Australian dollar	A$
Hong Kong dollar	HK$
Japanese yen	Y
Indonesian rupiah	Rps
Malaysian ringgit (dollar)	M$
New Zealand dollar	NZ$
Philippine peso	P$
Singapore dollar	Sin$
The Americas	
Brazilian cruzado	Cz$
Canadian dollar	C$
US dollar	US$
Europe	
British pound sterling	£
Danish krone	DKr
Dutch guilder	Dfl
Finnish mark	FIM
French franc	FFr
Irish punt	I£
Norwegian krone	NKr
Spanish peseta	Pta
Swedish krona	SKr
Swiss franc	SFr
West German Deutschmark	DM

Part I Australasia and Asia

Contents

1 Australia

Contents

Australian Stock Exchange (Sydney) Ltd

trading as the ASX Futures Market (ASX) and the Australian Options Market (AOM)

Address:

Exchange Centre
20 Bond Street
Sydney
New South Wales 2000
Australia

Telephone: (02) 227 0000
Fax: (02) 251 5525
Telex: STOCKEX AA20630

Exchange personnel

Manager (AOM): Bruce J. Donoghoe
Marketing Manager: Dan Wilkinson

Futures contracts available (traded on the ASX)
Australian Gold Stock Index
AOM Twenty Leaders Stock Index

Also available are futures contracts on 10 individual share issues, each contract having an underlying size of 10,000 shares. These are traded on one of the three quarterly expiry cycles (January, April, July, October; February, May, August, November; March, June, September, December). Trading hours are 10.00 a.m. – 4.00 p.m.

Options contracts on cash available (traded on the AOM)
AOM Twenty Leaders Stock Index
IOCC gold bullion
IOCC silver bullion

Also available are options on over 25 Australian equity issues, where each contract represents an underlying 1,000 shares. These are traded on one of the three quarterly expiry cycles (January, April, July, October; February, May, August, November; March, June, September, December). Trading hours are 10.00 a.m. – 4.00 p.m.

Clearing House:

Options Clearing House Pty Ltd.
International Options Clearing Corporation (IOCC)
(for gold and silver IOCC link contracts).
International Commodities Clearing House (for ASX futures contracts).

Method of trading:

Open outcry.

Commenced trading:

1976 for options and futures.

Exchange links:

Optiebeurs Amsterdam (EOE) – IOCC link.
The Montreal Exchange (ME) – IOCC link.
Vancouver Stock Exchange (VSE) – IOCC link.

A brief synopsis of the exchange:
The Australian Stock Exchange (Sydney) Ltd was formed as a result of the amalgamation of six regional exchanges (Sydney, Melbourne, Brisbane, Perth, Adelaide and Hobart) in 1987. Both AOM and ASX are wholly-owned subsidiaries of the Australian Stock Exchange (Sydney) Ltd. As short selling was not allowed in Australia until early in the 1980s, trading in put options did not start until 1982.

Through the IOCC's (International Options Clearing Corporation) precious metal options link that started in 1985 between Australia, Canada and the Netherlands, 18.5 hours a day trading is possible in gold and silver bullion. These traded instruments are fully fungible across the exchanges in the link and an electronic order book passes from exchange to exchange. Australia is the smallest of the link exchanges in terms of members.

The Australian Stock Exchange (Sydney) Ltd is one of only a handful of exchanges covered in this directory that permits trading in futures contracts in individual share issues, here through its ASX Futures Market subsidiary.

Australian Gold Stock Index futures

Contract size	A$20.00 multiplied by the Australian Gold Stock Index.
Standard delivery method	Cash settlement on the last trading day.
Trading months	The March, June, September and December cycle.
Trading hours	10.00 a.m. – 4.00 p.m. (pre-opening order input is available 8.30 a.m. – 10.00 a.m.).
Price quotation method	In Australian dollars (A$) per index point.
Minimum price move (value)	0.10 index points (A$2.00 per contract).
Daily price limits	None.
Position limits	None.
Last trading day	The last business day prior to the (settlement and) delivery day (i.e. the penultimate business day of the contract month).
Delivery day	The last business day of the contract month.
Initial (Variation) margin	Please consult the exchange or your broker for the current margin requirements.
Spread margin	Please consult the exchange or your broker for the current spread concessions.
Reuters Monitor (Quote)	N/a.
Telerate page	N/a.

AOM Twenty Leaders Stock Index futures

Contract size	A$100 multiplied by the AOM Twenty Leaders Stock Index.
Standard delivery method	Cash settlement on the last trading day.
Trading months	The March, June, September and December cycle.
Trading hours	10.00 a.m. – 4.00 p.m. (pre-opening order input is available 8.30 a.m. – 10.00 a.m.).
Price quotation method	In Australian dollars (A$) per index point.
Minimum price move (value)	0.10 index points (A$10.00 per contract).
Daily price limits	None.
Position limits	None.
Last trading day	The last business day prior to the (settlement and) delivery day (i.e. the penultimate business day of the contract month).
Delivery day	The last business day of the contract month.
Initial (Variation) margin	Please consult the exchange or your broker for the current margin requirements.
Spread margin	Please consult the exchange or your broker for the current spread concessions.
Reuters Monitor (Quote)	N/a.
Telerate page	N/a.

Option on AOM Twenty Leaders Stock Index

Contract size	A$100 multiplied by the AOM Twenty Leaders Stock Index.
Standard delivery method	Cash settlement at expiry. There is no facility for physical delivery of the stocks underlying the index.
Trading months	The nearby four consecutive calendar months.
Trading hours	10.00 a.m. – 4.00 p.m.
Price quotation method	In Australian dollars (A$) per index point.
Minimum price move (value)	One full index point (A$100 per contract).
Daily price limits	None.
Position limits	None.
Last trading day	The last business day prior to the delivery day (i.e. the penultimate business day of the contract month).
Delivery day	The last business day of the contract month.
Initial (Variation) margin	Not yet announced.
Spread margin	Not yet announced.
Strike price intervals	Not yet announced.
Option type	European style (the option may only be exercised at expiry and not at other times during its life).
Method of introduction of new strike prices	Not yet announced.
Reuters Monitor (Quote)	N/a.
Telerate page	N/a.

Option on IOCC gold bullion

Contract size	10 troy ounces of fine gold bullion of 0.995 fineness acceptable for good London delivery.
Standard delivery method	Physical delivery of the above with one of the five members of the London Gold Market or an institution acting as its delivery depot.
Trading months	The nearby three months of the February, May, August and November cycle.
Trading hours	The local dealing times of the IOCC link exchanges are as follows: AOM (Nov – Mar): 11.00 a.m. – 1.00 p.m. and 2.30 p.m. – 4.30 p.m. AOM (Apr – Oct): 10.30 a.m. – 12.30 p.m. and 2.00 p.m. – 4.00 p.m. Amsterdam: 10.30 a.m. – 4.30 p.m. Montreal: 9.00 a.m. – 2.30 p.m. Vancouver: 11.30 a.m. – 4.00 p.m.
Price quotation method	In US dollars (US$) and cents per troy ounce.
Minimum price move (value)	US$0.10 per troy ounce (US$1.00 per contract).
Daily price limits	None.

Position limits	5,000 contracts on the same side of the market.
Last trading day	The third Friday of the contract month. Trading ceases in the expiring contract at 4.00 p.m. (Amsterdam), 2.30 p.m. (Montreal), 4.00 p.m. (Vancouver) or 5.00 p.m. (Sydney) on the last trading day. These are all local times.
Delivery day	The business day following the last trading day. The option expires on the Monday following the third Friday of the contract month, this being the last time for exercise. Settlement is due on the fourth business day following the submission of tender notice.
Initial (Variation) margin	The option premium received plus a percentage of (if any) twice the intrinsic value of the option.
Spread margin	Not stated.
Strike price intervals	Gold price under US$400: US$10.00 intervals Gold price US$400 – US$600: US$20.00 intervals Gold price US$600 – US$900: US$30.00 intervals Gold price greater than US$900: US$40.00 intervals
Option type	American style (the option may be exercised on any business day up to and including the last trading day).
Method of introduction of new strike prices	Between four and five series are initially available. New series are introduced so as to allow there to be at least one in-the-money and one out-of-the-money series at all times. No new series are normally introduced in the last 20 business days before expiry. The other link exchanges take the lead from the EOE Amsterdam for introducing new strike prices.
Reuters Monitor (Quote)	YGDA – YGDP (EOE), MEGA – MEGB (ME), VEGA – VEGB (VSE), GDMB – GDMG.
Telerate page	N/a.

This contract is traded on the IOCC (International Options Clearing Corporation BV) link between the Australian Stock Exchange (Sydney) Ltd (AOM), the Montreal Exchange (ME), Optiebeurs Amsterdam (EOE) and the Vancouver Stock Exchange (VSE), allowing trading for 18.5 hours a day. A limit order book is passed from exchange to exchange. The contracts are fully fungible.

Option on IOCC silver bullion

Contract size	1,000 troy ounces 999 parts to 1,000 parts of good London delivery silver bullion.
Standard delivery method	Physical delivery of the above with one of the five members of the London Silver Market.
Trading months	The nearby three months of the March, June, September and December cycle.

Trading hours	The following are the local trading times for the IOCC link exchanges:

Amsterdam:	10.30 a.m. – 4.30 p.m.
Vancouver:	7.30 a.m. – 4.00 p.m.
AOM (Nov – Mar):	11.00 a.m. – 1.00 p.m. and 2.30 p.m. – 4.30 p.m.
AOM (Apr – Oct):	10.30 a.m. – 12.30 p.m. and 2.00 p.m. – 4.00 p.m.

Price quotation method
In US dollars (US$) and cents per troy ounce.

Minimum price move (value)
One US cent (US$0.01) per troy ounce (US$10.00 per contract).

Daily price limits
None.

Position limits
10,000 contracts on the same side of the market.

Last trading day
The third Friday of the contract month. Trading ceases in the expiring contract at 4.00 p.m. (Amsterdam and Vancouver) or 5.00 p.m. (Sydney), on the last trading day. These times are local times.

Delivery day
The business day following the last trading day. Options expire on the Monday following the third Friday of the contract month, which is the last time allowed for exercise.

Initial (Variation) margin
The option premium received plus a percentage of (if any) twice the intrinsic value of the option.

Spread margin
Not stated.

Strike price intervals

Silver price under US$5.00:	US$0.25 intervals
Silver price US$5.00 – US$15.00:	US$0.50 intervals
Silver price over US$15.00:	US$1.00 intervals

Option type
American style (the option may be exercised on any business day up to and including the last trading day).

Method of introduction of new strike prices
Between four and five series are initially available. New series are introduced so as to allow there to be at least one in-the-money and one out-of-the-money series at all times. No new series are normally introduced in the last 20 business days before expiry. The other link exchanges take the lead from the EOE Amsterdam in introducing new series.

Reuters Monitor (Quote)
YAQI – YAQP (EOE).

Telerate page
N/a.

This contract is traded on the IOCC (International Options Clearing Corporation BV) link between the Australian Stock Exchange (Sydney) Ltd (AOM), Optiebeurs Amsterdam (EOE) and the Vancouver Stock Exchange (VSE). Trading takes place therefore for 18.5 hours per day. An order book passes from exchange to exchange. The contracts are fully fungible.

Sydney Futures Exchange Ltd (SFE)

Address:	Grosvenor Street Sydney 2000 New South Wales Australia
Telephone:	(02) 256 0555
Fax:	(02) 256 0666
Telex:	AA 126713 SFEL

Exchange personnel

Chairman:	Bruce Hudson
Deputy Chairman:	Eric Spooner
Chief Executive:	Leslie V. Hosking
Manager, Education:	Craig Lambert

Domestic Representative Office
Level 1
10 Queen Street
Melbourne
Victoria 3000
Australia

Telephone:	(03) 629 1721
Fax:	(03) 629 1708
Telex:	N/a.

Chicago Representative Office
Information Bureau
Suite 1408
345 North Canal Street
Chicago
Illinois 60606
USA

Telephone:	(312) 559 5505
Fax:	(312) 559 5509
Telex:	350211
Marketing Director:	Barbara Diamond

Futures contracts available
All Ordinaries Share Price Index (SPI)
Australian dollar / US dollar currency
Five-year Semi-Government Bond
Greasy wool
Live cattle
90-day Bank Accepted Bills
10-year Commonwealth Treasury Bond
Three-year Commonwealth Treasury Bond

Options on futures contracts available
All Ordinaries Share Price Index future
Australian dollar / US dollar currency future
Five-year Semi-Government Bond future
90-day Bank Accepted Bank Bills future
10-year Commonwealth Treasury Bond future
Three-year Commonwealth Treasury Bond future

Clearing House:	International Commodities Clearing House (ICCH).
Method of trading:	Open outcry.
Commenced trading:	1960.
Exchange links:	London International Financial Futures Exchange (LIFFE) for US Government Treasury Bond and Eurodollar futures.

A brief synopsis of the exchange
The Sydney Futures Exchange is the oldest and the
leading financial futures and options exchange in
Australasia, having started in 1960 as the Sydney
Greasy Wool Futures Exchange. It changed its name
in 1982, and through its expansion over recent years
grew out of its original premises. Recently therefore,
the SFE moved to new purpose-built premises.

Financial products were first introduced in 1979
commencing with the Australian dollar / US dollar
currency future. The exchange provides a valuable
sector of the 24-hour trading clock on domestic and
international products of the American, European and
Asian time zones.

Fungible trading links were set up between the SFE
and COMEX (gold futures) and LIFFE (Eurodollar
and US Government Treasury Bond futures) in 1986,
although levels of turnover on these links are low. The
contract specifications are not shown in this section.
Please refer to LIFFE's contract specifications. The
Gold futures contract was delisted in 1989.

There are three categories of membership: Floor
Members (approximately 30), Associate Members –

full, market associate or broker associate (nearly 150), and Local Members (nearly 100).

The most recent developments at the exchange include the development of an electronic trading system, SYCOM, initially to extend trading hours outside the trading pit. New product plans include a replacement to the Australian Dollar futures contract.

All Ordinaries Share Price Index (SPI) futures

Contract size	A$100 multiplied by the Australian Stock Exchange's All Ordinaries Share Price Index (SPI*).
Standard delivery method	Cash settlement, based on the spot value of the All Ordinaries Share Price Index at 12.00 noon on the last trading day, calculated to one decimal point.
Trading months	The March, June, September and December cycle up to 18 months forward.
Trading hours	Two sessions daily: 9.30 a.m. – 12.30 p.m. and 2.00 p.m. – 4.10 p.m.
Price quotation method	In Australian dollars (A$) and cents per index point and tenths of an index point.
Minimum price move (value)	0.10 index points (A$10.00 per contract).
Daily price limits	None.
Position limits	None.
Last trading day	The last business day of the contract month.
Delivery day	The second business day following the last trading day.
Initial (Variation) margin	A$10,000 per contract (variation margin is due when the initial deposit margin has been eroded by more than 25%).
Spread margin	A$500 per spread position.
Reuters Monitor (Quote)	YALL, SYGN.
Telerate page	6183.

* The All Ordinaries Share Price Index (SPI) is a capitalisation weighted index of over 250 leading Australian stocks.

Australian dollar / US dollar currency futures

Contract size	A$100,000 traded against the US dollar (US$).
Standard delivery method	Cash settlement at expiry.
Trading months	The March, June, September and December cycle up to six months forward.
Trading hours	8.30 a.m. – 4.30 p.m. (no break).
Price quotation method	In terms of US dollars (US$) per Australian dollar (A$).
Minimum price move (value)	US$0.0001 per A$1.00 (US$10.00 per contract).
Daily price limits	None.
Position limits	None.
Last trading day	Two business days prior to the third Wednesday of the contract month. Trading ceases in the expiring contract at 3.00 p.m. on the last trading day.

Delivery day	The third Wednesday of the contract month.
Initial (Variation) margin	US$1,500 per contract (variation margin is due when the initial deposit margin has been eroded by more than 25%).
Spread margin	US$200 per spread position.
Reuters Monitor (Quote)	YAUD, SYIA.
Telerate page	6182 – 6184.

Five-year Semi-Government Bond futures

Contract size	A$100,000 nominal face value of Semi-Government Bonds with a notional coupon rate of 12% per annum, maturing in 1995.
Standard delivery method	Physical delivery of inscribed Semi-Government Bonds issued by authorities on the SFE list of approved issuers expiring in 1995*.
Trading months	The March, June, September and December cycle up to two years forward.
Trading hours	Two sessions daily: 8.30 a.m. – 12.30 p.m. and 2.00 p.m. – 4.30 p.m.
Price quotation method	In Australian dollars (A$) – 100.00 minus the annualised percentage yield.
Minimum price move (value)	0.01% per annum of nominal face value (approximately A$35.00 per contract, varying inversely with current rates of interest).
Daily price limits	None.
Position limits	None.
Last trading day	The 15th day of the contract month, or the next business day if the 15th is not a business day. Trading ceases in the expiring contract at 12.00 noon on the last trading day.
Delivery day	The fifth day following the last trading day.
Initial (Variation) margin	A$750 per contract.
Spread margin	A$200 per spread position.
Reuters Monitor (Quote)	YBSG, SYFD.
Telerate page	6193.

* The current SFE approved issuers with bonds eligible for delivery are as follows:
    Australian Telecommunications Corporation
    Government of the Northern Territory
    Melbourne & Metropolitan Board of Works
    New South Wales Treasury Corporation
    Queensland Treasury Corporation
    South Australian Government Financing Authority
    State Electricity Commission of Victoria
    Tasmanian Public Finance Corporation
    Victorian Public Authorities Finance Agency
    Western Australian Treasury Corporation.

Greasy wool futures

Contract size	2,500 kilograms clean weight of combing wool (approximately 23 bales of greasy wool).
Standard delivery method	Cash settlement according to the 22 micron Clean Wool Price Indicator published by the Australian Wool Corporation for the day prior to the last trading day, calculated to the nearest whole Australian cent per kilogram.
Trading months	The February, April, June, August, October and December cycle up to 18 months forward.
Trading hours	Two sessions daily: 10.30 a.m. – 12.30 p.m. and 2.00 p.m. – 4.00 p.m.
Price quotation method	In Australian cents per kilogram of clean weight.
Minimum price move (value)	One Australian cent (A$0.01) per kilogram (A$25.00 per contract).
Daily price limits	None.
Position limits	None.
Last trading day	The business day following the last day of the wool auction sales in the contract month. Trading ceases in the expiring contract at 12.00 noon on the last trading day.
Delivery day	The business day following the last trading day.
Initial (Variation) margin	A$1,500 per contract (variation margin is due when the initial deposit margin has been eroded by more than 25%).
Spread margin	US$100 per spread position.
Reuters Monitor (Quote)	YWOM, SYFF.
Telerate page	6188.

Live cattle futures

Contract size	10,000 kilograms liveweight of Cattle.
Standard delivery method	Cash settlement at expiry, based on the Live Cattle Index published by the Sydney Futures Exchange (SFE) for the day preceding the last trading day, calculated to the nearest 0.1% of a kilogram.
Trading months	Each consecutive calendar month up to 12 months forward.
Trading hours	Two sessions daily: 10.30 a.m. – 12.30 p.m. and 2.00 p.m. – 4.00 p.m.
Price quotation method	In Australian cents per kilogram liveweight.
Minimum price move (value)	0.1 Australian cents (A$0.001) per kilogram (A$10.00 per contract).
Daily price limits	None.
Position limits	None.

Last trading day	The second Wednesday of the contract month or the next business day if that day is not a business day.
Delivery day	The second business day following the last trading day.
Initial (Variation) margin	A$200 per contract (variation margin is due when the initial deposit margin has been eroded by more than 25%).
Spread margin	A$150 per spread position.
Reuters Monitor (Quote)	YCTM, SYFG.
Telerate page	N/a.

90-day Bank Accepted Bills futures

Contract size	A$500,000 nominal face value of 90-day Australian Bank Accepted Bills of Exchange.
Standard delivery method	Physical delivery of five Australian Bank Accepted Bills or Negotiable Certificates of Deposit (NCDs) each of a notional face value of A$100,000 or one NCD of A$500,000 maturing between 85 and 95 days from the settlement date.
Trading months	The March, June, September and December cycle up to three years forward.
Trading hours	Two sessions daily: 8.30 a.m. – 12.30 p.m. and 2.00 p.m. – 4.30 p.m.
Price quotation method	100.00 minus the annualised percentage yield calculated to two decimal points, quoted in Australian dollars (A$).
Minimum price move (value)	0.01% per annum (approximately A$11.50 per contract – the actual value of each tick varies inversely with the level of interest rates).
Daily price limits	None.
Position limits	None.
Last trading day	The business day immediately prior to the delivery day. Trading ceases in the expiring contract at 12.00 noon on the last trading day.
Delivery day	The second Friday of the contract month.
Initial (Variation) margin	A$500 per contract (variation margin is due when the initial deposit margin has been eroded by more than 25%).
Spread margin	A$250 per spread position.
Reuters Monitor (Quote)	YIRA.
Telerate page	6181.

10-year Commonwealth Treasury Bond futures

Contract size	A$100,000 nominal face value of Commonwealth Government Treasury Bonds, a notional coupon rate of 12% per annum and a term to maturity of 10 years.
Standard delivery method	Cash settlement at expiry, based on the average price between 12 brokers, dealers and banks at 11.30 a.m. on the last trading day (excluding the two highest and two lowest quotations). There is no facility for physical delivery of these bonds.
Trading months	The March, June, September and December cycle up to two years forward.
Trading hours	Two sessions daily: 8.30 a.m. – 12.30 p.m. and 2.00 p.m. – 4.30 p.m.
Price quotation method	100.00 minus the annualised yield per A$100 nominal face value.
Minimum price move (value)	0.005% per annum of nominal face value (approximately A$25.00 per contract – the actual value of each tick varies inversely with the level of interest rates), quoted in Australian dollars (A$).
Daily price limits	None.
Position limits	None.
Last trading day	The 15th day of the contract month, or the next business day if the 15th is not a business day. Trading ceases in the expiring contract at 12.00 noon on the last trading day.
Delivery day	The business day following the last trading day.
Initial (Variation) margin	A$1,000 per contract (variation margin is due when the initial deposit margin has been eroded by more than 25%).
Spread margin	A$200 per spread position. There is a spread concession of A$500 between the SFE 10-year Commonwealth Treasury Bond futures contract and the SFE Three-year Commonwealth Treasury Bond futures contract.
Reuters Monitor (Quote)	YBNE, SYGA.
Telerate page	6185.

Three-year Commonwealth Treasury Bond futures

Contract size	A$100,000 nominal face value of Commonwealth Treasury Bonds with a notional coupon rate of 12% per annum and a term to maturity of three years.
Standard delivery method	Cash settlement at expiry, based on the average price between 12 brokers, dealers and banks at 11.30 a.m. on the last trading day (excluding the two highest and two lowest quotes).

Trading months	The nearest three months from the March, June, September and December cycle.
Trading hours	Two sessions daily: 8.30 a.m. – 12.30 p.m. and 2.00 p.m. – 4.30 p.m.
Price quotation method	100.00 minus the annualised yield per A$100 nominal face value, quoted in Australian dollars (A$).
Minimum price move (value)	0.01% per annum of nominal face value (approximately A$25.00 per contract –the actual value of each tick varies inversely with the level of interest rates).
Daily price limits	None.
Position limits	None.
Last trading day	The 15th day of the contract month, or the next business day if the 15th is not a business day. Trading ceases in the expiring contract at 12.00 noon on the last trading day.
Delivery day	The business day following the last trading day.
Initial (Variation) margin	A$500 per contract (variation margin is due when the initial deposit margin has been eroded by more than 25%).
Spread margin	A$200 per spread position. There is a spread concession of A$500 between the SFE 10-year Commonwealth Treasury Bond futures contract and the SFE Three-year Commonwealth Treasury Bond futures contract.
Reuters Monitor (Quote)	YTYB, SYIN.
Telerate page	6182.

Option on SFE All Ordinaries Share Price Index (SPI) futures

Contract size	One SFE All Ordinaries Share Price Index (SPI) futures contract (of an underlying contract size of A$100 multiplied by the All Ordinaries Share Price Index).
Standard delivery method	Delivery of a long or short position in a futures contract at the strike price as above.
Trading months	At least the four nearest months of the March, June, September and December cycle.
Trading hours	Two sessions daily: 9.30 a.m. – 12.30 p.m. and 2.00 p.m. – 4.10 p.m.
Price quotation method	In Australian dollars (A$) per index point and tenths on an index point calculated to one decimal place.
Minimum price move (value)	0.10 index points (A$10.00 per contract).
Daily price limits	None.
Position limits	None.

Last trading day	The last business day of the contract month. Trading ceases in the expiring contract at 12.00 noon on the last trading day.
Delivery day	Two business days following the last trading day.
Initial (Variation) margin	Please consult the exchange or your broker for the current margin requirements.
Spread margin	Please consult the exchange or your broker for the current spread concessions.
Strike price intervals	At intervals of 25 points of the All Ordinaries Share Price Index.
Option type	American style (the option may be exercised on any business day up to and including the last trading day). In-the-money options are automatically exercised at expiry, unless specifically abandoned.
Method of introduction of new strike prices	New options series are automatically introduced as the underlying futures price moves.
Reuters Monitor (Quote)	YALH – YALK, SYGO – SYGZ.
Telerate page	22713 – 22716.

Option on SFE Australian dollar / US dollar currency futures

Contract size	One SFE Australian dollar / US dollar currency futures contract (of an underlying contract size of A$100,000 traded against the US dollar).
Standard delivery method	Delivery of a long or short position in a futures contract at the strike price as above.
Trading months	At least the nearest two months of the March, June, September and December cycle.
Trading hours	8.30 a.m. – 4.30 p.m. (no break).
Price quotation method	In terms of US dollars (US$) per Australian dollar (A$).
Minimum price move (value)	US$0.0001 per A$1.00 (US$10.00 per contract).
Daily price limits	None.
Position limits	None.
Last trading day	The second Friday prior to the third Wednesday of the contract month.
Delivery day	The business day following the last trading day.
Initial (Variation) margin	Please consult the exchange or your broker for the current margin requirements.
Spread margin	Please consult the exchange or your broker for the current spread concessions.
Strike price intervals	At intervals of US$0.01 per A$1.00.

Option type	American style (the option may be exercised on any business day up to and including the last trading day). In-the-money options are automatically exercised at expiry unless abandoned.
Method of introduction of new strike prices	New options series are automatically introduced as the underlying futures price moves.
Reuters Monitor (Quote)	YAUE – YAUH, SYIB – SYIM.
Telerate page	22717 – 22728.

Option on SFE five-year Semi-Government Bond futures

Contract size	One SFE five-year Semi-Government Bond futures contract (of an underlying contract size of A$100,000 nominal face value).
Standard delivery method	Delivery of a long or short position in a futures contract at the strike price as above.
Trading months	The March, June, September and December cycle.
Trading hours	Two sessions daily: 8.30 a.m. – 12.30 p.m. and 2.00 p.m. – 4.30 p.m.
Price quotation method	In Australian dollars (A$) – 100.00 minus the annualised percentage yield.
Minimum price move (value)	0.005% per annum of nominal face value (approximately A$17.50 per contract, varying inversely with the strike price).
Daily price limits	None.
Position limits	None.
Last trading day	Four business days prior to the close of trading in the underlying futures contract (which is the 15th day of the contract month).
Delivery day	The business day following the last trading day.
Initial (Variation) margin	Please consult the exchange or your broker for the current margin requirements.
Spread margin	Please consult the exchange or your broker for the current spread concessions.
Strike price intervals	At 0.25% annualised yield intervals.
Option type	American style (the option may be exercised on any business day up to and including the last trading day). In-the-money options are automatically exercised at expiry, unless specifically abandoned.
Method of introduction of new strike prices	New option series are created automatically as the underlying futures contract price moves.
Reuters Monitor (Quote)	N/a.
Telerate page	N/a.

Option on SFE 90-day Bank Accepted Bills futures

Contract size
One SFE 90-day Bank Accepted Bills futures contract (of an underlying contract size of A$500,000 nominal face value).

Standard delivery method
Delivery of a long or short position in a futures contract at the strike price as above.

Trading months
The four nearest months from the March, June, September and December cycle.

Trading hours
Two sessions daily: 8.30 a.m. – 12.30 p.m. and 2.00 p.m. – 4.30 p.m.

Price quotation method
In Australian dollars (A$) in terms of the annualised yield.

Minimum price move (value)
0.01% per annum (approximately A$11.50 per contract – the actual value of each tick varies inversely with the level of interest rates).

Daily price limits
None.

Position limits
None.

Last trading day
The Friday, one week prior to the delivery day for the underlying futures contract.

Delivery day
The business day following the last trading day.

Initial (Variation) margin
Please consult the exchange or your broker for the current margin requirements.

Spread margin
Please consult the exchange or your broker for the current spread concessions.

Strike price intervals
At intervals of 0.50% per annum yield.

Option type
American style (the option may be exercised on any business day up to and including the last trading day). In-the-money options are automatically exercised at expiry, unless specifically abandoned.

Method of introduction of new strike prices
New options series are automatically introduced as the underlying futures price moves.

Reuters Monitor (Quote)
YIRC – YIRH, SYUA – SYUZ.

Telerate page
22709 – 22712.

Option on SFE 10-year Commonwealth Treasury Bond futures

Contract size
One SFE 10-year Commonwealth Treasury Bond futures contract (of an underlying contract size of A$100,000 nominal face value).

Standard delivery method
Delivery of a long or short position in a futures contract at the strike price as above.

Trading months
The nearest two months of the March, June, September and December cycle.

Trading hours
Two sessions daily: 8.30 a.m. – 12.30 p.m. and 2.00 p.m. – 4.30 p.m.

Price quotation method	In Australian dollars (A$) – 100.00 minus the annualised percentage yield per A$100 nominal face value.
Minimum price move (value)	0.005% per annum of nominal value (approximately A$25.00 per contract varying inversely with the level of interest rates).
Daily price limits	None.
Position limits	None.
Last trading day	The 15th day of the contract month, or the next business day if the 15th is not a business day. Trading ceases at 12.00 noon on the last trading day.
Delivery day	The business day following the last trading day.
Initial (Variation) margin	Please consult the exchange or your broker for the current margin requirements.
Spread margin	Please consult the exchange or your broker for the current spread concessions.
Strike price intervals	At intervals of 0.25% yield per annum.
Option type	American style (the option may be exercised on any business day up to and including the last trading day). In-the-money options are automatically exercised at expiry, unless specifically abandoned.
Method of introduction of new strike prices	New options series are automatically introduced as the underlying futures contract price moves.
Reuters Monitor (Quote)	YBNF – YBNI, SYGB – SYGM.
Telerate page	22721 – 22724.

Option on SFE three-year Commonwealth Treasury Bond futures

Contract size	One SFE three-year Commonwealth Treasury Bond futures contract (of an underlying contract size of A$100,000 nominal face value).
Standard delivery method	Delivery of a long or short position in a futures contract at the strike price as above.
Trading months	At least the nearest two months of the March, June, September and December cycle.
Trading hours	Two sessions daily: 8.30 a.m. – 12.30 p.m. and 2.00 p.m. – 4.30 p.m.
Price quotation method	In Australian dollars (A$) in terms of the annualised percentage yield.
Minimum price move (value)	0.01% per annum (approximately A$25.00 per contract – the actual value of each tick varies inversely with the level of interest rates).
Daily price limits	None.
Position limits	None.

Last trading day	The 15th day of the contract month, or the next business day if the 15th is not a business day. Trading ceases in the expiring contract at 12.00 noon on the last trading day.
Delivery day	The business day following the last trading day.
Initial (Variation) margin	Please consult the exchange or your broker for the current margin requirements.
Spread margin	Please consult the exchange or your broker for the current spread concessions.
Strike price intervals	At intervals of 0.25% yield per annum.
Option type	American style (the option may be exercised on any business day up to and including the last trading day). In-the-money options are automatically exercised at expiry, unless specifically abandoned.
Method of introduction of new strike prices	New options series are automatically introduced as the underlying futures price moves.
Reuters Monitor (Quote)	YTYC – YTYD, SYIO – SYIZ.
Telerate page	22717 – 22720.

2 Hong Kong

Contents

Hong Kong Futures Exchange Ltd (HKFE)

Address:
Room 911, 9th floor
New World Tower
16/18 Queens Road
Central
Hong Kong

Telephone: (5) 251 005-8
Fax: (5) 810 5089
Telex: 65326 HKFE HX

Exchange personnel
Chairman: Ian Hay Davidson
Chief Executive: Douglas O. Ford
General Manager: Steven Yau
Information Officer: Candy Chan

Futures contracts available
Gold
Hang Seng Stock Index
Soyabeans
Raw sugar

Options contracts available
None

Clearing House: International Commodities Clearing House (ICCH).

Method of trading: Open outcry (for gold and HSI only).

Commenced trading: 1976.

Exchange links: None.

A brief synopsis of the exchange
The Hong Kong Futures Exchange started trading as the Hong Kong Commodity Exchange and changed its name in 1985. Beset by a series of scandals surrounding the Hang Seng Index futures contract, the exchange has flagged over the last few years, and has the further problem of increasing competition from the Japanese exchanges in financial products.

There are four categories of exchange membership: Full Members, Trade Affiliated Members, Market Members and Clearing (full or market) Members.

Future plans of the Hong Kong exchange include the introduction of a three month HIBOR (Hong Kong Dollar interest rate) futures contract, approval for which has recently been granted and trading is due to start in February 1990.

Gold futures

Contract size	100 troy ounces of refined gold bullion of not less than 995 fineness.
Standard delivery method	Physical delivery of the above, cast in 100-ounce, 50-ounce or one-kilo bars, at the seller's option in Hong Kong.
Trading months	The nearby three consecutive calendar months, plus months from the February, April, June, August, October and December cycle, up to two years and one month forward.
Trading hours	Two sessions daily: 9.00 a.m. – 12.00 noon and 2.00 p.m. – 5.30 p.m.
Price quotation method	In US dollars (US$) and cents per troy ounce.
Minimum price move (value)	10 US cents (US$0.10) per troy ounce (US$10.00 per contract).
Daily price limits	A movement of US$40.00 per troy ounce above or below the previous day's closing level halts trading for 30 minutes. Thereafter there are no limits for the rest of the day. There are no limits on the spot contract month.
Position limits	None.
Last trading day	At the close of the morning session on the last business day of the contract month.
Delivery day	Delivery may be made at the seller's choice on any business day during the contract month.
Initial (Variation) margin	Minimum initial margin: US$1,500 per contract.
Spread margin	Not stated.
Reuters Monitor (Quote)	HKCB, HKFG.
Telerate page	N/a.

Hang Seng Stock Index futures

Contract size	HK$50.00 multiplied by the Hang Seng Stock Index (HSI).
Standard delivery method	Cash settlement based on the average HSI quotations taken at five-minute intervals on the last trading day of the contract month, rounded down to the nearest full index point. There is no facility for physical delivery of the stocks underlying the index.
Trading months	The nearest four consecutive even months (from the February, April, June, August, October and December cycle).
Trading hours	Two sessions daily: 10.00 a.m. – 12.00 noon and 2.30 p.m. – 3.30 p.m.
Price quotation method	In Hong Kong dollars (HK$) per HSI point.

Minimum price move (value)	One full HSI point (HK$50.00 per contract).
Daily price limits	300 index points above or below the previous day's closing price. There is therefore a maximum daily limit of 600 points over the two daily sessions. These limits are able to be expanded. There are no limits on the spot contract month.
Position limits	None.
Last trading day	The penultimate business day of the contract month.
Delivery day	The business day following the last trading day.
Initial (Variation) margin	Minimum initial margin: HK$15,000 per contract, or approximately 15% of the underlying value of the contract.
Spread margin	Not stated.
Reuters Monitor (Quote)	HKFI.
Telerate page	N/a.

Soyabean futures

Contract size	500 bags of 60 kilograms each (total of 30,000 kilograms) of unselected China yellow soyabeans.
Standard delivery method	Physical delivery of the above, or unselected US yellow soyabeans produced in Indiana, Ohio or Michigan, in an approved godown in Tokyo or Kanagawa, Japan.
Trading months	The nearby six consecutive calendar months.
Trading hours	There are four sessions daily commencing at 9.50 a.m., 10.50 a.m., 12.50 p.m. and 2.50 p.m.
Price quotation method	In Hong Kong dollars (HK$) and cents per bag of 60 kilograms.
Minimum price move (value)	HK$0.20 per bag (HK$100 per contract).
Daily price limits	None.
Position limits	None.
Last trading day	At the close of the second morning session on the 15th calendar day of the contract month.
Delivery day	The business day following the last trading day.
Initial (Variation) margin	Minimum initial margin: HK$7,500 per contract.
Spread margin	Not stated.
Reuters Monitor (Quote)	HKCA, HKFF.
Telerate page	N/a.

Raw sugar futures

Contract size	50 long tons (112,000 pounds) net weight of raw cane sugar.
Standard delivery method	Physical delivery of the above (96° average polarisation), FOB stowed in bulk at designated ports in South-East Asian countries.
Trading months	The January, March, May, July, September and October cycle up to two years and one month forward.
Trading hours	Two sessions daily: 10.30 a.m. – 12.00 noon and 2.25 p.m. – 4.00 p.m.
Price quotation method	In US cents and one-hundredths (1/100) of a US cent per pound.
Minimum price move (value)	0.01 US cents (US$0.0001) per pound (US$11.20 per contract).
Daily price limits	If the contract price moves more than one US cent (US$0.01) per pound above or below the previous day's closing level, trading is halted for 30 minutes. Thereafter there are no limits for the rest of that day. There are no limits on the spot contract month.
Position limits	None.
Last trading day	The business day prior to the first day of the contract month.
Delivery day	Any business day throughout the contract month.
Initial (Variation) margin	Minimum initial margin: US$1,350 per contract.
Spread margin	Not stated.
Reuters Monitor (Quote)	HKCC, HKFH.
Telerate page	N/a.

3 Indonesia

Contents

Indonesian Commodity Exchange Board (ICEB) (Badan Pelaksana Bursa Komoditi)

Address:
Gedung Bursa
Jalan Medan Merdeka Seletan No 14
4th Floor
Jakarta Pusat 10110
Republic of Indonesia

Telephone: (021) 371921
Fax: (021) 380 4426
Telex: 441194 BPEBTI IA

Exchange personnel
Chairman: Rudy Lengkong
Secretary: Yanda Mohammad
Market Development: J. N. Tarigan
Promotion Division: H. P. Thompson

Futures contracts available
Coffee (robusta) – planned
Rubber (SIR) – planned
Rubber (RSS) – planned

Options contracts available
None

Clearing House: Indonesian Clearing House (PERSERO Kliring).

Method of trading: Open auction (outcry) system.

Commenced trading: Planned to start trading in 1990.

Exchange links: None.

A brief synopsis of the exchange:
The idea behind the Indonesian futures industry was inspired by the Association of Natural Rubber Producing Countries in 1970. Although not yet trading, contracts are expected to be launched in rubber (SIR and RSS) and coffee futures in 1990.

All trading will be supervised by an auction master for each grade of commodity to be traded in turn.

Indonesian
Commodity
Exchange Board
(ICEB)
Futures
Softs and
agricultural

Coffee (robusta) futures – planned

Contract size	5 metric tonnes (5,000 kilograms) of robusta coffee.
Standard delivery method	Physical delivery of the above, for local delivery.
Trading months	The nearby six consecutive calendar months.
Trading hours	Two sessions daily: 10.00 a.m. 12.00 noon and 2.30 p.m. – 3.30 p.m.
Price quotation method	In Indonesian rupiahs (Rps) per kilogram.
Minimum price move (value)	Rps5.00 per kilogram (Rps25,000 per contract).
Daily price limits	None.
Position limits	None.
Last trading day	The 10th business day of the contract month.
Delivery day	The 25th calendar day of the contract month.
Initial (Variation) margin	Not stated. Please consult the exchange for the current details.
Spread margin	Not stated. Please consult the exchange for the current details.
Reuters Monitor (Quote)	COFI-COFJ
Telerate page	N/a.

Rubber (SIR) futures – planned

Contract size	16 metric tonnes (16,000 kilograms) of natural rubber (SIR).
Standard delivery method	Physical delivery of SIR 3L, SIR 10 or SIR 20 rubber, either for local delivery or delivery FOB.
Trading months	The nearby six consecutive calendar months.
Trading hours	Two sessions daily: 10.00 a.m. – 12.00 noon and 2.30 p.m. – 3.30 p.m.
Price quotation method	In US dollars (US$) and cents per kilogram for FOB delivery, or in Indonesian rupiahs (Rps) per kilogram for local delivery.
Minimum price move (value)	One-eighth (1/8) of a US cent (US$0.00125) per kilogram (US$20.00 per contract) for FOB delivery or Rps5.00 per kilogram (Rps80,000 per contract) for local delivery.
Daily price limits	None.
Position limits	None.
Last trading day	The 10th business day of the contract month.
Delivery day	The 25th calendar day of the contract month.
Initial (Variation) margin	Not stated. Please consult the exchange for the current details.
Spread margin	Not stated. Please consult the exchange for the current details.
Reuters Monitor (Quote)	RURI-RURP
Telerate page	N/a.

Rubber (RSS) futures – planned

Indonesian
Commodity
Exchange Board
(ICEB)
Futures
Softs and
agricultural

Contract size	17 metric tonnes (17,000 kilograms) of natural rubber (RSS).
Standard delivery method	Physical delivery of ribbed smoked sheet (RSS) I or ribbed smoked sheet (RSS) III, either for local delivery or delivery FOB.
Trading months	The nearby six consecutive calendar months.
Trading hours	Two sessions daily: 10.00 a.m. – 12.00 noon and 2.30 p.m. – 3.30 p.m.
Price quotation method	In US dollars (US$) and cents per kilogram for FOB delivery, or in Indonesian rupiahs (Rps) per kilogram for local delivery.
Minimum price move (value)	One-eighth (1/8) of a US cent (US$0.00125) per kilogram (US$21.25 per contract) for FOB delivery or Rps5.00 per kilogram (Rps85,000 per contract) for local delivery.
Daily price limits	None.
Position limits	None.
Last trading day	The 10th business day of the contract month.
Delivery day	The 25th calendar day of the contract month.
Initial (Variation) margin	Not stated. Please consult the exchange for the current details.
Spread margin	Not stated. Please consult the exchange for the current details.
Reuters Monitor (Quote)	RURI-RURP
Telerate page	N/a.

4 Japan

Contents

Osaka Sugar Exchange (OSE)

Hokkaido Grain Exchange (HGE)

Address:	3 Oduri Nishi 5-Chome Chou-ku Sapparo Hokkaido 060 Japan
Telephone:	(011) 221 9131
Fax:	(011) 221 4964
Telex:	N/a.

Exchange personnel

President:	Minoru Ito
Managing Director:	Masao Moroto

Futures contracts available
Potato starch
Red beans
Soyabeans (domestic)
Soyabeans (imported)
White beans

Options contracts available
None

Clearing House:	Cleared by the exchange itself.
Method of trading:	By a competitive auction of concentrated bids and offers at a single contracted price. There is no continuous session, but several sessions each day.
Commenced trading:	History dates back to 1887.
Exchange links:	Member of the Japan Federation of Commodity Exchanges.

A brief synopsis of the exchange:
As with many other regional Japanese commodity exchanges, the development of the Hokkaido Grain Exchange can be traced back over many years, and through frequent name changes. Post-war, there was strong trading in fishery products, but this element closed in 1959. There are over 36 exchange members.

Commission rates

A range of customer commissions for the different contracts traded exists as follows depending on the contract price. Lower commissions are payable from members:

Potato starch	Y2,000 regardless of the contract price.
Red beans	From Y3,200 to Y4,000.
Soyabeans (domestic)	Y2,000 regardless of the contract price.
Soyabeans (imported)	From Y3,300 to Y5,500.
White beans	From Y3,000 to Y4,000.

Potato starch futures

Contract size	2,500 kilograms of potato starch.
Standard delivery method	Physical delivery of the above.
Trading months	The nearby three consecutive calendar months.
Trading hours	Six sessions daily (Monday to Saturday) commencing: (a) May to October – 8.50 a.m., 9.50 a.m., 10.50 a.m., 12.50 p.m., 1.50 p.m. and 2.50 p.m. and (b) November to April – 9.00 a.m., 10.00 a.m., 11.00 a.m., 1.00 p.m., 2.00 p.m. and 3.00 p.m.
Price quotation method	In Japanese yen (Y) per 25 kilograms.
Minimum price move (value)	Y1.00 per 25 kilograms (Y100 per contract).
Daily price limits	7% of the underlying contract value above or below the previous business day's closing price.
Position limits	None.
Last trading day	Not stated. Please consult the exchange for the latest details.
Delivery day	Not stated. Please consult the exchange for the latest details.
Initial (Variation) margin	Contract price under Y1,500: Y8,000 Contract price from Y1,500 to Y2,000: Y10,000 Contract price above Y2,000: Y12,000
Spread margin	Not stated. Please consult the exchange for the latest details.
Reuters Monitor (Quote)	N/a.
Telerate page	N/a.

Red beans futures

Contract size	2,400 kilograms of red beans.
Standard delivery method	Physical delivery of the above.
Trading months	The nearby nine consecutive calendar months.
Trading hours	Six sessions daily (Monday to Saturday) commencing: (a) May to October – 8.50 a.m., 9.50 a.m., 10.50 a.m., 12.50 p.m., 1.50 p.m. and 2.50 p.m. and (b) November to April – 9.00 a.m., 10.00 a.m., 11.00 a.m., 1.00 p.m., 2.00 p.m. and 3.00 p.m.
Price quotation method	In Japanese yen (Y) per 60 kilograms.
Minimum price move (value)	Y10.00 per 30 kilograms (Y800.00 per contract).
Daily price limits	7% of the underlying contract value above or below the previous business day's closing price.
Position limits	None.
Last trading day	Not stated. Please consult the exchange for the latest details.

Delivery day	Not stated. Please consult the exchange for the latest details.
Initial (Variation) margin	Contract price under Y14,000: Y50,000
	Contract price from Y14,000 to Y18,000: Y60,000
	Contract price above Y18,000: Y70,000
Spread margin	Not stated. Please consult the exchange for the latest details.
Reuters Monitor (Quote)	N/a.
Telerate page	N/a.

Soyabeans (domestic) futures

Contract size	2,400 kilograms of domestic soyabeans.
Standard delivery method	Physical delivery of the above.
Trading months	The nearby three consecutive calendar months.
Trading hours	Six sessions daily (Monday to Saturday) commencing: (a) May to October – 8.50 a.m., 9.50 a.m., 10.50 a.m., 12.50 p.m., 1.50 p.m. and 2.50 p.m. and (b) November to April – 9.00 a.m., 10.00 a.m., 11.00 a.m., 1.00 p.m., 2.00 p.m. and 3.00 p.m.
Price quotation method	In Japanese yen (Y) per 60 kilograms.
Minimum price move (value)	Y10.00 per 60 kilograms (Y400 per contract).
Daily price limits	7% of the underlying contract value above or below the previous business day's closing price.
Position limits	None.
Last trading day	Not stated. Please consult the exchange for the latest details.
Delivery day	Not stated. Please consult the exchange for the latest details.
Initial (Variation) margin	Contract price under Y3,000: Y8,000
	Contract price from Y3,000 to Y4,000: Y10,000
	Contract price above Y4,000: Y12,000
Spread margin	Not stated. Please consult the exchange for the latest details.
Reuters Monitor (Quote)	N/a.
Telerate page	N/a.

Soyabeans (imported) futures

Contract size	15,000 kilograms of imported soyabeans.
Standard delivery method	Physical delivery of the above.
Trading months	Every other six even months (the February, April, June, August, October and December cycle).
Trading hours	Six sessions daily (Monday to Saturday) commencing: (a) May to October – 8.50 a.m., 9.50 a.m., 10.50 a.m., 12.50 p.m., 1.50 p.m. and 2.50 p.m. and (b) November to April – 9.00 a.m., 10.00 a.m., 11.00 a.m., 1.00 p.m., 2.00 p.m. and 3.00 p.m.

Price quotation method	In Japanese yen (Y) per 60 kilograms.	
Minimum price move (value)	Y10.00 per 60 kilograms (Y2,500 per contract).	
Daily price limits	7% of the underlying contract value above or below the previous business day's closing price.	
Position limits	None.	
Last trading day	Not stated. Please consult the exchange for the latest details.	
Delivery day	Not stated. Please consult the exchange for the latest details.	
Initial (Variation) margin	Contract price under Y5,000:	Y70,000
	Contract price from Y5,000 to Y6,000:	Y80,000
	Contract price above Y6,000:	Y90,000
Spread margin	Not stated. Please consult the exchange for the latest details.	
Reuters Monitor (Quote)	N/a.	
Telerate page	N/a.	

White beans futures

Contract size	2,400 kilograms of white beans.	
Standard delivery method	Physical delivery of the above.	
Trading months	The nearby six consecutive calendar months.	
Trading hours	Six sessions daily (Monday to Saturday) commencing: (a) May to October – 8.50 a.m., 9.50 a.m., 10.50 a.m., 12.50 p.m., 1.50 p.m. and 2.50 p.m. and (b) November to April – 9.00 a.m., 10.00 a.m., 11.00 a.m., 1.00 p.m., 2.00 p.m. and 3.00 p.m.	
Price quotation method	In Japanese yen (Y) per 60 kilograms.	
Minimum price move (value)	Y10.00 per 60 kilograms (Y400 per contract).	
Daily price limits	7% of the underlying contract value above or below the previous business day's closing price.	
Position limits	None.	
Last trading day	Not stated. Please consult the exchange for the latest details.	
Delivery day	Not stated. Please consult the exchange for the latest details.	
Initial (Variation) margin	Contract price under Y13,000:	Y60,000
	Contract price from Y13,000 to Y18,000:	Y70,000
	Contract price above Y18,000:	Y80,000
Spread margin	Not stated. Please consult the exchange for the latest details.	
Reuters Monitor (Quote)	N/a.	
Telerate page	N/a.	

Kanmon Commodity Exchange (KCE)

Address:	1–5 Nabe-cho Shimonoseki Yamaguchi Pref. 20750 Japan
Telephone:	(0832) 31 1313–8
Fax:	(0832) 23 1947
Telex:	N/a.

Exchange personnel

President:	Takeharu Onishi
Executive Director:	Tadanao Oga
Managing Director:	Toshiaki Tameda

Futures contracts available
Potato starch
Raw sugar
Red beans
Refined white soft sugar
Soyabeans (imported)
White beans

Options contracts available
None

Clearing House:	Cleared by the exchange itself.
Method of trading:	By a competitive auction of concentrated bids and offers at a single contracted price. There is no continuous session, but several sessions each day.
Commenced trading:	Dates back to 1805.
Exchange links:	Member of the Japan Federation of Commodity Exchanges.

A brief synopsis of the exchange
From 1953, the old strength of the Kanmon Commodity Exchange of trading in rice futures was replaced by other grain-based commodities and then sugar. This is the only 'composite' commodity exchange in Japan; it is also the only exchange in the west of Japan and one of that country's four major sugar exchanges.

Commission rates

A range of customer commissions for the different contracts traded exist as follows depending on the contract price. Lower commissions are payable from members:

Potato starch	Y2,000 regardless of the contract price.
Raw sugar	From Y4,300 to Y4,700.
Red beans	From Y3,200 to Y4,000.
Refined white soft sugar	From Y4,000 to Y4,600.
Soyabeans (imported)	From Y3,300 to Y5,500.
White beans	From Y3,000 to Y4,000.

Kanmon
Commodity
Exchange (KCE)
Futures
Softs and
agricultural

Potato starch futures

Contract size	2,500 kilograms of potato starch.
Standard delivery method	Physical delivery of the above.
Trading months	The nearby three consecutive calendar months.
Trading hours	Six sessions daily (Monday to Saturday) commencing at 9.00 a.m., 10.00 a.m., 11.00 a.m., 1.00 p.m., 2.00 p.m. and 3.00 p.m.
Price quotation method	In Japanese yen (Y) per 25 kilograms.
Minimum price move (value)	Y1.00 per 25 kilograms (Y100 per contract).
Daily price limits	Within 10% of the underlying contract value above or below the previous business day's closing contract price.
Position limits	None.
Last trading day	Not stated. Please consult the exchange for the latest details.
Delivery day	Not stated. Please consult the exchange for the latest details.
Initial (Variation) margin	Contract price under Y1,500: Y8,000 Contract price from Y1,500 to Y2,000: Y10,000 Contract price above Y2,000: Y12,000
Spread margin	Not stated. Please consult the exchange for the latest details.
Reuters Monitor (Quote)	N/a.
Telerate page	N/a.

Raw sugar futures

Contract size	10,000 kilograms of raw sugar.
Standard delivery method	Physical delivery of the above.
Trading months	The nearby nine consecutive calendar months.
Trading hours	Four sessions daily (Monday to Saturday) commencing 9.30 a.m., 10.30 a.m., 1.30 p.m. and 2.30 p.m.
Price quotation method	In Japanese sen per kilogram.
Minimum price move (value)	10 Japanese sen (Y0.10) per kilogram (Y1,000 per contract).
Daily price limits	Less than Y10.00 per kilogram above or below the previous business day's closing contract price.
Position limits	None.
Last trading day	Not stated. Please consult the exchange for the latest details.
Delivery day	Not stated. Please consult the exchange for the latest details.

**Kanmon
Commodity
Exchange (KCE)
Futures
Softs and
agricultural**

Initial (Variation) margin	Contract price under Y100: Y50,000
	Contract price from Y100 to Y200: Y60,000
	Contract price above Y200: Y70,000
Spread margin	Not stated. Please consult the exchange for the latest details.
Reuters Monitor (Quote)	N/a.
Telerate page	N/a.

Red beans futures

Contract size	2,400 kilograms of red beans.
Standard delivery method	Physical delivery of the above.
Trading months	The nearby six consecutive calendar months.
Trading hours	Six sessions daily (Monday to Saturday) commencing 9.00 a.m., 10.00 a.m., 11.00 a.m., 1.00 p.m., 2.00 p.m. and 3.00 p.m.
Price quotation method	In Japanese yen (Y) per 30 kilograms.
Minimum price move (value)	Y10.00 per 30 kilograms (Y800 per contract).
Daily price limits	Within 10% of the underlying contract value above or below the previous business day's closing contract price.
Position limits	None.
Last trading day	Not stated. Please consult the exchange for the latest details.
Delivery day	Not stated. Please consult the exchange for the latest details.
Initial (Variation) margin	Contract price under Y14,000: Y50,000
	Contract price from Y14,000 to Y18,000: Y60,000
	Contract price above Y18,000: Y70,000
Spread margin	Not stated. Please consult the exchange for the latest details.
Reuters Monitor (Quote)	N/a.
Telerate page	N/a.

Refined white soft sugar futures

Contract size	9,000 kilograms of refined white soft sugar.
Standard delivery method	Physical delivery of the above.
Trading months	The nearby six consecutive calendar months.
Trading hours	Four sessions daily (Monday to Saturday) commencing 9.30 a.m., 10.30 a.m., 1.30 p.m. and 2.30 p.m.

Kanmon
Commodity
Exchange (KCE)
Futures
Softs and
agricultural

Price quotation method	In Japanese sen per kilogram.
Minimum price move (value)	10 Japanese sen (Y0.10) per kilogram (Y900 per contract).
Daily price limits	10% of the underlying contract value above or below the previous business day's closing contract price.
Position limits	None.
Last trading day	Not stated. Please consult the exchange for the latest details.
Delivery day	Not stated. Please consult the exchange for the latest details.
Initial (Variation) margin	Contract price under Y200: Y40,000 Contract price from Y200 to Y300: Y50,000 Contract price above Y300: Y60,000
Spread margin	Not stated. Please consult the exchange for the latest details.
Reuters Monitor (Quote)	N/a.
Telerate page	N/a.

Soyabeans (imported) futures

Contract size	15,000 kilograms of imported soyabeans.
Standard delivery method	Physical delivery of the above.
Trading months	The nearby six consecutive calendar months.
Trading hours	Six sessions daily (Monday to Saturday) commencing 9.00 a.m., 10.00 a.m., 11.00 a.m., 1.00 p.m., 2.00 p.m. and 3.00 p.m.
Price quotation method	In Japanese yen (Y) per 60 kilograms.
Minimum price move (value)	Y10.00 per 60 kilograms (Y2,500 per contract).
Daily price limits	Within 10% of the underlying contract value above or below the previous business day's closing contract price.
Position limits	None.
Last trading day	Not stated. Please consult the exchange for the latest details.
Delivery day	Not stated. Please consult the exchange for the latest details.
Initial (Variation) margin	Contract price under Y5,000: Y70,000 Contract price from Y5,000 to Y6,000: Y80,000 Contract price above Y6,000: Y90,000
Spread margin	Not stated. Please consult the exchange for the latest details.
Reuters Monitor (Quote)	N/a.
Telerate page	N/a.

Kanmon
Commodity
Exchange (KCE)
Futures
Softs and
agricultural

White beans futures

Contract size	2,400 kilograms of white beans.
Standard delivery method	Physical delivery of the above.
Trading months	The nearby six consecutive calendar months.
Trading hours	Six sessions daily (Monday to Saturday) commencing 9.00 a.m., 10.00 a.m., 11.00 a.m., 1.00 p.m., 2.00 p.m. and 3.00 p.m.
Price quotation method	In Japanese yen (Y) per 60 kilograms.
Minimum price move (value)	Y10.00 per 60 kilograms (Y400 per contract).
Daily price limits	Within 10% of the underlying contract value above or below the previous business day's closing contract price.
Position limits	None.
Last trading day	Not stated. Please consult the exchange for the latest details.
Delivery day	Not stated. Please consult the exchange for the latest details.
Initial (Variation) margin	Contract price under Y13,000: Y60,000 Contract price from Y13,000 to Y18,000: Y70,000 Contract price above Y18,000: Y80,000
Spread margin	Not stated. Please consult the exchange for the latest details.
Reuters Monitor (Quote)	N/a.
Telerate page	N/a.

Kobe Grain Exchange (KGE)

Address:	2-4-16 Honmachi Hyogo-ku Kobe 652 Japan
Telephone:	(078) 671 2901
Fax:	(078) 671 3837
Telex:	N/a.

Exchange personnel

President:	Shigeru Tamura
Managing Director:	Ikuo Kida

Futures contracts available
Red beans
Soyabeans (domestic)
Soyabeans (imported)
White beans

Options contracts available
None

Clearing House:	Cleared by the exchange itself.
Method of trading:	By a competitive auction of concentrated bids and offers at a single contracted price. There is no continuous session, but several sessions each day.
Commenced trading:	History dates back to 1892.
Exchange links:	Member of the Japan Federation of Commodity Exchanges.

A brief synopsis of the exchange
The exchange was initially known as the Hyogo Rice & Fertiliser Wholesale Co-operative, becoming a proper rice market in 1902. Rice futures were banned in 1926, but the exchange continued to trade in other grain products. The exchange has been in existence under its current name since 1952.

Commission rates

A range of customer commissions for the different contracts traded exists as follows depending on the contract price. Lower commissions are payable from members:

Red beans	From Y3,200 to Y4,000.
Soyabeans (imported)	From Y3,300 to Y5,500.
White beans	From Y3,000 to Y4,000.

Red beans futures

Contract size	2,400 kilograms of red beans.
Standard delivery method	Physical delivery of the above.
Trading months	The nearby six consecutive calendar months.
Trading hours	Six sessions daily (Monday to Saturday) commencing 9.00 a.m., 10.00 a.m., 11.00 a.m., 1.00 p.m., 2.00 p.m. and 3.00 p.m.
Price quotation method	In Japanese yen (Y) per 30 kilograms.
Minimum price move (value)	Y10.00 per 30 kilograms (Y800 per contract).
Daily price limits	Within 7% of the underlying contract value above or below the previous business day's closing contract price.
Position limits	None.
Last trading day	Not stated. Please consult the exchange for the latest details.
Delivery day	Not stated. Please consult the exchange for the latest details.
Initial (Variation) margin	Contract price under Y14,000: Y50,000 Contract price from Y14,000 to Y18,000: Y60,000 Contract price above Y18,000: Y70,000
Spread margin	Not stated. Please consult the exchange for the latest details.
Reuters Monitor (Quote)	N/a.
Telerate page	N/a.

Soyabeans (domestic) futures

Contract size	2,400 kilograms of domestic soyabeans.
Standard delivery method	Physical delivery of the above.
Trading months	The nearby six consecutive calendar months.
Trading hours	Six sessions daily (Monday to Saturday) commencing 9.00 a.m., 10.00 a.m., 11.00 a.m., 1.00 p.m., 2.00 p.m. and 3.00 p.m.
Price quotation method	In Japanese yen (Y) per 60 kilograms.
Minimum price move (value)	Y10.00 per 60 kilograms (Y400 per contract).
Daily price limits	Within 7% of the underlying contract value above or below the previous business day's closing contract price.
Position limits	None.
Last trading day	Not stated. Please consult the exchange for the latest details.
Delivery day	Not stated. Please consult the exchange for the latest details.

Initial (Variation) margin	Not stated. Please consult the exchange for the latest details.
Spread margin	Not stated. Please consult the exchange for the latest details.
Reuters Monitor (Quote)	N/a.
Telerate page	N/a.

Soyabeans (imported) futures

Contract size	15,000 kilograms of imported soyabeans.
Standard delivery method	Physical delivery of the above.
Trading months	Every other six uneven months.
Trading hours	Six sessions daily (Monday to Saturday) commencing 9.00 a.m., 10.00 a.m., 11.00 a.m., 1.00 p.m., 2.00 p.m. and 3.00 p.m.
Price quotation method	In Japanese yen (Y) per 60 kilograms.
Minimum price move (value)	Y10.00 per 60 kilograms (Y2,500 per contract).
Daily price limits	Within 7% of the underlying contract value above or below the previous business day's closing contract price.
Position limits	None.
Last trading day	Not stated. Please consult the exchange for the latest details.
Delivery day	Not stated. Please consult the exchange for the latest details.
Initial (Variation) margin	Contract price under Y5,000: Y70,000 Contract price from Y5,000 to Y6,000: Y80,000 Contract price above Y6,000: Y90,000
Spread margin	Not stated. Please consult the exchange for the latest details.
Reuters Monitor (Quote)	N/a.
Telerate page	N/a.

White beans futures

Contract size	2,400 kilograms of white beans.
Standard delivery method	Physical delivery of the above.
Trading months	The nearby six consecutive calendar months.
Trading hours	Six sessions daily (Monday to Saturday) commencing 9.00 a.m., 10.00 a.m., 11.00 a.m., 1.00 p.m., 2.00 p.m. and 3.00 p.m.
Price quotation method	In Japanese yen (Y) per 60 kilograms.

Minimum price move (value)	Y10.00 per 60 kilograms (Y400 per contract).
Daily price limits	Within 10% of the underlying contract value above or below the previous business day's closing contract price.
Position limits	None.
Last trading day	Not stated. Please consult the exchange for the latest details.
Delivery day	Not stated. Please consult the exchange for the latest details.
Initial (Variation) margin	Contract price under Y13,000: Y60,000
	Contract price from Y13,000 to Y18,000: Y70,000
	Contract price above Y18,000: Y80,000
Spread margin	Not stated. Please consult the exchange for the latest details.
Reuters Monitor (Quote)	N/a.
Telerate page	N/a.

Kobe Raw Silk Exchange (KRSE)

Address:	126 Higashi-Machi Chou-ku Kobe 650 Japan
Telephone:	(078) 331 7171/4
Fax:	(078) 331 7145
Telex:	N/a.

Exchange personnel

President:	Kan Nanba
Managing Directors:	Reizo Tamenaga, Haruo Miyairi

Futures contracts available
Raw silk

Options contracts available
None

Clearing House:	Cleared by the exchange itself.
Method of trading:	By a competitive auction of concentrated bids and offers at a single contracted price. There is no continuous session, but several sessions each day.
Commenced trading:	Dates back to 1871.
Exchange links:	Member of the Japan Federation of Commodity Exchanges.

A brief synopsis of the exchange
Like many other Japanese exchanges, the history at Kobe tells of involvement in rice futures in the last century. The exchange closed during the war, and has traded under its present name, mainly as a domestic exchange, since 1951.

Commission rates

A range of customer commissions exists as follows depending on the contract price. Lower commissions are payable from members:

Contract value	*Commission*
Contract price under Y13,500	Y4,900.
Contract price over Y13,500	Additional Y500 for each Y2,000.

Raw silk futures

Contract size	300 kilograms (or five bales or 10 cases) of raw silk.
Standard delivery method	Physical delivery of one of the above categories of raw silk.
Trading months	The nearby six consecutive calendar months.
Trading hours	Four sessions daily (Monday to Saturday) commencing at 9.15 a.m., 11.10 a.m., 1.15 p.m. and 3.10 p.m.
Price quotation method	In Japanese yen (Y) per kilogram.
Minimum price move (value)	Y1.00 per kilogram (Y300 per contract).
Daily price limits	Within 5% of the underlying value of the contract above or below the previous day's closing price.
Position limits	None.
Last trading day	Not stated. Please consult the exchange for the latest details.
Delivery day	Not stated. Please consult the exchange for the latest details.
Initial (Variation) margin	Contract price under Y11,500: Y25,000 Contract price from Y11,500 to Y13,500: Y30,000 Contract price above Y13,500: Y35,000
Spread margin	Not stated. Please consult the exchange for the latest details.
Reuters Monitor (Quote)	N/a.
Telerate page	N/a.

Kobe Rubber Exchange (KRE)

Address: 49 Harima-cho
Chou-ku
Kobe 650
Japan

Telephone: (078) 331 4211
Fax: (078) 332 1622
Telex: N/a.

Exchange personnel
President: Takeshi Ohira
Managing Director: Keiichiro Hayashi

Futures contracts available
International No.3 ribbed smoked sheet (RSS3) rubber

Options contracts available
None

Clearing House: Cleared by the exchange itself.

Method of trading: By a competitive auction of concentrated bids and offers at a single contracted price. There is no continuous session, but several sessions each day.

Commenced trading: 1885 (1952 under the present name).

Exchange links: Member of the Japan Federation of Commodity Exchanges.

A brief synopsis of the exchange
The Kobe Rubber Exchange is a non-profit organisation, comprising three categories of membership: Regular, Commission and Associate members. Rubber as an industry in Kobe dates back to the nineteenth century, and the city is the major producer of rubber in Japan. The introduction of Associate membership (non-residents) in 1984 and a later trading session was part of the exchange's program of internationalisation.

Commission rates

A range of customer commissions exist as follows depending on the contract price. Lower commissions are payable from members:

Contract value	*Commission*
Contract price under Y250	Y3,500.
Contract price Y250 – Y300	Y3,800.
Contract price Y300 – Y350	Y4,100.
Contract price Y350 – Y400	Y4,400.
Contract price over Y400	Y50 for each Y300 increase in the contract price.

International No.3 ribbed smoked sheet (RSS3) rubber futures

Contract size	5,000 kilograms of standard grade (No.3) ribbed smoked sheet (RSS3) rubber conforming to international standards.
Standard delivery method	Physical delivery of the above.
Trading months	The current month, the next three consecutive calendar months and the following two even months from the February, April, June, August, October and December cycle.
Trading hours	Six sessions daily (Monday to Saturday) commencing at 9.30 a.m., 10.30 a.m., 1.30 p.m., 2.30 p.m., 3.30 p.m. and 5.00 p.m.
Price quotation method	In Japanese yen (Y) per kilogram.
Minimum price move (value)	Y0.10 per kilogram (Y500 per contract).
Daily price limits	An amount in the ranges Y6.00–Y10.00 per kilogram which is predetermined based on the average contract price during the previous month.
Position limits	None.
Last trading day	The day that is five business days counting from the last day of the contract month. The final contract settlement price comes from the second session's price on the last trading day.
Delivery day	The last business day of the contract month.
Initial (Variation) margin	Contract price less than Y130: Y30,000 Contract price between Y130 and Y160: Y40,000 Contract price between Y160 and Y190: Y50,000 Contract price between Y190 and Y210: Y60,000 Contract price greater than Y210: Y70,000
Spread margin	No concessions.
Reuters Monitor (Quote)	RUJC–RUJF, KREQ–KRES.
Telerate page	N/a.

Maebashi Dried Cocoon Exchange (MDCE)

Address:	1-49-1 Furuichi-machi Maebashi 371 Japan
Telephone:	(0272) 52 1401
Fax:	(0272) 51 8270
Telex:	N/a.

Exchange personnel

President:	Kimkiji Kuribara
Executive Director:	Maseo Yamamura
Managing Director:	Yukio Saito

Futures contracts available
Dried cocoons

Options contracts available
None

Clearing House: Cleared by the exchange itself.

Method of trading: By a competitive auction of concentrated bids and offers at a single contracted price. There is no continuous session, but several sessions each day.

Commenced trading: 1952.

Exchange links: Member of the Japan Federation of Commodity Exchanges.

A brief synopsis of the exchange
Dried cocoons are raw cocoons dried for preservation, and used as the raw material for raw silk. The exchange is important for the hedging needs of the silk yarn industries and the cocoons traded at the MDCE are both domestic and international in origin. There has been an increased speculative use of this contract in recent years.

Commission rates

A range of customer commissions exist as follows depending on the contract price. Lower commissions are payable from members:

Contract value	Commission
Contract price under Y13,500	Y4,900.
Contract price over Y13,500	Y500 for each additional Y2,000.

Maebashi Dried
Cocoon Exchange
(MDCE)
Futures
Softs and
agricultural

Dried cocoon futures

Contract size	300 kilograms of dried cocoons.
Standard delivery method	Physical delivery of the above.
Trading months	The nearby six consecutive calendar months.
Trading hours	Four sessions daily (Monday to Saturday) commencing 9.20 a.m., 11.20 a.m., 1.20 p.m. and 3.20 p.m.
Price quotation method	In Japanese yen (Y) per kilogram.
Minimum price move (value)	Y1.00 per kilogram (Y300 per contract).
Daily price limits	Y130 per kilogram above or below the previous day's closing level.
Position limits	None.
Last trading day	Not stated. Please consult the exchange for the latest details.
Delivery day	Not stated. Please consult the exchange for the latest details.
Initial (Variation) margin	Contract price under Y5,800: Y60,000
	Contract price from Y5,800 to Y6,400: Y70,000
	Contract price above Y6,400: Y80,000
Spread margin	Not stated. Please consult the exchange for the latest details.
Reuters Monitor (Quote)	SKJB–SKJE.
Telerate page	17110.

Nagoya Grain and Sugar Exchange (NGSE)

Address:

2-3-2 Maieki-Minami
Nakamura-ku
Nagoya 450
Japan

Telephone:
Fax:
Telex:

(052) 571 8161
(052) 581 4653
N/a.

Exchange personnel

President:
Managing Director:

Shouzou Takahashi
Fujio Nagano

Futures contracts available
Potato starch
Red beans
Refined white soft sugar
Soyabeans (domestic)
Soyabeans (imported)
Sweet potato starch
White beans

Options contracts available
None

Clearing House:

Cleared by the exchange itself.

Method of trading:

By a competitive auction of concentrated bids and offers at a single contracted price. There is no continuous session, but several sessions each day.

Commenced trading:

Dates back to 1877.

Exchange links:

Member of the Japan Federation of Commodity Exchanges.

A brief synopsis of the exchange
One of several Japanese exchanges that trace their origins back to rice futures, Nagoya is centrally located in the heart of Japan. Nagoya plans to develop further from grains and sugar into a more general commodity exchange.

Commission rates

A range of customer commissions exists for each contract as follows depending on the contract price. Lower commissions are payable from members:

Potato starch	Y2,000 regardless of the contract price.
Red beans	Y3,200 – Y4,000.
Refined white soft sugar	Y4,000–Y4,600 increasing by Y300 for each Y50 increase in the contract price.
Soyabeans (domestic)	Y2,000 regardless of the contract price.
Soyabeans (imported)	Y3,500–Y4,000.
Sweet potato starch	Y2,000 regardless of the contract price.
White beans	Y3,000 – Y4,000.

Nagoya Grain &
Sugar Exchange
(NGSE)
Futures
Softs and
agricultural

Potato starch futures

Contract size	2,500 kilograms of potato starch.
Standard delivery method	Physical delivery of the above.
Trading months	The nearby three consecutive calendar months.
Trading hours	Six sessions daily (Monday to Saturday) commencing at 9.00 a.m., 10.00 a.m., 11.00 a.m., 1.00 p.m., 2.00 p.m. and 3.00 p.m.
Price quotation method	In Japanese yen (Y) per kilogram.
Minimum price move (value)	Y1.00 per 25 kilograms (Y100 per contract).
Daily price limits	Within 7% of the underlying contract value of the previous business day's closing price.
Position limits	None.
Last trading day	Not stated. Please consult the exchange for the latest details.
Delivery day	Not stated. Please consult the exchange for the latest details.
Initial (Variation) margin	Contract price under Y1,500: Y8,000
	Contract price from Y1,500 to Y2,000: Y9,000
	Contract price above Y2,000: Y10,000
Spread margin	Not stated. Please consult the exchange for the latest details.
Reuters Monitor (Quote)	N/a.
Telerate page	N/a.

Red beans futures

Contract size	2,400 kilograms of red beans.
Standard delivery method	Physical delivery of the above.
Trading months	The nearby six consecutive calendar months.
Trading hours	Six sessions daily (Monday to Saturday) commencing at 9.00 a.m., 10.00 a.m., 11.00 a.m., 1.00 p.m., 2.00 p.m. and 3.00 p.m.
Price quotation method	In Japanese yen (Y) per kilogram.
Minimum price move (value)	Y10.00 per 30 kilograms (Y800 per contract).
Daily price limits	Within 7% of the underlying contract value of the previous business day's closing price.
Position limits	None.
Last trading day	Not stated. Please consult the exchange for the latest details.
Delivery day	Not stated. Please consult the exchange for the latest details.

**Nagoya Grain &
Sugar Exchange
(NGSE)
Futures
Softs and
agricultural**

Initial (Variation) margin	Contract price under Y14,000: Y50,000
	Contract price from Y14,000 to Y18,000: Y60,000
	Contract price above Y18,000: Y70,000
Spread margin	Not stated. Please consult the exchange for the latest details.
Reuters Monitor (Quote)	N/a.
Telerate page	N/a.

Refined white soft sugar futures

Contract size	9,000 kilograms of refined white soft sugar.
Standard delivery method	Physical delivery of the above.
Trading months	The nearby six consecutive calendar months.
Trading hours	Four sessions daily (Monday to Saturday) commencing at 9.30 a.m., 10.30 a.m., 1.30 p.m. and 2.30 p.m.
Price quotation method	In Japanese sen per kilogram.
Minimum price move (value)	10 Japanese sen (Y0.10) per kilogram (Y900 per contract).
Daily price limits	Within 7% of the underlying contract value of the previous business day's closing price.
Position limits	None.
Last trading day	Not stated. Please consult the exchange for the latest details.
Delivery day	Not stated. Please consult the exchange for the latest details.
Initial (Variation) margin	Contract price under Y200: Y40,000
	Contract price from Y200 to Y300: Y50,000
	Contract price above Y300: Y60,000
Spread margin	Not stated. Please consult the exchange for the latest details.
Reuters Monitor (Quote)	N/a.
Telerate page	N/a.

Soyabeans (domestic) futures

Contract size	2,400 kilograms of domestic soyabeans.
Standard delivery method	Physical delivery of the above.
Trading months	The nearby three consecutive calendar months.
Trading hours	Six sessions daily (Monday to Saturday) commencing at 9.00 a.m., 10.00 a.m., 11.00 a.m., 1.00 p.m., 2.00 p.m. and 3.00 p.m.
Price quotation method	In Japanese yen (Y) per kilogram.

Minimum price move *(value)*	Y10.00 per 60 kilograms (Y400 per contract).
Daily price limits	Within 7% of the underlying contract value of the previous business day's closing price.
Position limits	None.
Last trading day	Not stated. Please consult the exchange for the latest details.
Delivery day	Not stated. Please consult the exchange for the latest details.
Initial (Variation) margin	Contract price under Y3,000: Y8,000 Contract price from Y3,000 to Y4,000: Y10,000 Contract price above Y4,000: Y12,000
Spread margin	Not stated. Please consult the exchange for the latest details.
Reuters Monitor (Quote)	N/a.
Telerate page	N/a.

Soyabeans (imported) futures

Contract size	15,000 kilograms of imported soyabeans.
Standard delivery method	Physical delivery of the above.
Trading months	Every other six odd months (the January, March, May, July, September and November cycle).
Trading hours	Six sessions daily (Monday to Saturday) commencing at 9.00 a.m., 10.00 a.m., 11.00 a.m., 1.00 p.m., 2.00 p.m. and 3.00 p.m.
Price quotation method	In Japanese yen (Y) per kilogram.
Minimum price move *(value)*	Y10.00 per 60 kilograms (Y2,500 per contract).
Daily price limits	Within 7% of the underlying contract value of the previous business day's closing price.
Position limits	None.
Last trading day	Not stated. Please consult the exchange for the latest details.
Delivery day	Not stated. Please consult the exchange for the latest details.
Initial (Variation) margin	Contract price under Y5,000: Y70,000 Contract price from Y5,000 to Y6,000: Y80,000 Contract price above Y6,000: Y90,000
Spread margin	Not stated. Please consult the exchange for the latest details.
Reuters Monitor (Quote)	N/a.
Telerate page	N/a.

**Nagoya Grain &
Sugar Exchange
(NGSE)
Futures
Softs and
agricultural**

Sweet potato starch futures

Contract size	2,500 kilograms of sweet potato starch.
Standard delivery method	Physical delivery of the above.
Trading months	The nearby three consecutive calendar months.
Trading hours	Six sessions daily (Monday to Saturday) commencing at 9.00 a.m., 10.00 a.m., 11.00 a.m., 1.00 p.m., 2.00 p.m. and 3.00 p.m.
Price quotation method	In Japanese yen (Y) per kilogram.
Minimum price move (value)	Y1.00 per 25 kilograms (Y100 per contract).
Daily price limits	Within 7% of the underlying contract value of the previous business day's closing price.
Position limits	None.
Last trading day	Not stated. Please consult the exchange for the latest details.
Delivery day	Not stated. Please consult the exchange for the latest details.
Initial (Variation) margin	Contract price under Y1,500: Y7,000
	Contract price from Y1,500 to Y2,000: Y8,000
	Contract price above Y2,000: Y9,000
Spread margin	Not stated. Please consult the exchange for the latest details.
Reuters Monitor (Quote)	N/a.
Telerate page	N/a.

White beans futures

Contract size	2,400 kilograms of white beans.
Standard delivery method	Physical delivery of the above.
Trading months	The nearby six consecutive calendar months.
Trading hours	Six sessions daily (Monday to Saturday) commencing at 9.00 a.m., 10.00 a.m., 11.00 a.m., 1.00 p.m., 2.00 p.m. and 3.00 p.m.
Price quotation method	In Japanese yen (Y) per kilogram.
Minimum price move (value)	Y10.00 per 60 kilograms (Y400 per contract).
Daily price limits	Within 7% of the underlying contract value of the previous business day's closing price.
Position limits	None.
Last trading day	Not stated. Please consult the exchange for the latest details.
Delivery day	Not stated. Please consult the exchange for the latest details.

Initial (Variation) margin	Contract price under Y13,000:	Y60,000
	Contract price from Y13,000 to Y18,000:	Y70,000
	Contract price above Y18,000:	Y80,000
Spread margin	Not stated. Please consult the exchange for the latest details.	
Reuters Monitor (Quote)	N/a.	
Telerate page	N/a.	

Nagoya Stock Exchange (NSX)

Address:	3-3-17 Sakae Nakaa-ku Nagoya 450 Japan
Telephone:	(052) 262 31791
Fax:	N/a.
Telex:	N/a.

Exchange personnel

President:	Not known.
Managing Director:	Not known.

Futures contracts available
None

Options contracts on cash/physical available
NSX Option 25 Stock Index

Clearing House:	Cleared by the exchange itself.
Method of trading:	By a competitive auction of concentrated bids and offers at a single contracted price.
Commenced trading:	1988 in index options.
Exchange links:	None.

Commission rates
A range of customer commissions exists as follows depending on the contract price. Lower commissions are payable from members:

Amount of premium received or paid (or exercise value)	*Commission due*
Under Y1,000,000	2.00%
From Y1,000,000 to Y3,000,000	1.50% + Y5,000
From Y3,000,000 to Y5,000,000	1.00% + Y20,000
From Y5,000,000 to Y10,000,000	0.75% + Y32,500
From Y10,000,000 to Y30,000,000	0.60% + Y47,500
From Y30,000,000 to Y50,000,000	0.45% + Y92,500
Over Y50,000,000	0.30% + Y167,500

Option on the NSX Option 25 Stock Index

Contract size	Y10,000 multiplied by the NSX Option 25 Stock Index*.
Standard delivery method	Cash settlement on the last trading day. There is no facility for physical delivery of the shares underlying the index.
Trading months	The nearby four consecutive calendar months.
Trading hours	Two sessions daily (Monday to Saturday): 9.00 a.m. – 11.15 a.m. and 12.30 p.m. – 3.15 p.m. Trading ceases in the expiring contract at 3.00 p.m. on the last trading day.
Price quotation method	In Japanese yen (Y) per index point.
Minimum price move (value)	0.5 index points (Y5,000 per contract) for spot index quotations under 100 and one full index point (Y10,000 per contract) for all higher quotations.
Daily price limits	Around 3% of the underlying value of the TOPIX index (the range being between 30 and 120 index points). The exchange may alter limits at its discretion with regard to the volatility of the underlying index.
Position limits	None.
Last trading day	The business day prior to the second Friday of the contract month or the nearest business day if that day is a non-business day.
Delivery day	The business day following the last trading day. Premiums must be paid by 9.00 a.m. on the third business day following the day of the transaction and margins by 9.00 a.m. on the second day following the day of the transaction.
Initial (Variation) margin	For uncovered short positions, the minimum margin is the greater of (a) Y6,000,000 and (b) the option premium received plus 9% of the strike price. Maintenance margin must be deposited when the initial deficiency becomes 3% of the strike price.
Spread margin	Not stated.
Strike price intervals	At 0.5 index point intervals.
Option type	European style (the option may be exercised only on the last trading day and not at other times during its life). Any series that are in-the-money are automatically exercised on expiry.
Method of introduction of new strike prices	Five series are issued initially around the current index level. New series are introduced as the underlying index moves, although no new series are normally introduced in the month in which the option expires.
Reuters Monitor (Quote)	N/a.
Telerate page	N/a.

* The NSX Option 25 Index is a price weighted index according to the market value of 25 underlying securities each with an underlying market value of at least Y200 billion.

Nagoya Textile Exchange (NTE)

Address:

2-15, Nishiki 3 chome
Nakaku
Nagoya 460
Japan

Telephone: (052) 951 2171
Fax: (052) 961 6407
Telex: N/a.

Exchange personnel

President: Hanshichi Toyoshima
Executive Director: Minoru Kimbara
Managing Director: Hiroo Harada

Futures contracts available
Cotton yarn
Staple fibre yarn (spun rayon yarn)
Woollen yarn

Options contracts available
None

Clearing House: Cleared by the exchange itself.

Method of trading: By a competitive auction of concentrated bids and offers at a single contracted price. There is no continuous session, but several sessions each day.

Commenced trading: Dates back to 1877.

Exchange links: Member of the Japan Federation of Commodity Exchanges.

A brief synopsis of the exchange
The exchange was established as the third commodity exchange in Japan in 1951, initially listing only staple fibre yarn. Nagoya is centrally located in Japan, and is part of a prosperous woollen industry.

Commission rates
A range of customer commissions exists for each contract as follows depending on the contract price. Lower commissions are payable from members:

Nagoya Textile Exchange (NTE)

Cotton yarn	Contract price under Y330	Y4,500.
	Contract price Y330 – Y410	Y4,800.
	Contract price over Y410	Y5,100.
Staple fibre yarn	Contract price under Y220	Y3,300.
	Contract price Y220 – Y280	Y3,600.
	Contract price over Y280	Y3,900.
Woollen Yarn	Contract price under Y2,000	Y3,500.
	Contract price Y2,000 – Y2,500	Y4,000.
	Contract price over Y2,500	Y4,500.

Cotton yarn futures

Contract size	4,000 pounds (1,814.36 kilograms) of cotton yarn.
Standard delivery method	Physical delivery of the above.
Trading months	The nearby six consecutive calendar months.
Trading hours	Four sessions daily (Monday to Saturday) commencing at 9.20 a.m., 10.30 a.m., 1.10 p.m. and 2.20 p.m.
Price quotation method	In Japanese sen per pound.
Minimum price move (value)	10 Japanese sen (Y0.10) per pound (Y400 per contract).
Daily price limits	3% of the underlying contract value above or below the previous day's closing price.
Position limits	None.
Last trading day	Not stated. Please consult the exchange for the latest details.
Delivery day	Not stated. Please consult the exchange for the latest details.
Initial (Variation) margin	Contract price under Y300: Y40,000 Contract price between Y300 and Y400: Y45,000 Contract price over Y400: Y50,000
Spread margin	Not stated. Please consult the exchange for the latest details.
Reuters Monitor (Quote)	N/a.
Telerate page	N/a.

Staple fibre yarn (spun rayon yarn) futures

Contract size	5,000 pounds (2,267.95 kilograms) of staple fibre yarn (spun rayon yarn).
Standard delivery method	Physical delivery of the above.
Trading months	The nearby six consecutive calendar months.
Trading hours	Four sessions daily (Monday to Saturday) commencing at 9.55 a.m., 11.05 a.m., 1.55 p.m. and 3.00 p.m.
Price quotation method	In Japanese sen per pound.
Minimum price move (value)	10 Japanese sen (Y0.10) per pound (Y500 per contract).
Daily price limits	5% of the underlying contract value above or below the previous day's closing price.
Position limits	None.
Last trading day	Not stated. Please consult the exchange for the latest details.
Delivery day	Not stated. Please consult the exchange for the latest details.

Initial (Variation) margin	Contract price under Y220:	Y30,000
	Contract price between Y220 and Y280:	Y37,000
	Contract price over Y280:	Y44,000

Spread margin   Not stated. Please consult the exchange for the latest details.

Reuters Monitor (Quote)   N/a.

Telerate page   N/a.

Woollen yarn futures

Contract size   500 kilograms of woollen yarn.

Standard delivery method   Physical delivery of the above.

Trading months   The nearby six consecutive calendar months.

Trading hours   Four sessions daily (Monday to Saturday) commencing at 9.40 a.m., 10.50 a.m., 1.30 p.m. and 2.40 p.m.

Price quotation method   In Japanese yen (Y) per kilogram.

*Minimum price move
   (value)*   Y1.00 per kilogram (Y500.00 per contract).

Daily price limits   3% of the underlying contract value above or below the previous day's closing price.

Position limits   None.

Last trading day   Not stated. Please consult the exchange for the latest details.

Delivery day   Not stated. Please consult the exchange for the latest details.

Initial (Variation) margin	Contract price under Y2,000:	Y35,000
	Contract price between Y2,000 and Y2,500:	Y40,000
	Contract price over Y2,500:	Y45,000

Spread margin   Not stated. Please consult the exchange for the latest details.

Reuters Monitor (Quote)   N/a.

Telerate page   N/a.

Osaka Grain Exchange (OGE)

Address:

1-10-14 Awaza
Nishi-ku
Osaka 550
Japan

Telephone: (06) 531 7931
Fax: (06) 541 9343
Telex: N/a.

Exchange personnel

President: Osamu Osugi
Executive Director: Kiyoshi Hirai

Futures contracts available
Potato starch
Red beans
Soyabeans (domestic)
Soyabeans (imported)
White beans

Options contracts available
None

Clearing House: Cleared by the exchange itself.

Method of trading: By a competitive auction of concentrated bids and offers at a single contracted price. There is no continuous session, but several sessions each day.

Commenced trading: Dates back to 1640.

Exchange links: Member of the Japan Federation of Commodity Exchanges.

A brief synopsis of the exchange
The oldest exchange in Japan, the Osaka Grain Exchange traces its origins back to 1640 and the Dojima Rice Exchange. It began trading under its new name in 1952 as the 15th Japanese commodity exchange specialising in the cereal markets. There are around 100 exchange members.

Commission rates

A range of customer commissions exists for each contract as follows depending on the contract price. Lower commissions are payable from members:

Potato starch	Y2,000 regardless of contract price.
Red beans	Y3,200 – Y4,000.
Soyabeans (domestic)	Y2,000 regardless of contract price.
Soyabeans (imported)	Y3,300 – Y5,500.
White beans	Y3,000 – Y4,000.

Potato starch futures

Contract size	2,500 kilograms of potato starch.
Standard delivery method	Physical delivery of the above.
Trading months	The nearby three consecutive calendar months.
Trading hours	Six sessions daily (Monday to Saturday) commencing at 9.00 a.m., 10.00 a.m., 11.00 a.m., 1.00 p.m., 2.00 p.m. and 3.00 p.m.
Price quotation method	In Japanese yen (Y) per kilogram.
Minimum price move (value)	Y1.00 per 25 kilograms (Y100 per contract).
Daily price limits	Within 7% of the underlying contract value of the previous business day's closing price.
Position limits	None.
Last trading day	Not stated. Please consult the exchange for the latest details.
Delivery day	Not stated. Please consult the exchange for the latest details.
Initial (Variation) margin	Contract price under Y1,500: Y8,000 Contract price from Y1,500 to Y2,000: Y10,000 Contract price above Y2,000: Y12,000
Spread margin	Not stated. Please consult the exchange for the latest details.
Reuters Monitor (Quote)	N/a.
Telerate page	N/a.

Red beans futures

Contract size	2,400 kilograms of red beans.
Standard delivery method	Physical delivery of the above.
Trading months	The nearby six consecutive calendar months.
Trading hours	Six sessions daily (Monday to Saturday) commencing at 9.00 a.m., 10.00 a.m., 11.00 a.m., 1.00 p.m., 2.00 p.m. and 3.00 p.m.
Price quotation method	In Japanese yen (Y) per kilogram.
Minimum price move (value)	Y10.00 per 30 kilograms (Y800 per contract).
Daily price limits	Within 7% of the underlying contract value of the previous business day's closing price.
Position limits	None.
Last trading day	Not stated. Please consult the exchange for the latest details.
Delivery day	Not stated. Please consult the exchange for the latest details.

Initial (Variation) margin	Contract price under Y14,000:	Y50,000
	Contract price from Y14,000 to Y18,000:	Y60,000
	Contract price above Y18,000:	Y70,000

Spread margin Not stated. Please consult the exchange for the latest details.

Reuters Monitor (Quote) N/a.
Telerate page N/a.

Soyabeans (domestic) futures

Contract size 2,400 kilograms of domestic soyabeans.
Standard delivery method Physical delivery of the above.
Trading months The nearby three consecutive calendar months.
Trading hours Six sessions daily (Monday to Saturday) commencing at 9.00 a.m., 10.00 a.m., 11.00 a.m., 1.00 p.m., 2.00 p.m. and 3.00 p.m.
Price quotation method In Japanese yen (Y) per kilogram.
Minimum price move (value) Y10.00 per 60 kilograms (Y400 per contract).
Daily price limits Within 7% of the underlying contract value of the previous business day's closing price.
Position limits None.
Last trading day Not stated. Please consult the exchange for the latest details.
Delivery day Not stated. Please consult the exchange for the latest details.

Initial (Variation) margin	Contract price under Y3,000:	Y8,000
	Contract price from Y3,000 – Y4,000:	Y10,000
	Contract price above Y4,000:	Y12,000

Spread margin Not stated. Please consult the exchange for the latest details.

Reuters Monitor (Quote) N/a.
Telerate page N/a.

Soyabeans (imported) futures

Contract size 15,000 kilograms of imported soyabeans.
Standard delivery method Physical delivery of the above.
Trading months Every other six even months (the February, April, June, August, October and December cycle).
Trading hours Six sessions daily (Monday to Saturday) commencing at 9.00 a.m., 10.00 a.m., 11.00 a.m., 1.00 p.m., 2.00 p.m. and 3.00 p.m.

Price quotation method	In Japanese yen (Y) per kilogram.	
Minimum price move (value)	Y10.00 per 60 kilograms (Y2,500 per contract).	
Daily price limits	Within 7% of the underlying contract value of the previous business day's closing price.	
Position limits	None.	
Last trading day	Not stated. Please consult the exchange for the latest details.	
Delivery day	Not stated. Please consult the exchange for the latest details.	
Initial (Variation) margin	Contract price under Y5,000:	Y70,000
	Contract price from Y5,000 to Y6,000:	Y80,000
	Contract price above Y6,000:	Y90,000
Spread margin	Not stated. Please consult the exchange for the latest details.	
Reuters Monitor (Quote)	N/a.	
Telerate page	N/a.	

White beans futures

Contract size	2,400 kilograms of white beans.	
Standard delivery method	Physical delivery of the above.	
Trading months	The nearby six consecutive calendar months.	
Trading hours	Six sessions daily (Monday to Saturday) commencing at 9.00 a.m., 10.00 a.m., 11.00 a.m., 1.00 p.m., 2.00 p.m. and 3.00 p.m.	
Price quotation method	In Japanese yen (Y) per kilogram.	
Minimum price move (value)	Y10.00 per 60 kilograms (Y400 per contract).	
Daily price limits	Within 7% of the underlying contract value of the previous business day's closing price.	
Position limits	None.	
Last trading day	Not stated. Please consult the exchange for the latest details.	
Delivery day	Not stated. Please consult the exchange for the latest details.	
Initial (Variation) margin	Contract price under Y13,000:	Y60,000
	Contract price from Y13,000 to Y18,000:	Y70,000
	Contract price above Y18,000:	Y80,000
Spread margin	Not stated. Please consult the exchange for the latest details.	
Reuters Monitor (Quote)	N/a.	
Telerate page	N/a.	

Osaka Securities Exchange (OSX)

Address:	8-16 Kitahama 1-chome Chou-ku Osaka 541 Japan
Telephone:	(06) 229 8641/3
Fax:	(06) 231 2639 / 227 0445
Telex:	5222215

Exchange personnel

President:	Hiroshi Yamanouchi
Chairman:	Munekazu Yano
Information Officer:	Minoru Nakamura

Futures contracts available
Nikkei 225 Stock Average
OSF 50 Stock Index

Options contracts on cash/physical available
Nikkei 225 Stock Average

Clearing House:	Cleared by the exchange itself.
Method of trading:	Futures are traded through a computerised trading system while options are traded by open outcry.
Commenced trading:	1987 for futures, 1989 for options.
Exchange links:	None.

A brief synopsis of the exchange
The Osaka Securities Exchange is one of the oldest securities exchanges in Japan, its predecesor the Osaka Stock Exchange being founded in 1878. Trading in the OSF 50, the first stock index futures contract in Japan began in June 1987, based on physical delivery procedures. In May 1988, Japanese law was revised to allow stock index futures and options trading based on cash settlement. The Nikkei 225 Stock Average futures and options were later introduced. This was Japan's first stock index options market. Osaka is an important worldwide financial centre and the exchange ranks fourth in terms of market capitalisation after Tokyo, New York and London.

There are nearly 100 full exchange members and
approximately the same number of floor brokers.

Commission rates

Contract value	*Commission*
Up to Y100 million	0.04%
Y100 m – Y300 m	0.03% + Y10,000
Y300 m – Y500 m	0.02% + Y40,000
Y500 m – Y1 billion	0.01% + Y90,000
Over Y1 billion	0.005% + Y140,000

Nikkei 225 stock average futures

Contract size	Y1,000 multiplied by the Nikkei 225 Stock Average.
Standard delivery method	Cash settlement on the last trading day (see below).* There is no facility for physical delivery of the stocks underlying the index.
Trading months	The March, June, September and December cycle (with the nearest five contract months available for trading at any one time).
Trading hours	Two sessions daily (Monday to Saturday): 9.00 a.m. – 11.15 a.m. and 12.30 p.m. – 3.15 p.m.
Price quotation method	In Japanese yen (Y) per index point.
Minimum price move (value)	Y10.00 per index point (Y10,000 per contract).
Daily price limits	About 3% of the underlying contract value above or below the previous day's closing index level.
Position limits	None.
Last trading day	The business day prior to the second Friday of the contract month. Trading ceases in the expiring contract at 3.00 p.m. on the last trading day.
Delivery day	The fourth business day following the last trading day.
Initial (Variation) margin	9% (with a minimum of 3% in cash) of the underlying contract value with a minimum of Y6,000,000. Additional margin is necessary when a 'paper loss' exceeds 3% of the contract value.
Spread margin	There are no spread concessions.
Reuters Monitor (Quote)	OQOG – OGOH.
Telerate page	N/a.

* The final settlement price (the 'Special Nikkei Stock Average') is based on the total opening prices of each component issue in the Nikkei Stock Average on the business day following the last trading day.

OSF 50 Stock Index futures

Contract size	The sum total of the number of shares representing one trading unit (basket) of each of the 50 underlying index stocks in the cash market (usually 1,000 shares).
Standard delivery method	Physical delivery of the above basket of 50 stocks.
Trading months	The March, June, September and December cycle (with the nearest five contract months available for trading at any time).
Trading hours	Two sessions daily (Monday to Saturday): 9.00 a.m. – 11.15 a.m. and 1.00 p.m. – 3.15 p.m.
Price quotation method	One fifty-thousandth (1/50,000) of the total of the per share price of each underlying stock multiplied by the number of shares per trading unit.

Minimum price move *(value)*	Y0.50 per trading unit (a minimum value of Y25,000 per contract).
Daily price limits	Base index level under Y1,000: Y30.00
	Base index level Y1,000 – Y2,000: Y60.00
	Base index level Y2,000 – Y3,000: Y90.00
	Base index level Y3,000 – Y4,000: Y120.00
	Base index level over Y4,000: Y150.00
Position limits	None.
Last trading day	The sixth business day prior to the delivery day of the contract month.
Delivery day	The 15th day of the contract month, or the next available business day, if the 15th is not a business day.
Initial (Variation) margin	9% (with a minimum of 3% in cash) of the underlying contract value with a minimum of Y6,000,000. Additional margin is necessary when a 'paper loss' exceeds 3% of the contract value.
Spread margin	There are no spread concessions.
Reuters Monitor (Quote)	N/a.
Telerate page	N/a.

Option on Nikkei 225 Stock Average

Contract size	Y1,000 multiplied by the Nikkei 225 Stock Average.
Standard delivery method	Cash settlement on the last trading day. There is no facility for physical delivery of the stocks underlying the index.
Trading months	The nearest four consecutive calendar months.
Trading hours	Two sessions daily (Monday to Saturday): 9.00 a.m. – 11.15 a.m. and 12.30 p.m. – 3.15 p.m. For those expiry months that overlap with a Nikkei 225 futures contract (the March, June, September and December cycle), the afternoon session closes at 3.00 p.m.
Price quotation method	In Japanese yen (Y) per index point.
Minimum price move *(value)*	Up to Y1,000: Y5.00 per index point (Y5,000 per contract). Over Y1,000: Y10.00 per index point (Y10,000 per contract).
Daily price limits	About 3% of the underlying contract value above or below the previous day's closing index level.
Position limits	None.
Last trading day	The business day before the second Friday of each expiry month.
Delivery day	The business day following the last trading day.

Initial (Variation) margin	(The option price + strike price × 9%) multiplied by Y1,000, subject to a minimum of Y6,000,000 per contract. Additional margin is necessary when the shortage of deposits exceeds 3% of the strike price × Y1,000.
Spread margin	There are no spread concessions.
Strike price intervals	At Y500 per index point intervals.
Option type	American style (the option may be exercised on any business day up to and including the last trading day). However, at present, options may only be exercised on Thursdays and the last trading day.
Method of introduction of new strike prices	Five or six series will be issued initially, with two more around the current Nikkei 225 Stock Average. No new strike prices are normally introduced in the last month before expiry.
Reuters Monitor (Quote)	OROA – OROU.
Telerate page	N/a.

Osaka Sugar Exchange (OSE)

Address: 3-32-1 Kitakyutaro-machi
Higashi-ku
Osaka 541
Japan

Telephone: (06) 254 2261
Fax: (06) 245 2264
Telex: N/a.

Exchange personnel
President: Moriyoshi Ueno
Managing Director: Yoshiharu Nonozaki

Futures contracts available
Raw sugar
Refined white soft sugar

Options contracts available
None currently, but options are being planned.

Clearing House: Cleared by the exchange itself.

Method of trading: By a competitive auction of concentrated bids and offers at a single contracted price. There is no continuous session, but several sessions each day.

Commenced trading: 1925.

Exchange links: Member of the Japan Federation of Commodity Exchanges.

A brief synopsis of the exchange
The exchange, established in 1925, closed in 1939 and reopened in 1952. The exchange shares the same dealing floor as the Osaka Textile Exchange, becoming in 1980 the first collective exchange in Japan. Transactions in raw sugar are for settlement as bulk cargo. There are around 100 exchange members.

Raw sugar

Refined white soft sugar

Commission rates

A range of customer commissions exist for each contract as follows depending on the contract price. Lower commissions are payable from members:

From Y4,300 for a contract price under Y100, and then an additional Y200 for each Y50 increase in the contract price.

From Y4,000 for a contract price under Y200, and then an additional Y300 for each Y50 increase in the contract price.

Raw sugar futures

Contract size	10,000 kilograms of raw sugar.
Standard delivery method	Physical delivery of the above.
Trading months	The nearby nine consecutive calendar months.
Trading hours	Four sessions daily (Monday to Saturday), beginning at 9.30 a.m., 10.30 a.m., 1.30 p.m. and 2.30 p.m.
Price quotation method	In Japanese sen per kilogram.
Minimum price move (value)	10 Japanese sen (Y0.10) per kilogram (Y1,000 per contract).
Daily price limits	10% of the underlying contract value above or below the previous day's settlement price.
Position limits	None.
Last trading day	Not stated. Please consult the exchange for the latest details.
Delivery day	Not stated. Please consult the exchange for the latest details.

Initial (Variation) margin

Contract price under Y50:	Y50,000
Contract price between Y50 and Y100:	Y60,000
Contract price greater than Y100:	Y70,000

Spread margin	Not stated. Please consult the exchange for the latest details.
Reuters Monitor (Quote)	N/a.
Telerate page	N/a.

Refined white soft sugar futures

Contract size	9,000 kilograms of refined white soft sugar.
Standard delivery method	Physical delivery of the above.
Trading months	The nearby six consecutive calendar months.
Trading hours	Four sessions daily (Monday to Saturday), beginning at 9.30 a.m., 10.30 a.m., 1.30 p.m. and 2.30 p.m.
Price quotation method	In Japanese sen per kilogram.
Minimum price move (value)	10 Japanese sen (Y0.10) per kilogram (Y1,000 per contract).
Daily price limits	10% of the underlying contract value above or below the previous day's settlement price.
Position limits	None.
Last trading day	Not stated. Please consult the exchange for the latest details.
Delivery day	Not stated. Please consult the exchange for the latest details.

Initial (Variation) margin

Contract price under Y200:	Y40,000
Contract price between Y200 and Y300:	Y50,000
Contract price greater than Y300:	Y60,000

Osaka Sugar Exchange (OSE) Futures Softs and agricultural	*Spread margin*	Not stated. Please consult the exchange for the latest details.
	Reuters Monitor (*Quote*)	N/a.
	Telerate page	N/a.

Osaka Textile Exchange (OTE)

Address:	2-5-28 Kyutaro Chou-ku Osaka 541 Japan
Telephone: Fax: Telex:	(06) 253 0031 (06) 253 0034 N/a.

Exchange personnel

President:	Shinichi Arai
Executive Director:	Kouji Murata
Managing Director:	Ninpei Kitagawa

Futures contracts available
Cotton yarn (20s single Z-twist)
Cotton yarn (30s single Z-twist)
Cotton yarn (40s single Z-twist)
Staple fibre yarn
Woollen yarn

Options contracts available
None

Clearing House:	Cleared by the exchange itself.
Method of trading:	By a competitive auction of concentrated bids and offers at a single contracted price. There is no continuous session, but several sessions each day.
Commenced trading:	1984.
Exchange links:	Member of the Japan Federation of Commodity Exchanges.

A brief synopsis of the exchange
Trading in cotton and related products has been a feature of the Japanese commodity markets since 1893, through the Osaka Sampin Exchange, a predecessor to the current exchange. Primary users of the exchange's products include spinning companies, textile manufacturers, etc.

Commission rates

A range of customer commissions exists for each contract as follows depending on the contract price. Lower commissions are payable from members:

Cotton yarn 20s	From Y2,000 to Y2,400.
Cotton yarn 40s	From Y4,500 to Y5,100.
Staple fibre yarn	From Y3,300 to Y3,900.
Woollen yarn	From Y3,500 to Y4,500.

Cotton yarn (20s single Z-twist) futures

Contract size	2,000 pounds (907.18 kilograms) of cotton yarn (20s single Z-twist).
Standard delivery method	Physical delivery of the above.
Trading months	The nearby six consecutive calendar months.
Trading hours	Four sessions daily (Monday to Saturday) commencing at 9.45 a.m., 10.45 a.m., 1.45 p.m. and 2.45 p.m.
Price quotation method	In Japanese sen per pound (0.45359 kilograms).
Minimum price move (value)	10 Japanese sen (Y0.10) per pound (Y200 per contract).
Daily price limits	3% of the underlying contract value above or below the previous day's closing price.
Position limits	None.
Last trading day	The last four business days of the contract month including the last business day.
Delivery day	Delivery must be made by the end of the contract month.
Initial (Variation) margin	Contract price under Y220: Y15,000
	Contract price between Y220 and Y320: Y20,000
	Contract price over Y320: Y25,000
Spread margin	There are no spread concessions.
Reuters Monitor (Quote)	N/a.
Telerate page	N/a.

Cotton yarn (30s single Z-twist) futures

Contract size	2,000 pounds (907.18 kilograms) of cotton yarn (30s single Z-twist).
Standard delivery method	Physical delivery of the above.
Trading months	The nearby six consecutive calendar months.
Trading hours	Two sessions daily (Monday to Saturday) commencing at 9.45 a.m. and 1.45 p.m.
Price quotation method	In Japanese sen per pound (0.45359 kilograms).
Minimum price move (value)	10 Japanese sen (Y0.10) per pound (Y200 per contract).
Daily price limits	3% of the underlying contract value above or below the previous day's closing price.
Position limits	None.
Last trading day	The last four business days of the contract month including the last business day.
Delivery day	Delivery must be made by the end of the contract month.
Initial (Variation) margin	Contract price under Y300: Y20,000
	Contract price between Y300 and Y340: Y25,000
	Contract price between Y340 and Y380: Y30,000
	Contract price over Y380: Y35,000

Spread margin	There are no spread concessions.
Reuters Monitor (Quote)	N/a.
Telerate page	N/a.

Cotton yarn (40s single Z twist) futures

Contract size	4,000 pounds (1,814.36 kilograms) of cotton yarn (40s single Z-twist).
Standard delivery method	Physical delivery of the above.
Trading months	The nearby six consecutive calendar months.
Trading hours	Four sessions daily (Monday to Saturday) commencing at 9.45 a.m., 10.45 a.m., 1.45 p.m. and 2.45 p.m.
Price quotation method	In Japanese sen per pound (0.45359 kilograms).
Minimum price move (value)	10 Japanese sen (Y0.10) per pound (Y400 per contract).
Daily price limits	3% of the underlying contract value above or below the previous day's closing price.
Position limits	None.
Last trading day	The last four business days of the contract month including the last business day.
Delivery day	Delivery must be made by the end of the contract month.
Initial (Variation) margin	Contract price under Y350: Y40,000
	Contract price between Y350 and Y390: Y45,000
	Contract price over Y390: Y50,000
Spread margin	There are no spread concessions.
Reuters Monitor (Quote)	N/a.
Telerate page	N/a.

Staple fibre yarn futures

Contract size	5,000 pounds (2,267.95 kilograms) of staple fibre yarn.
Standard delivery method	Physical delivery of the above.
Trading months	The nearby six consecutive calendar months.
Trading hours	Two sessions daily (Monday to Saturday) commencing at 9.45 a.m. and 1.45 p.m.
Price quotation method	In Japanese sen per pound (0.45359 kilograms).
Minimum price move (value)	10 Japanese sen (Y0.10) per pound (Y500 per contract).
Daily price limits	3% of the underlying contract value above or below the previous day's closing price.
Position limits	None.
Last trading day	The last four business days of the contract month including the last business day.

Delivery day	Delivery must be made by the end of the contract month.	
Initial (Variation) margin	Contract price under Y210:	Y30,000
	Contract price between Y210 and Y250:	Y37,000
	Contract price over Y250:	Y44,000
Spread margin	There are no spread concessions.	
Reuters Monitor (Quote)	N/a.	
Telerate page	N/a.	

Woollen yarn futures

Contract size	500 kilograms of woollen yarn.	
Standard delivery method	Physical delivery of the above.	
Trading months	The nearby six consecutive calendar months.	
Trading hours	Four sessions daily (Monday to Saturday) commencing at 9.20 a.m., 11.20 a.m., 2.20 a.m. and 3.20 p.m.	
Price quotation method	In Japanese yen (Y) per kilogram.	
Minimum price move (value)	Y1.00 per kilogram (Y500 per contract).	
Daily price limits	3% of the underlying contract value above or below the previous day's closing price.	
Position limits	None.	
Last trading day	The last four business days of the contract month including the last business day.	
Delivery day	Delivery must be made by the end of the contract month.	
Initial (Variation) margin	Contract price under Y2,200:	Y35,000
	Contract price between Y2,200 and Y2,500:	Y40,000
	Contract price over Y2,500:	Y45,000
Spread margin	There are no spread concessions.	
Reuters Monitor (Quote)	N/a.	
Telerate page	N/a.	

Tokyo Commodity Exchange for Industry (TOCOM)

Address:	10-8 Nihonbashi-Horidome 1-chome Chou-ku Tokyo 103 Japan
Telephone: Fax: Telex:	(03) 661 9191 (03) 661 7568 N/a.

Exchange personnel

President:	Naozo Mabuchi
General Manager:	Toshihisa Koboyashi
Executive Director:	Yonosuke Ariga
Managing Directors:	Toshiyuki Mase, Tatsuo Oka, Hideo Tsuboi

Futures contracts available
Cotton yarn (40s single Z-twist)
Gold
Platinum
Rubber (No.3 international ribbed smoked sheet)
Silver
Woollen yarn

Options contracts available
None

Clearing House:	Cleared by the exchange itself.
Method of trading:	By a competitive auction of concentrated bids and offers at a single contracted price. There is no continuous session, but several sessions each day.
Commenced trading:	1984.
Exchange links:	Member of the Japan Federation of Commodity Exchanges.

A brief synopsis of the exchange

TOCOM was established as the unification of the Tokyo Textile Exchange, the Tokyo Rubber Exchange and the Tokyo Gold Exchange, the first of these dating back to 1918. Precious metal trading was new to Japan in the early 1980s when there was a rapid increase in imported gold.

TOCOM records the largest futures trade in Japan and is a major exchange in the worldwide rankings. There are over 200 exchange members.

Commission rates

A range of customer commissions exists for each contract as follows depending on the contract price. Lower commissions are payable from members:

Cotton yarn	From Y4,500 to Y5,100.
Gold	From Y7,800 for contract prices below Y2,800 and increasing by Y1,200 for Y400 increases thereafter.
Platinum	From Y4,900 for contract prices below Y3,000 and increasing by Y700 for Y400 increases thereafter.
Rubber (RSS3)	From Y3,500 for contract prices below Y250 and increasing by Y300 for Y50 increases thereafter.
Silver	From Y3,500 for contract prices below Y90 and increasing by Y700 for Y20 increases thereafter.
Woollen yarn	From Y3,500 to Y4,500.

Cotton yarn (40s single Z-twist) futures

Contract size	4,000 pounds (1,814.36 kilograms) of cotton yarn (40s single Z-twist).
Standard delivery method	Physical delivery of the above.
Trading months	The nearest six consecutive calendar months.
Trading hours	Four sessions daily (Monday to Saturday) commencing at 8.50 a.m., 10.00 a.m., 12.50 p.m. and 3.10 p.m.
Price quotation method	In Japanese sen per pound (0.45359 kilograms).
Minimum price move (value)	10 Japanese sen (Y0.10) per pound (Y400 per contract).
Daily price limits	At 3% of the underlying contract value above or below the previous day's closing price.
Position limits	None.
Last trading day	Not stated. Please consult the exchange for the latest details.
Delivery day	Not stated. Please consult the exchange for the latest details.
Initial (Variation) margin	Contract price under Y350: Y20,000
	Contract price from Y350 to Y390: Y22,500
	Contract price above Y390: Y25,000
Spread margin	Not stated. Please consult the exchange for the latest details.
Reuters Monitor (Quote)	TCXF.
Telerate page	17101.

Gold futures

Contract size	One kilogram (1,000 grams) of fine gold bullion.
Standard delivery method	Physical delivery of the above.
Trading months	The nearby seven consecutive calendar months.
Trading hours	Six sessions daily (Monday to Saturday) commencing at 9.10 a.m., 10.30 a.m., 11.30 a.m., 1.10 p.m., 2.30 p.m. and 3.45 p.m.
Price quotation method	In Japanese yen (Y) per gram.
Minimum price move (value)	Y1.00 per gram (Y1,000 per contract).
Daily price limits	Y130 per gram above or below the previous day's settlement price.
Position limits	None.
Last trading day	Not stated. Please consult the exchange for the latest details.
Delivery day	Not stated. Please consult the exchange for the latest details.

Initial (Variation) margin	Contract price under Y3,000:	Y135,000
	Contract price from Y3,000 to Y3,400:	Y150,000
	Contract price from Y3,400 to Y3,800:	Y165,000
	Contract price above Y3,800:	Y180,000

Spread margin — Not stated. Please consult the exchange for the latest details.

Reuters Monitor (Quote) — TCXB.

Telerate page — N/a.

Platinum futures

Contract size — 500 grams (0.50 kilograms) of platinum.

Standard delivery method — Physical delivery of the above.

Trading months — The nearby seven consecutive calendar months.

Trading hours — Four sessions daily (Monday to Saturday) commencing immediately after those of the silver futures which follow the first two morning and first and last afternoon sessions of the gold futures, which start at 9.10 a.m., 10.30 a.m., 1.10 p.m., and 3.45 p.m.

Price quotation method — In Japanese yen (Y) per gram.

Minimum price move (value) — Y1.00 per gram (Y500 per contract).

Daily price limits — Y130 per gram above or below the previous day's settlement price.

Position limits — None.

Last trading day — Not stated. Please consult the exchange for the latest details.

Delivery day — Not stated. Please consult the exchange for the latest details.

Initial (Variation) margin	Contract price under Y3,000:	Y66,000
	Contract price from Y3,000 to Y3,400:	Y72,000
	Contract price from Y3,400 to Y3,800:	Y78,000
	Contract price above Y3,800:	Y84,000

Spread margin — Not stated. Please consult the exchange for the latest details.

Reuters Monitor (Quote) — TCXD.

Telerate page — N/a.

Rubber (No. 3 international ribbed smoked sheet) futures

Contract size — 5,000 kilograms of No.3 international ribbed smoked sheet (RSS3) rubber.

Standard delivery method — Physical delivery of the above.

Trading months — The nearby nine consecutive calendar months.

Trading hours	Five sessions daily (Monday to Saturday) commencing at 9.45 a.m., 10.45 a.m., 1.45 p.m., 2.45 p.m. and 3.30 p.m.
Price quotation method	In Japanese sen per kilogram.
Minimum price move (value)	10 Japanese sen (Y0.10) per kilogram (Y500 per contract).
Daily price limits	5% of the underlying contract value above or below the previous day's closing price.
Position limits	None.
Last trading day	Not stated. Please consult the exchange for the latest details.
Delivery day	Not stated. Please consult the exchange for the latest details.
Initial (Variation) margin	Contract price under Y250: Y70,000 Contract price from Y250 to Y280: Y80,000 Contract price from Y280 to Y310: Y90,000 Contract price from Y310 to Y340: Y100,000 Contract price above Y340: Y110,000
Spread margin	Not stated. Please consult the exchange for the latest details.
Reuters Monitor (Quote)	TCXE.
Telerate page	17104.

Silver futures

Contract size	10 kilograms of silver bullion.
Standard delivery method	Physical delivery of the above.
Trading months	The nearby seven consecutive calendar months.
Trading hours	Four sessions daily (Monday to Saturday) commencing immediately after the first two morning and first and last afternoon sessions of the gold futures, which start at 9.10 a.m., 10.30 a.m., 1.10 p.m., and 3.45 p.m.
Price quotation method	In Japanese sen per gram.
Minimum price move (value)	10 Japanese sen (Y0.10) per gram (Y1,000 per contract).
Daily price limits	Y2.50 per gram above or below the previous day's settlement price.
Position limits	None.
Last trading day	Not stated. Please consult the exchange for the latest details.
Delivery day	Not stated. Please consult the exchange for the latest details.
Initial (Variation) margin	Contract price under Y90: Y42,000 Contract price from Y90 to Y110: Y51,000 Contract price from Y110 to Y130: Y60,000 Contract price above Y130: Y69,000

Spread margin	Not stated. Please consult the exchange for the latest details.
Reuters Monitor (Quote)	TCXC.
Telerate page	N/a.

Woollen yarn futures

Contract size	500 kilograms of woollen yarn.
Standard delivery method	Physical delivery of the above.
Trading months	The nearby six consecutive calendar months.
Trading hours	Four sessions daily (Monday to Saturday) commencing after the cotton yarn futures sessions, which begin at 8.50 a.m., 10.00 a.m., 12.50 p.m. and 3.10 p.m.
Price quotation method	In Japanese yen (Y) per kilogram.
Minimum price move (value)	Y1.00 per kilogram (Y500 per contract).
Daily price limits	At 3% of the underlying contract value above or below the previous day's closing price.
Position limits	None.
Last trading day	Not stated. Please consult the exchange for the latest details.
Delivery day	Not stated. Please consult the exchange for the latest details.
Initial (Variation) margin	Contract price under Y2,200: Y17,500
	Contract price from Y2,200 – Y2,500: Y20,000
	Contract price above Y2,500: Y22,500
Spread margin	Not stated. Please consult the exchange for the latest details.
Reuters Monitor (Quote)	TCXG.
Telerate page	17101.

Tokyo Grain Exchange (TGE)

Address:
1-12-5 Kakigara-cho
Nihonbashi
Chou-ku
Tokyo 103
Japan

Telephone: (03) 668 9311
Fax: (03) 668 9566
Telex: N/a.

Exchange personnel
President/Chairman: Akira Ishida
Executive Director: Seigi Nakagawa

Futures contracts available
American soyabeans
Chinese soyabeans
Domestic soyabeans
Potato starch
Red beans
White beans

Options contracts available
None

Clearing House: Cleared by the exchange itself.

Method of trading: By a competitive auction of concentrated bids and offers at a single contracted price. There is no continuous session, but several sessions each day.

Commenced trading: 1952.

Exchange links: Member of the Japan Federation of Commodity Exchanges.

A brief synopsis of the exchange
The exchange was established following the Commodity Exchange Law of 1950, trading a wide range of bean products, both domestic and international in origin. Rice futures are planned when Government control is relaxed. There are around 150 exchange members.

	Commission rates
	A range of customer commissions exists for each contract as follows depending on the contract price. Lower commissions are payable from members:
American or Chinese soyabeans	From Y3,300 to Y5,500.
Domestic soyabeans	Y2,000 regardless of contract price.
Potato starch	Y2,000 regardless of contract price.
Red beans	Contract price under Y14,000 Y3,200.
	Contract price under Y18,000 Y3,600.
	Contract price over Y18,000 Y4,000.
White beans	Contract price under Y20,000 Y3,000.
	Contract price under Y30,000 Y3,500.
	Contract price over Y30,000 Y4,000.

American soyabeans futures

Contract size	15,000 kilograms of American soyabeans.
Standard delivery method	Physical delivery of the above.
Trading months	Every other six even months (the February, April, June, August, October and December cycle).
Trading hours	Six sessions daily (Monday to Saturday) commencing at 9.00 a.m., 10.00 a.m., 11.00 a.m., 1.00 p.m., 2.00 p.m. and 3.00 p.m.
Price quotation method	In Japanese yen (Y) per kilogram.
Minimum price move (value)	Y10.00 per 60 kilograms (Y2,500 per contract).
Daily price limits	Within 7% of the underlying contract value above or below the previous business day's closing price.
Position limits	None.
Last trading day	Not stated. Please consult the exchange for the latest details.
Delivery day	Not stated. Please consult the exchange for the latest details.
Initial (Variation) margin	Contract price under Y5,000: Y70,000 Contract price from Y5,000 to Y6,000: Y80,000 Contract price above Y6,000: Y90,000
Spread margin	Not stated. Please consult the exchange for the latest details.
Reuters Monitor (Quote)	TGEA – TGED.
Telerate page	17108.

Chinese soyabeans futures

Contract size	15,000 kilograms of Chinese soyabeans.
Standard delivery method	Physical delivery of the above.
Trading months	The nearby six consecutive calendar months.
Trading hours	Six sessions daily (Monday to Saturday) commencing at 9.00 a.m., 10.00 a.m., 11.00 a.m., 1.00 p.m., 2.00 p.m. and 3.00 p.m.
Price quotation method	In Japanese yen (Y) per kilogram.
Minimum price move (value)	Y10.00 per 60 kilograms (Y2,500 per contract).
Daily price limits	Within 7% of the underlying contract value above or below the previous business day's closing price.
Position limits	None.
Last trading day	Not stated. Please consult the exchange for the latest details.
Delivery day	Not stated. Please consult the exchange for the latest details.

Initial (Variation) margin	Contract price under Y5,000: Y70,000
	Contract price from Y5,000 to Y6,000: Y80,000
	Contract price above Y6,000: Y90,000
Spread margin	Not stated. Please consult the exchange for the latest details.
Reuters Monitor (Quote)	TGEB – TGEE.
Telerate page	17107.

Domestic soyabeans futures

Contract size	2,400 kilograms of domestic soyabeans.
Standard delivery method	Physical delivery of the above.
Trading months	The nearby three consecutive calendar months.
Trading hours	Six sessions daily (Monday to Saturday) commencing at 9.00 a.m., 10.00 a.m., 11.00 a.m., 1.00 p.m., 2.00 p.m. and 3.00 p.m.
Price quotation method	In Japanese yen (Y) per kilogram.
Minimum price move (value)	Y10.00 per 60 kilograms (Y400 per contract).
Daily price limits	Within 7% of the underlying contract value above or below the previous business day's closing price.
Position limits	None.
Last trading day	Not stated. Please consult the exchange for the latest details.
Delivery day	Not stated. Please consult the exchange for the latest details.
Initial (Variation) margin	Contract price under Y3,000: Y8,000
	Contract price from Y3,000 to Y4,000: Y10,000
	Contract price above Y4,000: Y12,000
Spread margin	Not stated. Please consult the exchange for the latest details.
Reuters Monitor (Quote)	N/a.
Telerate page	17106.

Potato starch futures

Contract size	2,500 kilograms of potato starch.
Standard delivery method	Physical delivery of the above.
Trading months	The nearby three consecutive calendar months.
Trading hours	Six sessions daily (Monday to Saturday) commencing at 9.00 a.m., 10.00 a.m., 11.00 a.m., 1.00 p.m., 2.00 p.m. and 3.00 p.m.
Price quotation method	In Japanese yen (Y) per kilogram.

Minimum price move (value)	Y1.00 per 25 kilograms (Y100 per contract).
Daily price limits	Within 7% of the underlying contract value above or below the previous business day's closing price.
Position limits	None.
Last trading day	Not stated. Please consult the exchange for the latest details.
Delivery day	Not stated. Please consult the exchange for the latest details.
Initial (Variation) margin	Contract price under Y1,500: Y8,000
	Contract price from Y1,500 to Y2,000: Y10,000
	Contract price above Y2,000: Y12,000
Spread margin	Not stated. Please consult the exchange for the latest details.
Reuters Monitor (Quote)	N/a.
Telerate page	N/a.

Red beans futures

Contract size	2,400 kilograms of red beans.
Standard delivery method	Physical delivery of the above.
Trading months	The nearby six consecutive calendar months.
Trading hours	Six sessions daily (Monday to Saturday) commencing at 9.00 a.m., 10.00 a.m., 11.00 a.m., 1.00 p.m., 2.00 p.m. and 3.00 p.m.
Price quotation method	In Japanese yen (Y) per kilogram.
Minimum price move (value)	Y10.00 per 30 kilograms (Y800 per contract).
Daily price limits	Within 7% of the underlying contract value above or below the previous business day's closing price.
Position limits	None.
Last trading day	Not stated. Please consult the exchange for the latest details.
Delivery day	Not stated. Please consult the exchange for the latest details.
Initial (Variation) margin	Contract price under Y14,000: Y50,000
	Contract price from Y14,000 to Y18,000: Y60,000
	Contract price above Y18,000: Y70,000
Spread margin	Not stated. Please consult the exchange for the latest details.
Reuters Monitor (Quote)	TGEC – TGEF.
Telerate page	17106.

White beans futures

Contract size	2,400 kilograms of white beans.
Standard delivery method	Physical delivery of the above.
Trading months	The nearby six consecutive calendar months.
Trading hours	Six sessions daily (Monday to Saturday) commencing at 9.00 a.m., 10.00 a.m., 11.00 a.m., 1.00 p.m., 2.00 p.m. and 3.00 p.m.
Price quotation method	In Japanese yen (Y) per kilogram.
Minimum price move (value)	Y10.00 per 60 kilograms (Y400 per contract).
Daily price limits	Within 7% of the underlying contract value above or below the previous business day's closing price.
Position limits	None.
Last trading day	Not stated. Please consult the exchange for the latest details.
Delivery day	Not stated. Please consult the exchange for the latest details.
Initial (Variation) margin	Contract price under Y13,000: Y60,000 Contract price from Y13,000 to Y18,000: Y70,000 Contract price above Y18,000: Y80,000
Spread margin	Not stated. Please consult the exchange for the latest details.
Reuters Monitor (Quote)	N/a.
Telerate page	17106.

Tokyo International Financial Futures Exchange (TIFFE)

Address:
2-2 Otemachi 2-chrome
Chiyoda-ku
Tokyo 100
Japan

Telephone: (03) 275 2111
Fax: (03) 275 4840
Telex: 2226612 TIFFE J

Exchange personnel
President: Hiroyoshi Ono
Managing Director: Takashi Okada
Information Officer: Yoshiyuki Ohhara
Senior Manager: Kazuo Fuse
Chief Secretary: Fuminori Yano

Futures contracts available
Japanese yen / US dollar currency
Three month Eurodollar interest rate
Three month Euro-yen interest rate

Options contracts available
None

Clearing House: In-house clearing by the exchange.

Method of trading: Automated with computerised matching of telephone orders.

Commenced trading: June 1989.

Exchange links: None.

A brief synopsis of the exchange
This was the first specialised financial futures exchange in Japan, with trading in interest-rate and currency contracts commencing in June 1989. The membership comprises around 100 clearing members and over 160 general (non-clearing) members.

Commission rates

The following commission rates are applicable to transactions on TIFFE:

Number of contracts In one transaction:	*Yen commission per contract*
Up to 4	Y3,090
5 to 10	Y2,060
11 to 50	Y1,330
51 and over	Y1,030

Japanese yen / US dollar currency futures

Contract size	Y12,500,000 traded against the US dollar (US$).
Standard delivery method	Physical delivery of Japanese yen in Tokyo and US dollars in New York.
Trading months	The March, June, September and December cycle (with the nearest five expiry months available for trading at one time).
Trading hours	Two sessions daily (Monday to Saturday): 9.00 a.m. – 12.00 noon and 1.30 p.m. – 3.30 p.m. (trading ceases in the expiring contract at 10.45 a.m. on the last trading day).
Price quotation method	In terms of US dollars (US$) per Japanese yen (Y).
Minimum price move (value)	US$0.000001 per Y1.00 (US$12.50 per contract).
Daily price limits	None.
Position limits	None.
Last trading day	Two business days prior to the third Wednesday of the contract month.
Delivery day	The third Wednesday of the contract month.
Initial (Variation) margin	US$2,000 per contract (US$1,500) – the same margin requirements are applicable for hedgers and speculators.
Spread margin	There are no spread concessions.
Reuters Monitor (Quote)	TFEC, TIFE
Telerate page	9945 – 9948.

Three-month Eurodollar interest rate futures

Contract size	US$1,000,000 nominal value.
Standard delivery method	Cash settlement on the last trading day.
Trading months	The March, June, September and December cycle up to eight expiry months (two years) forward.
Trading hours	Two sessions daily (Monday to Saturday): 9.00 a.m. – 12.00 noon and 1.30 p.m. – 3.30 p.m. (trading ceases in the expiring contract at 11.00 a.m. on the last trading day).
Price quotation method	100.00 minus the annualised interest rate, calculated to two decimal places and quoted in US dollars (US$).
Minimum price move (value)	0.01% of nominal face value (US$25.00 per contract).
Daily price limits	None.
Position limits	None.
Last trading day	Two business days prior to the third Wednesday of the contract month.

Delivery day
Initial (Variation) margin

The first business day after the last trading day.
US$800 per contract (US$500) – the same margin
requirements are applicable for hedgers and
speculators.

Spread margin
Reuters Monitor (Quote)
Telerate page

There are no spread concessions.
TFEB – TFEE, TIFE
9945 – 9948

*There are similar futures contracts traded in London,
Chicago, Singapore and Sydney.*

Three-month Euro-yen interest rate futures

Contract size
Standard delivery method
Trading months

Trading hours

Y100,000,000 nominal value.
Cash settlement on the last trading day.
The March, June, September and December cycle up
to eight expiry months (two years) forward.
Two sessions daily (Monday to Saturday): 9.00 a.m. –
12.00 noon and 1.30 p.m. – 3.30 p.m.* (trading ceases
in the expiring contract at 11.00 a.m. on the last
trading day).

Price quotation method

100.00 minus the annualised rate of interest, calculated
to two decimal places quoted in Japanese yen (Y).

Minimum price move
(value)
Daily price limits
Position limits
Last trading day

0.01% of nominal face value (Y2,500 per contract).

None.
None.
Two business days prior to the third Wednesday of the
contract month.

Delivery day
Initial (Variation) margin

The first business day after the last trading day.
Y80,000 per contract (Y50,000) – the same margin
requirements are applicable for hedgers and
speculators.

Spread margin
Reuters Monitor (Quote)
Telerate page

There are no spread concessions.
TFEA – TFEF, TIFE
9945 – 9948

* The second daily trading session is expected to be extended to
close at 6.00 p.m. presently.

Tokyo Stock Exchange (TSX)

Address:	2 1 Kabuto Cho Nihombashi Chou-Ku Tokyo 103 Japan
Telephone: Fax: Telex:	(03) 666 0141 (03) 661 3240 / 663 0625 02 52 2759 TKOOSE

Exchange personnel

President:	Minoru Nagaoka
Vice-President:	Shiro Uramatsu
Managing Director:	Mitsuo Sato
Public Relations:	Kazue Suzuki
Index Products Manager:	Noriaka Ushijima

New York Representative Office
TSX New York Research Office
100 Wall Street
New York
NY 10005
USA

Telephone: Fax: Telex:	(212) 363 2350 (212) 363 2354 N/a.

Futures contracts available
10-year Japanese Government Treasury Bond
Tokyo Stock Price Index (TOPIX)
20-year Japanese Government Treasury Bond
US Government Treasury Bond

Options contracts on cash/physical available
Tokyo Stock Price Index (TOPIX)

Clearing House:	Tokyo and Japanese Securities Clearing Corporation.
Method of trading:	Automated screen trading.

Tokyo Stock Exchange (TSX)

Commenced trading: 1985.

Exchange links: None.

A brief synopsis of the exchange

The Tokyo Stock Exchange started trading in its first derivative product in 1985, the 10-year Japanese Government Bond future. Trading is carried out by nearly 100 Japanese securities houses and around 150 special participants.

There is no exchange dealing floor and trading takes place by telephone. The exchange has over 100 members.

10-year Japanese Government Treasury Bond futures

Contract size	Y100,000,000 nominal face value of a 6% coupon, 10-year notional Japanese Government Treasury Bond.
Standard delivery method	Physical delivery of the above Japanese Bonds with a life to maturity of between seven and 11 years, at the seller's option.
Trading months	The March, June, September and December cycle, with the nearest five contract months available for trading at any one time.
Trading hours	Two sessions daily (Monday to Saturday): 9.00 a.m. – 11.00 a.m. and 1.00 p.m. – 3.00 p.m.
Price quotation method	In Japanese yen (Y) per cent of par.
Minimum price move (value)	One-hundredth (1/100) of a point per 100 points (Y10,000 per contract).
Daily price limits	Two points above or below the previous day's closing price (a value of Y2,000,000 per contract).
Position limits	None.
Last trading day	The ninth business day prior to the start of the delivery day.
Delivery day	The 20th calendar day of the contract month or the next business day if the 20th is not a business day.
Initial (Variation) margin	The greater of either 3% of the nominal value of the contract or Y6,000,000. This is due on the second business day following the day of the transaction. Margin may take the form of securities as well as cash, as long as a minimum of 1% is in the form of cash.
Spread margin	Not stated. Please consult the exchange for the latest details.
Reuters Monitor (Quote)	JPMC.
Telerate page	9777-9780.

Commissions

Nominal transaction value	Commission
Up to Y0.5 billion	0.015%
Y0.5 billion – Y1.0 billion	0.01% + Y25,000
Y1.0 billion – Y5.0 billion	0.005% + Y75,000
Over Y5.0 billion	0.0025% + Y200,000

A similar contract is traded on the London International Financial Futures Exchange (LIFFE).

Tokyo Stock Price Index (TOPIX) futures

Contract size	Y10,000 multiplied by the Tokyo Stock Price Index* (TOPIX), disregarding decimal fractions.
Standard delivery method	Cash settlement on the last trading day. There is no facility for physical delivery of the shares underlying the index.

Trading months	The March, June, September and December cycle, with the nearest five contract months always available.
Trading hours	Two sessions daily (Monday to Saturday): 9.00 a.m. – 11.15 a.m. and 1.00 p.m. – 3.15 p.m. Trading ceases in the expiring contract at 3.00 p.m. on the last trading day.
Price quotation method	In Japanese yen (Y) per index point.
Minimum price move (value)	One full point of the TOPIX index (Y10,000 per contract).
Daily price limits	Around 3% of the underlying value of the contract above or below the previous day's closing level.
Position limits	None.
Last trading day	The third business day prior to the delivery day.
Delivery day	The 10th calendar day of the contract month, or the next business day if the 10th is not a business day.
Initial (Variation) margin	The greater of either 9% of the underlying value of the contract or Y6,000,000. Securities may be accepted as margin as long as a minimum of 3% of the underlying value of the contract is deposited in cash. Margin is due on the second business day following the day of the transaction.
Spread margin	Not stated. Please consult the exchange for the latest details.
Reuters Monitor (Quote)	TPXA – TPXB.
Telerate page	N/a.

Commissions

Contract value	Commission	
Up to Y100 million	0.04%	
Y100 million – Y300 million	0.03%	+ Y10,000
Y300 million – Y500 million	0.02%	+ Y40,000
Y500 million – Y1 billion	0.01%	+ Y90,000
Over Y1 billion	0.005%	+ Y140,000

* The Tokyo Stock Price Index (TOPIX) is a weighted index according to market value, calculated every 60 seconds throughout the trading day. There are around 1,100 issues from the First Section comprising the index. The index is formally reported six times a day: 9.15 a.m., 10.00 a.m., 11.00 a.m., 1.15 p.m., 2.00 p.m. and 3.00 p.m.

20-year Japanese Government Treasury Bond futures

Contract size	Y100,000,000 nominal face value of a 6% coupon, 20 year notional Japanese Government Treasury Bond.
Standard delivery method	Physical delivery of the above Japanese Bonds with a life to maturity of between 15 and 21 years, at the seller's option.
Trading months	The March, June, September and December cycle, with the nearest five contract months available for trading at all times.

Trading hours	Two sessions daily (Monday to Saturday): 9.00 a.m. – 11.00 a.m. and 1.00 p.m. – 3.00 p.m.
Price quotation method	In Japanese yen (Y) per cent of par.
Minimum price move (value)	One-hundredth (1/100) of a point per 100 points (Y10,000 per contract).
Daily price limits	Three points above or below the previous day's closing price (a value of Y3,000,000 per contract).
Position limits	None.
Last trading day	The ninth business day prior to the delivery day.
Delivery day	The 20th calendar day of the contract month or the next business day if the 20th is not a business day.
Initial (Variation) margin	The greater of either 4.5% of the nominal value of the contract or Y6,000,000. This is due on the second business day following the day of the transaction. Margin may take the form of securities as well as cash, as long as a minimum of 1.5% is in the form of cash.
Spread margin	Not stated. Please consult the exchange for the latest details.
Reuters Monitor (Quote)	TQOD.
Telerate page	9777-9780.

Commissions

Nominal transaction value	Commission
Up to Y0.5 billion	0.015%
Y0.5 billion – Y1.0 billion	0.01% + Y25,000
Y1.0 billion – Y5.0 billion	0.005% + Y75,000
Over Y5.0 billion	0.0025% + Y200,000

Option on Tokyo Stock Price Index (TOPIX)

Contract size	Y10,000 multiplied by the Tokyo Stock Price Index (TOPIX).*
Standard delivery method	Cash settlement at the strike price on the last trading day. There is no facility for physical delivery of the shares underlying the index.
Trading months	The nearby four consecutive calendar months.
Trading hours	Two sessions daily (Monday to Saturday): 9.00 a.m. – 11.15 a.m. and 1.00 p.m. – 3.15 p.m. Trading ceases in the expiring contract at 3.00 p.m. on the last trading day.
Price quotation method	In Japanese yen (Y) per index point.
Minimum price move (value)	One half of one point of the TOPIX index (Y5,000 per contract).
Daily price limits	Around 3% of the underlying value of the TOPIX index (the range being between 60 and 90 index points).
Position limits	None.

Last trading day	The business day prior to the second Friday of the contract month.
Delivery day	The option expires on the business day prior to the last Friday of the contract month, or in the case of March, June, September and December, on the second Friday of the contract month. The latest time for exercise is 1.45 p.m. on any business day.
Initial (Variation) margin	For uncovered short positions, the greater of either Y6,000,000 or the transaction value of the option contract plus 9% of the exercise price multiplied by Y10,000 multiplied by the number of short contracts. Margin must be maintained on a fall of 3%.
Spread margin	Not stated. Please consult the exchange for the latest details.
Strike price intervals	At 50 TOPIX index point intervals.
Option type	American style (the option may be exercised on any business day up to and including the last trading day). Any option series that are in-the-money by at least 0.3% are automatically exercised on expiry.
Method of introduction of new strike prices	Five series will be issued initially around the current underlying TOPIX index. New series are introduced ∴ the underlying TOPIX index is 25 index points greater than (less than) the current highest (lowest) available strike price. No new exercise prices are normally introduced in the month preceding expiry.
Reuters Monitor (Quote)	N/a.
Telerate page	N/a.

* The Tokyo Stock Price Index (TOPIX) is a weighted index according to market value calculated every 60 seconds throughout the trading day. There are around 1,100 issues from the First Section comprising the index. The index is formally reported six times a day: 9.15 a.m., 10.00 a.m., 11.00 a.m., 1.15 p.m., 2.00 p.m. and 3.00 p.m.

Tokyo Sugar Exchange (TSUG)

Address:	9-4 Nihonbashi Kaomi-cho Chou-ku Tokyo 103 Japan
Telephone:	(03) 666 0201
Fax:	(03) 661 4596
Telex:	N/a.

Exchange personnel

Chairman:	Kojiro Yada
Managing Directors:	Mioya Ohashi and Teruo Kodaira

Futures contracts available
Raw sugar
Refined white soft sugar

Options contracts available
None

Clearing House:	Cleared by the exchange itself.
Method of trading:	By a competitive auction of concentrated bids and offers at a single contracted price. There is no continuous session, but several sessions each day.
Commenced trading:	1952.
Exchange links:	Member of the Japan Federation of Commodity Exchanges.

A brief synopsis of the exchange
The exchange was established following the liberalisation of rationing in 1951 in Japan, in order to have a medium for preservation of a free market and price for sugar. Sugar is traded for delivery in bulk, and this normally takes place in Tokyo at the seller's option. Associate membership was introduced in 1985 to allow the entry of international participants. There are around 100 exchange members. A raw sugar options contract is planned as a future project.

Raw sugar

Refined white soft sugar

Commission rates

A range of customer commissions exists for each contract as follows depending on the contract price. Lower commissions are payable from members:

From Y4,300 on contract prices below Y100 rising by Y200 for each additional Y50 increase in the contract price.

From Y4,000 on contract prices below Y200 rising by Y300 for each additional Y50 increase in the contract price.

Raw sugar futures

Contract size	10,000 kilograms of raw sugar.
Standard delivery method	Physical delivery of the above in bulk.
Trading months	The nearby nine consecutive calendar months.
Trading hours	Four sessions daily (Monday to Saturday) commencing at 9.30 a.m., 10.30 a.m., 1.30 p.m. and 2.30 p.m.
Price quotation method	In Japanese sen per kilogram.
Minimum price move (value)	10 Japanese sen (Y0.10) per kilogram (Y1,000 per contract).
Daily price limits	10% of the underlying value of the contract above or below the previous day's closing level.
Position limits	None.
Last trading day	Not stated. Please consult the exchange for the latest details.
Delivery day	Not stated. Please consult the exchange for the latest details.
Initial (Variation) margin	Contract price under Y50: Y50,000 Contract price from Y50 to Y100: Y60,000 Contract price above Y100: Y70,000
Spread margin	Not stated. Please consult the exchange for the latest details.
Reuters Monitor (Quote)	TSGA.
Telerate page	17100.

Refined white soft sugar futures

Contract size	9,000 kilograms of refined white soft sugar.
Standard delivery method	Physical delivery of the above in bulk.
Trading months	The nearby six consecutive calendar months.
Trading hours	Four sessions daily (Monday to Saturday) commencing at 9.30 a.m., 10.30 a.m., 1.30 p.m. and 2.30 p.m.
Price quotation method	In Japanese sen per kilogram.
Minimum price move (value)	10 Japanese sen (Y0.10) per kilogram (Y900 per contract).
Daily price limits	10% of the underlying value of the contract above or below the previous day's closing level.
Position limits	None.
Last trading day	Not stated. Please consult the exchange for the latest details.
Delivery day	Not stated. Please consult the exchange for the latest details.
Initial (Variation) margin	Contract price under Y200: Y40,000 Contract price from Y200 to Y300: Y50,000 Contract price above Y300: Y60,000

**Tokyo Sugar
Exchange (TSUG)
Futures
Softs and
agricultural**

Spread margin

Reuters Monitor (Quote)
Telerate page

Not stated. Please consult the exchange for the latest details.

TSGB.
17100.

Toyohashi Dried Cocoon Exchange (TDCE)

Address:

52-2 Ekimae odori
Toyohashi 440
Japan

Telephone: (0532) 52 6231
Fax: (0532) 55 1529
Telex: N/a.

Exchange personnel
President: Keikichi Kawai
Managing Director: Masanori Mori

Futures contracts available
Dried cocoons

Options contracts available
None

Clearing House: Cleared by the exchange itself.

Method of trading: By a competitive auction of concentrated bids and offers at a single contracted price. There is no continuous session, but several sessions each day.

Commenced trading: 1937.

Exchange links: Member of the Japan Federation of Commodity Exchanges.

A brief synopsis of the exchange
The exchange was the eighth exchange to re open after the war, with Toyohashi being a major centre of the Japanese silk yarn industry. In the 1950s business declined, but after imported cocoons became eligible for delivery in the 1960s, there was a rapid recovery of business. There are around 50 exchange members.

Commission rates
Customer commissions of Y4,200 exist per contract. Lower commissions are payable from members.

Dried cocoon futures

Contract size	300 kilograms of dried cocoons.
Standard delivery method	Physical delivery of the above.
Trading months	The nearby six consecutive calendar months.
Trading hours	Four sessions daily (Monday to Saturday) commencing at 9.30 a.m., 11.15 a.m., 1.30 p.m. and 3.15 p.m.
Price quotation method	In Japanese yen (Y) per kilogram.
Minimum price move (value)	Y1.00 per kilogram (Y300 per contract).
Daily price limits	Y130 per kilogram above or below the previous day's closing price.
Position limits	None.
Last trading day	The last business day of the contract month.
Delivery day	The business day following the last trading day.
Initial (Variation) margin	Contract price under Y5,800: Y60,000
	Contract price between Y5,800 and Y6,400: Y70,000
	Contract price over Y6,400: Y80,000
Spread margin	There are no spread concessions.
Reuters Monitor (Quote)	N/a.
Telerate page	N/a.

Yokohama Raw Silk Exchange (YRSE)

Address:	Silk Center 1 Yamashita-cho Naka-ku Yokohama 231 Japan
Telephone:	(045) 641 1341
Fax:	(045) 641 1346
Telex:	N/a.

Exchange personnel

President:	Chikao Matsumura
Secretary General:	Katsusuke Ohtake

Futures contracts available
Raw silk

Options contracts available
None

Clearing House:	Cleared by the exchange itself.
Method of trading:	By a competitive auction of concentrated bids and offers at a single contracted price. There is no continuous session, but several sessions each day.
Commenced trading:	1894 (re-established in 1951).
Exchange links:	Member of the Japan Federation of Commodity Exchanges.

A brief synopsis of the exchange
The exchange has origins dating back to the rice futures markets of the last century. The exchange provides an index price for the world market in raw silk, and also a domestic price.

Commission rates

A range of customer commissions exists for each contract as follows depending on the contract price. Lower commissions are payable from members:

Contract value	Commission
Contract price under Y13,500	Y4,900.
Contract price Y13,500 – Y15,500	Y5,400.
Increases thereafter of Y2,000	Y500 per Y2,000.

Yokohama Raw
Silk Exchange
(YRSE)
Futures
Softs and
agricultural

Raw silk futures

Contract size	300 kilograms (or five bales or 10 cases) of raw silk.
Standard delivery method	Physical delivery of one of the above categories of raw silk.
Trading months	The nearby six consecutive calendar months.
Trading hours	Four sessions daily (Monday to Saturday) commencing 9.30 a.m., 11.00 a.m., 1.30 p.m. and 3.00 p.m.
Price quotation method	In Japanese yen (Y) per kilogram.
Minimum price move (value)	Y1.00 per kilogram (Y300 per contract).
Daily price limits	Y150 per kilogram above or below the previous day's closing level.
Position limits	None.
Last trading day	Not stated. Please consult the exchange for the latest details.
Delivery day	Not stated. Please consult the exchange for the latest details.
Initial (Variation) margin	Y50,000 per contract irrespective of the prevailing contract price.
Spread margin	Not stated. Please consult the exchange for the latest details.
Reuters Monitor (Quote)	SKJF – SKJI.
Telerate page	17109.

5 Malaysia

Contents

Kuala Lumpur Commodity Exchange (KLCE)

Address:	4th Floor Citypoint Dayabumi Complex Jalam Sultan Hishamuddin PO Box 11260 50740 Kuala Lumpur Malaysia
Telephone: Fax: Telex:	(603) 293 6822 (603) 274 2215 MA 31472 KLCE

Exchange personnel

Chairman:	Tan Sri Lee Boon Chim
Chief Executive:	Syed Abdul Jabbar Shahabudin
Public Relations Officer:	Juli Murshidah Munassor

Futures contracts available
Cocoa
Crude palm oil
Rubber (SMR 20)
Tin

Options contracts available
None

Clearing House:	Malaysian Futures Clearing Corporation Sdn Bhd.
Method of trading:	Open outcry.
Commenced trading:	1980.
Exchange links:	None.

A brief synopsis of the exchange
The Kuala Lumpur Commodity Exchange was
restructured in 1985 following a major default and now
closely resembles other major international futures
exchanges in terms of its rules and regulations. The

first futures contract was introduced in 1980 on Crude palm oil. Planned future contracts include a future on the Kuala Lumpur Stock Exchange Composite Stock Index.

There are currently around 100 member corporations with over 130 clearing memberships, which are freely transferable.

Kuala Lumpur
Commodity
Exchange (KLCE)
Futures
Softs and
agricultural

Cocoa futures

Contract size	10 tonnes of cocoa.
Standard delivery method	Physical delivery of the above.
Trading months	The January, March, May, July, September, November and December cycle.
Trading hours	Two sessions daily: 11.15 a.m. – 12.00 noon and 4.00 p.m. – 7.00 p.m.
Price quotation method	In US dollars (US$) and cents per tonne.
Minimum price move (value)	US$1.00 per tonne (US$10.00 per contract).
Daily price limits	US$80.00 per tonne above or below the previous day's settlement price, expandable to US$100 on the second limit day, US$120 on the third limit day, no limits on the fourth day, reverting to the basic limit of US$80.00 on the fifth day. There are no price limits on the current (spot) contract month.
Position limits	None.
Last trading day	The 20th calendar day of the contract month or the preceding business day if the 20th is a non-market day.
Delivery day	The delivery period is from the first business day of the contract month to the last business day of the contract month.
Initial (Variation) margin	Initial deposits are required for all contracts traded, and are marked to market daily.
Spread margin	No concessions.
Reuters Monitor (Quote)	KLCO.
Telerate page	N/a.

Crude palm oil futures

Contract size	25 tonnes of crude palm oil.
Standard delivery method	Physical delivery of the above, in bulk unbleached, in port tank installations at the option of the seller in Prai/Butterworth, Port Kelang or Pasir Gudang.
Trading months	The current (spot) month, the next five consecutive calendar months plus alternate months (the February, April, June, August, October and December cycle) up to 12 months forward.
Trading hours	Two sessions daily: 11.00 a.m. – 12.30 p.m. and 3.30 p.m. – 6.00 p.m.
Price quotation method	In Malaysian ringgits (M$) per tonne.
Minimum price move (value)	M$1.00 per tonne (M$25.00 per contract).

**Kuala Lumpur
Commodity
Exchange (KLCE)
Futures
Softs and
agricultural**

Daily price limits	M$50.00 per tonne above or below the previous day's settlement price, expandable to M$75.00 on the second limit day, M$100 on the third limit day, no limit on the fourth day and reverting back to M$50.00 on the fifth day. There are no price limits on the current (spot) contract month.
Position limits	Reportable at 100 contracts, with a limit of 500 contracts long or short in any one contract month. There is also a single transaction limit of 25 contracts.
Last trading day	The 15th day of the contract month (or the preceding business day if the 15th is a non-market day). Trading in the expiring contract ceases at 12.00 noon on the last trading day.
Delivery day	The delivery period is from the first business day of the contract month to the 20th calendar day of a contract month, or the preceding business day if the 20th is a non-market day.
Initial (Variation) margin	Initial deposits are required for all contracts traded, and are marked to market daily.
Spread margin	A margin deposit is payable on only one side of a spread position.
Reuters Monitor (Quote)	KLPK – KLPO.
Telerate page	N/a.

Rubber (SMR 20) futures

Contract size	10 tonnes of rubber (SMR 20) for single contract months or 30 tonnes of rubber (SMR 20) for delivery quarters.
Standard delivery method	Physical delivery of the above.
Trading months	The current (spot) calendar month, the next two consecutive calendar months and two distant quarter months (from the March, June, September and December cycle).
Trading hours	10.00 a.m. – 1.00 p.m. and 4.00 p.m. – 6.00 p.m.
Price quotation method	In Malaysian sen per kilogram.
Minimum price move (value)	0.25 Malaysian sen (M$0.0025) per kilogram (M$25.00 per contract for single contract months and M$75.00 per contract for delivery quarters).
Daily price limits	10 Malaysian sen (M$0.10) per kilogram above or below the previous day's settlement price. When these limits are traded at for the nearby two calendar months, trading for all months is halted for 15 minutes, after which time new 10 Malaysian sen (M$0.10) per kilogram limits are introduced. This process is repeated through the day as new limits are reached. There are no price limits in the current (spot) contract month.

Position limits	None.
Last trading day	The last business day of the month preceding the contract month.
Delivery day	The tender day is the last business day of the month preceding the contract month and the delivery day is the second business day of the contract month.
Initial (Variation) margin	Initial deposits are required for all contracts traded, and are marked to market daily.
Spread margin	A margin is payable on only one side of a spread position.
Reuters Monitor (Quote)	KLRU – KLRX, RUQE – RUQG.
Telerate page	N/a.

Tin futures

Contract size	Five tonnes of not less than 99.85% tin.
Standard delivery method	Physical delivery of five tonnes of the above, plus or minus not more than 2%, on warrants issued by an exchange-approved warehouse in Pinang or Singapore at the seller's choice.
Trading months	The nearest (spot) calendar month, the next three consecutive calendar months plus alternate months (from the February, April, June, August, October and December cycle) up to 12 months forward.
Trading hours	Two sessions daily: 12.15 p.m. – 1.00 p.m. and 4.00 p.m. – 7.00 p.m.
Price quotation method	In US Dollars (US$) and cents per tonne.
Minimum price move (value)	US$5.00 per tonne (US$25.00 per contract).
Daily price limits	US$250 above or below the previous day's settlement price. When prices for the nearest three consecutive contract months trade at a limit, trading halts for 15 minutes, after which time new price limits of US$250 are set. After three limit-up or limit-down days, on the fourth day the limits are removed, but are reintroduced on the fifth day. There are no price limits on the current (spot) contract month.
Position limits	None.
Last trading day	The business day immediately before the last two business days of the contract month. Trading ceases in the expiring contract at 12.00 noon on the last trading day.
Delivery day	The delivery period is from the first business day of the contract month up to and including the last business day of the contract month.
Initial (Variation) margin	Initial deposits are required for all contracts traded, and are marked to market daily.

Kuala Lumpur Commodity Exchange (KLCE) Futures Softs and agricultural

Spread margin   A margin is payable on only one side of a spread position.

Reuters Monitor (Quote)   KULT and KULU.

Telerate page   N/a.

6 New Zealand

Contents

New Zealand Futures Exchange Ltd (NZFE)

Address:
PO Box 6734
Wellesley Street
Auckland 1
New Zealand

Telephone: (9) 398 308
Fax: (9) 398 817
Telex: NZ 63359

Exchange personnel

Chairman: Gavin Kennedy
Managing Director: Len Ward
Marketing Manager: Lincoln Gould
Manager, Finance &
  Operations: Wendie Hall

Futures contracts available
Barclays Share Price Index
Five-year New Zealand Government stock No.2
New Zealand dollar / US dollar currency
90-day Bank Accepted Bills
US dollar / New Zealand dollar currency

Options contracts on futures available
Barclays Share Price Index futures
Five-year New Zealand Government stock No.2
futures
New Zealand dollar / US dollar currency futures

Clearing House: International Commodities Clearing House (ICCH).

Method of trading: Automated (screen) trading through the ATS (Automated Trading System) developed and operated by ICCH.

Commenced trading: 1985.

Exchange links: None.

A brief synopsis of the exchange

The New Zealand Futures Exchange was one of the first successfully to implement computerised trading via the Automated Trading System (ATS) as an alternative to floor trading through the open-outcry system. This was developed with the exchange's clearing house, the ICCH. Trading commenced in its first futures contract – the New Zealand dollar traded against the US dollar future in 1985. Agricultural contracts (wheat and wool) have recently been delisted due to insufficient turnover. Currently the most active contract is futures on New Zealand Government stock.

There are two types of exchange member: trading members and affiliate members (who must trade through a trading member). There are over 40 trading members and affiliate members.

The NZFE has the dubious honour to be the first exchange worldwide to open daily.

Barclays Share Price Index (BSI) futures

Contract size	NZ$20.00 multiplied by the Barclays Share Price Index (40 shares, capitalisation weighted).
Standard delivery method	Cash settlement at expiry based on the quotation at 9.00 a.m. of the Barclays Share Price Index on the business day following the last trading day.
Trading months	The March, June, September and December cycle up to one year forward.
Trading hours	9.00 a.m. – 4.50 p.m.
Price quotation method	In terms of New Zealand dollars (NZ$) per index point.
Minimum price move (value)	One full index point (NZ$20.00 per contract).
Daily price limits	None.
Position limits	None.
Last trading day	The second to last business day of the contract month.
Delivery day	The business day following the last trading day.
Initial (Variation) margin	Please consult the exchange or your broker for the current margin requirements.
Spread margin	Please consult the exchange or your broker for the current spread concessions.
Reuters Monitor (Quote)	SIZE.
Telerate page	2478.

Five-year Government Stock No. 2 (GSK) futures

Contract size	NZ$100,000 nominal face value of New Zealand Government stock with a coupon rate of 10% and a term to maturity of five years.
Standard delivery method	Cash settlement at 11.30 a.m. on the last trading day based on mid-rate quotations obtained from ten randomly selected Government-approved stock dealers for buying and selling yields, after disregarding both any quotations with a spread over 0.15 and the two highest and two lowest quotations. The settlement price is announced at 3.00 p.m. on the last trading day. There is no provision for physical delivery.
Trading months	The March, June, September and December cycle up to one year forward.
Trading hours	8.00 a.m. – 5.00 p.m. (trading ceases in the expiring contract at 12.00 noon on the last trading day).
Price quotation method	100.00 minus the annualised yield per NZ$100 face value, quoted in New Zealand dollars (NZ$).

Minimum price move (value)	0.01% of nominal face value (NZ$10.00 per contract).
Daily price limits	None.
Position limits	None.
Last trading day	The first Wednesday after the ninth day of the contract month.
Delivery day	The second business day after the last trading day.
Initial (Variation) margin	Please consult the exchange or your broker for the current margin requirements.
Spread margin	Please consult the exchange or your broker for the current spread concessions.
Reuters Monitor (Quote)	GSZE.
Telerate page	2478, 6205.

New Zealand dollar / US dollar currency (KWI) futures

Contract size	NZ$100,000 traded against the US dollar (US$).
Standard delivery method	Cash settlement based on the average mid-rate of six spot NZ$/US$ quotations obtained by the ICCH at 11.30 a.m. on the last trading day from randomly selected licensed foreign exchange dealers after disregarding the two highest and two lowest quoted rates and those with a spread greater than 0.15%. There is no facility for physical delivery.
Trading months	The spot month plus the next three consecutive calendar months, then financial quarters (the March, June, September and December cycle) up to one year forward.
Trading hours	8.15 a.m. – 4.45 p.m.
Price quotation method	In US dollars (US$) per New Zealand dollar (NZ$).
Minimum price move (value)	US$0.0001 per NZ$1.00 (US$10.00 per contract).
Daily price limits	None.
Position limits	None.
Last trading day	Two business days before the third Wednesday of the contract month. Trading ceases in the expiring contract at 2.30 p.m. on the last trading day.
Delivery day	The business day following the last trading day.
Initial (Variation) margin	Please consult the exchange or your broker for the current margin requirements.
Spread margin	Please consult the exchange or your broker for the current spread concessions.
Reuters Monitor (Quote)	JYSE.
Telerate page	2478.

90-day Bank Accepted Bill (BBC) futures

Contract size	NZ$500,000 nominal face value of 90-day Bank Accepted Bills of Exchange.
Standard delivery method	Cash settlement at 10.00 a.m. on the last trading day based on the average mid-rate quotations obtained from a random selection of 10 approved dealers, disregarding the two highest and the two lowest quotations and those quotations with a spread wider than 0.25%. The settlement price is announced at 1.30 p.m. on the last trading day. There are no facilities for physical delivery.
Trading months	The spot month, the next two consecutive calendar months, then months from the March, June, September and December cycle up to two years forward.
Trading hours	8.10 a.m. – 4.50 p.m.
Price quotation method	In terms of an annualised yield per NZ$100 face value, quoted in New Zealand dollars (NZ$).
Minimum price move (value)	0.01% per annum of nominal face value (approximately NZ$11.50 per contract varying inversely with interest rates).
Daily price limits	None.
Position limits	None.
Last trading day	The first Wednesday after the ninth day of the contract month. Trading ceases in the expiring contract at 12.30 p.m. on the last trading day.
Delivery day	The first business day following the last trading day.
Initial (Variation) margin	Please consult the exchange or your broker for the current margin requirements.
Spread margin	Please consult the exchange or your broker for the current spread concessions.
Reuters Monitor (Quote)	BBZE.
Telerate page	2478, 6204.

US dollar / New Zealand dollar currency (USD) futures

Contract size	US$50,000 traded against the New Zealand dollar (NZ$).
Standard delivery method	Cash settlement of the above in New Zealand dollars (NZ$) based on the mid-rate of six quotations obtained by the Clearing House at 2.30 p.m. on the last trading day from licensed foreign exchange dealers, after disregarding the highest and lowest quoted rates.
Trading months	The spot month plus the next three consecutive calendar months, then financial quarters (the March, June, September and December cycle) up to one year forward.

Trading hours	8.15 a.m. – 4.45 p.m.
Price quotation method	In New Zealand dollars (NZ$) per US dollar (US$).
Minimum price move (value)	NZ$0.0001 per US$1.00 (NZ$5.00 per contract).
Daily price limits	None.
Position limits	None.
Last trading day	The first Wednesday after the ninth day of the contract month.
Delivery day	Two business days following the last trading day.
Initial (Variation) margin	Please consult the exchange or your broker for the current margin requirements.
Spread margin	Please consult the exchange or your broker for the current spread concessions.
Reuters Monitor (Quote)	USZE – USZF.
Telerate page	2478, 6203.

Option on NZFE Barclays Share Price Index (BSO) futures

Contract size	One NZFE Barclays Share Price Index futures contract (of an underlying contract size of NZ$20.00 multiplied by the index).
Standard delivery method	Delivery of a long or short position in a futures contract at the strike price as above.
Trading months	The March, June, September and December cycle up to six months forward.
Trading hours	9.00 a.m. – 4.50 p.m.
Price quotation method	In terms of New Zealand dollars (NZ$) per index point.
Minimum price move (value)	One full index point (NZ$20.00 per contract).
Daily price limits	None.
Position limits	None.
Last trading day	That of the underlying futures contract (the second to last business day of the contract month).
Delivery day	The business day following the last trading day.
Initial (Variation) margin	Calculated according to daily published risk factors multiplied by the initial deposit margin of the underlying futures contract. Initial margin cannot exceed the value of the option premium.
Spread margin	Margin requirements are reduced for options and options on futures combinations.
Strike price intervals	At 50 index point intervals.
Option type	American style (the option may be exercised on any business day up to and including the last trading day).
Method of introduction of new strike prices	Not stated.
Reuters Monitor (Quote)	N/a.
Telerate page	2478.

Option on NZFE five-year Government stock No. 2 (GSO) futures

Contract size	One NZFE five-year Government stock No.2 futures contract (of an underlying contract size of NZ$100,000 nominal face value).
Standard delivery method	Delivery of a long or short position in a futures contract at the strike price as above.
Trading months	The March, June, September and December cycle up to six months forward.
Trading hours	8.00 a.m. – 5.00 p.m.
Price quotation method	100.00 minus the annualised percentage yield, quoted in New Zealand dollars (NZ$).
Minimum price move (value)	0.01% per annum of nominal face value (NZ$10.00 per contract).
Daily price limits	None.
Position limits	None.
Last trading day	The last trading day of the underlying futures contract (the first Wednesday after the ninth day of the contract month). Trading ceases in the expiring contract at 12.00 noon on the last trading day.
Delivery day	The business day following the last trading day.
Initial (Variation) margin	Calculated according to daily published risk factors multiplied by the initial deposit margin of the underlying futures contract. Initial margin cannot exceed the value of the option premium.
Spread margin	Margin requirements are reduced for options and options on futures combinations.
Strike price intervals	At 0.25% per annum intervals.
Option type	American style (the option may be exercised on any business day up to and including the last trading day).
Method of introduction of new strike prices	Not stated.
Reuters Monitor (Quote)	GSZF – GSZI.
Telerate page	2478.

Option on NZFE New Zealand dollar / US dollar currency (KWO) futures

Contract size	One NZFE New Zealand dollar / US dollar currency futures contract (of an underlying contract size of NZ$100,000 traded against the US dollar).
Standard delivery method	Delivery of a long or short position in a futures contract at the strike price as above.
Trading months	The March, June, September and December cycle up to six months forward.
Trading hours	8.15 a.m. – 4.45 p.m.

Price quotation method	In US dollars (US$) per New Zealand dollar (NZ$).
Minimum price move (value)	US$0.0001 per NZ$1.00 (US$10.00 per contract).
Daily price limits	None.
Position limits	None.
Last trading day	That of the underlying futures contract (two business days before the third Wednesday of the contract month). Trading ceases in the expiring contract at 2.30 p.m. on the last trading day.
Delivery day	The business day following the last trading day.
Initial (Variation) margin	Calculated according to daily published risk factors multiplied by the initial deposit margin of the underlying futures contract. Initial margin cannot exceed the value of the option premium.
Spread margin	Margin requirements are reduced for options and options on futures combinations.
Strike price intervals	At 50 points of US$0.005 per NZ$1.00 intervals.
Option type	American style (the option may be exercised on any business day up to and including the last trading day). All in-the-money options are automatically exercised at expiry.
Method of introduction of new strike prices	Not stated.
Reuters Monitor (Quote)	KWZF – KWZH.
Telerate page	2478.

7 The Philippines

Contents

Manila International Futures Exchange (MIFEX)

Manila International Futures Exchange (MIFEX)

Address:	7th Floor Producers Bank Centre Paseo de Roxas Makati Metro Manila The Philippines
Telephone:	818 54 96
Fax:	818 55 29
Telex:	63092 MMS PN

Exchange personnel

Chairman:	Francisco S. Sumulong
President:	Peter Choi Yau Man
Information Officer:	U. A. McInnes

Futures contracts available
Coffee
Copra
Soyabeans
Sugar

Options contracts available
None

Clearing House:	Manila International Clearing House.
Method of trading:	Group trading system.
Commenced trading.	1986.
Exchange links:	None.

A brief synopsis of the exchange
No historic information has been received from the exchange.

Coffee futures

Contract size	5,000 kilograms of robusta coffee.
Standard delivery method	Physical delivery robusta CTMAL standard coffee, FOB stowed in bags at designated ports in the following countries: Indonesia, Ivory Coast, Angola, Cameroons, Sierra Leone, Tanzania, Ghana, Guinea, India, Nigeria, Togo, Trinidad, Uganda, Philippines, Malagasy Republic, Central African Republic and Zaire. Premiums and discounts are in force for alternative delivery grades.
Trading months	The nearby six consecutive calendar months.
Trading hours	Four sessions daily commencing at 9.30 a.m., 10.30 a.m., 1.30 p.m. and 2.30 p.m.
Price quotation method	In Philippine pesos (P$) and cents per kilogram.
Minimum price move (value)	5 Philippine cents (P$0.05) per kilogram (P$250 per contract).
Daily price limits	On the first and second days: P$1.60 per kilogram above or below the previous day's settlement price; on the third day: P$2.40 per kilogram above or below the previous day's settlement price.
Position limits	None.
Last trading day	The first business day prior to the first day of the contract month.
Delivery day	The first business day of the contract month.
Initial (Variation) margin	Not stated. Please consult the exchange for the current details.
Spread margin	Not stated. Please consult the exchange for the current details.
Reuters Monitor (Quote)	MIFU.
Telerate page	N/a.

Copra futures

Contract size	20,000 kilograms of copra.
Standard delivery method	Physical delivery of Philippine originated FPA content of resultant oil basis 4% copra, stowed in bulk, designated Philippine ports, with premiums and discounts applicable for alternative grades as established by the exchange from time to time.
Trading months	The nearby six consecutive calendar months.
Trading hours	Four sessions daily commencing at 9.00 a.m., 10.00 a.m., 1.00 p.m. and 2.00 p.m.
Price quotation method	In Philippine pesos (P$) and cents per kilogram.
Minimum price move (value)	1 Philippine cent (P$0.01) per kilogram (P$200 per contract).

Daily price limits	On the first and second days: P$0.40 per kilogram above or below the previous day's settlement price; on the third day: P$0.60 per kilogram above or below the previous day's settlement price.
Position limits	None.
Last trading day	The first business day prior to the first day of the contract month.
Delivery day	The first business day of the contract month.
Initial (Variation) margin	Not stated. Please consult the exchange for the current details.
Spread margin	Not stated. Please consult the exchange for the current details.
Reuters Monitor (Quote)	PCOP, MIFR.
Telerate page	N/a.

Soyabean futures

Contract size	500 bags each of 60 kilograms of soyabeans (30,000 kilograms in total).
Standard delivery method	Physical delivery of either (a) unselected or selected yellow Chinese soyabeans shipped from Dai Ren or Chin Wang Tao, China, or (b) selected US yellow soyabeans produced in Indiana, Ohio or Michigan state.
Trading months	The nearby six consecutive calendar months.
Trading hours	Four sessions daily commencing at 9.45 a.m., 10.45 a.m., 1.45 p.m. and 2.45 p.m.
Price quotation method	In Philippine pesos (P$) and cents per bag.
Minimum price move (value)	50 Philippine cents (P$0.50) per bag (P$250 per contract).
Daily price limits	On the first and second days: P$20 per kilogram above or below the previous day's settlement price; on the third day: P$30 per kilogram above or below the previous day's settlement price.
Position limits	None.
Last trading day	The first business day prior to the first day of the contract month.
Delivery day	The first business day of the contract month.
Initial (Variation) margin	Not stated. Please consult the exchange for the current details.
Spread margin	Not stated. Please consult the exchange for the current details.
Reuters Monitor (Quote)	MIFI – MIFJ.
Telerate page	N/a.

**Manila
International
Futures Exchange
(MIFEX)
Futures
Softs and
agricultural**

Sugar futures

Contract size	112,000 pounds of raw sugar.
Standard delivery method	Physical delivery of raw centrifugal cane sugar of average 96° polarisation, with premiums and discounts applicable for other grades, as established by the exchange from time to time.
Trading months	The nearby six consecutive calendar months.
Trading hours	Four sessions daily commencing at 9.15 a.m., 10.15 a.m., 1.15 p.m. and 2.15 p.m.
Price quotation method	In Philippine pesos (P$) and cents per pound.
Minimum price move (value)	20 Philippine cents (P$0.20) per pound (P$22,400 per contract).
Daily price limits	On the first and second days: P$0.10 per pound above or below the previous day's settlement price; on the third day: P$0.15 per pound above or below the previous day's settlement price.
Position limits	None.
Last trading day	The first business day prior to the first day of the contract month.
Delivery day	The first business day of the contract month.
Initial (Variation) margin	Not stated. Please consult the exchange for the current details.
Spread margin	Not stated. Please consult the exchange for the current details.
Reuters Monitor (Quote)	MIFE.
Telerate page	N/a.

8 Singapore

Contents

Singapore International Monetary Exchange (SIMEX)

Address:

1 Raffles Place
Suite 07-00
OUB Centre
Singapore 0104

Telephone: 535 7382
Fax: 535 7282
Telex: RS 38000 SINMEX

Exchange personnel

Chairman: Elizabeth Sam
President: Ang Swee Tian
SVP, Marketing: Liaw Hong Peng
Information Officer: Benjamin Foo

Futures contracts available
British pound / US dollar currency
Deutschmark / US dollar currency
High sulphur fuel oil
Japanese yen / US dollar currency
Nikkei 225 Stock Average
100-ounce gold
Three-month Eurodollar interest rate
Three-month Euro-yen interest rate

Options contracts on futures available
Deutschmark / US dollar currency future
Japanese yen / US dollar currency future
Three-month Eurodollar interest rate future

Clearing House: SIMEX Clearing House.

Method of trading: Open outcry.

Commenced trading: 1984.

Exchange links: Mutual offset link with the Chicago Mercantile Exchange (CME) in Eurodollar and currency futures.

A brief synopsis of the exchange

SIMEX was originally established as the Gold Exchange of Singapore, but in 1984 became the first specialist financial futures exchange in Asia. Eurodollar and currency futures are traded under the 'mutual offset system' fungible link with the Chicago Mercantile Exchange (CME). The Nikkei 225 Average futures are traded by SIMEX under a sub-licence from the CME who own the right to trade the Nikkei 225 Average futures outside of Japan. Although the US Government Treasury Bond futures contract traded on SIMEX was identical to that traded at the CBOT, there was no mutual offset and the contract has subsequently closed. The contract specification for the gold futures is currently under review.

There are five categories of membership (Corporate Clearing Member - over 30, Corporate Non-Clearing Member – over 40, Commercial Associate Member, Individual Non-Clearing Member and Individual Trading Permit Holder) with over 460 members in total.

The major competitors to SIMEX are the SFE and the Japanese exchanges. Trading in a local Singapore stock market index futures contract on SIMEX is planned.

Singapore
International
Monetary Exchange
(SIMEX)
Futures
Currencies

British pound / US dollar currency (BP) futures

Contract size	£62,500 traded against the US dollar (US$).
Standard delivery method	Physical delivery of the currencies concerned.
Trading months	The spot (nearby calendar) month plus months from the March, June, September and December cycle.
Trading hours	8.25 a.m. – 5.15 p.m.
Price quotation method	In US dollars (US$) per pounds sterling (£).
Minimum price move (value)	US$0.0002 per £1.00 (US$12.50 per contract).
Daily price limits	None.
Position limits	None.
Last trading day	The second business day preceding the third Wednesday of the contract month.
Delivery day	The third Wednesday of the contract month.
Initial (Variation) margin	US$2,750 per contract (US$2,000).
Spread margin	Not stated.
Reuters Monitor (Quote)	BPSE.
Telerate page	N/a.

This contract has the same specifications as and is mutually offsettable against the Chicago Mercantile Exchange's British pound / US dollar currency futures contract.

Deutschmark / US dollar currency (DM) futures

Contract size	DM125,000 traded against the US dollar (US$).
Standard delivery method	Physical delivery of the currencies concerned.
Trading months	The spot (nearby calendar) month plus months from the March, June, September and December cycle.
Trading hours	8.20 a.m. – 5.10 p.m.
Price quotation method	In US dollars (US$) per Deutschmark (DM).
Minimum price move (value)	US$0.0001 per DM1.00 (US$12.50 per contract).
Daily price limits	None.
Position limits	None.
Last trading day	The second business day preceding the third Wednesday of the contract month.
Delivery day	The third Wednesday of the contract month.
Initial (Variation) margin	US$1,788 per contract (US$1,300).
Spread margin	Not stated.
Reuters Monitor (Quote)	MKSE.
Telerate page	6177.

This contract has the same specifications as and is mutually offsettable against the Chicago Mercantile Exchange's Deutschmark / US dollar currency futures contract.

**Singapore
International
Monetary Exchange
(SIMEX)
Futures
Currencies**

High sulphur fuel oil (SF) futures

Contract size	100 metric tons of high sulphur fuel oil.
Standard delivery method	Physical delivery FOB, ex-tank, in-tank transfer or ex-ship (a cash settlement alternative is available for delivery positions under 10 contracts).
Trading months	The nearby six consecutive calendar months.
Trading hours	Two sessions daily: 9.30 a.m. – 12.30 p.m. and 2.30 p.m. – 6.00 p.m.
Price quotation method	In US dollars (US$) and cents per metric ton.
Minimum price move (value)	US$0.10 per metric ton (US$10.00 per contract).
Daily price limits	For the month prior to the contract month: a movement of US$5.00 per metric ton (US$500 per contract) above or below the previous day's settlement price holds for 30 minutes. Thereafter there are no further limits for the rest of the day. There are no limits in the last hour of trading, except where an upper or lower limit is reached prior to the last hour of trading. For months other than the above: a movement of US$5.00 per ton (US$500 per contract) above or below the previous day's settlement price holds for 30 minutes. Thereafter the limit is raised to US$10.00 per metric ton (US$1,000 per contract). If the settlement price reaches the US$10.00 limit on two consecutive days, there is no limit on the third day, and on the fourth day limits are reinstated.
Position limits	Net position of 1,000 contracts. Gross position of 4,000 contracts except in the last ten days of a contract's life where the limit is reduced to 100 contracts for speculators or 400 contracts for hedgers.
Last trading day	The last business day of the month preceding the contract month.
Delivery period	From the day after the fifth business day to the 25th calendar day of the contract month.
Initial (Variation) margin	Prior to the month preceding the contract month: US$700 per contract (US$500). During the month preceding the contract month: US$1,100 per contract (US$800). From the fifth business day prior to the last trading day: US$1,400 per contract (US$1,000).
Spread margin	Various inter-commodity straddle margin concessions are available.
Reuters Monitor (Quote)	SFSE.
Telerate page	N/a.

Japanese yen / US dollar currency (JY) futures

Singapore
International
Monetary Exchange
(SIMEX)
Futures
Stock indices

Contract size	Y12,500,000 traded against the US dollar (US$).
Standard delivery method	Physical delivery of the currencies concerned.
Trading months	The spot (nearby calendar) month plus months from the March, June, September and December cycle.
Trading hours	8.15 a.m. – 5.05 p.m.
Price quotation method	In US dollars (US$) per Japanese yen (Y).
Minimum price move (value)	US$0.0001 per Y100.00 (US$12.50 per contract).
Daily price limits	None.
Position limits	None.
Last trading day	The second business day preceding the third Wednesday of the contract month.
Delivery day	The third Wednesday of the contract month.
Initial (Variation) margin	US$2,750 per contract (US$2,000).
Spread margin	Not stated.
Reuters Monitor (Quote)	JYSE.
Telerate page	6176.

This contract has the same specifications as and is mutually offsettable against the Chicago Mercantile Exchange's Japanese yen / US dollar currency futures contract.

Nikkei 225 Stock Average (NK) futures

Contract size	Y500 multiplied by the capitalisation-weighted Nikkei 225 Stock Average futures price.
Standard delivery method	Cash settlement (there is no facility for physical delivery of the underlying stocks to the index).
Trading months	The spot (nearby calendar) month plus months from the March, June, September and December cycle.
Trading hours	8.00 a.m. – 2.15 p.m.
Price quotation method	In Japanese yen (Y) per index point.
Minimum price move (value)	5.0 index points (Y2,500 per contract).
Daily price limits	10% above or below the previous day's settlement price (for 30 minutes), then the limit is extended to 15% above or below the previous day's settlement price for the rest of the day. If the upper limit is reached on the next two successive business days, there will be no limit on the fourth day, after which normal limits resume. There are no limits on the last trading day.
Position limits	For speculative positions: 1,000 contracts net.

**Singapore
International
Monetary Exchange
(SIMEX)
Futures
Stock indices**

Last trading day	The third Wednesday of the contract month.
Delivery day	The business day following the last trading day.
Initial (Variation) margin	Y1,200,000 per contract (Y1,000,000).
Spread margin	Not stated.
Reuters Monitor (Quote)	NKSE.
Telerate page	N/a.

100-ounce gold futures

Contract size	100 fine troy ounces of gold bullion.
Standard delivery method	Physical delivery of the above.
Trading months	The March, June, September and December cycle up to 12 months forward.
Trading hours	9.30 a.m. – 5.15 p.m.
Price quotation method	In US dollars (US$) and cents per troy ounce.
Minimum price move (value)	US$0.10 per troy ounce (US$10.00 per contract).
Daily price limits	250 basis points (US$25.00 per ounce) above or below the previous day's settlement price.
Position limits	A speculative limit of 2,500 applies.
Last trading day	The business day preceding the fifth to last business day of the contract month.
Delivery day	The penultimate business day of the contract month.
Initial (Variation) margin	US$1,600 per contract (US$1,200).
Spread margin	Not stated.
Reuters Monitor (Quote)	GDSE.
Telerate page	N/a.

Three-month Eurodollar interest rate (ED) futures

Contract size	US$1,000,000 nominal value.
Standard delivery method	Cash settlement on the last trading day.
Trading months	The March, June, September and December cycle.
Trading hours	7.45 a.m. – 5.20 p.m.
Price quotation method	100.00 minus the annualised rate of interest calculated to two decimal places, and quoted in US dollars (US$).
Minimum price move (value)	0.01% per annum of nominal face value (US$25.00 per contract).
Daily price limits	None.

Singapore
International
Monetary Exchange
(SIMEX)
Futures
Interest rates

Position limits	The limit on speculative positions is 1,000 contracts.
Last trading day	The second London business day preceding the third Wednesday of the contract month.
Delivery day	The third Wednesday of the contract month.
Initial (Variation) margin	US$1,050 per contract (US$750).
Spread margin	Not stated.
Reuters Monitor (Quote)	EDSE.
Telerate page	6175.

This contract has the same specifications as and is mutually offsettable against the Chicago Mercantile Exchange's three-month Eurodollar interest rate futures contract.

Three-month Euro-yen interest rate (EY) futures

Contract size	Y100,000,000 nominal value.
Standard delivery method	Cash settlement at the final settlement price* on the third Wednesday of the contract month.
Trading months	The March, June, September and December cycle up to two years forward.
Trading hours	8.00 a.m. – 5.00 p.m. Trading ceases in the expiring contract at 10.00 a.m. on the last trading day.
Price quotation method	100.00 minus the annualised rate of interest calculated to two decimal places, and quoted in Japanese yen (Y).
Minimum price move (value)	0.01% per annum of nominal face value (Y2,500 per contract).
Daily price limits	None.
Position limits	3,000 contracts net long or short in all contract months. Higher limits are available to bona fide hedgers on application to the exchange.
Last trading day	The second business day immediately preceding the third Wednesday of the contract month.
Delivery day	The third Wednesday of the contract month.
Initial (Variation) margin	Y65,000 per contract (Y50,000).
Spread margin	Straddle margin concessions exist between SIMEX Eurodollar and Euro-yen futures contracts.
Reuters Monitor (Quote)	EJSE.
Telerate page	6173.

* The final settlement price is calculated as the Singapore Interbank Offered Rate (SIBOR) for three-month Euro-yen funds quoted by major banks at a random time in the last 90 minutes of trading on the last trading day. The final settlement price will be 100.00 minus the arithmetic mean at that time.

Singapore
International
Monetary Exchange
(SIMEX)
Options on futures
Currencies

Option on SIMEX Deutschmark / US dollar currency futures

Contract size	One SIMEX Deutschmark / US dollar currency futures contract (of an underlying contract size of DM125,000 traded against the US dollar).
Standard delivery method	Delivery of a long or short position in a futures contract at the strike price as above.
Trading months	The spot (nearby calendar) month plus months from the March, June, September and December cycle.
Trading hours	8.20 a.m. – 5.10 p.m.
Price quotation method	In US cents per Deutschmark (DM) – a premium of US$0.005 represents an option price of US$625.
Minimum price move (value)	US$0.0001 per DM1.00 (US$12.50 per contract).
Daily price limits	None.
Position limits	None.
Last trading day	Two Fridays before the third Wednesday of the contract month (or the preceding day if this is an exchange holiday).
Delivery day	The business day following the last trading day.
Initial (Variation) margin	Please contact the exchange for the current margin requirements.
Spread margin	Please contact the exchange for the current spread concessions.
Strike price intervals	At intervals of one US cent (US$0.01) per DM1.00 – e.g. US$0.42, US$0.43, US$0.44, etc.
Option type	American style (the option may be exercised on any business day up to and including the last trading day).
Method of introduction of new strike prices	Not stated.
Reuters Monitor (Quote)	SMQA – SMQZ.
Telerate page	N/a.

Option on SIMEX Japanese yen / US dollar currency futures

Contract size	One SIMEX Japanese yen / US dollar currency futures contract (of an underlying contract size of Y12,500,000 traded against the US dollar).
Standard delivery method	Delivery of a long or short position in a futures contract at the strike price as above.
Trading months	The spot (nearby calendar) month, the next two consecutive calendar months plus months from the March, June, September and December cycle.
Trading hours	8.15 a.m. – 5.05 p.m.

Singapore
International
Monetary Exchange
(SIMEX)
Options on futures
Interest rates

Price quotation method	In US cents per Japanese yen (Y) – a premium of US$0.00005 represents an option price of US$625.
Minimum price move (value)	US$0.0001 per Y100 (US$12.50 per contract). Trades may also occur at a total price of US$1,000 if this results in a liquidation of positions for both parties to the trade.
Daily price limits	None.
Position limits	None.
Last trading day	Two Fridays before the third Wednesday of the contract month (or the preceding day if this is an exchange holiday).
Delivery day	The business day following the last trading day.
Initial (Variation) margin	Please contact the exchange for the current margin requirements.
Spread margin	Please contact the exchange for the current spread concessions.
Strike price intervals	At intervals of one US cent (US$0.01) per Y100 – e.g. US$0.0042, US$0.0043, etc.
Option type	American style (the option may be exercised on any business day up to and including the last trading day).
Method of introduction of new strike prices	Not stated.
Reuters Monitor (Quote)	SMRA – SMRZ.
Telerate page	N/a.

Option on SIMEX three-month Eurodollar interest rate futures

Contract size	One SIMEX three-month Eurodollar futures contract (of an underlying contract size of US$1,000,000 nominal value).
Standard delivery method	Delivery of a long or short position in a futures contract at the strike price as above.
Trading months	The March, June, September and December cycle.
Trading hours	8.30 a.m. – 5.20 p.m.
Price quotation method	100.00 minus the annualised rate of interest calculated to two decimal places, quoted in US dollars (US$).
Minimum price move (value)	0.01 Eurodollar futures point (US$25.00 per contract) except that trades may occur at a total price of US$1,000 if this results in a liquidation of positions for both parties to the trade.
Daily price limits	None.
Position limits	None.
Last trading day	The second London business day preceding the third Wednesday of the contract month.

Delivery day	The third Wednesday of the contract month.
Initial (Variation) margin	Please contact the exchange for the current margin requirements.
Spread margin	Please contact the exchange for the current spread concessions.
Strike price intervals	At 50 basis point (0.50%) intervals for Eurodollar futures levels below 88-00 and at 25 basis point (0.25%) intervals for Eurodollar futures levels above 88-00 (eg. 88-25, 88-50, 88-75, etc).
Option type	American style (the option may be exercised on any business day up to and including the last trading day). All in-the-money options are automatically exercised at expiry unless contrary instructions are received.
Method of introduction of new strike prices	A new strike price is listed when the underlying futures price touches within half a strike price of either the second highest or lowest existing strike price. No new series will normally be introduced in the last 10 calendar days prior to expiry.
Reuters Monitor (Quote)	SMOA – SMOZ.
Telerate page	27800 – 27840.

Part II The Americas

Contents

9 Bermuda

Contents

International Futures Exchange (Bermuda) (INTEX)

10 Brazil

Contents

Bolsa de Mercadorias de São Paulo (BMSP) (São Paulo Commodity Exchange)

Address:	Rua Libero Badaro 471 4th Floor CX Postal 1442 São Paulo CEP 1009 Brazil
Telephone:	(55–11) 32–3101
Fax:	(55–11) 32–4244
Telex:	N/a.

Exchange personnel

President:	Ney Castro Alves
Vice-President:	Julio Cesar de Toledo Piza Junior
Vice-President:	Jose Antonio Esteve
General Superintendent:	Francisco Jose Monteiro Esperante
Research Department:	Irene Goldenberg

Futures contracts available
Arabica coffee
British pound / Brazilian cruzado currency
BTN (Brazilian Treasury Bills)
CDB (Banking Certificates of Deposit)
Cocoa
Coffee (Robusta / Connillon)
Corn
Cotton
Deutschmark / Brazilian cruzado currency
Feeder cattle
FGV-100 Stock Index
Frozen chickens
Gold
Japanese yen / Brazilian cruzado currency
Live cattle
Soyabean meal
Soyabean oil
Soyabeans
US dollar / Brazilian cruzado currency

Options contracts on futures available
Arabica coffee futures
Gold futures
Live cattle futures
US dollar / Brazilian cruzado currency futures

Options contracts on cash/physical available
Gold

Clearing House: Caixe Nacional de Liquidacao de Negocios a Termo e
                               Disponivel SA.

Method of trading: Simultaneous auctions transmitted by telephone.

Commenced trading: 1918.

Exchange links: Other regional exchanges in Brazil.

A brief synopsis of the exchange:
Cotton was the most traded commodity until the mid-1970s when a wide series of new contracts was introduced, including agricultural products, financials and options. Gold, cattle and coffee are the most actively traded contracts.

In 1988, high rates of Brazilian inflation led to the launch of the Adjusted Futures Market (AFM) for coffee, cattle and gold, allowing investors to hedge effectively despite the rate of inflation. There is also now an AFM for soyabeans.

The BMSP is the largest futures exchange in Brazil, accounting for three-quarters of Brazil's total turnover. Three small regional exchanges make up the remainder. Simultaneous auctions by telephone connect the four exchanges and the country's futures markets are therefore very nationalistic. There are nearly 40 clearing members and approximately 140 brokers.

Arabica coffee futures

Contract size	100 bags of 60 kilograms each (6,000 kilograms in total) of arabica coffee.
Standard delivery method	Physical delivery of the above.
Trading months	The March, May, July, September and December cycle.
Trading hours	10.00 a.m. – 3.20 pm.
Price quotation method	In Brazilian cruzados (Cz$) per bag of coffee.
Minimum price move (value)	Cz$0.01 per bag of coffee (Cz$1.00 per contract).
Daily price limits	There are no price limits on the spot month. For the second month limits are twice the daily price limit. For all other months limits are 4% of the average weighted price of the three months with the largest open interest. Limits can be expanded by up to 50%.
Position limits	None.
Last trading day	The 13th business day before the end of the contract month.
Delivery day	The fifth business day before the last day of the contract month.
Initial (Variation) margin	10% of the underlying value of the contract. For speculators: three times the daily price limit. For hedgers: 75% of the speculators' margin.
Spread margin	Not stated.
Reuters Monitor (Quote)	N/a.
Telerate page	N/a.

British pound / Brazilian cruzado currency futures

Contract size	£5,000 traded against the Brazilian cruzado (Cz$).
Standard delivery method	Physical exchange of the currencies concerned.
Trading months	The first six consecutive calendar months followed by the first and/or third contract month from the next quarterly period (the March, June, September and December cycle).
Trading hours	10.15 a.m. – 4.00 p.m.
Price quotation method	In terms of Brazilian cruzados (Cz$) per pounds sterling (£).
Minimum price move (value)	Cz$0.001 per £1.00 (Cz$5.00 per contract).
Daily price limits	For the first month the limit is tripled. For the second month the limit is twice the daily price limit. For all other months the limit is 3% of the average weighted price of the months with the largest open interest. The limits may be expanded by up to 100%.

Position limits	None.
Last trading day	The last business day of the month before the contract month.
Delivery day	The business day following the last trading day.
Initial (Variation) margin	10% of the underlying value of the contract. For speculators: three times the daily price limit. For hedgers: 75% of the speculators' margin.
Spread margin	Not stated.
Reuters Monitor (Quote)	N/a.
Telerate page	N/a.

BTN (Brazilian Treasury Bills) futures

Contract size	1,000 BTNs (Brazilian Treasury Bills).
Standard delivery method	Not stated.
Trading months	All consecutive calendar months.
Trading hours	10.30 a.m. – 4.00 p.m.
Price quotation method	In Brazilian cruzados (Cz$) per BTN.
Minimum price move (value)	Cz$0.10 per BTN (Cz$100 per contract).
Daily price limits	For the first month the limit is tripled. For the second month limits are twice the daily price limit. For all other months limits are 1% of the average weighted price of the three months with the largest open interest. The limits may be expanded by up to 100%.
Position limits	None.
Last trading day	The first business day of the contract month.
Delivery day	The first business day after the last trading day.
Initial (Variation) margin	10% of the underlying value of the contract. For speculators: three times the daily price limit. For hedgers: 75% of the speculators' margin.
Spread margin	Not stated.
Reuters Monitor (Quote)	N/a.
Telerate page	N/a.

CDB (Banking Certificates of Deposit) futures

Contract size	Cz$500,000 nominal face value of Brazilian Banking Certificates of Deposit.
Standard delivery method	Physical delivery of the above.
Trading months	The January, March, May, July, September and November cycle.
Trading hours	Not stated as the contract is inactive.
Price quotation method	In Brazilian cruzados (Cz$) per nominal face value.

São Paulo
Commodity
Exchange (BMSP)
Futures
Softs and
agricultural

Minimum price move (value)	Not stated as the contract is inactive.
Daily price limits	There are no price limits on the spot month. For the second month limits are twice the daily price limit. For all other months the limit is 0.10 of the average weighted price of the three months with the largest open interest. Limits can be expanded by up to 100%.
Position limits	None.
Last trading day	The first business day before the second Wednesday of the contract month.
Delivery day	The tenth business day after the last trading day.
Initial (Variation) margin	10% of the underlying value of the contract. For speculators: three times the daily price limit. For hedgers: 75% of the speculators' margin.
Spread margin	Not stated.
Reuters Monitor (Quote)	N/a.
Telerate page	N/a.

Cocoa futures

Contract size	50 bags of 60 kilograms each (3,000 kilograms in total) of cocoa type II.
Standard delivery method	Physical delivery of the above.
Trading months	The March, May, July, September and December cycle.
Trading hours	2.00 p.m. – 3.30 p.m.
Price quotation method	In Brazilian cruzados (Cz$) per bag.
Minimum price move (value)	Cz$0.01 per bag (Cz$0.50 per contract).
Daily price limits	There are no price limits on the spot month. For the second month limits are twice the daily price limit. For all other months limits are 3% of the average weighted price of the three months with the largest open interest. Limits can be expanded by up to 60%.
Position limits	None.
Last trading day	The 13th business day before the end of the contract month.
Delivery day	The third business day before the last day of the contract month.
Initial (Variation) margin	10% of the underlying value of the contract. For speculators: three times the daily price limit. For hedgers: 75% of the speculators' margin.
Spread margin	Not stated
Reuters Monitor (Quote)	N/a.
Telerate page	N/a.

São Paulo
Commodity
Exchange (BMSP)
Futures
Softs and
agricultural

Coffee (Robusta/Connillon) futures

Contract size	100 bags of 60 kilograms each (6,000 kilograms in total) of Robusta/Connillon coffee.
Standard delivery method	Physical delivery of the above.
Trading months	The March, May, July, September and December cycle.
Trading hours	10.00 a.m. – 3.20 p.m.
Price quotation method	In Brazilian cruzados (Cz$) per bag of coffee.
Minimum price move (value)	Cz$0.01 per bag of coffee (Cz$1.00 per contract).
Daily price limits	There are no price limits on the spot month. For the second month limits are twice the daily price limit. For all other months limits are 4% of the average weighted price of the three months with the largest open interest. Limits can be expanded by up to 50%.
Position limits	None.
Last trading day	The 13th business day before the end of the contract month.
Delivery day	The fifth business day before the last day of the contract month.
Initial (Variation) margin	10% of the underlying value of the contract. For speculators: three times the daily price limit. For hedgers: 75% of the speculators' margin.
Spread margin	Not stated.
Reuters Monitor (Quote)	N/a.
Telerate page	N/a.

Corn futures

Contract size	60 metric tons of corn.
Standard delivery method	Physical delivery of the above.
Trading months	The January, March, May, July, September and November cycle.
Trading hours	Not stated as the contract is inactive.
Price quotation method	In Brazilian cruzados (Cz$) per metric ton.
Minimum price move (value)	Not stated as the contract is inactive.
Daily price limits	There are no price limits on the spot month. For the second month limits are twice the daily price limit. For all other months limits are 3% of the average weighted price of the three months with the largest open interest. Limits can be expanded by up to 60%.
Position limits	None.

Last trading day	The 13th business day before the end of the contract month.
Delivery day	The fifth business day before the last day of the contract month.
Initial (Variation) margin	10% of the underlying value of the contract. For speculators: three times the daily price limit. For hedgers: 75% of the speculators' margin.
Spread margin	Not stated.
Reuters Monitor (Quote)	N/a.
Telerate page	N/a.

Cotton futures

Contract size	500 arrobas (1 arroba = 15 kilograms) of cotton.
Standard delivery method	Physical delivery of the above.
Trading months	The March, May, July, October and December cycle.
Trading hours	11.00 a.m. – 12.00 noon.
Price quotation method	In Brazilian cruzados (Cz$) per arroba.
Minimum price move (value)	Cz$0.01 per arroba (Cz$5.00 per contract).
Daily price limits	There are no price limits on the spot month. For the second month limits are twice the daily price limit. For all other months limits are 3% of the average weighted price of the three months with the largest open interest. Limits can be expanded by up to 60%.
Position limits	None.
Last trading day	The 13th business day before the end of the contract month.
Delivery day	The third business day before the last day of the contract month.
Initial (Variation) margin	10% of the underlying value of the contract. For speculators: three times the daily price limit. For hedgers: 75% of the speculators' margin.
Spread margin	Not stated.
Reuters Monitor (Quote)	N/a.
Telerate page	N/a.

Deutschmark / Brazilian cruzado currency futures

Contract size	DM10,000 traded against the Brazilian cruzado (Cz$).
Standard delivery method	Physical exchange of the currencies concerned.
Trading months	The first six consecutive calendar months followed by the first and/or third contract month from the next quarterly period (the March, June, September and December cycle).

Trading hours	10.15 a.m. – 4.00 p.m.
Price quotation method	In Brazilian cruzados (Cz$) per Deutschmark (DM).
Minimum price move (value)	Cz$0.001 per DM1.00 (Cz$10.00 per contract).
Daily price limits	For the first month the limit is tripled. For the second month the daily price limit is doubled. For all other months limits are 3% of the average weighted price of the months with the largest open interest. The limits may be expanded by up to 100%.
Position limits	None.
Last trading day	The last business day of the month before the contract month.
Delivery day	The business day following the last trading day.
Initial (Variation) margin	10% of the underlying value of the contract. For speculators: three times the daily price limit. For hedgers: 75% of the speculators' margin.
Spread margin	Not stated.
Reuters Monitor (Quote)	N/a.
Telerate page	N/a.

Feeder cattle futures

Contract size	27 heads of feeder cattle.
Standard delivery method	Physical delivery of the above.
Trading months	The January, March, May, July, September and November cycle.
Trading hours	3.00 p.m. – 4.05 p.m.
Price quotation method	In Brazilian cruzados (Cz$) per head of feeder cattle.
Minimum price move (value)	Cz$0.01 per head of feeder cattle (Cz$0.27 per contract).
Daily price limits	There are no price limits on the spot month. For the second month the limits are twice the daily price limit. For all other months the limits are 3% of the average weighted price of the three months with the largest open interest. Limits can be expanded by up to 60%.
Position limits	None.
Last trading day	The 13th business day before the end of the contract month.
Delivery day	The fifth business day before the last day of the contract month.
Initial (Variation) margin	10% of the underlying value of the contract. For speculators: three times the daily price limit. For hedgers: 75% of the speculators' margin.
Spread margin	Not stated.
Reuters Monitor (Quote)	N/a.
Telerate page	N/a.

FGV-100 Stock Index futures

São Paulo
Commodity
Exchange (BMSP)
Futures
Softs and
agricultural

Contract size	One portfolio equivalent to five theoretical portfolios of the FGV-100 Stock Index.
Standard delivery method	Cash settlement at expiry. There is no facility for physical delivery of the stocks underlying the index.
Trading months	All consecutive calendar months.
Trading hours	Not stated as the contract is inactive.
Price quotation method	In Brazilian cruzados (Cz$) per index point.
Minimum price move (value)	10 index points (Cz$50.00 per contract).
Daily price limits	There are no price limits on the spot month. For the second month limits are four times the daily price limit. For all other months limits are 3% of the average weighted price of the three months with the largest open interest. Limits can be expanded by up to 60%.
Position limits	None.
Last trading day	The last business day before the third Wednesday of the contract month.
Delivery day	The third business day before the last day of the contract month.
Initial (Variation) margin	10% of the underlying value of the contract. For speculators: three times the daily price limit. For hedgers: 75% of the speculators' margin.
Spread margin	Not stated.
Reuters Monitor (Quote)	N/a.
Telerate page	N/a.

Frozen chicken futures

Contract size	12 tons of frozen chickens.
Standard delivery method	Physical delivery of the above.
Trading months	The February, April, June, August, October and December cycle.
Trading hours	Not stated as the contract is inactive.
Price quotation method	In Brazilian cruzados (Cz$) per ton.
Minimum price move (value)	Not stated as the contract is inactive.
Daily price limits	There are no limits on the spot month. For the second month the daily price limit is doubled. For all other months the limit is 3% of the average weighted price of the month with the largest open interest. Limits can be expanded by up to 100%.
Position limits	None.
Last trading day	The 13th business day before the end of the contract month.
Delivery day	The fifth business day before the last day of the contract month.

São Paulo
Commodity
Exchange (BMSP)
Futures
Soft and
agricultural

Initial (Variation) margin	10% of the underlying value of the contract. For speculators: three times the daily price limit. For hedgers: 75% of the speculators' margin.
Spread margin	Not stated.
Reuters Monitor (Quote)	N/a.
Telerate page	N/a.

Gold futures

Contract size	250 grams (0.25 kilograms) of fine gold bullion.
Standard delivery method	Physical delivery of the above.
Trading months	The February, April, June, August, October and December cycle.
Trading hours	10.00 a.m. – 3.30 p.m.
Price quotation method	In Brazilian cruzados (Cz$) per gram.
Minimum price move (value)	Cz$0.01 per gram (Cz$2.50 per contract).
Daily price limits	There are no price limits on the spot month. For the second month the daily price limit doubles. For all other months the limit is 5% of the average weighted price of the month with the largest open interest. Limits can be expanded by up to 100%.
Position limits	None.
Last trading day	The 13th business day before the end of the contract month.
Delivery day	The third business day before the last day of the contract month.
Initial (Variation) margin	10% of the underlying value of the contract. For speculators: three times the daily price limit. For hedgers: 75% of the speculators' margin.
Spread margin	Not stated.
Reuters Monitor (Quote)	N/a.
Telerate page	N/a.

Japanese yen / Brazilian cruzado currency futures

Contract size	Y1,000,000 traded against the Brazilian cruzado (Cz$).
Standard delivery method	Physical exchange of the currencies concerned.
Trading months	The first six consecutive calendar months followed by the first and/or third contract month from the next quarterly period (the March, June, September and December cycle).
Trading hours	10.15 a.m. – 4.00 p.m.

São Paulo
Commodity
Exchange (BMSP)
Futures
Softs and
agricultural

Price quotation method	In terms of Brazilian cruzados (Cz$) per Japanese yen (Y).
Minimum price move (value)	Cz$0.001 per Y100 (Cz$10.00 per contract).
Daily price limits	For the first month the limit is tripled. For the second month limits are twice the daily price limit. For all other months limits are 3% of the average weighted price of the months with the largest open interest. The limits may be expanded by up to 100%.
Position limits	None.
Last trading day	The last business day of the month before the contract month.
Delivery day	The business day following the last trading day.
Initial (Variation) margin	10% of the underlying value of the contract. For speculators: three times the daily price limit. For hedgers: 75% of the speculators' margin.
Spread margin	Not stated.
Reuters Monitor (Quote)	N/a.
Telerate page	N/a.

Live cattle futures

Contract size	330 arrobas (1 arroba = 15 kilograms) of live cattle.
Standard delivery method	Physical delivery of the above.
Trading months	The February, April, June, August, October and December cycle.
Trading hours	3.00 p.m. – 4.05 p.m.
Price quotation method	In Brazilian cruzados (Cz$) per arroba.
Minimum price move (value)	Cz$0.01 per arroba (Cz$3.30 per contract).
Daily price limits	There are no limits on the spot month. For the second month limits are twice the daily price limit. For all other months the limits are 3% of the average weighted price of the three months with the largest open interest. Limits can be expanded by up to 60%.
Position limits	None.
Last trading day	The 13th business day before the end of the contract month.
Delivery day	The fifth business day before the last day of the contract month.
Initial (Variation) margin	10% of the underlying value of the contract. For speculators: three times the daily price limit. For hedgers: 75% of the speculators' margin.
Spread margin	Not stated.
Reuters Monitor (Quote)	N/a.
Telerate page	N/a.

São Paulo
Commodity
Exchange (BMSP)
Futures
Softs and
agricultural

Soyabean meal futures

Contract size	25 metric tons of soyabean meal.
Standard delivery method	Physical delivery of the above.
Trading months	The January, March, May, July, September and November cycle.
Trading hours	11.30 a.m. – 3.15 p.m.
Price quotation method	In Brazilian cruzados (Cz$) per metric ton.
Minimum price move (value)	Not stated as the contract is inactive.
Daily price limits	There are no price limits on the spot month. For the second month limits are twice the daily price limit. For all other months limits are 3% of the average weighted price of the three months with the largest open interest. Limits can be expanded by up to 60%.
Position limits	None.
Last trading day	The 13th business day before the end of the contract month.
Delivery day	The fifth business day before the last day of the contract month.
Initial (Variation) margin	10% of the underlying value of the contract. For speculators: three times the daily price limit. For hedgers: 75% of the speculators' margin.
Spread margin	Not stated.
Reuters Monitor (Quote)	N/a.
Telerate page	N/a.

Soyabean oil futures

Contract size	12.5 metric tons of soyabean oil.
Standard delivery method	Physical delivery of the above.
Trading months	The January, March, May, July, September and November cycle.
Trading hours	11.30 a.m. – 3.15 p.m.
Price quotation method	In Brazilian cruzados (Cz$) per metric ton.
Minimum price move (value)	Not stated as the contract is inactive.
Daily price limits	There are no price limits on the spot month. For the second month limits are twice the daily price limit. For all other months the limit is 3% of the average weighted price of the three months with the largest open interest. Limits can be expanded by up to 60%.
Position limits	None.
Last trading day	The 13th business day before the end of the contract month.
Delivery day	The fifth business day before the last day of the contract month.

Initial (Variation) margin	10% of the underlying value of the contract. For speculators: three times the daily price limit. For hedgers: 75% of the speculators' margin.
Spread margin	Not stated.
Reuters Monitor (Quote)	N/a.
Telerate page	N/a.

Soyabeans futures

Contract size	30 metric tons of soyabeans.
Standard delivery method	Physical delivery of the above.
Trading months	The January, March, May, July, September and November cycle.
Trading hours	11.30 a.m. – 3.15 p.m.
Price quotation method	In Brazilian cruzados (Cz$) per kilogram.
Minimum price move (value)	Cz$0.01 per 60 kilograms.
Daily price limits	There are no price limits on the spot month. For the second month limits are twice the daily price limit. For all other months the limits are 3% of the average weighted price of the three months with the largest open interest. Limits can be expanded by up to 60%.
Position limits	None.
Last trading day	The 13th business day before the end of the contract month.
Delivery day	The fifth business day before the last day of the contract month.
Initial (Variation) margin	10% of the underlying value of the contract. For speculators: three times the daily price limit. For hedgers: 75% of the speculators' margin.
Spread margin	Not stated.
Reuters Monitor (Quote)	N/a.
Telerate page	N/a.

US dollar / Brazilian cruzado currency futures

Contract size	US$5,000 traded against the Brazilian cruzado (Cz$).
Standard delivery method	Physical exchange of the currencies concerned.
Trading months	The first six consecutive calendar months followed by the first and/or third contract month from the next quarterly period (the March, June, September and December cycle).
Trading hours	10.15 a.m. – 4.00 p.m.
Price quotation method	In Brazilian cruzados (Cz$) per US dollar (US$).

Minimum price move (value)	Cz$0.001 per US$1.00 (Cz$5.00 per contract).
Daily price limits	For the first month the limit is tripled. For the second month the price limit is doubled. For all other months the limit is 3% of the average weighted price of the months with the largest open interest. The limits may be expanded by up to 100%.
Position limits	None.
Last trading day	The last business day of the month before the contract month.
Delivery day	The business day following the last trading day.
Initial (Variation) margin	10% of the underlying value of the contract. For speculators: three times the daily price limit. For hedgers: 75% of the speculators' margin.
Spread margin	Not stated.
Reuters Monitor (Quote)	N/a.
Telerate page	N/a.

Option on BMSP Arabica coffee futures

Contract size	One BMSP Arabica coffee futures contract (of an underlying contract size of 100 bags of 60 kilograms each).
Standard delivery method	Delivery of a long or short position in a futures contract at the strike price as above.
Trading months	The March, May, July, September and December cycle.
Trading hours	10.00 a.m. – 3.30 p.m.
Price quotation method	In Brazilian cruzados (Cz$) per bag of coffee.
Minimum price move (value)	Cz$0.01 per bag of coffee (Cz$1.00 per contract).
Daily price limits	None.
Position limits	None.
Last trading day	The 10th business day before the first business day of the contract month of the underlying futures contract.
Delivery day	The business day following the last trading day.
Initial (Variation) margin	Not stated. Please consult the exchange for the current margin requirements.
Spread margin	Not stated.
Strike price intervals	Not stated.
Option type	Not stated.
Method of introduction of new strike prices	Not stated.
Reuters Monitor (Quote)	N/a.
Telerate page	N/a.

São Paulo
Commodity
Exchange (BMSP)
Options on futures
Softs and
agricultural

Option on BMSP gold futures

Contract size	One BMSP gold futures contract (of an underlying contract size of 0.25 kilograms).
Standard delivery method	Delivery of a long or short position in a futures contract at the strike price as above.
Trading months	The February, April, June, August, October and December cycle.
Trading hours	10.00 a.m. – 3.50 p.m.
Price quotation method	In Brazilian cruzados (Cz$) per gram.
Minimum price move (value)	Cz$0.01 per gram (Cz$2.50 per contract).
Daily price limits	None.
Position limits	None.
Last trading day	The 10th business day before the first business day of the contract month of the underlying futures contract.
Delivery day	The business day following the last trading day.
Initial (Variation) margin	Not stated. Please consult the exchange for the current margin requirements.
Spread margin	Not stated.
Strike price intervals	Not stated.
Option type	Not stated.
Method of introduction of new strike prices	Not stated.
Reuters Monitor (Quote)	N/a.
Telerate page	N/a.

Option on BMSP live cattle futures

Contract size	One BMSP live cattle futures contract (of an underlying contract size of 330 arrobas).
Standard delivery method	Delivery of a long or short position in a futures contract at the strike price as above.
Trading months	The February, April, June, August, October and December cycle.
Trading hours	3.00 p.m. – 4.05 p.m.
Price quotation method	In Brazilian cruzados (Cz$) per arroba.
Minimum price move (value)	Cz$0.01 per arroba (Cz$3.30 per contract).
Daily price limits	None.
Position limits	None.
Last trading day	The 10th business day before the first business day of the contract month of the underlying futures contract.
Delivery day	The business day following the last trading day.
Initial (Variation) margin	Not stated. Please consult the exchange for the current margin requirements.
Spread margin	Not stated.

São Paulo
Commodity
Exchange (BMSP)
Options on futures
Softs and
agricultural

Strike price intervals	Not stated.
Option type	Not stated.
Method of introduction of new strike prices	Not stated.
Reuters Monitor (Quote)	N/a.
Telerate page	N/a.

Option on BMSP US dollar / Brazilian cruzado currency futures

Contract size	One BMSP US dollar / Brazilian cruzado futures contract (of an underlying contract size of US$5,000 traded against the Brazilian cruzado (Cz$)).
Standard delivery method	Delivery of a long or short position in a futures contract at the strike price as above.
Trading months	The first six consecutive calendar months followed by the first and/or third contract month from the next quarterly period (the March, June, September and December cycle).
Trading hours	10.15 a.m. – 4.00 p.m.
Price quotation method	In Brazilian cruzados (Cz$) per US dollar (US$).
Minimum price move (value)	Cz$0.001 per US$1.00 (Cz$5.00 per contract).
Daily price limits	None.
Position limits	None.
Last trading day	The business day before the last day of the contract month of the underlying futures contract.
Delivery day	The business day following the last trading day.
Initial (Variation) margin	Not stated. Please consult the exchange for the current margin requirements.
Spread margin	Not stated.
Strike price intervals	Not stated.
Option type	Not stated.
Method of introduction of new strike prices	Not stated.
Reuters Monitor (Quote)	N/a.
Telerate page	N/a.

Option on gold

Contract size	250 grams (0.25 kilograms) of gold bullion.
Standard delivery method	Physical delivery of the above.
Trading months	The January, March, May, July, September and November cycle.
Trading hours	10.00 a.m. – 3.50 p.m.

Price quotation method	In Brazilian cruzados (Cz$) per gram.	**São Paulo Commodity Exchange (BMSP) Options on cash/physical Precious metals**
Minimum price move (value)	Not stated as the contract is inactive.	
Daily price limits	None.	
Position limits	None.	
Last trading day	Not stated as the contract is inactive.	
Delivery day	Not stated as the contract is inactive.	
Initial (Variation) margin	Not stated. Please consult the exchange for the current margin requirements.	
Spread margin	Not stated.	
Strike price intervals	Not stated.	
Option type	Not stated.	
Method of introduction of new strike prices	Not stated.	
Reuters Monitor (Quote)	N/a.	
Telerate page	N/a.	

Bolsa Mercantil & de Futuros (BM&F) (Mercantile & Futures Exchange)

Address:

Praca Antonio Prado 48
01010–São Paulo
Brazil

Telephone: (5511) 239.5511, 36.6182, 37.9959
Fax: (5511) 35.2541
Telex: (11) 26928

Exchange personnel

Chairman: Luiz Masagao Ribeiro
President: Eduardo da Rocha Azevedo
Market Development: Alberto Amaral Lyra, Jr
General Manager: Horacio de Mendonca Netto
Chief Executive Officer: Dorival Rodrigues Alves
Marketing Manager: Patricia Maria Brighenti

Futures contracts available
Bovespa (São Paulo Stock Exchange) Stock Index
'Brazilian' coffee (traded in both Brazilian cruzados or US dollars)
Brazilian cruzado / Deutschmark currency
Brazilian cruzado / Japanese yen currency
Brazilian cruzado / US dollar currency
Brazilian Government Treasury Bonds
Broiler chickens (frozen/chilled)
Domestic Certificates of Deposit (60- and 90-day)
Gold (also forward, 'odd-lot' spot and 'round-lot' spot)
Live cattle
Live hogs

Options contracts on cash/physical available
Brazilian cruzado / US dollar (cash)
Gold

Clearing House: Cleared by the exchange itself.

Method of trading: Open outcry.

Commenced trading: 1986.

Exchange links:

Other regional Brazilian futures exchanges:
Bolsa de Mercadorias de Parana
Bolsa de Mercadorias do Rio Grande do Sul
Bolsa Mercantil de Minas

A brief synopsis of the exchange:
In the first 36 months of trading the exchange traded nearly 28 million contracts. It was founded by the São Paulo Stock Exchange and has 75 clearing members, over 20 local traders, 150 commodity brokerage houses and 1,400 licensed floor brokers. In addition to futures and options, both forward and spot contracts are available on the exchange on gold. The exchange claims to be the largest and most modern in Brazil.

Bovespa (São Paulo Stock Exchange) Stock Index futures

Contract size	Cz$0.50 multiplied by the Bovespa (São Paulo Stock Exchange) Stock Index level.
Standard delivery method	Cash settlement at expiry. There is no facility for physical delivery of the stocks underlying the index.
Trading months	Even months (the February, April, June, August, October, December cycle).
Trading hours	9.30 a.m. – 1.15 p.m.
Price quotation method	In Brazilian cruzados (Cz$) per index point.
Minimum price move (value)	Five index points (Cz$2.50 per contract).
Daily price limits	5% of the underlying value of the third contract month, above or below the previous day's settlement price.
Position limits	None.
Last trading day	The Wednesday nearest to the 15th calendar day of the contract month.
Delivery day	The business day following the last trading day.
Initial (Variation) margin	Cz$9,600 per contract (marked to market daily for variation margin purposes).
Spread margin	There are no spread concessions.
Reuters Monitor (Quote)	N/a.
Telerate page	N/a.

'Brazilian' coffee futures

Contract size	100 bags (6,000 kilograms) of 'Brazilian' coffee.*
Standard delivery method	Cash settlement at expiry. There is no facility for physical delivery.
Trading months	The March, May, July, September and December cycle.
Trading hours	10.45 a.m. – 4.00 p.m.
Price quotation method	In Brazilian cruzados (Cz$) per bag.
Minimum price move (value)	Cz$0.01 per bag (Cz$1.00 per contract).
Daily price limits	5% of the underlying value of the third contract month above or below the previous day's settlement price.
Position limits	None.
Last trading day	The last business day of the contract month.
Delivery day	The business day following the last trading day.
Initial (Variation) margin	Please consult the exchange or your broker for the current margin requirements.
Spread margin	Please consult the exchange or your broker for the current spread concessions.

Reuters Monitor (Quote)	N/a.
Telerate page	N/a.

* Brazilian coffee may also be traded denominated in US dollars. The contract specifications are identical with the following exceptions:
1. Tick size: US$0.01 per bag (US$1.00 per contract)
2. Last trading day: The sixth business day of the contract month.

Brazilian cruzado / Deutschmark currency futures

Contract size	DM10,000 traded against the Brazilian cruzado (Cz$).
Standard delivery method	Cash settlement at expiry. There is no facility for the physical exchange of the currencies concerned.
Trading months	All consecutive calendar months.
Trading hours	10.00 a.m. – 3.45 p.m.
Price quotation method	In terms of Brazilian cruzados (Cz$) per Deutschmark (DM).
Minimum price move (value)	Cz$0.001 per DM1.00 (Cz$10.00 per contract).
Daily price limits	5% of the underlying value of the third contract month above or below the previous day's settlement price.
Position limits	None.
Last trading day	The first business day of the contract month.
Delivery day	The business day following the last trading day.
Initial (Variation) margin	Cz$16,000 per contract (marked to market daily for variation margin purposes).
Spread margin	There are no spread concessions.
Reuters Monitor (Quote)	N/a.
Telerate page	N/a.

Brazilian cruzado / Japanese yen currency futures

Contract size	Y1,000,000 traded against the Brazilian cruzado (Cz$).
Standard delivery method	Cash settlement at expiry. There is no facility for the physical exchange of the currencies concerned.
Trading months	All consecutive calendar months.
Trading hours	10.00 a.m. – 3.45 p.m.
Price quotation method	In terms of Brazilian cruzados (Cz$) per Japanese yen (Y).
Minimum price move (value)	Cz$0.00001 per Y1.00 (Cz$10.00 per contract).
Daily price limits	5% of the underlying value of the third contract month above or below the previous day's settlement price.
Position limits	None.

Last trading day	The first business day of the contract month.
Delivery day	The business day following the last trading day.
Initial (Variation) margin	Cz$16,000 per contract (marked to market daily for variation margin purposes).
Spread margin	There are no spread concessions.
Reuters Monitor (Quote)	N/a.
Telerate page	N/a.

Brazilian cruzado / US dollar currency futures

Contract size	US$5,000 traded against the Brazilian cruzado (Cz$).
Standard delivery method	Cash settlement at expiry. There is no facility for physical exchange of the currencies concerned.
Trading months	All consecutive calendar months.
Trading hours	10.00 a.m. – 3.45 p.m.
Price quotation method	In terms of Brazilian cruzados (Cz$) per US dollar (US$).
Minimum price move (value)	Cz$0.001 per US$1.00 (Cz$5.00 per contract).
Daily price limits	5% of the underlying value of the third contract month above or below the previous day's settlement price.
Position limits	None.
Last trading day	The first business day of the contract month.
Delivery day	The business day following the last trading day.
Initial (Variation) margin	Cz$16,000 per contract (marked to market daily for variation margin purposes).
Spread margin	There are no spread concessions.
Reuters Monitor (Quote)	N/a.
Telerate page	N/a.

Brazilian Government Treasury Bond futures

Contract size	Cz$5,000 nominal face value of Brazilian Government Treasury Bonds.
Standard delivery method	Cash settlement at expiry. There is no facility for physical delivery of the underlying bonds.
Trading months	All consecutive calendar months.
Trading hours	Not stated – please consult the exchange for the current trading hours.
Price quotation method	In Brazilian cruzados (Cz$) per Cz$1,000 nominal face value.
Minimum price move (value)	Cz$1.00 per Cz$1,000 nominal face value (Cz$5.00 per contract).

Daily price limits	None.
Position limits	None.
Last trading day	The first business day of the contract month.
Delivery day	The business day following the last trading day.
Initial (Variation) margin	5% of the underlying value of the third contract month.
Spread margin	Please consult the exchange or your broker for the current spread concessions.
Reuters Monitor (Quote)	N/a.
Telerate page	N/a.

Broiler chickens (frozen/chilled) futures

Contract size	12 metric tons of broiler chickens (frozen/chilled).
Standard delivery method	Cash settlement at expiry. There is no facility for physical delivery of the produce.
Trading months	Even months (the February, April, June, August, October and December cycle).
Trading hours	Two sessions daily: 2.15 p.m. – 2.35 p.m. and 2.40 p.m. – 3.00 p.m.
Price quotation method	In Brazilian cruzados (Cz$) per kilogram.
Minimum price move (value)	Cz$0.01 per kilogram (Cz$12.00 per contract).
Daily price limits	5% of the underlying value of the third contract month above or below the previous day's settlement price.
Position limits	None.
Last trading day	The last business day of the contract month.
Delivery day	The business day following the last trading day.
Initial (Variation) margin	Cz$24,000 per contract (marked to market daily for variation margin purposes).
Spread margin	There are no spread concessions.
Reuters Monitor (Quote)	N/a.
Telerate page	N/a.

Domestic Certificates of Deposit (60- and 90-day) futures

Contract size	Cz$10,000 nominal face value of 60- or 90-day Domestic Brazilian Certificates of Deposit (CDs).
Standard delivery method	Cash settlement at expiry. There is no facility for physical delivery of the underlying CDs.
Trading months	All consecutive calendar months.
Trading hours	Two sessions daily: 11.45 a.m. – 12.30 p.m. and 3.15 p.m. – 4.00 p.m.

Price quotation method	In Brazilian Cruzados (Cz$) per Cz$100 nominal face value.
Minimum price move *(value)*	One full point (Cz$100 per contract).
Daily price limits	None.
Position limits	None.
Last trading day	The third Wednesday of the contract month or the following business day if the third Wednesday is a non-trading day.
Delivery day	The business day following the last trading day.
Initial (Variation) margin	Please consult the exchange or your broker for the current margin requirements.
Spread margin	Please consult the exchange or your broker for the current spread concessions.
Reuters Monitor (Quote)	N/a.
Telerate page	N/a.

Gold futures

Contract size	250 grams (0.25 kilograms) of gold bullion.*
Standard delivery method	Cash settlement at maturity. There is no facility for physical delivery of gold.
Trading months	The spot month, the next two consecutive calendar months, plus months from the February, April, June, August, October and December cycle.
Trading hours	10.00 a.m. – 4.00 p.m.
Price quotation method	In Brazilian cruzados (Cz$) per gram.
Minimum price move *(value)*	Cz$0.01 per gram (Cz$2.50 per contract).
Daily price limits	5% of the underlying value of the third contract month above or below the previous day's settlement price.
Position limits	None.
Last trading day	The last business day of the month preceding the contract month.
Delivery day	The business day following the last trading day.
Initial (Variation) margin	Cz$24,000 per contract (marked to market daily for variation margin purposes).
Spread margin	There are no spread concessions.
Reuters Monitor (Quote)	N/a.
Telerate page	N/a.

* The Bolsa Mercantil & Futuros also trades gold forward contracts and both 'round-lot' and 'odd-lot' spot gold.
Gold forwards are traded with the same contract specifications as above, except that they have rolling five-day expiries and multiples of five days. There is no minimum price movement or daily price limits for gold forwards.
The contract size of 'round-lot' spot gold is 250 grams, whilst the size of 'odd-lot' spot gold is 0.225 grams. There are no daily price limits.

Live cattle futures

Contract size	330 net arrobas (4,950 kilograms) of live cattle.
Standard delivery method	Cash settlement at expiry. There is no facility for physical delivery.
Trading months	Even months (the February, April, June, August, October and December cycle).
Trading hours	3.30 p.m. – 4.30 p.m.
Price quotation method	In Brazilian cruzados (Cz$) per net arroba.
Minimum price move (value)	Cz$0.10 per net arroba (Cz$33.00 per contract).
Daily price limits	5% of the underlying value of the third contract month above or below the previous day's settlement price.
Position limits	None.
Last trading day	The last business day of the contract month.
Delivery day	The business day following the last trading day.
Initial (Variation) margin	Cz$24,000 per contract (marked to market daily for variation margin purposes).
Spread margin	There are no spread concessions.
Reuters Monitor (Quote)	N/a.
Telerate page	N/a.

Live hogs futures

Contract size	8,000 net kilograms of live hogs.
Standard delivery method	Cash settlement at expiry. There is no facility for physical delivery.
Trading months	Even months (the February, April, June, August, October and December cycle).
Trading hours	Two sessions daily: 2.15 p.m. – 2.35 p.m. and 2.40 p.m. – 3.00 p.m.
Price quotation method	In Brazilian cruzados (Cz$) per net kilogram.
Minimum price move (value)	Cz$0.01 per kilogram (Cz$80.00 per contract).
Daily price limits	5% of the underlying value of the third contract month above or below the previous day's settlement price.
Position limits	None.
Last trading day	The last business day of the contract month.
Delivery day	The business day following the last trading day.
Initial (Variation) margin	Cz$16,000 per contract (marked to market daily for variation margin purposes).
Spread margin	There are no spread concessions.
Reuters Monitor (Quote)	N/a.
Telerate page	N/a.

Option on Brazilian cruzado / US dollar (cash)

Contract size	US$5,000 traded against the Brazilian cruzado (Cz$).
Standard delivery method	Cash settlement at expiry at the strike price. There is no facility for the physical exchange of the currencies concerned.
Trading months	All consecutive calendar months.
Trading hours	10.00 a.m. – 3.45 p.m.
Price quotation method	In terms of Brazilian cruzados (Cz$) per US dollar (US$).
Minimum price move (value)	Cz$0.001 per US$1.00 (Cz$5.00 per contract).
Daily price limits	None
Position limits	None.
Last trading day	The first business day of the contract month.
Delivery day	The business day following the last trading day.
Initial (Variation) margin	For uncovered short positions, Cz$16,000 per contract (marked to market daily for variation margin purposes).
Spread margin	There are no spread concessions.
Strike price intervals	Not stated. Please consult the exchange for full details.
Option type	Not stated. Please consult the exchange for full details.
Method of introduction of new strike prices	Not stated. Please consult the exchange for full details.
Reuters Monitor (Quote)	N/a.
Telerate page	N/a.

Option on gold (physical)

Contract size	250 grams of gold bullion.
Standard delivery method	Cash settlement at expiry at the strike price. There is no facility for physical delivery of the gold.
Trading months	Odd months (the January, March, May, July, September, November cycle).
Trading hours	10.00 a.m. – 4.00 p.m.
Price quotation method	In terms of Brazilian cruzados (Cz$) per gram.
Minimum price move (value)	Cz$0.01 per gram (Cz$2.50 per contract).
Daily price limits	None.
Position limits	None.
Last trading day	The third Friday of the contract month or the previous business day if the third Friday is not a business day.
Delivery day	The business day following the last trading day.
Initial (Variation) margin	For uncovered short positions, 1.5 times the premium received.
Spread margin	There are no spread concessions.
Strike price intervals	At Cz$0.10 per gram intervals.

Option type	Not stated. Please consult the exchange for full details.
Method of introduction of new strike prices	Not stated. Please consult the exchange for full details.
Reuters Monitor (Quote)	N/a.
Telerate page	N/a.

11 Canada

Contents

Vancouver Stock Exchange (VSX)   11/19

Winnipeg Commodity Exchange (WCE)   11/25

The Montreal Exchange (ME)
(Le Bourse de Montreal)

Address:	The Stock Exchange Tower PO Box 61 800 Victoria Square Montreal Quebec H4Z 1A9 Canada
Telephone:	(514) 871 2424
Fax:	(514) 871 3533
Telex:	055–60586

Exchange personnel

Chairman:	Terence C. W. Reid
President & CEO:	Bruno Riverin
Director Derivative Products:	Bich N. Pham
VP, Public Relations:	Marcel Barthe

Futures contracts available
Canadian Bankers' Acceptances
Canadian Government Treasury Bond (CGB)

Options contracts on cash/physical available
Bellweather Canadian Government Treasury Bonds
IOCC gold bullion
IOCC platinum (*dormant*)

Options contracts on futures available
Canadian Government Treasury Bond (CGB) futures
(*planned for mid-1990*)

*Also available are traded options on over 30 Canadian
equities with an underlying contract size of 100 shares
and three- and five-month expiries.*

Clearing House:	International Options Clearing Corporation (IOCC) and Trans Canada Options Corporation Inc.
Method of trading:	Open outcry.
Commenced trading:	1975 (1984 for futures).

Exchange links:

The following exchanges form with the Montreal Exchange the IOCC precious metals trading link:
Optiebeurs NV (EOE) Amsterdam
Vancouver Stock Exchange (VSX)
Australian Stock Exchange (Sydney) Ltd. (AOM)

A brief synopsis of the exchange

The Montreal Exchange is Canada's oldest stock exchange dating back to 1874, and was the first exchange in Canada to trade options in 1975 and is now Canada's leading options market-place. The most active options contract is on Canadian Treasury Bonds.

The main IOCC link with Vancouver, Amsterdam and Sydney provides round-the-clock trading in fully fungible precious metal options, with an electronic limit order book passing from exchange to exchange.

More recently, the ME has introduced futures contracts on Canadian Bankers' Acceptances and Canadian Treasury Bonds which are traded on the ME's Mercantile Division.

There are nearly 100 specialist traders on the market floor.

Canadian Bankers' Acceptances (BAX) futures

Contract size	C$1,000,000 nominal face value of three-month Canadian Bankers' Acceptances.
Standard delivery method	Cash settlement based on a final settlement price of the average of three-month Canadian Bankers' Acceptances as quoted on Reuters page CDOR on the last trading day at 10.00 a.m. (EST/EDT), excluding the two highest and two lowest quotations.
Trading months	The March, June, September and December cycle, up to two years forward.
Trading hours	8.30 a.m. – 3.00 p.m.
Price quotation method	As an index of 100.00 minus the annualised yield of three-month Bankers' Acceptances, quoted in Canadian dollars (C$).
Minimum price move (value)	0.01% per annum of nominal face value (C$25.00 per contract).
Daily price limits	None.
Position limits	5,000 contracts (reportable at 300 contracts).
Last trading day	The second London business day prior to the third Wednesday of the contract month. Trading ceases in the expiring contract at 11.00 a.m. on the last trading day.
Delivery day	The business day following the last trading day.
Initial (Variation) margin	Speculators: C$1,500 per contract. Hedgers: C$1,000 per contract.
Spread margin	C$625 per spread position.
Reuters Monitor (Quote)	CDOR, MBQA.
Telerate page	N/a.

Canadian Government Treasury Bond (CGB) futures

Contract size	C$100,000 nominal face value of a notional Canadian Government Treasury Bond with a 9% coupon rate.
Standard delivery method	Physical delivery of any Canadian Government Treasury Bond with between 6.5 and 10 years remaining to maturity (or when callable) from the first day of the contract month, deliverable during the contract month, as determined by the Montreal Exchange, through the Canadian Depository for Securities. An alternative coupon-rated bond may be substituted at the seller's choice.

Trading months	The March, June, September and December cycle up to two years forward.
Trading hours	8.20 a.m. – 3.00 p.m.
Price quotation method	In Canadian dollars (C$) and cents per C$100 nominal face value of par.
Minimum price move (value)	0.01% per annum of nominal face value (C$10.00 per contract).
Daily price limits	3.0 points (C$3,000 per contract) above or below the previous day's settlement price.
Position limits	4,000 contracts (reportable at 250 contracts).
Last trading day	The seventh business day preceding the last business day of the contract month.
Delivery day	Any business day in the contract month at the seller's choice up to 4.00 p.m. on the fifth business day preceding the last day of the contract month (the last Notice Day).
Initial (Variation) margin	Speculators: C$1,500 per contract. Hedgers: C$1,000 per contract.
Spread margin	C$300 per spread position.
Reuters Monitor (Quote)	MCBF – MCBG.
Telerate page	N/a.

Option on specific issues of bellweather Canadian Government Treasury Bonds

Contract size	C$25,000 nominal face value of a specific class of Government of Canada Treasury Bonds, with an outstanding issue size of at least C$500,000,000. The current tradable bonds are as follows: 9.5% October 2001 (OBA) 10.25% February 2004 (OBD) 9.0% March 2011 (OBK) 10.25% February 1994 (OBT)
Standard delivery method	Physical delivery of the specified bond via the Security Settlement Service of CDS.
Trading months	The nearest three consecutive calendar months plus the next two months from the March, June, September and December expiry cycle.
Trading hours	8.20 a.m. – 4.00 p.m.
Price quotation method	In Canadian dollars (C$) per cent of par per C$100 nominal face value.
Minimum price move (value)	0.01% of nominal face value (C$2.50 per contract).
Daily price limits	None.
Position limits	4,000 contracts on the same side of the market, or 1,000 contracts in the case of uncovered short call positions.

Last trading day	The third Friday of the contract month.
Delivery day	The business day following the last trading day. The options expire on the Saturday following the third Friday of the contract month. Delivery is to be made within five days of the exercise tender notice.
Initial (Variation) margin	Please consult the exchange or your broker for the current details.
Spread margin	Please consult the exchange or your broker for the current details.
Strike price intervals	At intervals of 1.00 point.
Option type	Please consult the exchange or your broker for the current details.
Method of introduction of new strike prices	There will be two to three strike prices around the current market price of each bond.
Reuters Monitor (Quote)	TBVU – TBWF.
Telerate page	N/a.

Option on IOCC gold bullion

Contract size	10 troy ounces of fine gold bullion of 0.995 fineness acceptable for good London delivery.
Standard delivery method	Physical delivery of the above with one of the five members of the London Gold Market or an institution acting as its delivery depot.
Trading months	The nearest three months of the February, May, August and November cycle.
Trading hours	The local dealing times on the IOCC link exchanges are as follows:

AOM (Nov – Mar): 11.00 a.m. – 1.00 p.m. and
2.30 p.m. – 4.30 p.m.

AOM (Apr – Oct): 10.30 a.m. – 12.30 p.m. and
2.00 p.m. – 4.00 p.m.

EOE: 10.30 a.m. – 4.30 p.m.

ME: 9.00 a.m. – 2.30 p.m.

VSX: 11.30 a.m. – 4.00 p.m.

Price quotation method	In US dollars (US$) and cents per troy ounce.
Minimum price move (value)	US$0.10 per troy ounce (US$1.00 per contract).
Daily price limits	None.
Position limits	5,000 contracts on the same side of the market.
Last trading day	The third Friday of the contract month. Trading ceases in the expiring contract at 4.00 p.m. (Amsterdam), 2.30 p.m. (Montreal), 4.00 p.m. (Vancouver) or 5.00 p.m. (Sydney) on the last trading day. These are all local times.

Delivery day	The business day following the last trading day. The options expire on the Monday following the third Friday of the contract month, this being the last time for exercise. Settlement is due on the fourth business day following the submission of tender notice.
Initial (Variation) margin	The option premium received plus a percentage of (if any) twice the intrinsic value of the option.
Spread margin	Not stated.
Strike price intervals	Gold price under US$400: US$10.00 intervals.
	Gold price US$400 – US$600: US$20.00 intervals.
	Gold price US$600 – US$900: US$30.00 intervals.
	Gold price over US$900: US$40.00 intervals.
Option type	American style (the option may be exercised on any business day up to and including the last trading day).
Method of introduction of new strike prices	Between four and five series are initially available. New series are introduced so as to allow there to be at least one in-the-money and one out-of-the-money series at all times. No new series are normally introduced in the last 20 business days before expiry. The other link exchanges take the lead from the EOE Amsterdam in introducing new strike prices.
Reuters Monitor (Quote)	YGDA – YGDP (EOE), MEGA – MEGB (Montreal), VEGA – VEGB (Vancouver), GDMB – GDMG.
Telerate page	N/a.

This contract is traded on the IOCC (International Options Clearing Corporation BV) link between the Australian Stock Exchange (Sydney) Ltd (AOM), the Montreal Exchange (ME), Optiebeurs Amsterdam (EOE) and the Vancouver Stock Exchange (VSX), allowing trading for 18.5 hours a day. A limit order book is passed from exchange to exchange. The contracts are fully fungible.

Option on IOCC platinum (*dormant*)

Contract size	10 troy ounces of platinum of a minimum 0.9995 fineness.
Standard delivery method	Physical delivery of the above in a form specified by the IOCC with an institution acting as its delivery depot.
Trading months	The nearest three months of the March, June, September and December cycle.
Trading hours	ME: 9.30 a.m. – 2.30 p.m.
	VSX: 11.30 a.m. – 4.00 p.m.
Price quotation method	In US dollars (US$) and cents per troy ounce.
Minimum price move (value)	US$0.10 per troy ounce (US$1.00 per contract).

Daily price limits	None.
Position limits	500 contracts on the same side of the market for clients (1,000 options for professionals).
Last trading day	The third Friday of the contract month at the close of the local trading session.
Delivery day	The business day following the last trading day. The option expires on the Monday following the third Friday of the contract month, which is the last available time to exercise.
Initial (Variation) margin	Not stated.
Spread margin	Not stated.
Strike price intervals	At US$10.00 per troy ounce intervals.
Option type	American style (the option may be exercised on any business day up to and including the last trading day).
Method of introduction of new strike prices	Introduced in co-ordination with the other link exchanges. The VSX follows the lead of the EOE Amsterdam in introducing new series.
Reuters Monitor (Quote)	N/a.
Telerate page	N/a.

This contract is traded on the IOCC (International Options Clearing Corporation BV) link between Optiebeurs Amsterdam (EOE), the Montreal Exchange (ME) and the Vancouver Stock Exchange (VSX). A limit order book is passed from exchange to exchange. The contracts are fully fungible.

Option on ME Canadian Government Treasury Bond (CGB) futures (*planned for mid-1990*)

Contract size	One ME Canadian Government Bond (CGB) futures contract (of an underlying contract size of C$100,000 nominal face value).
Standard delivery method	Delivery of a long or short position in a futures contract at the strike price as above.
Trading months	The March, June, September and December cycle up to two years forward.
Trading hours	8.20 a.m. – 3.00 p.m.
Price quotation method	In Canadian dollars (C$) and cents per C$100 nominal face value of par.
Minimum price move (value)	0.01% of nominal face value (C$10.00 per contract).
Daily price limits	None.
Position limits	None.
Last trading day	Not yet announced.
Delivery day	Not yet announced.
Initial (Variation) margin	Not yet announced.
Spread margin	Not yet announced.

Strike price intervals	Not yet announced.
Option type	Not yet announced.
Method of introduction of new strike prices	Not yet announced.
Reuters Monitor (*Quote*)	N/a.
Telerate page	N/a.

Toronto Stock Exchange (TSE)

incorporating Toronto Futures Exchange (TFE) (a division of the Toronto Stock Exchange)

Address:	The Exchange Tower 2 First Canadian Place Toronto Ontario M5X 1J2 Canada
Telephone:	(416) 947 4700 – TSE (416) 947 4487 – TFE
Fax:	(416) 947 4788 – TFE
Telex:	06217759

Exchange personnel

TSE
President: J. P. Bunting
Chairman: D. Scott

TFE
Chairman: Tristram Lett
President: Andrew Glademenos
Marketing Manager: Sonja Kokal / John McDonald

Futures contracts available on the TFE
Government of Canada Treasury Bills
Long-term Canadian Government Treasury Bonds
Mid-term Canadian Government Treasury Bonds
Toronto 35 Stock Index
TSE 300 Composite Spot Stock Index

Options contracts on physical/cash available on the TFE
Canadian Government Treasury Bonds
Silver

Options contracts on physical/cash available on the TSE
Toronto 35 Stock Index

| **Toronto Stock Exchange (TSE)**

Clearing House:	Trans Canada Options Corporation Inc.
Method of trading:	Open outcry.
Commenced trading:	1852 (for the TSE), 1984 (for the TFE).
Exchange links:	None.

A brief synopsis of the exchange

The Toronto Futures Exchange opened in 1984 as the futures division of the Toronto Stock Exchange, and it is now operated as a separate entity. They do, however, occupy a shared trading floor. The main success of the TFE has been in stock-index-related products, with precious metals, currencies and interest-rate instruments being less successful. Most Canadian interest-rate futures and options trading activity takes place on the Montreal Exchange (ME).

There are three classes of exchange membership: Dealer Members, Trader Members and Sponsor Members, with a total of 260 TFE seats held by over 190 members.

The clearing house, Trans Canada Options, is owned jointly by the Toronto, Vancouver and Montreal exchanges.

Government of Canada Treasury Bill (CTB) futures

Contract size	C$1,000,000 nominal face value of Government of Canada Treasury Bills.
Standard delivery method	Physical delivery of the above bills with maturities ranging from 88 to 93 days with a discounted value of C$1,000,000 at maturity.
Trading months	The spot month plus months from the March, June, September and December cycle.
Trading hours	9.00 a.m. – 3.15 p.m.
Price quotation method	On a yield basis in terms of the Treasury Bill Index (100.00 minus the Treasury Bill yield on a 365-day year basis), quoted in Canadian dollars (C$).
Minimum price move (value)	0.01% (C$24.00 per contract).
Daily price limits	0.60% (C$1,440 per contract) above or below the previous day's settlement price, expandable to 0.90% (C$2,160 per contract).
Position limits	Speculators: 300 contracts in total.
	Hedgers: 3,000 contracts in total (750 in any one contract month).
	Reporting limits: 100 contracts (speculators) and 300 contracts (hedgers).
Last trading day	The day of the Bank of Canada auction preceding the last Friday of the contract month.
Delivery day	Any of the last three Fridays of the contract month, provided that a delivery notice has been submitted on the previous business day.
Initial (Variation) margin	Hedgers: C$1,000 per contract.
	Speculators: C$1,500 per contract.
Spread margin	C$625 per spread position.
Reuters Monitor (Quote)	N/a.
Telerate page	3153.

Long-term Canadian Government Treasury Bond (GCB) futures

Contract size	C$100,000 nominal face value of a notional 9% coupon long-term Canadian Government Treasury Bond.
Standard delivery method	Physical delivery of eligible bonds, which must not be callable (or mature) for at least 15 years from the date of delivery.
Trading months	The March, June, September and December cycle.

Trading hours	9.00 a.m. – 3.15 p.m. Trading ceases in the expiring contract at 11.00 a.m. on the last trading day.
Price quotation method	In Canadian dollars (C$) per cent of par in increments of thirty-seconds (1/32).
Minimum price move (value)	One thirty-second (1/32) of a point (C$31.25 per contract).
Daily price limits	Two points (C$2,000 per contract) above or below the previous day's settlement price, expandable to three points (C$3,000 per contract).
Position limits	Speculators: 1,200 contracts in total, reportable at 400 contracts in total.
	Hedgers: 6,000 contracts in total, reportable at 600 contracts in total.
Last trading day	The sixth to last business day of the contract month.
Delivery day	The fifth business day following the tender of a delivery notice. Delivery notices may be tendered on any business day from five business days prior to the first business day of the contract month up to and including the sixth to last business day of the contract month.
Initial (Variation) margin	Speculators: C$2,000 per contract.
	Hedgers: C$1,000 per contract.
Spread margin	C$625 per spread position.
Reuters Monitor (Quote)	N/a.
Telerate page	3153.

Mid-term Canadian Government Treasury Bond (MCB) futures

Contract size	C$50,000 nominal face value of a mid-term Canadian Government Treasury Bond, with a notional coupon rate of 9%.
Standard delivery method	Physical delivery of eligible bonds, with a maturity of no less than four years and no more than six years from the date of delivery, with a face value of C$50,000 and a coupon of 9%.
Trading months	The March, June, September and December cycle.
Trading hours	9.00 a.m. – 3.15 p.m.
Price quotation method	In Canadian Dollars (C$) and cents per cent of par in increments of thirty-seconds (1/32).
Minimum price move (value)	One thirty-second (1/32) of a point (C$15.625 per contract).
Daily price limits	Two points (C$1,000 per contract) above or below the previous day's settlement price, expandable to three points (C$1,500 per contract).

Position limits	500 contracts for any one month (reportable at 380 contracts), or 1,200 in total (reportable at 900 contracts).
Last trading day	The sixth to last business day of the contract month.
Delivery day	The fifth business day following the tender of a delivery notice. Delivery notices may be tendered at the seller's option on any business day from five business days prior to the first business day of the contract month up to and including the sixth to last business day of the contract month.
Initial (Variation) margin	Speculators: C$1,000 per contract. Hedgers: C$500 per contract.
Spread margin	C$300 per spread position.
Reuters Monitor (Quote)	N/a.
Telerate page	3153.

Toronto 35 Stock Index (TXF) futures

Contract size	C$500 multiplied by the Toronto 35 Stock Index futures price.
Standard delivery method	Cash settlement based on the opening index level on the third Friday of the contract month. There is no facility for physical delivery of the stocks underlying the index.
Trading months	The three nearest consecutive calendar months.
Trading hours	9.30 a.m. – 4.15 p.m.
Price quotation method	In Canadian dollars (C$) per index point calculated to two decimal places.
Minimum price move (value)	0.02 index points (C$10.00 per contract).
Daily price limits	Nine index points (C$4,500 per contract) above or below the previous day's settlement price, expandable to 13.5 index points (C$6,750 per contract).
Position limits	Hedgers: 2,200 contracts net. Speculators: 1,000 contracts net. Reportable limits: 300 contracts.
Last trading day	The Thursday before the third Friday of the contract month.
Delivery day	The second business day following the last trading day.
Initial (Variation) margin	Hedgers: C$5,000 per contract. Speculators: C$9,000 per contract (approximately 5% of the underlying value of the contract).
Spread margin	C$1,200 per spread position.
Reuters Monitor (Quote)	IDTE.
Telerate page	3153.

TSE 300 Composite Spot Stock Index (TSE) futures

Contract size	C$10.00 multiplied by the TSE 300 Composite Stock Index.
Standard delivery method	Cash settlement at the daily expiry. There is no physical delivery of the stocks underlying the index.
Trading months	Each day – at the end of each day all open positions will be marked to market to two decimal places and terminated by cash settlement.
Trading hours	9.20 a.m. – 4.10 p.m.
Price quotation method	In Canadian dollars (C$) per whole index point.
Minimum price move (value)	One index point (C$10.00 per contract).
Daily price limits	None.
Position limits	2,000 contracts in total, reportable at 300 contracts in total.
Last trading day	Every business day.
Delivery day	The business day following the day of trading.
Initial (Variation) margin	Hedgers: C$1,000 per contract. Speculators: C$1,500 per contract.
Spread margin	There are no spread concessions.
Reuters Monitor (Quote)	IDTE.
Telerate page	3153.

Option on Canadian Government Treasury Bonds

Contract size	C$25,000 nominal face value at maturity of a specific issue of Government of Canada Treasury Bonds.
Standard delivery method	Physical delivery of the above eligible bonds.
Trading months	The nearest three months from the March, June, September and December cycle.
Trading hours	9.00 a.m. – 4.00 p.m.
Price quotation method	In Canadian dollars (C$) per cent of par.
Minimum price move (value)	0.5% of C$100 nominal face value when the premium is under C$2.00 (C$125.00 per contract), and one-eighth (1/8) of C$100 nominal face value for premiums over C$2.00 (C$31.25 per contract). A premium of 2.75 represents a cost of C$687.50 per contract.
Daily price limits	None.
Position limits	2,000 contracts per class, on the same side of the market when the size of the underlying bond issue is less than C$2 billion, or 4,000 contracts for larger underlying bond issues. A limit of 25% of the above is imposed for uncovered short call positions.
Last trading day	The third Friday of the contract month.

Delivery day	Within five days of the tender of an exercise notice.
Initial (Variation) margin	Please consult the exchange or your broker for the current details.
Spread margin	Please consult the exchange or your broker for the current details.
Strike price intervals	At 2.5 point intervals for long-term bonds and 2.0 point intervals for mid-term bonds to bracket the current market price of the underlying bond.
Option type	American style (the option may be exercised on any business day up to and including the last trading day).
Method of introduction of new strike prices	New series are introduced as the underlying bond's market price approaches an existing strike price.
Reuters Monitor (Quote)	N/a.
Telerate page	3153.

Option on silver (SVR)

Contract size	100 troy ounces of 0.999 fineness silver bullion.
Standard delivery method	Physical delivery of the above in the form of a silver certificate issued by an approved depository.
Trading months	The two nearby consecutive calendar months and the next two expiry months from the March, June, September and December cycle.
Trading hours	9.05 a.m. – 4.00 p.m.
Price quotation method	In US dollars (US$) and cents per troy ounce.
Minimum price move (value)	One US cent (US$0.01) per troy ounce (US$1.00 per contract).
Daily price limits	None.
Position limits	20,000 puts and calls on the same side of the market. Reportable limit: 500 contracts of one class.
Last trading day	The third Friday of the contract month.
Delivery day	The fifth business day following receipt of the exercise notice.
Initial (Variation) margin	Please consult the exchange or your broker for the current details.
Spread margin	Please consult the exchange or your broker for the current details.
Strike price intervals	Strike prices under US$5.00: US$0.25 Strike prices US$5.00 – US$15.00: US$0.50 Strike prices over US$15.00: US$1.00
Option type	American style (the option may be exercised on any business day up to and including the last trading day).
Method of introduction of new strike prices	Not stated.
Reuters Monitor (Quote)	SITE – SITJ.
Telerate page	N/a.

Option on the Toronto 35 Stock Index (TXO)

Contract size	C$100 multiplied by the Toronto 35 Stock Index.
Standard delivery method	Cash settlement based on the opening index level on the third Friday of the contract month. There is no facility for physical delivery of the stocks underlying the index.
Trading months	The three nearest consecutive calendar months.
Trading hours	9.30 a.m. – 4.15 p.m.
Price quotation method	In Canadian dollars (C$) per index point.
Minimum price move (value)	Premiums under C$0.10: C$0.01 (C$1.00 per contract). Premiums under C$5.00: C$0.05 (C$5.00 per contract). Premiums over C$5.00: C$0.125 (C$12.50 per contract).
Daily price limits	None.
Position limits	8,000 contracts on the same side of the market.
Last trading day	The Thursday before the third Friday of the contract month. The official opening index on the next business day is used for settlement purposes.
Delivery day	Two business days after the last trading day.
Initial (Variation) margin	Please consult the exchange or your broker for the current details.
Spread margin	Please consult the exchange or your broker for the current details.
Strike price intervals	At 5 index point intervals around the Toronto 35 Stock Index.
Option type	European style (the option may only be exercised on the day after the last trading day and not at other times during its life). All in-the-money options are automatically exercised at expiry.
Method of introduction of new strike prices	New series are introduced when the Toronto 35 Stock Index closes at or beyond the last currently available strike price.
Reuters Monitor (Quote)	QCJO – QCJR.
Telerate page	3153.

Vancouver Stock Exchange (VSX)

Address:	Stock Exchange Tower PO Box 10333 609 Granville Street Vancouver British Columbia V7Y 1H1 Canada
Telephone:	(604) 689 3334
Fax:	(604) 688 6051
Telex:	(04) 55480

Exchange personnel

Chairman:	J. L. Mathers
President:	Donald J. Hudson
Options Co-ordinator:	David Taylor
Information Officer:	Joyce Courtney

Futures contracts available
None

Options contracts on cash/physical available
IOCC gold bullion
IOCC platinum
IOCC silver bullion

Also available are options on around 20 Canadian equities, in each case the contract size being 100 shares underlying. These options trade on one of the following three cycles:
    January, April, July and October
    February, May, August and November
    March, June, September and December.
The trading hours are 6.30 a.m. – 1.00 p.m. and the options expire on the third Friday of the contract month.

Clearing House:	Trans Canada Options Clearing Corporation (TCO) and International Options Clearing Corporation (IOCC).
Method of trading:	Open outcry and automated trading (approximately 90% of Vancouver's trading is conducted through the computer system).

Vancouver Stock Exchange (VSX)

Commenced trading: 1982 (for commodity options), 1984 (for equity options).

Exchange links: The following exchanges with the Vancouver Stock Exchange form the IOCC precious metals trading link:
Optiebeurs NV (EOE) Amsterdam
Montreal Exchange (ME)
Australian Stock Exchange (Sydney) Ltd (AOM).

A brief synopsis of the exchange:
One of the four Canadian exchanges, the Vancouver Stock Exchange is part of the International Options Clearing Corporation (IOCC) precious metals options link between Vancouver, Montreal, Amsterdam and Sydney allowing fungible trading for nearly 20 hours a day. An electronic limit book passes from exchange to exchange. This link accounts for little of the VSX's turnover and the VSX in turn only represents under 5% of total IOCC link turnover.

There are around 70 exchange members, with membership carrying the right to trade both equities and options, four firms of which are specialist primary and secondary market-makers in the commodity and equity options.

Option on IOCC gold bullion

Contract size	10 troy ounces of fine gold bullion of 0.995 fineness acceptable for good London delivery.
Standard delivery method	Physical delivery of the above with one of the five members of the London Gold Market or an institution acting as its delivery depot.
Trading months	The nearest three months of the February, May, August and November cycle.
Trading hours	The local dealing times for the IOCC link exchanges are as follows:

AOM (Nov – Mar):   11.00 a.m. –   1.00 p.m. and
                          2.30 p.m. –   4.30 p.m.
AOM (Apr – Oct):   10.30 a.m. – 12.30 p.m. and
                          2.00 p.m. –   4.00 p.m.
EOE: 10.30 a.m. –   4.30 p.m.
ME: 9.00 a.m. –   2.30 p.m.
VSX: 11.30 a.m. –   4.00 p.m.

Price quotation method	In US dollars (US$) and cents per troy ounce.
Minimum price move (value)	US$0.10 per troy ounce (US$1.00 per contract).
Daily price limits	None.
Position limits	5,000 contracts on the same side of the market.
Last trading day	The third Friday of the contract month. Trading ceases in the expiring contract at 4.00 p.m. (Amsterdam), 2.30 p.m. (Montreal), 4.00 p.m. (Vancouver) or 5.00 p.m. (Sydney) on the last trading day. These are all local times.
Delivery day	The business day following the last trading day. The options expire on the Monday following the third Friday of the contract month, this being the last time for exercise. Settlement is due on the fourth business day following the submission of tender notice.
Initial (Variation) margin	The option premium received plus a percentage of (if any) twice the intrinsic value of the option.
Spread margin	Not stated.
Strike price intervals	Gold price under US$400: US$10.00 intervals.
Gold price US$400 – US$600:   US$20.00 intervals.
Gold price US$600 – US$900:   US$30.00 intervals.
Gold price over US$900:   US$40.00 intervals.
Option type	American style (the option may be exercised on any business day up to and including the last trading day).
Method of introduction of new strike prices	Between four and five series are initially available. New series are introduced so as to allow there to be at least one in-the-money and one out-of-the-money series at all times. No new series are normally introduced in

the last 20 business days before expiry. The other link exchanges take the lead from the EOE Amsterdam in introducing new series.

Reuters Monitor (Quote)   YGDA – YGDP (EOE), MEGA – MEGB (ME), VEGA – VEGB (VSX), GDMB – GDMG.

Telerate page   N/a.

This contract is traded on the IOCC (International Options Clearing Corporation BV) link between the Australian Stock Exchange (Sydney) Ltd (AOM), the Montreal Exchange (ME), Optiebeurs Amsterdam (EOE) and the Vancouver Stock Exchange (VSX), allowing trading for 18.5 hours a day. A limit order book is passed from exchange to exchange. The contracts are fully fungible.

Option on IOCC platinum

Contract size   10 troy ounces of platinum of a minimum 0.9995 fineness.

Standard delivery method   Physical delivery of the above in a form specified by the IOCC with an institution acting as its delivery depot.

Trading months   The nearest three months of the March, June, September and December cycle.

Trading hours   ME: 9.30 a.m. – 2.30 p.m.
VSX: 11.30 a.m. – 4.00 p.m.

Price quotation method   In US dollars (US$) and cents per troy ounce.

Minimum price move (value)   US$0.10 per troy ounce (US$1.00 per contract).

Daily price limits   None.

Position limits   500 options on the same side of the market for clients (1,000 options for professionals).

Last trading day   The third Friday of the contract month at the close of the local trading session.

Delivery day   The business day following the last trading day. The option expires on the Monday following the third Friday of the contract month, which is the last available time for exercise.

Initial (Variation) margin   The option premium received plus a percentage of (if any) twice the intrinsic value of the option.

Spread margin   Not stated.

Strike price intervals   At US$10.00 per troy ounce intervals.

Option type   American style (the option may be exercised on any business day up to and including the last trading day).

Method of introduction of new strike prices   Introduced in co-ordination with the other link exchanges. The VSX follows the lead of the EOE in this respect.

| Reuters Monitor (Quote) | N/a. |
| Telerate page | N/a. |

This contract is traded on the IOCC (International Options Clearing Corporation BV) link between the Montreal Exchange (ME), the Vancouver Stock Exchange (VSX) and Optiebeurs Amsterdam (EOE). A limit order book is passed from exchange to exchange. The contracts are fully fungible.

Option on IOCC silver bullion

Contract size	1,000 troy ounces, 999 parts to 1,000 parts, of good London delivery silver bullion.
Standard delivery method	Physical delivery of the above with one of the five members of the London Silver Market.
Trading months	The nearest three months of the March, June, September and December cycle.
Trading hours	The following are the local trading times for the IOCC link exchanges:

EOE:	10.30 a.m. – 4.30 p.m.
VSX:	7.30 a.m. – 4.00 p.m.
AOM (Nov – Mar):	11.00 a.m. – 1.00 p.m. and
	2.30 p.m. – 4.30 p.m.
AOM (Apr – Oct):	10.30 a.m. – 12.30 p.m. and
	2.00 p.m. – 4.00 p.m.

Price quotation method	In US dollars (US$) and cents per troy ounce.
Minimum price move (value)	One US cent (US$0.01) per troy ounce (US$10.00 per contract).
Daily price limits	None.
Position limits	10,000 contracts on the same side of the market.
Last trading day	The third Friday of the contract month. Trading ceases in the expiring contract at 4.00 p.m. (Amsterdam and Vancouver) or 5.00 p.m. (Sydney), on the last trading day. These times are local times.
Delivery day	The business day following the last trading day. Options expire on the Monday following the third Friday of the contract month, which is the last time allowed for exercise.
Initial (Variation) margin	The option premium received plus a percentage of (if any) twice the intrinsic value of the option.
Spread margin	Not stated.
Strike price intervals	Silver price US$0 – US$5.00: US$0.25 intervals.
	Silver price US$5.00 – US$15.00: US$0.50 intervals.
	Silver price over US$15.00: US$1.00 intervals.
Option type	American style (the option may be exercised on any business day up to and including the last trading day).

Method of introduction of new strike prices

Between four and five series are initially available. New series are introduced so as to allow there to be at least one in-the-money and one out-of-the-money series at all times. No new series are introduced in the last 20 business days before expiry. The other link exchanges take the lead from the EOE Amsterdam in introducing new strike prices.

Reuters Monitor (Quote)

YAQI – YAQP (EOE), VSIA – VSIB (VSX).

Telerate page

N/a.

This contract is traded on the IOCC (International Options Clearing Corporation BV) link between the Australian Stock Exchange (Sydney) Ltd (AOM), Optiebeurs Amsterdam (EOE) and the Vancouver Stock Exchange (VSX). Trading takes place therefore for 18.5 hours per day. An order book passes from exchange to exchange. The contracts are fully fungible.

Winnipeg Commodity Exchange (WCE)

Address:	500 Commodity Exchange Tower 360 Main Street Winnipeg Manitoba R3C 3Z4 Canada
Telephone:	(204) 949 0495
Fax:	(204) 943 5448
Telex:	N/a.

Exchange personnel

Chairman:	Eric Wood
President:	Robert Purves
Information Officer:	Elsa Bukoski

Futures contracts available
Canola
Canola (cash call)
Domestic feed barley
Domestic feed wheat
Flaxseed
Oats
Rye
Western domestic feed barley

Options contracts available
None

Clearing House:	Winnipeg Clearing Corporation Ltd.
Method of trading:	Open outcry.
Commenced trading:	1887.
Exchange links:	None.

A brief synopsis of the exchange
The Winnipeg Commodity Exchange was founded in 1887 and is the oldest exchange in Canada, specialising in the grain markets. There are over 300 exchange members. Futures were first introduced in 1904 on wheat and then other grain products.

Gold futures were first introduced in 1972 and gold options followed in 1979.

The WCE set up the Canadian Financial Futures Market (CFFM) in 1981 to trade the precious metals and other financial derivatives. Turnover in precious metals and interest-rate contracts fell to very low levels and these contracts have been deactivated to concentrate on the strength in grain products.

Winnipeg
Commodity
Exchange (WCE)
Futures
Softs and
agricultural

Canola (RS) futures

Contract size	100 tons (in board lots) or 20 tons (in job lots) of Canola.
Standard delivery method	Physical delivery of No.1 Canola at par or No.2 Canola at C$13.00 per ton discount at Vancouver, or alternative delivery points.
Trading months	The January, March, June, September and November cycle.
Trading hours	9.30 a.m. – 1.15 p.m.
Price quotation method	In Canadian dollars (C$) and cents per ton.
Minimum price move (value)	C$0.10 per ton (C$10.00 per contract – board lots, C$2.00 per contract – job lots).
Daily price limits	C$10.00 per ton above or below the previous day's close. Following two successive limit closes in the same direction for two of the nearest three trading contract months, limits are expanded by 50% for the next two days, and by 100% for the next two days after that. When no two of the nearest three trading contract months close at their expanded daily limit, the daily limit returns to normal.
Position limits	None.
Last trading day	The eighth business day before the end of the contract month.
Delivery day	Any business day during the contract month. Delivery to points alternative to Vancouver is only permitted until the eighth business day before the end of the contract month.
Initial (Variation) margin	Regular: C$300 per contract (C$200). Hedgers: C$200 per contract (C$200).
Spread margin	C$100 per spread position (C$100).
Reuters Monitor (Quote)	GNXH, FRWE.
Telerate page	N/a.

Canola – cash call (RC) futures

Contract size	One railcar lot (66.5 – 73.5 tons) of Canola.
Standard delivery method	Physical delivery of No.1 Canola at par or No.2 Canola at C$13.00 per ton discount at Vancouver.
Trading months	Any calendar month named at the time of dealing.
Trading hours	1.30 p.m. – 2.00 p.m.
Price quotation method	In Canadian dollars (C$) and cents per ton.
Minimum price move (value)	C$0.10 per ton (C$6.65 – C$7.35 per contract).
Daily price limits	None.
Position limits	None.

Last trading day	The eighth business day before the end of the designated contract month.
Delivery day	Any business day during the contract month.
Initial (Variation) margin	Regular: C$300 per contract (C$200).
	Hedgers: C$200 per contract (C$200).
Spread margin	C$100.00 per contract (C$100).
Reuters Monitor (Quote)	GNXH, FRWE.
Telerate page	N/a.

Domestic feed barley (B) futures

Contract size	100 tons (in board lots) or 20 tons (in job lots) of domestic feed barley.
Standard delivery method	Physical delivery of No.1 CW at par or No.2 CW at a C$5.00 per ton discount at Thunder Bay.
Trading months	The March, May, July, October, November and December cycle.
Trading hours	9.30 a.m. – 1.15 p.m.
Price quotation method	In Canadian dollars (C$) and cents per ton.
Minimum price move (value)	C$0.10 per ton (C$10.00 per contract – board lots, C$2.00 per contract – job lots).
Daily price limits	C$5.00 per ton above or below the previous day's close. Following two successive limit closes in the same direction for two of the nearest three trading months, limits are expanded by 50% for the next two days, and by 100% for the next two days after that. When no two of the nearest three trading contract months close at their expanded daily limit, the daily limit returns to normal.
Position limits	None.
Last trading day	The last business day of the contract month.
Delivery day	Any business day during the contract month.
Initial (Variation) margin	Regular: C$120 per contract (C$100).
	Hedgers: C$100 per contract (C$100).
Spread margin	C$50.00 per spread position (C$50.00).
Reuters Monitor (Quote)	CNXG, BRWE.
Telerate page	926.

Domestic feed wheat (W) futures

Contract size	100 tons (in board lots) or 20 tons (in job lots) of domestic feed wheat.
Standard delivery method	Physical delivery of No.3 CWRS at par or No.2 Prairie Spring, No.1 CWU, No.2 CWU or CW feed at C$5.00 per ton discount at Thunder Bay.

Trading months	The March, May, July, October, November and December cycle.
Trading hours	9.30 a.m. – 1.15 p.m.
Price quotation method	In Canadian dollars (C$) and cents per ton.
Minimum price move (value)	C$0.10 per ton (C$10.00 per contract – board lots, C$2.00 per contract – job lots).
Daily price limits	C$5.00 per ton above or below the previous day's close. Following two successive limit closes in the same direction for two of the nearest three trading contract months, limits are expanded by 50% for the next two days, and by 100% for the next two days after that. When no two of the nearest three trading contract months close at their expanded daily limit, the daily limit returns to normal.
Position limits	None.
Last trading day	The last business day of the contract month.
Delivery day	Any business day during the contract month.
Initial (Variation) margin	Regular: C$120 per contract (C$100). Hedgers: C$100 per contract (C$100).
Spread margin	C$50.00 per contract (C$50.00).
Reuters Monitor (Quote)	N/a.
Telerate page	925.

Flaxseed (F) futures

Contract size	100 tons (in board lots) or 20 tons (in job lots) of flaxseed.
Standard delivery method	Physical delivery of No.1 CW at par or No.2 CW at C$2.00 per ton discount at Thunder Bay, or alternative delivery points.
Trading months	The March, May, July, October and December cycle.
Trading hours	9.30 a.m. – 1.15 p.m.
Price quotation method	In Canadian dollars (C$) and cents per ton.
Minimum price move (value)	C$0.10 per ton (C$10.00 per contract – board lots, C$2.00 per contract – job lots).
Daily price limits	C$10.00 per ton above or below the previous day's close. Following two successive limit closes in the same direction for two of the nearest three trading contract months, limits are expanded by 50% for the next two days, and by 100% for the next two days after that. When no two of the nearest three trading contract months close at their expanded daily limit, the daily limit returns to normal.
Position limits	None.
Last trading day	The last business day of the contract month.

**Winnipeg
Commodity
Exchange (WCE)
Futures
Softs and
agricultural**

Delivery day	Any business day during the contract month. Delivery to alternative delivery points is only permitted until the eighth business day before the end of the contract month.
Initial (Variation) margin	Regular: C$300 per contract (C$200).
	Hedgers: C$200 per contract (C$200).
Spread margin	C$100 per spread position (C$100).
Reuters Monitor (Quote)	GNXH, CSME.
Telerate page	926.

Oats (O) futures

Contract size	100 tons (in board lots) or 20 tons (in job lots) of oats.
Standard delivery method	Physical delivery of No.3 CW at par or No.4 CW at C$5.00 per ton discount at Thunder Bay.
Trading months	The March, May, July, October, November and December cycle.
Trading hours	9.30 a.m. – 1.15 p.m.
Price quotation method	In Canadian dollars (C$) and cents per ton.
Minimum price move (value)	C$0.10 per ton (C$10.00 per contract – board lots, C$2.00 per contract – job lots).
Daily price limits	C$5.00 per ton above or below the previous day's close. Following two successive limit closes in the same direction for two of the nearest three trading contract months, limits are expanded by 50% for the next two days, and by 100% for the next two days after that. When no two of the nearest three trading contract months close at their expanded daily limit, the daily limit returns to normal.
Position limits	None.
Last trading day	The last business day of the contract month.
Delivery day	Any business day during the contract month.
Initial (Variation) margin	Regular: C$120 per contract (C$100).
	Hedgers: C$100 per contract (C$100).
Spread margin	C$50.00 per spread position (C$50.00).
Reuters Monitor (Quote)	GNXG.
Telerate page	N/a.

Rye (R) futures

Contract size	100 tons (in board lots) or 20 tons (in job lots) of rye.
Standard delivery method	Physical delivery of No.1 CW at par or No.2 CW at C$2.00 per ton discount at Thunder Bay.
Trading months	The March, May, July, October and December cycle.
Trading hours	9.30 a.m. – 1.15 p.m.

Price quotation method	In Canadian dollars (C$) and cents per ton.
Minimum price move (value)	C$0.10 per ton (C$10.00 per contract – board lots, C$2.00 per contract – job lots).
Daily price limits	C$5.00 per ton above or below the previous day's close. Following two successive limit closes in the same direction for two of the nearest three trading contract months, limits are expanded by 50% for the next two days, and by 100% for the next two days after that. When no two of the nearest three trading contract months close at their expanded daily limit, the daily limit returns to normal.
Position limits	None.
Last trading day	The last business day of the contract month.
Delivery day	Any business day during the contract month.
Initial (Variation) margin	Regular: C$120 per contract (C$100). Hedgers: C$100 per contract (C$100).
Spread margin	C$50.00 per spread position (C$50.00).
Reuters Monitor (Quote)	RYWE.
Telerate page	N/a.

Western domestic feed barley (AB) futures

Contract size	20 tons of Western domestic feed barley.
Standard delivery method	Physical delivery of the above at Lethbridge.
Trading months	The February, May, August and November cycle.
Trading hours	9.30 a.m. – 1.15 p.m.
Price quotation method	In Canadian dollars (C$) and cents per ton.
Minimum price move (value)	C$0.10 per ton (C$2.00 per contract).
Daily price limits	C$5.00 per ton above or below the previous day's close. Following two successive limit closes in the same direction for two of the nearest three trading contract months, limits are expanded by 50% for the next two days, and by 100% for the next two days after that. When no two of the nearest three trading contract months close at their expanded daily limit, the daily limit returns to normal.
Position limits	None.
Last trading day	The first Monday of the contract month.
Delivery day	Any business day during the contract month.
Initial (Variation) margin	Regular: C$120 per contract (C$100). Hedgers: C$100 per contract (C$100).
Spread margin	C$50.00 per spread position (C$50.00).
Reuters Monitor (Quote)	BRWW.
Telerate page	N/a.

12 United States of America

Contents

Chicago

Mid-American Commodity Exchange (MACE) (affiliated to the CBOT)

Sub. Chicago Rice & Cotton Exchange (CRCE) (a division of the MACE)

New York

Commodity Exchange Inc. (COMEX) 12/105

New York Cotton Exchange Inc. (NYCE)

Citrus Associates of the New York Cotton Exchange (CA) (an affiliate of the NYCE)

Financial Instrument Exchange (FINEX) (a division of the NYCE)

New York Mercantile Exchange (NYMEX)

New York Stock Exchange (NYSE) 12/133

New York Futures Exchange (NYFE) (a subsidiary of the NYSE)

Philadelphia

Philadelphia Stock Exchange (PHLX) 12/141

Philadelphia Board of Trade (PBOT) (a subsidiary of the PHLX)

Elsewhere

Kansas City Board of Trade (KBOT)

Minneapolis Grain Exchange (MGE)

Chicago Board of Trade (CBOT)

Address:	141 West Jackson Boulevard Chicago Illinois 60604 USA
Telephone:	(312) 435 3500
Fax:	(312) 435 7170
Telex:	253223 CBOT VR

Exchange personnel

Chairman:	Karsten Mahlmann
Vice Chairman:	Patrick Arbor
President & CEO:	Thomas R. Donovan
Vice President, Public Relations:	Raymond W. Carmichael

Washington Representative Office

Address:	1455 Pennsylvania Avenue NW Suite 1225 Washington DC 20004 USA
Telephone:	(202) 783 1190
Fax:	(202) 393 3310
Telex:	N/a.
Contact:	Celesta Jurkovich

UK Representative Office

Address:	52–54 Gracechurch Street London EC3V 0EH United Kingdom
Telephone:	(01) 929 0021
Fax:	(01) 929 0058
Telex:	9413558
Managing Director:	Peter Donnelly
Public Relations Manager:	Suzanne Matus

Address:

Asia/Pacific Representative Office
Imperial Tower 6–A–12
1–1–1 Uchisaiwaicho
Chiyoda-ku
Tokyo 100
Japan

Telephone: (03) 593 2600
Fax: (03) 593 8013
Telex: N/a.
Managing Director: William D Grossman

Futures contracts available
CBOE 250 Stock Index
Corn
5,000-ounce Silver
Five-year US Government Treasury Notes
Kilo gold (32.15 tr. oz)
Long-term Municipal Bond Index
Major Market Stock Index (XMI)
Mortgage-backed securities (MBS)
Oats
100-ounce gold
1,000-ounce silver
Soyabeans
Soyabean meal
Soyabean oil
30-day interest rate
US Government Treasury Notes
US Government Treasury Bonds
Wheat

Options contracts on futures available
Corn futures
Long-term Municipal Bond Index futures
Mortgage-backed securities (MBS) futures
1,000-ounce silver futures
Soyabean futures
Soyabean meal futures
Soyabean oil futures
US Government Treasury Note futures
US Government Treasury Bond futures
Wheat futures

Clearing House:

Board of Trade Clearing Corporation (founded in 1925).

Method of trading:

Open outcry.

Commenced trading:

1848.

Exchange links:

Mid-American Commodity Exchange (MACE)
Chicago Rice & Cotton Exchange (CRCE)
Chicago Board Options Exchange (CBOE)

A brief synopsis of the exchange

The Chicago Board of Trade is the oldest and largest specialist futures exchange worldwide, and its product range covers agricultural, metal and financial instruments. It was founded in the mid-1800s to allow grain producers and consumers alike to hedge their forward price payments and receipts that were at the time highly volatile due to vagaries of pestilence and weather. To this day, grain contracts are of major importance to the exchange.

The CBOT introduced the first interest-rate futures worldwide in 1975, on the Government National Mortgage Association (GNMA). Two years later in 1977, it launched the contract that was to become the world's largest in terms of turnover, the US Government Treasury Bond futures contract. This was soon followed by another first, options on futures on the US Government Treasury Bond.

The CBOT has over 1,400 full members, and around 700 associate members (who may only trade the non-agricultural contracts), and of the full members around 150 are full clearing members. At 32,000 square feet the total trading area of the exchange is larger than an American football field.

The exchange has the Mid-American Commodity Exchange (MACE) and the Chicago Rice & Cotton Exchange (CRCE) as affiliates, both of which trade on the same dealing floor as the CBOT, and in 1973, the now independent Chicago Board Options Exchange (CBOE) was founded.

To enhance internationalisation, an evening trading session began in April 1987. The exchange currently trades around one-half of the total US futures market volume and it is a self-regulated exchange.

Also in 1987, the CBOT introduced gold and silver bullion futures contracts in direct competition to the major world precious metals futures market, COMEX Inc., in New York, but as is often the case with the early leader, COMEX reigns supreme, with the CBOT making little inroad into this area of activity.

Future plans include internationalisation of the product range with a Japanese yen bond futures (awaiting CFTC approval), a Japanese stock index product (probably on the TOPIX Index) and even a futures contract on fertiliser.

CBOE 250 Stock index futures

Contract size	US$500 multiplied by the CBOE 250 Stock Index (i.e. if the CBOE 250 Index stands at 325.00, the underlying value of the futures contract is US$162,500).
Standard delivery method	Cash settlement on the last trading day. There is no facility for physical delivery of the stocks underlying the index.
Trading months	The nearest three consecutive calendar months, then the next three months from the March, June, September and December cycle.
Trading hours	8.15 a.m. – 3.15 p.m.
Price quotation method	In US dollars (US$) and cents per index point.
Minimum price move (value)	0.05 index points (US$25.00 per contract).
Daily price limits	50 index points above or below the previous day's settlement price, with an initial limit of 30 index points below the previous day's settlement price.
Position limits	5,000 contracts in total (500 reportable in any one month).
Last trading day	The first business day prior to the first Saturday following the third Friday of the contract month.
Delivery day	The business day following the last trading day.
Initial (Variation) margin	Speculators: US$18,000 per contract (US$10,000). Hedgers: US$10,000 per contract (US$10,000). These minimum margin requirements increase by 50% when daily price limits are increased.
Spread margin	A wide range of straddle, spread, or intra-commodity spread concessions is available. Please contact the exchange or your broker for full details.
Reuters Monitor (Quote)	IVCE.
Telerate page	8498.

Corn futures

Contract size	5,000 bushels of US No.2 yellow corn.
Standard delivery method	Physical delivery of the above.
Trading months	The March, May, July, September and December cycle.
Trading hours	9.30 a.m. – 1.15 p.m. (trading ceases in the expiring contract at 12.00 noon on the last trading day).
Price quotation method	In US cents and quarter-cents per bushel.
Minimum price move (value)	One quarter (1/4) of a US cent per bushel (US$12.50 per contract).

Daily price limits	10 US cents (US$0.10) per bushel (US$500 per contract) above or below the previous day's settlement price. There are no limits on the spot month.
Position limits	100 contracts on the same side of the market.
Last trading day	Seven business days before the last business day of the contract month.
Delivery day	The last delivery day is the last business day of the contract month.
Initial (Variation) margin	Speculators: US$700 per contract (US$500). Hedgers: US$500 per contract (US$500). These minimum margin requirements increase by 50% when daily price limits are increased.
Spread margin	A wide range of straddle, spread, or intra-commodity spread concessions is available. Please contact the exchange or your broker for full details.
Reuters Monitor (Quote)	GNXO.
Telerate page	926.

5,000-ounce silver futures

Contract size	5,000 troy ounces of refined (999 fineness) silver.
Standard delivery method	Physical delivery of the above through a receipt issued by a CBOT-approved vault in Chicago.
Trading months	The current month, the next two consecutive calendar months and then months from the February, April, June, August, October and December cycle.
Trading hours	7.25 a.m. – 1.25 p.m. Monday to Friday and evening session 5.00 p.m. – 8.30 p.m. (CST) or 6.00 p.m. – 9.30 p.m. (when on Central Daylight Saving time) Sunday to Thursday.
Price quotation method	In US dollars (US$) and cents per troy ounce.
Minimum price move (value)	0.10 US cents (US$0.001) per troy ounce (US$5.00 per contract).
Daily price limits	US$1.00 per troy ounce (US$5,000 per contract) above or below the previous day's settlement price.
Position limits	15,000,000 troy ounces (in either CBOT 1,000-ounce silver futures or CBOT 5,000-ounce silver futures or both).
Last trading day	The fourth to last business day of the contract month.
Delivery day	The delivery process in the contract month is as follows: first business day – seller gives notice of intention to deliver, second business day – buyer is notified; last business day – buyer receives vault receipts and must pay promptly.
Initial (Variation) margin	Speculators: US$1,750 per contract (US$1,250). Hedgers: US$1,250 per contract (US$1,250). These minimum margin requirements increase by 50% when daily price limits are increased.

Spread margin	A wide range of straddle, spread, or intra-commodity spread concessions is available. Please contact the exchange or your broker for full details.
Reuters Monitor (Quote)	N/a.
Telerate page	N/a.

Five-year US Government Treasury Notes futures

Contract size	US$100,000 nominal face value of a notional five-year US Government Treasury Note.
Standard delivery method	Physical delivery of the above notes, being any of the four most recently auctioned five-year Treasury Notes with an original maturity of not more than five years and three months and not less than four years and three months, as of the first day of the contract month.
Trading months	The March, June, September and December cycle.
Trading hours	7.20 a.m. – 2.00 p.m.
Price quotation method	In percent of par in increments of one thirty-second (1/32) of a point, quoted in US dollars (US$).
Minimum price move (value)	One sixty-fourth (1/64) of a point (US$15.625 per contract).
Daily price limits	Three points above or below the previous day's settlement price (expandable to 4.5 points).
Position limits	5,000 contracts in total (200 reportable in any one month).
Last trading day	The eighth to last business day of the contract month.
Delivery day	The last business day of the contract month.
Initial (Variation) margin	Speculators: US$1,250 per contract (US$750). Hedgers: US$750 per contract (US$750). These minimum margin requirements increase by 50% when daily price limits are increased.
Spread margin	A wide range of straddle, spread, or intra-commodity spread concessions is available. Please contact the exchange or your broker for full details.
Reuters Monitor (Quote)	TOCB.
Telerate page	N/a.

Kilo gold futures

Contract size	One kilogram (32.15 troy ounces) of refined (995 fineness) gold.
Standard delivery method	Physical delivery of the above, through a vault receipt issued by a CBOT-approved vault in Chicago or New York.

Trading months	The current month, the next two consecutive calendar months and then months from the February, April, June, August, October and December cycle.
Trading hours	7.20 a.m. – 1.40 p.m.
Price quotation method	In US dollars (US$) and cents per troy ounce.
Minimum price move (value)	US$0.10 per ounce (US$3.215 per contract).
Daily price limits	US$50.00 per troy ounce (US$1,607.50 per contract) above or below the previous day's settlement price.
Position limits	241,125 troy ounces (in either CBOT one kilo gold futures or CBOT 100 ounce gold futures or both).
Last trading day	The fourth business day before the end of the contract month.
Delivery day	The delivery process in the contract month is as follows: first business day – seller gives notice of intention to deliver, second business day – buyer is notified, last business day – buyer receives vault receipts and must pay promptly.
Initial (Variation) margin	Speculators: US$500 per contract (US$300). Hedgers: US$300 per contract (US$300). These minimum margin requirements increase by 50% when daily price limits are increased.
Spread margin	A wide range of straddle, spread, or intra-commodity spread concessions is available. Please contact the exchange or your broker for full details.
Reuters Monitor (Quote)	GDCE.
Telerate page	N/a.

Long-term Municipal Bond Index futures

Contract size	US$1,000 multiplied by Bond Buyer Municipal Bond Index* (a price of 85-16 reflects a contract size of US$85,500).
Standard delivery method	Cash settlement at the index level on the last trading day. There is no facility for physical delivery.
Trading months	The March, June, September and December cycle.
Trading hours	7.20 a.m. – 2.00 p.m.
Price quotation method	In US dollars (US$) per index point and thirty-seconds (1/32) of a point.
Minimum price move (value)	One thirty-second (1/32) of an index point (US$31.25 per contract).
Daily price limits	Three full index points (US$3,000 per contract) above or below the previous day's settlement price.
Position limits	5,000 contracts in total (500 reportable in any one month).
Last trading day	The eighth to last business day of the contract month.
Delivery day	The business day following the last trading day.

Initial (Variation) margin

Speculators: US$1,250 per contract (US$750).
Hedgers: US$750 per contract (US$750).
These minimum margin requirements increase by 50%
when daily price limits are increased.

Spread margin

A wide range of straddle, spread, or intra-commodity
spread concessions is available. Please contact the
exchange or your broker for full details.

Reuters Monitor (Quote)

MBCE.

Telerate page

894.

* The Bond Buyer Municipal Bond Index comprises 40 actively
traded general obligation and revenue bonds, that are rated A- or
better by Standard & Poors or rated A or better by Moody's. The
issue size must be of US$50 million or greater, have a remaining life
to maturity of at least 19 years, be callable prior to maturity with the
first call between 7 and 16 years upon inclusion in the index and
have a fixed coupon with semi-annual interest payments.

Major Market Stock Index (XMI) futures

Contract size

US$250 multiplied by the value of the Major Market
Index (XMI)* (i.e. if the XMI stands at 435.00, the
underlying value of the futures contract is
US$108,750).

Standard delivery method

Cash settlement at the final index level of the XMI on
the last trading day. There is no facility for physical
delivery of the stocks underlying the index.

Trading months

All consecutive calendar months.

Trading hours

8.15 a.m. – 3.15 p.m.

Price quotation method

In US dollars (US$) and cents per index point.

*Minimum price move
(value)*

0.05 index points (US$12.50 per contract).

Daily price limits

None.

Position limits

20,000 contracts in total (500 reportable in any one
month).

Last trading day

The third Friday of the contract month.

Delivery day

The business day following the last trading day.

Initial (Variation) margin

Speculators: US$15,000 per contract (US$10,000) –
approximately 5% of the underlying
value of the contract.
Hedgers: US$10,000 per contract (US$10,000).
These minimum margin requirements increase by 50%
when daily price limits are increased.

Spread margin

A wide range of straddle, spread, or intra-commodity
spread concessions is available. Please contact the
exchange or your broker for full details.

Reuters Monitor (Quote)

MMCG – MMCH (C₂BC*).

Telerate page

N/a.

* The Major Market Index (XMI) is a price-weighted index based
on equal weighting factors to each of the following current
constituents:

American Express · · · AT&T · · · · Chevron
Coca-Cola · · · · · · Dow Chemical · Du Pont
Eastman Kodak · · · Exxon · · · · · General Electric
General Motors · · · IBM · · · · · · International Paper
Johnson & Johnson · Merck & Co. · · Minnesota Mining & Mfg
Mobil · · · · · · · Philip Morris · Procter & Gamble
Sears, Roebuck · · · USX

Mortgage-backed securities (MBS) futures

Contract size	US$100,000 nominal face value of mortgage-backed securities – each month the coupon for the newly introduced future will be the prevailing GNMA (Government National Mortgage Association) coupon – therefore there may be as many as four different coupons trading.
Standard delivery method	Cash settlement on the last trading day, based on the Mortgage-Backed Price Survey. There is no facility for physical delivery.
Trading months	The four nearby consecutive calendar months.
Trading hours	7.20 a.m. – 2.00 p.m. Trading ceases in the expiring contract at 1.00 p.m. on the last trading day.
Price quotation method	In US dollars (US$) and cents per point and thirty-seconds (1/32) of a point.
Minimum price move (value)	One thirty-second (1/32) of a point (US$31.25 per contract).
Daily price limits	Three points above or below the previous day's closing price (US$3,000 per contract).
Position limits	None.
Last trading day	The Friday preceding the third Wednesday of the contract month.
Delivery day	The business day following the last trading day.
Initial (Variation) margin	Not stated. Please consult the exchange for the current details.
Spread margin	Not stated. Please consult the exchange for the current details.
Reuters Monitor (Quote)	GMCG – GMCH.
Telerate page	906.

Oat futures

Contract size	5,000 bushels of No.2 heavy oats or No.1 oats at par.
Standard delivery method	Physical delivery of one of the above grades of oats.
Trading months	The March, May, July, September and December cycle.

Trading hours	9.30 a.m. – 1.15 p.m. (trading ceases in the expiring contract at 12.00 noon on the last trading day).
Price quotation method	In US cents and quarters (1/4) of a US cent per bushel.
Minimum price move (value)	One quarter (1/4) of a US cent per bushel (US$12.50 per contract).
Daily price limits	10 US cents (US$0.10) per bushel (US$500 per contract) above or below the previous day's settlement price. There are no limits on the spot month.
Position limits	60 contracts on the same side of the market.
Last trading day	Seven business days before the last business day of the contract month.
Delivery day	The business day following the last trading day.
Initial (Variation) margin	Speculators: US$700 per contract (US$500). Hedgers: US$500 per contract (US$500). These minimum margin requirements increase by 50% when daily price limits are increased.
Spread margin	A wide range of straddle, spread, or intra-commodity spread concessions is available. Please contact the exchange or your broker for full details.
Reuters Monitor (Quote)	OACE.
Telerate page	926.

100-ounce gold futures

Contract size	100 troy ounces of refined (995 fineness) gold.
Standard delivery method	Physical delivery of the above, through a vault receipt from a CBOT-approved vault in Chicago or New York.
Trading months	The current (spot) month, the next two consecutive calendar months and then months from the February, April, June, August, October and December cycle.
Trading hours	7.20 a.m. – 1.40 p.m. Monday to Friday and evening session 5.00 p.m. – 8.30 p.m. (CST) or 6.00 p.m. – 9.30 p.m. (when on Central Daylight Saving time) Sunday to Thursday.
Price quotation method	In US dollars (US$) and cents per troy ounce.
Minimum price move (value)	US$0.10 per troy ounce (US$10.00 per contract).
Daily price limits	US$50.00 per troy ounce (US$5,000 per contract) above or below the previous day's settlement price.
Position limits	241,125 troy ounces (in either CBOT one kilo gold futures or CBOT 100 ounce gold futures or both).
Last trading day	The fourth business day before the last business day of the contract month.
Delivery day	The delivery process in the contract month is as follows: first business day – seller gives notice of intention to deliver, second business day – buyer is

	notified; last business day – buyer receives vault receipts and must pay promptly.
Initial (Variation) margin	Speculators: US$1,250 per contract (US$1,000). Hedgers: US$1,000 per contract (US$1,000). These minimum margin requirements increase by 50% when daily price limits are increased.
Spread margin	A wide range of straddle, spread, or intra-commodity spread concessions is available. Please contact the exchange or your broker for full details.
Reuters Monitor (Quote)	GDCG – GDCH.
Telerate page	N/a.

1,000-ounce silver futures

Contract size	1,000 troy ounces of refined (999 fineness) silver.
Standard delivery method	Physical delivery of the above, through a receipt issued by a CBOT-approved vault in Chicago.
Trading months	The current (spot) month, the next two consecutive calendar months and then months from the February, April, June, August, October and December cycle.
Trading hours	7.25 a.m. – 1.25 p.m.
Price quotation method	In US dollars (US$) and cents per troy ounce.
Minimum price move (value)	0.10 US cents per troy ounce (US$1.00 per contract).
Daily price limits	US$1.00 per troy ounce (US$1,000 per contract) above or below the previous day's settlement price.
Position limits	15,000,000 troy ounces (in either CBOT 1,000-ounce silver futures or CBOT 5,000-ounce silver futures or both).
Last trading day	The fourth to last business day of the contract month.
Delivery day	The delivery process in the contract month is as follows: first business day – seller gives notice of intention to deliver; second business day – buyer is notified; last business day – buyer recieves vault receipts and must pay promptly.
Initial (Variation) margin	Speculators: US$350 per contract (US$250). Hedgers: US$250 per contract (US$250). These minimum margin requirements increase by 50% when daily price limits are increased.
Spread margin	A wide range of straddle, spread, or intra-commodity spread concessions is available. Please contact the exchange or your broker for full details.
Reuters Monitor (Quote)	N/a.
Telerate page	N/a.

Soyabean futures

Contract size	5,000 bushels of US No.2 yellow soyabeans.
Standard delivery method	Physical delivery of the above.
Trading months	The January, March, May, July, August, September and November cycle.
Trading hours	9.30 a.m. – 1.15 p.m. (trading ceases in the expiring contract at 12.00 noon on the last trading day).
Price quotation method	In US cents and quarters (1/4) of a US cent per bushel.
Minimum price move (value)	One quarter (1/4) of a US cent per bushel (US$12.50 per contract).
Daily price limits	30 US cents (US$0.30) per bushel (US$1,500 per contract) above or below the previous day's settlement price. There are no limits on the spot month.
Position limits	100 contracts on the same side of the market.
Last trading day	Seven business days before the last business day of the contract month.
Delivery day	The business day following the last trading day
Initial (Variation) margin	Speculators: US$1,500 per contract (US$1,250). Hedgers: US$1,250 per contract (US$1,250). These minimum margin requirements increase by 50% when daily price limits are increased.
Spread margin	A wide range of straddle, spread, or intra-commodity spread concessions is available. Please contact the exchange or your broker for full details.
Reuters Monitor (Quote)	GNXA.
Telerate page	927.

Soyabean meal futures

Contract size	100 tons (2,000 pounds per ton) of soyabean meal with minimum protein of 44%.
Standard delivery method	Physical delivery of the above.
Trading months	The January, March, May, July, August, September, October and December cycle.
Trading hours	9.30 a.m. – 1.15 p.m. (trading ceases in the expiring contract at 12.00 noon on the last trading day).
Price quotation method	In US dollars (US$) and cents per ton.
Minimum price move (value)	10 US cents (US$0.10) per ton (US$10.00 per contract).
Daily price limits	US$10.00 per ton (US$1,000 per contract) above or below the previous day's settlement price. There are no limits on the spot month.
Position limits	200 contracts on the same side of the market.
Last trading day	Seven business days before the last business day of the contract month.
Delivery day	The business day following the last trading day.

Initial (Variation) margin	Speculators: US$1,000 per contract (US$800).
	Hedgers: US$800 per contract (US$800).
	These minimum margin requirements increase by 50% when daily price limits are increased.
Spread margin	A wide range of straddle, spread, or intra-commodity spread concessions is available. Please contact the exchange or your broker for full details.
Reuters Monitor (Quote)	GNXC.
Telerate page	928.

Soyabean oil futures

Contract size	60,000 pounds of crude soyabean oil.
Standard delivery method	Physical delivery of the above.
Trading months	The January, March, May, July, August, September, October and December cycle.
Trading hours	9.30 a.m. – 1.15 p.m. (trading ceases in the expiring contract at 12.00 noon on the last trading day).
Price quotation method	In US cents and one-hundredths (1/100) of a US cent per pound.
Minimum price move (value)	One-hundredth (1/100) of a US cent per pound (US$6.00 per contract).
Daily price limits	One US cent (US$0.01) per pound (US$600 per contract) above or below the previous day's settlement price. There are no limits on the spot month.
Position limits	200 contracts on the same side of the market.
Last trading day	Seven business days before the last business day of the contract month.
Delivery day	The business day following the last trading day.
Initial (Variation) margin	Speculators: US$600 per contract (US$500).
	Hedgers: US$500 per contract (US$500).
	These minimum margin requirements increase by 50% when daily price limits are increased.
Spread margin	A wide range of straddle, spread, or intra-commodity spread concessions is available. Please contact the exchange or your broker for full details.
Reuters Monitor (Quote)	GNXB.
Telerate page	928.

30-day interest rate futures

Contract size	US$5,000,000 nominal value.
Standard delivery method	Cash settlement against the average Fed Funds rate for the contract month, as reported daily by the Federal Reserve Bank of New York. There is no facility for physical delivery.

Trading months	The first seven consecutive calendar months, and the first two months from the March, June, September and December cycle.
Trading hours	7.20 a.m. – 2.00 p.m.
Price quotation method	100.00 minus the monthly (30 days) average overnight Fed Funds rate, quoted in US dollars (US$).
Minimum price move (value)	0.01% of US$5,000,000 on a 30-day basis (US$41.67 per contract).
Daily price limits	150 basis points (expandable to 225 basis points for successive periods of three days, if three or more contracts trade at their limit). There are no limits in the spot month.
Position limits	3,000 contracts in total (500 reportable in any one month).
Last trading day	The last business day of the contract month.
Delivery day	The business day following the last trading day.
Initial (Variation) margin	Speculators: US$800 per contract (US$600). Hedgers: US$600 per contract (US$600). These minimum margin requirements increase by 50% when daily price limits are increased.
Spread margin	A wide range of straddle, spread, or intra-commodity spread concessions is available. Please contact the exchange or your broker for full details.
Reuters Monitor (Quote)	IRCE.
Telerate page	N/a.

US Government Treasury Note futures

Contract size	US$100,000 nominal face value of a notional US Government Treasury Note.
Standard delivery method	Physical delivery of the above notes, maturing in at least 6.5 years, but not more than 10 years from the first day of the contract month, with a nominal 8% coupon rate.
Trading months	The March, June, September and December cycle.
Trading hours	7.20 a.m. – 2.00 p.m. Monday to Friday and an evening session 5.00 p.m. – 8.30 p.m. (CST) or 6.00 p.m. – 9.30 p.m. (when on Central Daylight Saving time) Sunday to Thursday.
Price quotation method	In US dollars (US$) per thirty-seconds (1/32) per cent of par.
Minimum price move (value)	One thirty-second (1/32) of 1% (US$31.25 per contract).
Daily price limits	Three points above or below the previous day's settlement price.
Position limits	5,000 contracts in total (500 reportable in any one month).

Last trading day	Seven business days prior to the last business day of the contract month.
Delivery day	The last business day of the contract month. Delivery may take place on any business day during the contract month.
Initial (Variation) margin	Speculators: US$1,500 per contract (US$1,000). Hedgers: US$1,000 per contract (US$1,000). These minimum margin requirements increase by 50% when daily price limits are increased.
Spread margin	US$200 per spread position (US$200). A wide range of straddle, spread, or intra-commodity spread concessions is available. Please contact the exchange or your broker for full details.
Reuters Monitor (Quote)	TOCA.
Telerate page	905.

US Government Treasury Bond futures

Contract size	US$100,000 nominal face value of a notional long-term US Government Treasury Bond.
Standard delivery method	Physical delivery of the above bonds, maturing at least 15 years from the first day of the contract month, with a notional coupon of 8%.
Trading months	The March, June, September and December cycle.
Trading hours	7.20 a.m. – 2.00 p.m. Monday to Friday and an evening session 5.00 p.m. – 8.30 p.m. (CST) or 6.00 p.m. – 9.30 p.m. (when on Central Daylight Saving time) Sunday to Thursday.
Price quotation method	In terms of US dollars (US$) and cents in thirty-seconds (1/32) per cent of par.
Minimum price move (value)	One thirty-second (1/32) of 1% (US$31.25 per contract).
Daily price limits	Three points above or below the previous day's settlement price.
Position limits	10,000 contracts in total (300 reportable in any one month).
Last trading day	Seven business days prior to the last business day of the contract month.
Delivery day	The last business day of the contract month. Delivery may take place on any business day during the contract month.
Initial (Variation) margin	Speculators: US$2,000 per contract (US$1,500). Hedgers: US$1,500 per contract (US$1,500). These minimum margin requirements increase by 50% when daily price limits are increased.

Spread margin

US$200 per spread position (US$200). A wide range of straddle, spread, or intra-commodity spread concessions is available. Please contact the exchange or your broker for full details.

Reuters Monitor (Quote)
TBCA – TBCN (C$_2$ US*).

Telerate page
912.

Similar contracts are traded in London, Sydney and Tokyo.

Wheat futures

Contract size

5,000 bushels of No.2 soft red, No.2 hard red winter wheat, No.2 dark northern spring wheat or No.1 northern spring wheat at par.

Standard delivery method
Physical delivery of one of the above grades of wheat.

Trading months
The March, May, July, September and December cycle.

Trading hours
9.30 a.m. – 1.25 p.m. (trading ceases in the expiring contract at 12.00 noon on the last trading day).

Price quotation method
In US cents and quarters (1/4) of a US cent per bushel.

Minimum price move (value)
One quarter (1/4) of a US cent per bushel (US$12.50 per contract).

Daily price limits
20 US cents (US$0.20) per bushel (US$1.00 per contract) above or below the previous day's settlement price. There are no limits on the spot month.

Position limits
100 contracts on the same side of the market.

Last trading day
Seven business days before the last business day of the contract month.

Delivery day
The business day following the last trading day.

Initial (Variation) margin
Speculators: US$1,000 per contract (US$700).
Hedgers: US$700 per contract (US$700).
These minimum margin requirements increase by 50% when daily price limits are increased.

Spread margin
A wide range of straddle, spread, or intra-commodity spread concessions is available. Please contact the exchange or your broker for full details.

Reuters Monitor (Quote)
GNXC.

Telerate page
925.

Option on CBOT corn futures

Contract size

One CBOT corn futures contract of a specified contract month (of an underlying contract size of 5,000 bushels).

Standard delivery method

Delivery of a long or short position in a futures contract of a specified contract month at the strike price as above.

Trading months	The March, May, July, September and December cycle.
Trading hours	9.30 a.m. – 1.15 p.m. (trading ceases in the expiring contract at 12.00 noon on the last trading day).
Price quotation method	In US cents and one-eighths (1/8) of a US cent per bushel.
Minimum price move (value)	One-eighth (1/8) of a cent per bushel (US$6.25 per contract).
Daily price limits	10 US cents (US$0.10) per bushel (US$500 per contract) above or below the previous day's settlement premium. There are no limits on the spot month.
Position limits	100 contracts on the same side of the market.
Last trading day	The last Friday preceding the first notice day of the underlying corn futures contract by at least five business days. Unexercised options expire at 10.00 a.m. on the Saturday following the last trading day.
Delivery day	The business day following the last trading day.
Initial (Variation) margin	Uncovered short positions pay a margin equal to the premium received plus the greater of: (a) the current initial margin for the underlying futures contract less half the amount by which the option is out-of-the-money; or (b) half the current initial margin for the underlying futures contract.
Spread margin	A wide series of spread, straddle and intra-commodity margin concessions is available. Please contact the exchange or your broker for full details.
Strike price intervals	At one US cent (US$0.01) per bushel intervals.
Option type	American style (the option may be exercised on any business day up to and including the last trading day).
Method of introduction of new strike prices	Not stated.
Reuters Monitor (Quote)	N/a.
Telerate page	N/a.

Option on CBOT Long-term Municipal Bond Index futures

Contract size	One CBOT long-term Municipal Bond Index futures contract of a specified contract month (of an underlying contract size of US$1,000 multiplied by the index).
Standard delivery method	Delivery of a long or short position in a futures contract of a specified contract month at the strike price as above.
Trading months	The March, June, September and December cycle.
Trading hours	7.20 a.m. – 2.00 p.m.
Price quotation method	In US dollars (US$) and cents per index point.

Minimum price move (value)	One sixty-fourth (1/64) of a point (US$15.625 per contract).
Daily price limits	Three full index points (US$3,000 per contract) above or below the previous day's settlement premium.
Position limits	None.
Last trading day	The last day of trading of the relevant futures contract – the eighth to last business day of the contract month.
Delivery day	The business day following the last trading day.
Initial (Variation) margin	Uncovered short positions pay a margin equal to the premium received plus the greater of: (a) the current initial margin for the underlying futures contract less half the amount by which the option is out-of-the-money; or (b) half the current initial margin for the underlying futures contract.
Spread margin	A wide series of spread, straddle and intra-commodity margin concessions is available. Please contact the exchange or your broker for full details.
Strike price intervals	At two index points intervals (e.g. 92-00, 94-00, 96-00, etc.).
Option type	American style (options may be exercised on any business day (up to 8.00 p.m.) up to and including the last trading day). In-the-money options are automatically exercised on expiry.
Method of introduction of new strike prices	Not stated.
Reuters Monitor (Quote)	N/a.
Telerate page	N/a.

Option on CBOT mortgage-backed securities (MBS) futures

Contract size	One CBOT mortgage-backed securities futures contract of a specified contract month and a specified coupon (of an underlying contract size of US$100,000 nominal face value).
Standard delivery method	Delivery of a long or short position in a futures contract at the strike price as above.
Trading months	The four nearby consecutive calendar months.
Trading hours	7.20 a.m. – 2.00 p.m. Trading ceases in the expiring contract at 8.00 a.m. on the last trading day.
Price quotation method	In sixty-fourths (1/64) of 1% of a US$100,000 mortgage-backed security futures contract, quoted in US dollars (US$).
Minimum price move (value)	One sixty-fourth (1/64) of a point (US$15.625 per contract).

Daily price limits	Three points above or below the previous day's settlement premium (US$3,000 per contract).
Position limits	None.
Last trading day	At 8.00 p.m. on the last trading day of the underlying futures contract (the Friday preceding the third Wednesday of the contract month). All in-the-money options are automatically exercised at expiry.
Delivery day	The business day following the last trading day.
Initial (Variation) margin	Uncovered short positions pay a margin equal to the premium received plus the greater of: (a) the current initial margin for the underlying futures contract less half the amount by which the option is out-of-the-money; or (b) half the current initial margin for the underlying futures contract.
Spread margin	A wide series of spread, straddle and intra-commodity margin concessions is available. Please contact the exchange or your broker for full details.
Strike price intervals	At intervals of one point (US$1,000 per contract).
Option type	American style (the option may be exercised on any business day up to and including the last trading day).
Method of introduction of new strike prices	Not stated. Please consult the exchange for the current details.
Reuters Monitor (Quote)	N/a.
Telerate page	N/a.

Option on CBOT 1,000-ounce silver futures

Contract size	One CBOT 1,000 ounce silver futures contract of a specified contract month (of an underlying contract size of 1,000 ounces).
Standard delivery method	Delivery of a long or short position in a futures contract of a specified contract month at the strike price as above.
Trading months	The February, April, June, August, October and December cycle. There is no trading in months where there is not an underlying futures contract trading at the CBOT.
Trading hours	7.25 a.m. – 1.25 p.m.
Price quotation method	In multiples of one-tenths (1/10) of a US cent per troy ounce.
Minimum price move (value)	0.10 US cents (US$0.001) per troy ounce (US$1.00 per contract).
Daily price limits	US$1.00 per troy ounce above or below the previous day's settlement premium.
Position limits	None.

Last trading day	The last Friday before the first notice day of the underlying futures contract by at least five business days. The option expires at 10.00 a.m. on the Saturday following the last trading day.
Delivery day	The business day following the last trading day.
Initial (Variation) margin	Uncovered short positions pay a margin equal to the premium received plus the greater of: (a) the current initial margin for the underlying futures contract less half the amount by which the option is out-of-the-money; or (b) half the current initial margin for the underlying futures contract.
Spread margin	A wide series of spread, straddle and intra-commodity margin concessions is available. Please contact the exchange or your broker for full details.
Strike price intervals	Strike prices below US$8.00: US$0.25. Strike prices from US$8.00 to US$20.00: US$0.50. Strike prices over US$20.00: US$1.00.
Option type	American style (the option may be exercised on any business day up to and including the last trading day).
Method of introduction of new strike prices	Not stated.
Reuters Monitor (Quote)	N/a.
Telerate page	N/a.

Option on CBOT soyabean futures

Contract size	One CBOT soyabean futures contract of a specified contract month (of an underlying contract size of 5,000 bushels).
Standard delivery method	Delivery of a long or short position in a futures contract of a specified contract month at the strike price as above.
Trading months	The January, March, May, July, August, September and November cycle.
Trading hours	9.30 a.m. – 1.15 p.m. (trading ceases in the expiring contract at 12.00 noon on the last trading day).
Price quotation method	In US cents and one-eighths (1/8) of a US cent per bushel.
Minimum price move (value)	One eighth (1/8) of a US cent per bushel (US$6.25 per contract).
Daily price limits	30 US cents (US$0.30) per bushel (US$1,500 per contract) above or below the previous day's settlement premium. There are no limits on the spot month.
Position limits	100 contracts on the same side of the market.
Last trading day	The last Friday before the first notice day of the underlying soyabeans futures contract by at least five business days. Unexercised options expire at 10.00 a.m. on the Saturday following the last trading day.

Delivery day	The business day following the last trading day.
Initial (Variation) margin	Uncovered short positions pay a margin equal to the premium received plus the greater of: (a) the current initial margin for the underlying futures contract less half the amount by which the option is out-of-the-money; or (b) half the current initial margin for the underlying futures contract.
Spread margin	A wide series of spread, straddle and intra-commodity margin concessions is available. Please contact the exchange or your broker for full details.
Strike price intervals	At intervals of 25 US cents (US$0.25) per bushel.
Option type	American style (the option may be exercised on any business day up to and including the last trading day).
Method of introduction of new strike prices	There are generally 11 available strike prices around the underlying futures contract price. New series are introduced when the underlying futures contract trades at least halfway above (below) the highest (lowest) currently available strike price and the next strike price due to be introduced. No new strike prices are normally added during the month in which the option expires.
Reuters Monitor (Quote)	SOXG – SOYZ.
Telerate page	N/a.

Option on CBOT soyabean meal futures

Contract size	One CBOT soyabean meal futures contract of a specified contract month (of an underlying contract size of 100 tons).
Standard delivery method	Delivery of a long or short position in a futures contract of a specified contract month at the strike price as above.
Trading months	The January, March, May, July, August, September, October and December cycle.
Trading hours	9.30 a.m. – 1.15 p.m. (trading ceases in the expiring contract at 12.00 noon on the last trading day).
Price quotation method	In US dollars (US$) and cents per ton.
Minimum price move (value)	5 US cents (US$0.05) per ton (US$5.00 per contract).
Daily price limits	US$10.00 per ton (US$1,000 per contract) above or below the previous day's settlement premium. There are no limits on the spot month.
Position limits	200 contracts on the same side of the market.
Last trading day	The last Friday before the first notice day of the underlying soyabeans futures contract by at least five business days. Unexercised options expire at 10.00 a.m. on the Saturday following the last trading day.
Delivery day	The business day following the last trading day.

Initial (Variation) margin	Uncovered short positions pay a margin equal to the premium received plus the greater of: (a) the current initial margin for the underlying futures contract less half the amount by which the option is out-of-the-money; or (b) half the current initial margin for the underlying futures contract.
Spread margin	A wide series of spread, straddle and intra-commodity margin concessions is available. Please contact the exchange or your broker for full details.
Strike price intervals	At US$5.00 per ton intervals when the futures price is less than US$200 per ton, thereafter at intervals of US$10.00 per ton.
Option type	American style (the option may be exercised on any business day up to and including the last trading day).
Method of introduction of new strike prices	There are generally 11 available strikes around the underlying futures contract price. New series are introduced when the underlying futures contract trades at least halfway above (below) the highest (lowest) currently available strike price and the next strike price due to be introduced. No new strike prices are normally added during the month in which the option expires.
Reuters Monitor (Quote)	SYXA – SYYZ.
Telerate page	N/a.

Option on CBOT soyabean oil futures

Contract size	One CBOT soyabean oil futures contract of a specified contract month (of an underlying contract size of 60,000 pounds).
Standard delivery method	Delivery of a long or short position in a futures contract of a specified contract month at the strike price as above.
Trading months	The January, March, May, July, August, September, October and December cycle.
Trading hours	9.30 a.m. – 1.15 p.m. (trading ceases in the expiring contract at 12.00 noon on the last trading day).
Price quotation method	In US cents and one-thousandths (1/1000) of a US cent per pound.
Minimum price move (value)	Five-thousandths (5/1000) of a US cent per pound (US$3.00 per contract).
Daily price limits	One US cent (US$0.01) per pound (US$600 per contract) above or below the previous day's settlement premium. There are no limits on the spot month.
Position limits	200 contracts on the same side of the market.
Last trading day	The last Friday before the first notice day of the underlying soyabeans futures contract by at least five business days. Unexercised options expire at 10.00 a.m. on the Saturday following the last trading day.

Delivery day	The business day following the last trading day.
Initial (Variation) margin	Uncovered short positions pay a margin equal to the premium received plus the greater of: (a) the current initial margin for the underlying futures contract less half the amount by which the option is out-of-the-money; or (b) half the current initial margin for the underlying futures contract.
Spread margin	A wide series of spread, straddle and intra-commodity margin concessions is available. Please contact the exchange or your broker for full details.
Strike price intervals	At one US cent (US$0.01) per pound intervals.
Option type	American style (the option may be exercised on any business day up to and including the last trading day).
Method of introduction of new strike prices	There are generally eleven available strikes around the underlying futures contract price. New series are introduced when the underlying futures contract trades at least halfway above (below) the highest (lowest) currently available strike price and the next strike price due to be introduced. No new strike prices are normally added during the month in which the option expires.
Reuters Monitor (Quote)	SYQU – SYRZ.
Telerate page	N/a.

Option on CBOT US Government Treasury Note futures

Contract size	One CBOT US Government Treasury Note futures contract of a specified contract month (of an underlying contract size of US$100,000 nominal face value).
Standard delivery method	Delivery of a long or short position in a futures contract of a specified contract month at the strike price as above.
Trading months	The March, June, September and December cycle.
Trading hours	7.20 a.m. – 2.00 p.m. Monday to Friday and an evening session 5.00 p.m. – 8.30 p.m. (CST) or 6.00 p.m. – 9.30 p.m. (when on Central Daylight Saving time) Sunday to Thursday.
Price quotation method	In US dollars (US$) in terms of sixty-fourths (1/64) of percent of par.
Minimum price move (value)	One sixty-fourth (1/64) of 1% (US$15.625 per contract).
Daily price limits	Three points above or below the previous day's settlement premium. Limits do not apply during the option's expiry month.
Position limits	A position of 100 or more contracts is reportable.

Last trading day	The last Friday preceding by at least five business days the first notice day for the underlying futures contract. Trading ceases in the expiring contract at 12.00 noon on the last trading day.
Delivery day	The business day following the last trading day. Options expire on the Saturday following the last trading day.
Initial (Variation) margin	Uncovered short positions pay a margin equal to the premium received plus the greater of: (a) the current initial margin for the underlying futures contract less half the amount by which the option is out-of-the-money; or (b) half the current initial margin for the underlying futures contract.
Spread margin	A wide series of spread, straddle and intra-commodity margin concessions is available. Please contact the exchange or your broker for full details.
Strike price intervals	At one point intervals (e.g. 86-00, 87-00, etc.).
Option type	American style (option may be exercised on any business day (up to 8.00 p.m.) up to and including the last trading day). Options that are in-the-money by at least two points are automatically exercised.
Method of introduction of new strike prices	There are generally seven available strike prices around the underlying futures contract price. New series are introduced when a trade occurs at the previous highest or lowest currently available strike price. No new strike prices are normally added during the month in which the option expires.
Reuters Monitor (Quote)	1TNA – 1TNN.
Telerate page	955 – 956.

Option on CBOT US Government Treasury Bond futures

Contract size	One CBOT US Government Treasury Bond futures contract of a specified contract month (of an underlying contract value of US$100,000 nominal face value).
Standard delivery method	Delivery of a long or short position in a futures contract of a specified contract month at the strike price as above.
Trading months	The March, June, September and December cycle.
Trading hours	7.20 a.m. – 2.00 p.m. Monday to Friday and an evening session 5.00 p.m. – 8.30 p.m. (CST) or 6.00 p.m. – 9.30 p.m. (when on Central Daylight Saving time) Sunday to Thursday.
Price quotation method	In US dollars (US$) and cents per sixty-fourths (1/64) per cent of par.

Minimum price move (value)	One sixty-fourth (1/64) of 1% (US$15.625 per contract).
Daily price limits	Three points above or below the previous day's settlement premium. Limits do not apply during the option's expiry month.
Position limits	A position of 100 or more contracts is reportable.
Last trading day	The last Friday preceding by at least five business days the first notice day for the underlying futures contract. Trading ceases in the expiring contract at 12.00 noon on the last trading day.
Delivery day	The business day following the last trading day. Options expire on the Saturday following the last trading day.
Initial (Variation) margin	Uncovered short positions pay a margin equal to the premium received plus the greater of: (a) the current initial margin for the underlying futures contract less half the amount by which the option is out-of-the-money; or (b) half the current initial margin for the underlying futures contract.
Spread margin	A wide series of spread, straddle and intra-commodity margin concessions is available. Please contact the exchange or your broker for full details.
Strike price intervals	At two point intervals (e.g. 96-00, 98-00, etc.).
Option type	American style (option may be exercised on any business day (up to 8.00 p.m.) up to and including the last trading day). Options that are in-the-money by at least two points at expiry are automatically exercised.
Method of introduction of new strike prices	There are generally seven available strike prices around the underlying futures contract price. New series are introduced when a trade occurs at the previous highest or lowest currently available strike price. No new strike prices are normally added during the month in which the option expires.
Reuters Monitor (Quote)	1TBA – 1TBP.
Telerate page	9521 onwards.

Option on CBOT wheat futures

Contract size	One CBOT wheat futures contract of a specified contract month (of an underlying contract size of 5,000 bushels).
Standard delivery method	Delivery of a long or short position in a futures contract of a specified contract month at the strike price as above.
Trading months	The March, May, July, September and December cycle.

Chicago Board of Trade (CBOT)
Options on futures
Softs and agricultural

Trading hours	9.30 a.m. – 1.25 p.m. (trading ceases in the expiring contract at 12.00 noon on the last trading day).
Price quotation method	In US cents and quarters (1/4) of a US cent per bushel.
Minimum price move (value)	One-eighth (1/8) of a US cent per bushel (US$6.25 per contract).
Daily price limits	20 US cents (US$0.20) above or below the previous day's settlement premium (US$1,000 per contract).
Position limits	100 contracts on the same side of the market.
Last trading day	The last Friday preceding the first notice day of the underlying wheat futures contract by at least five business days. Unexercised options expire at 10.00 a.m. on the Saturday following the last trading day.
Delivery day	The business day following the last trading day.
Initial (Variation) margin	Uncovered short positions pay a margin equal to the premium received plus the greater of: (a) the current initial margin for the underlying futures contract less half the amount by which the option is out-of-the-money; or (b) half the current initial margin for the underlying futures contract.
Spread margin	A wide series of spread, straddle and intra-commodity margin concessions is available. Please contact the exchange or your broker for full details.
Strike price intervals	At 10 US cents (US$0.10) per bushel intervals.
Option type	American style (the option may be exercised on any business day up to and including the last trading day).
Method of introduction of new strike prices	Not stated.
Reuters Monitor (Quote)	WHQG – WHQZ.
Telerate page	N/a.

Chicago Board Options Exchange (CBOE)

Address:	La Salle at Van Buren Chicago Illinois 60605 USA
Telephone:	(312) 786 5600
Fax:	(312) 786 7413
Telex:	201203

Exchange personnel

Chairman:	Alger Chapman
President:	Charles Henry
Information Officer:	Warren Moulds

UK Representative Office

Address:	2nd Floor 43 London Wall London EC2 United Kingdom
Telephone:	(01) 374 8253
Fax:	(01) 374 2016
Telex:	N/a.
Contact:	Jonelle Daniels
Managing Director:	Stephen Schoess

Futures contracts available
None

Options contracts on physical/cash available
Five-year US Government Treasury Notes
Long-term (30-year) US Government Treasury Bonds
Long-term US interest rate
S&P 100 Stock Index
S&P 500 Stock Index
Short-term US interest rate

The CBOE also trades over 200 US equity options, each option representing 100 underlying shares of that issue. Trade takes place on the nearest two months and then on the quarterly cycle. Trading hours are 8.30 a.m.–3.15 p.m.

Clearing House:	Options Clearing Corporation (OCC).
Method of trading:	Open outcry.
Commenced trading:	1973.
Exchange links:	Chicago Board of Trade (CBOT).

A brief synopsis of the exchange

The CBOE was formed as the specialist options division of the CBOT in 1973 and although now totally independent, it works closely with the CBOT to develop mutual products.

The CBOE is the world's largest specialist options exchange accounting for roughly half of stock options transactions in the USA and since 1987 has been affiliated to the Cincinatti Stock Exchange. There are over 2,000 memberships (seats) and in addition there is an automatic execution system that handles the smaller orders (under 10 contracts).

The lead contract of the CBOE is the S&P 100 Index option, with a turnover severalfold that of its nearest rival, the Major Market Index option at AMEX. Since the change in contract specifications on the S&P 500 Index options from American style to European style the somewhat lagging volume of trade on this contract has sharply increased.

Possibilities exist that the CBOE will go an international route, commencing with an option on the Japanese TOPIX Index, currently only traded domestically in Tokyo.

Chicago Board
Options Exchange
(CBOE)
Options on
cash/physical
Interest rates

Option on five-year US Government Treasury Notes

Contract size	US$100,000 nominal face value of a specific issue of US Government Treasury Notes with approximately five years to maturity. Generally two or three issues are listed at one time.
Standard delivery method	Physical delivery of the above.
Trading months	The nearest two consecutive calendar months and the next two months from the March, June, September and December cycle.
Trading hours	8.00 a.m. – 2.00 p.m.
Price quotation method	In US dollars (US$) per one thirty-second (1/32) of par.
Minimum price move (value)	One thirty-second (1/32) of a point (US$31.25 per contract).
Daily price limits	None.
Position limits	4,000 contracts when the issue size is greater than US$4 billion.
Last trading day	The third Friday of the contract month.
Delivery day	The business day following the last trading day. The option expires on the Saturday following the third Friday of the contract month.
Initial (Variation) margin	For uncovered short positions, 100% of the option premium received plus 3% of the underlying principal, less any out-of-the-money element, with a minimum of 0.5% of the underlying principal.
Spread margin	Various spread and intra-market margin concessions are available. Please consult the exchange or your broker for full details.
Strike price intervals	At one point intervals, stated in percentage of par.
Option type	American style (the option may be exercised on any business day up to and including the last trading day).
Method of introduction of new strike prices	Set to bracket the current market prices of the individual issues.
Reuters Monitor (Quote)	N/a.
Telerate page	15000.

Option on long-term (30-year) US Government Treasury Bonds

Contract size	US$100,000 nominal face value of a specific issue of US Government Treasury Bonds with approximately 30 years to maturity. Generally three issues will be listed at any one time.
Standard delivery method	Physical delivery of the above.

Trading months	The nearest two months from the March, June, September and December cycle.
Trading hours	8.00 a.m. – 2.00 p.m.
Price quotation method	In US dollars (US$) and cents per one thirty-second (1/32) of par.
Minimum price move (value)	One thirty-second (1/32) of a point (US$31.25 per contract).
Daily price limits	None.
Position limits	None.
Last trading day	The third Friday of the contract month.
Delivery day	The business day following the last trading day. The option expires on the Saturday following the third Friday of the contract month.
Initial (Variation) margin	For naked short positions, 100% of the option premium received plus 3.5% of the underlying principal, less any out-of-the-money element, with a minimum of 0.5% of the underlying principal.
Spread margin	Various spread and intra-market margin concessions are available. Please consult the exchange or your broker for full details.
Strike price intervals	At two point intervals, stated in percentage of par.
Option type	American style (the option may be exercised on any business day up to and including the last trading day).
Method of introduction of new strike prices	Set to bracket the current market prices of the individual issues.
Reuters Monitor (Quote)	N/a.
Telerate page	15000.

Option on long-term interest rate (LTX)

Contract size	US$100 multiplied by 10 times the average yield to maturity of a portfolio of six US Government securities (the two most recently auctioned 7-year, 10-year and 30-year US Treasury issues). For example, if the average yield of these underlying issues were 9.25%, the composite index level would be 92.50.
Standard delivery method	Cash settlement at expiry. There is no facility for physical delivery.
Trading months	Monthly and quarterly from the March, June, September and December cycle.
Trading hours	7.20 a.m. – 2.00 p.m.
Price quotation method	In US dollars (US$) and cents per point and fractions of a point.
Minimum price move (value)	One-sixteenth (1/16) for premiums below US$3.00 (US$6.25 per contract), and one-eighth (1/8) for all higher premiums (US$12.50 per contract).
Daily price limits	None.

Chicago Board
Options Exchange
(CBOE)
Options on
cash/physical
Stock indices

Position limits	25,000 contracts on the same side of the market.
Last trading day	The third Friday of the contract month.
Delivery day	The business day following the last trading day. Options expire on the Saturday following the third Friday of the contract month.
Initial (Variation) margin	For uncovered short positions, 100% of the option premium received plus 3.5% of the underlying principal, less any out-of-the-money element, with a minimum of 0.5% of the underlying principal.
Spread margin	Various spread and intra-market margin concessions are available. Please consult the exchange or your broker for full details.
Strike price intervals	At 2.5 composite point intervals, to bracket the current composite value.
Option type	European style (the option may only be exercised at expiry at the exercise settlement price and not at other times during its life).
Method of introduction of new strike prices	Not stated. Please contact the exchange for full details.
Reuters Monitor (Quote)	N/a.
Telerate page	N/a.

Option on S&P 100 Stock Index (OEX)

Contract size	US$100 multiplied by the Standard & Poors 100 (S&P 100) Stock Index.
Standard delivery method	Cash settlement based on the difference between the closing US dollar value of the index and the strike price on the last trading day. There is no facility for physical delivery of the stocks underlying the index.
Trading months	The nearby (spot) month plus the next three months from the March, June, September and December cycle.
Trading hours	8.30 a.m. – 3.15 p.m.
Price quotation method	In US dollars (US$) and cents per unit of the index.
Minimum price move (value)	One-sixteenth (1/16) of a point for premiums under US$3.00 (US$6.25 per contract) and one-eighth (1/8) of a point for all higher premiums (US$12.50 per contract).
Daily price limits	None.
Position limits	15,000 contracts on either side of the market.
Last trading day	The third Friday of the contract month.
Delivery day	The business day following the last trading day. The options expire on the Saturday following the third Friday of the contract month.

**Chicago Board
Options Exchange
(CBOE)
Options on
cash/physical
Stock indices**

Initial (Variation) margin	For uncovered short positions, 100% of the option premium received plus 5% of the underlying index value, less any out-of-the-money element, with a minimum of 2% of the underlying index value.
Spread margin	Various spread and intra-market margin concessions are available. Please consult the exchange or your broker for full details.
Strike price intervals	At five index point intervals.
Option type	American style (the option may be exercised on any business day up to and including the last trading day).
Method of introduction of new strike prices	New series are introduced when the underlying index approaches the limits of the existing strikes.
Reuters Monitor (Quote)	1SPA – 1SQD.
Telerate page	N/a.

Option on S&P 500 Stock Index (NSX)

Contract size	US$100 multiplied by the Standard & Poors 500 (S&P 500) Stock Index.
Standard delivery method	Cash settlement on the business day following the last trading day (usually a Friday) based on the difference between the opening value of the index on that day and the strike price. There is no facility for physical delivery of the stocks underlying the index.
Trading months	The nearby two months plus the next three months from the March, June, September and December cycle.
Trading hours	8.30 a.m. – 3.15 p.m.
Price quotation method	In US dollars (US$) and cents per unit of the index.
Minimum price move (value)	One full index point (US$100 per contract).
Daily price limits	None.
Position limits	15,000 contracts on either side of the market.
Last trading day	The third Friday of the contract month. The opening price of the S&P 500 Index (after all stocks have opened) is taken as the final settlement level.
Delivery day	The business day following the last trading day. The options expire on the Saturday following the third Friday of the contract month.
Initial (Variation) margin	For uncovered short positions, 100% of the option premium received plus 5% of the underlying index value, less any out-of-the-money element, with a minimum of 2% of the underlying index value.
Spread margin	Various spread and intra-market margin concessions are available. Please consult the exchange or your broker for full details.
Strike price intervals	At five index point intervals.

Chicago Board
Options Exchange
(CBOE)
Options on
cash/physical
Interest rates

Option type	European style (the option may only be exercised at expiry and not at other stages during its life).
Method of introduction of new strike prices	Not stated. Please contact the exchange for full details.
Reuters Monitor (Quote)	SPQA – SPQZ.
Telerate page	N/a.

Option on short-term interest rate (IRX)

Contract size	US$100 multiplied by 10 times the yield (annualised discount rate) on the most recently auctioned 13 week US Government Treasury Bills. For example, if the yield on the 13-week T-Bill were 8.5%, the composite index level would be 85-00.
Standard delivery method	Cash settlement at expiry. There is no facility for physical delivery.
Trading months	Monthly and quarterly from the March, June, September and December cycle.
Trading hours	7.20 a.m. – 2.00 p.m.
Price quotation method	In US dollars (US$) and cents per point and fractions of a point.
Minimum price move (value)	One-sixteenth (1/16) for premiums below US$3.00 (US$6.25 per contract), and one-eighth (1/8) for all higher premiums (US$12.50 per contract).
Daily price limits	None.
Position limits	5,000 contracts on the same side of the market.
Last trading day	The third Friday of the contract month.
Delivery day	The business day following the last trading day. Options expire on the Saturday following the third Friday of the contract month.
Initial (Variation) margin	For uncovered short positions, 100% of the option premium received plus 3.5% of the underlying principal, less any out-of-the-money element, with a minimum of 0.5% of the underlying principal.
Spread margin	Various spread and intra-market margin concessions are available. Please consult the exchange or your broker for full details.
Strike price intervals	At 2.5 composite points, to bracket the current composite value.
Option type	European style (the option may only be exercised at expiry at the exercise settlement price and not at other times during its life).
Method of introduction of new strike prices	Not stated. Please contact the exchange for full details.
Reuters Monitor (Quote)	N/a.
Telerate page	N/a.

Chicago Mercantile Exchange (CME)

incorporating Index and Options Market (IOM) and International Monetary Market (IMM)

Address: 30 South Wacker Drive
Chicago
Illinois 60606
USA

Telephone: (312) 930 1000
Fax: (312) 930 8219
Telex: 255 123

Exchange personnel
Chairman: Leo Melamed
President & CEO: William Brodsky
Information Officer: Andrew Yemma
Marketing Manager: Monica Butler

Japan Representative Office
Address: 3–3–1 Kasumigaseki
Chiyoda-ku
Tokyo 100
Japan

Telephone: (03) 595 2251
Fax: (03) 595 2244
Telex: N/a.
Contact: Takeo Arakawa

London Representative Office
Address: 27 Throgmorton Street
London
EC2N 2AN
United Kingdom

Telephone: (01) 920 0722
Fax: (01) 920 0978
Telex: 892577
Deputy Managing Director: Robin Brown

Address:

New York Representative Office
67 Wall Street
New York
New York 10005
USA

Telephone: (212) 363 7000
Fax: (212) 425 1337
Telex: N/a.
Contact: Ira Kawaller

Washington Representative Office

Address: 2000 Pennsylvania Avenue
Washington
DC 20006
USA

Telephone: (202) 223 6905
Fax: (202) 466 3049
Telex: N/a.

Futures contracts available
Australian dollar / US dollar currency
British pound / US dollar currency
Canadian dollar / US dollar currency
Deutschmark / US dollar currency
ECU / US dollar currency (*dormant*)
Feeder cattle
French franc / US dollar currency
Frozen pork bellies
Japanese yen / US dollar currency
Live cattle
Live hogs
One-month LIBOR (London Interbank Offered Rate)
interest rate (*planned*)
Random-length lumber
S&P 500 Stock Index
Swiss franc / US dollar currency
Three-month Eurodollar time deposit
Three-month Euro-rate differential (US dollar–
Deutschmark)
Three-month Euro-rate differential (US dollar–pound
sterling)
Three-month Euro-rate differential (US dollar–yen)
Three-month (90-day) US Government Treasury Bills

Options contracts on futures available
Australian dollar / US dollar currency futures
British pound / US dollar currency futures

Canadian dollar / US dollar currency futures
Deutschmark / US dollar currency futures
Eurodollar time deposit futures
Feeder cattle futures
Frozen pork bellies futures
Japanese yen / US dollar currency futures
Live cattle futures
Live hogs futures
Random-length lumber futures
S&P 500 Stock Index futures
Swiss franc / US dollar currency futures
US Treasury Bill futures

Clearing House:	Chicago Mercantile Exchange Clearing House.
Method of trading:	Open outcry on exchange floor.
Commenced trading:	1874 (as the Chicago Produce Exchange) and in 1919 as the CME.
Exchange links:	Singapore International Monetary Exchange (SIMEX) – fungible trading link (see below). Marché à terme International de France (MATIF) with regard to the GLOBEX automated trading and execution project.

A brief synopsis of the exchange
The Chicago Mercantile Exchange is the second
largest futures exchange in the world behind the
CBOT, providing international markets for futures and
options in agricultural commodities, foreign currencies,
interest rates and stock indices. Its history traces back
to 1874 as the Chicago Produce Exchange, and to 1898
with the Chicago Butter and Egg Board. These entities
became one in 1919. Its trading floor now occupies
40,000 square feet, and is perhaps one of the most
diversified of all US exchanges.

The CME was the first exchange to offer futures
contracts on financial instruments in 1972 on foreign
currencies, and was also the first exchange to introduce
the concept of cash settlement on its three month
Eurodollar contract in 1981.

A 29-strong Board of Governors produces policy for
the exchange and its divisions, the International
Monetary Market (established in 1972) and the Index
and Options Market (established in 1982), through 50
different committees. The exchange has a staff of over
800, and more than 2,700 traders (who clear through
one of the 80-plus clearing member firms) daily on the
exchange floor which can actually accommodate over
4,500 individuals on a busy day.

The most active contract at the CME is the S&P 500 Stock Index futures which additionally is the world's largest stock index futures contract.

The three divisions of the Chicago Mercantile Exchange are the CME, specialising in agricultural products, the Index and Options Market (IOM), whose role is self-explanatory, and the International Monetary Market (IMM), for all other financially based contracts. These three different forms of membership confer trading rights to the specific divisions of the CME or, in the case of full CME membership, to all contracts.

There are mutual offset facilities with SIMEX in Eurodollar, Deutschmark, Japanese yen and British pound currency futures that allow these contracts to trade in a fungible manner into the Far Eastern time zone.

As well as the CBOT, the CME has filed for permission to trade Japanese products in Chicago. The CME in conjunction with Reuters has nearly completed extensive development into an (initially) pre- and post-hours computerised trading system called GLOBEX. The MATIF is also engaged in this project, although it is the only overseas exchange to remain involved.

Australian dollar / US dollar currency (AD) futures

Contract size	A$100,000 traded against the US dollar (US$).
Standard delivery method	Physical delivery of currencies concerned as above.
Trading months	The nearby (spot) month plus months from the January, March, April, June, July, September, October and December cycle.
Trading hours	7.20 a.m. – 2.00 p.m. (trading ceases in the expiring contract at 9.16 a.m. on the last trading day).
Price quotation method	In US dollars (US$) per Australian dollar (A$).
Minimum price move (value)	US$0.0001 per A$1.00 (US$10.00 per contract).
Daily price limits	The opening limit between 7.20 a.m. and 7.35 a.m. only is 150 points (US$0.015 per A$1.00).
Position limits	None.
Last trading day	The second business day before the third Wednesday of the contract month.
Delivery day	The third Wednesday of the contract month.
Initial (Variation) margin	Hedgers: US$1,000 per contract (US$1,000). Speculators: US$1,375 per contract (US$1,250).
Spread margin	Zero.
Reuters Monitor (Quote)	AD31, AUSD.
Telerate page	N/a.

British pound / US dollar currency (BP) futures

Contract size	£62,500 traded against the US dollar (US$).
Standard delivery method	Physical delivery of currencies concerned as above.
Trading months	The March, June, September, and December cycle.
Trading hours	7.20 a.m. – 2.00 p.m. (trading ceases in the expiring contract at 9.16 a.m. on the last trading day).
Price quotation method	In US dollars (US$) per pounds sterling (£).
Minimum price move (value)	US$0.0002 per £1.00 (US$12.50 per contract)
Daily price limits	The opening limit between 7.20 a.m. and 7.35 a.m. only is 400 points (US$0.04 per £1.00).
Position limits	None.
Last trading day	The second business day before the third Wednesday of the contract month.
Delivery day	The third Wednesday of the contract month.
Initial (Variation) margin	Hedgers: US$2,000 per contract (US$2,000). Speculators: US$2,750 per contract (US$2,500).
Spread margin	Zero.
Reuters Monitor (Quote)	STIE (C$_1$ BP*).
Telerate page	914.

Canadian dollar / US dollar currency (CD) futures

Contract size	C$100,000 traded against the US dollar (US$).
Standard delivery method	Physical delivery of currencies concerned as above.
Trading months	The March, June, September, and December cycle.
Trading hours	7.20 a.m. – 2.00 p.m. (trading ceases in the expiring contract at 9.16 a.m. on the last trading day).
Price quotation method	In US dollars (US$) per Canadian dollar (C$).
Minimum price move (value)	US$0.0001 per C$1.00 (US$10.00 per contract).
Daily price limits	The opening limit between 7.20 a.m. and 7.35 a.m. only is 100 points (US$0.01 per C$1.00).
Position limits	None.
Last trading day	The second business day before the third Wednesday of the contract month.
Delivery day	The third Wednesday of the contract month.
Initial (Variation) margin	Hedgers: US$500 per contract (US$500). Speculators: US$688 per contract (US$625).
Spread margin	Zero.
Reuters Monitor (Quote)	CDIE (C$_1$ CD*).
Telerate page	915.

Deutschmark / US dollar currency futures

Contract size	DM125,000 traded against the US dollar (US$).
Standard delivery method	Physical delivery of currencies concerned as above.
Trading months	The March, June, September, and December cycle.
Trading hours	7.20 a.m. – 2.00 p.m. (trading ceases in the expiring contract at 9.16 a.m. on the last trading day).
Price quotation method	In US dollars (US$) per Deutschmark (DM).
Minimum price move (value)	US$0.0001 per DM1.00 (US$12.50 per contract).
Daily price limits	The opening limit between 7.20 a.m. and 7.35 a.m. only is 150 points (US$0.015 per DM1.00).
Position limits	None.
Last trading day	The second business day before the third Wednesday of the contract month.
Delivery day	The third Wednesday of the contract month.
Initial (Variation) margin	Hedgers: US$1,300 per contract (US$1,300). Speculators: US$1,788 per contract (US$1,625).
Spread margin	Zero.
Reuters Monitor (Quote)	MKIE (C$_1$ DM*).
Telerate page	914.

European Currency Unit/ US dollar currency (EC) futures (*dormant*)

Contract size	ECU125,000 traded against the US dollar (US$).
Standard delivery method	Physical delivery of currencies concerned as above.
Trading months	The March, June, September and December cycle.
Trading hours	7.10 a.m. – 2.00 p.m. (trading ceases in the expiring contract at 9.00 a.m. on the last trading day).
Price quotation method	In US dollars (US$) per European Currency Unit (ECU).
Minimum price move (*value*)	US$0.0001 per ECU1.00 (US$12.50 per contract).
Daily price limits	The opening limit between 7.20 a.m. and 7.35 a.m. only is 150 points (US$0.015 per ECU1.00).
Position limits	None.
Last trading day	The second business day before the third Wednesday of the contract month.
Delivery day	The third Wednesday of the contract month.
Initial (*Variation*) margin	Not stated. Please contact the exchange for full details.
Spread margin	Not stated.
Reuters Monitor (*Quote*)	ECIE.
Telerate page	915.

Feeder cattle (FC) futures

Contract size	44,000 pounds of feeder cattle in 600–800-pound steers.
Standard delivery method	Cash settlement at expiry at the United States Feeder Steer price as calculated by Cattle Fax (there is no facility for physical delivery).
Trading months	The January, March, April, May, August, September, October and November cycle.
Trading hours	9.05 a.m. – 1.00 p.m. (trading ceases in the expiring contract at 12.00 noon on the last trading day).
Price quotation method	In US dollars (US$) and cents per pound.
Minimum price move (*value*)	2.5 US cents (US$0.025) per 100 pounds (US$11.00 per contract).
Daily price limits	1.5 US cents (US$0.015) per pound (US$660 per contract) above or below the previous day's settlement price.
Position limits	None.
Last trading day	The last Thursday of the contract month, subject to special provisions.
Delivery day	The business day following the last trading day.
Initial (*Variation*) margin	US$800 per contract (US$600).
Spread margin	Hedgers: US$600 per spread position (US$600). Speculators: US$863 per spread position (US$750).
Reuters Monitor (*Quote*)	FDIE.
Telerate page	931.

French franc / US dollar currency futures

Contract size	FFr250,000 traded against the US dollar (US$).
Standard delivery method	Physical delivery of currencies concerned as above.
Trading months	The March, June, September, and December cycle.
Trading hours	7.20 a.m. – 2.00 p.m. (trading ceases in the expiring contract at 9.16 a.m. on the last trading day).
Price quotation method	In US dollars (US$) per French franc (FFr).
Minimum price move (value)	US$0.00005 per FF1.00 (US$12.50 per contract).
Daily price limits	The opening limit between 7.20 a.m. and 7.35 a.m. only is 500 points (US$0.005 per FFr1.00).
Position limits	None.
Last trading day	The second business day before the third Wednesday of the contract month.
Delivery day	The third Wednesday of the contract month.
Initial (Variation) margin	Hedgers: US$500 per contract (US$500). Speculators: US$688 per contract (US$625).
Spread margin	Zero.
Reuters Monitor (Quote)	FRIE (C_1 FR*).
Telerate page	915.

Frozen pork bellies (PB) futures

Contract size	40,000 pounds of USDA-inspected, 12–14-pound or 14–16-pound frozen pork bellies.
Standard delivery method	Physical delivery of the above at approved warehouses in Chicago at par, or outside Chicago by arrangement through the exchange.
Trading months	The February, March, May, July and August cycle.
Trading hours	9.10 a.m. – 1.00 p.m. (trading ceases in the expiring contract at 12.00 noon on the last trading day).
Price quotation method	In US dollars (US$) and cents per pound.
Minimum price move (value)	2.5 US cents (US$0.025) per 100 pounds (US$10.00 per contract).
Daily price limits	2 US cents (US$0.02) per pound (US$400 per contract).
Position limits	None.
Last trading day	The business day immediately preceding the last five business days of the contract month.
Delivery day	The first business day following the last trading day. Delivery may be made on any business day during the contract month.
Initial (Variation) margin	US$1,000 per contract (US$700).
Spread margin	Hedgers: US$700 per spread position (US$700). Speculators: US$1,006 per spread position (US$875).
Reuters Monitor (Quote)	PBIE.
Telerate page	931.

Japanese yen / US dollar currency futures

Contract size	Y12,500,000 traded against the US dollar (US$).
Standard delivery method	Physical delivery of currencies concerned as above.
Trading months	The March, June, September, and December cycle.
Trading hours	7.20 a.m. – 2.00 p.m. (trading ceases in the expiring contract at 9.16 a.m. on the last trading day).
Price quotation method	In US dollars (US$) per Japanese yen (Y).
Minimum price move (value)	US$0.000001 per Y1.00 (US$12.50 per contract).
Daily price limits	The opening limit between 7.20 a.m. and 7.35 a.m. only is 150 points (US$0.00015 per Y1.00).
Position limits	None.
Last trading day	The second business day before the third Wednesday of the contract month.
Delivery day	The third Wednesday of the contract month.
Initial (Variation) margin	Hedgers: US$2,000 per contract (US$2,000). Speculators: US$2,750 per contract (US$2,500).
Spread margin	Zero.
Reuters Monitor (Quote)	JYIE (C_1 JY*).
Telerate page	914.

Live cattle (LC) futures

Contract size	40,000 pounds of live cattle (choice grade steers of 1,050 – 1,200 pounds per head average weight).
Standard delivery method	Physical delivery of the above in Sioux City, Omaha, Joliet, Greeley, Dodge City or Amarillo at par.
Trading months	The February, April, June, August, September, October and December cycle.
Trading hours	9.05 a.m. – 1.00 p.m. (trading ceases in the expiring contract at 12.00 noon on the last trading day).
Price quotation method	In US dollars (US$) and cents per pound.
Minimum price move (value)	2.5 US cents (US$0.025) per 100 pounds (US$10.00 per contract).
Daily price limits	1.5 US cents (US$0.015) per pound (US$600 per contract) above or below the previous day's closing level.
Position limits	None.
Last trading day	The 20th calendar day of the contract month or the previous business day if the 20th is not a business day, subject to special provisions.
Delivery day	The first business day following the last trading day, subject to special provisions. Delivery may take place on any business day during the contract month except the day preceding a holiday.
Initial (Variation) margin	US$800 per contract (US$600).
Spread margin	Hedgers: US$600 per spread position (US$600). Speculators: US$863 per spread position (US$750).
Reuters Monitor (Quote)	LCIE.
Telerate page	931.

Live hogs (LH) futures

Contract size	30,000 pounds of USDA No.1, No.2 or No.3 grade barrows and gilts of 210–240 pounds per head average weight of live hogs.
Standard delivery method	Physical delivery of the above at Peoria at par or other delivery points at various discounts.
Trading months	The February, April, June, August, September, October and December cycle.
Trading hours	9.10 a.m. – 1.00 p.m. (trading ceases in the expiring contract at 12.00 noon on the last trading day).
Price quotation method	In US dollars (US$) and cents per pound.
Minimum price move (value)	2.5 US cents (US$0.025) per 100 pounds (US$7.50 per contract).
Daily price limits	1.5 US cents (US$0.015) per pound (US$450 per contract) above or below the previous day's settlement price.
Position limits	None.
Last trading day	The 20th calendar day of the contract month or the immediately preceding business day if the 20th is not a business day, subject to special provisions.
Delivery day	The first business day following the last trading day, subject to special provisions. Delivery may take place on any business day of the contract month, except Fridays or any day preceding a holiday.
Initial (Variation) margin	US$600 per contract (US$400).
Spread margin	Hedgers: US$400 per spread position (US$400). Speculators: US$575 per spread position (US$500).
Reuters Monitor (Quote)	LHIE.
Telerate page	931.

One-month LIBOR (London Interbank Offered Rate) interest rate futures (*planned*)

Contract size	US$3,000,000 nominal value.
Standard delivery method	Cash settlement at expiry. There is no facility for physical delivery.
Trading months	The six nearby consecutive calendar months plus months from the March, June, September and December cycle.
Trading hours	7.20 a.m. – 2.00 p.m. Trading in the expiring contract ceases at 3.30 p.m. on the last trading day.
Price quotation method	100.00 minus the annualised yield calculated to two decimal places and quoted in US dollars (US$).
Minimum price move (value)	0.01% per annum of nominal face value (US$25.00 per contract).

Daily price limits	None.
Position limits	None.
Last trading day	Two business days before the third Wednesday of the contract month.
Delivery day	The business day following the last trading day.
Initial (Variation) margin	Not available yet.
Spread margin	Not available yet.
Reuters Monitor (Quote)	Not available yet.
Telerate page	Not available yet.

Random-length lumber (LB) futures

Contract size	150,000 board feet of random length (8–20 feet) lumber.
Standard delivery method	Physical delivery of the above (construction or standard grades No.1 or No.2 or better) of alpine fir, Engleman spruce, hem fir, Lodgepole pine and/or Spruce pine fir, manufactured from mills in California, Idaho, Montana, Nevada, Oregon, Washington or Wyoming in the USA or British Columbia or Alberta in Canada.
Trading months	The January, March, May, July, September and November cycle.
Trading hours	9.00 a.m. – 1.05 p.m. (trading ceases in the expiring contract at 12.05 p.m. on the last trading day).
Price quotation method	In US dollars (US$) and cents per thousand board feet (MBF).
Minimum price move (value)	10 US cents (US$0.10) per MBF (US$15.00 per contract).
Daily price limits	US$5.00 per MBF above or below the previous day's settlement price (there is no price limit on the nearby (spot) month.
Position limits	None.
Last trading day	The business day immediately preceding the 16th calendar day of the contract month.
Delivery day	Any business day after the last trading day up to and including the last business day of the month.
Initial (Variation) margin	US$800 per contract (US$600).
Spread margin	Hedgers: US$600 per spread position (US$600). Speculators: US$803 per spread position (US$750).
Reuters Monitor (Quote)	LUIE.
Telerate page	N/a.

Standard & Poors 500 Stock Index (SP) futures

Contract size	US$500 multiplied by the Standard & Poors 500 (S&P 500) Stock Index.
Standard delivery method	Cash settlement based on a special opening quotation on the Friday following the last trading day (there is no facility for physical delivery of the stocks underlying the index).
Trading months	The March, June, September and December cycle.
Trading hours	8.30 a.m. – 3.15 p.m.
Price quotation method	In US dollars (US$) and cents per index point.
Minimum price move (value)	0.05 index points (US$25.00 per contract).
Daily price limits	1. Five index point opening SHOCK ABSORBER limit from previous night's settlement price – limit applies for 10 minutes. 2. 20 index point SHOCK ABSORBER limit during the day – limit applies for one hour (if this limit is hit after 1.30 pm, it will remain in force for the rest of that day). 3. 30 index point CIRCUIT BREAKER limit following the one-hour period elapsing if the DJIA falls 250 points – remains in force for the rest of that day. For further details consult the CME Special Executive Report.
Position limits	5,000 contracts on the same side of the market.
Last trading day	The Thursday prior to the third Friday of the contract month.
Delivery day	The business day following the last trading day.
Initial (Variation) margin	Approximately 5% of the underlying value of the contract. Hedgers: US$6,000 per contract (US$6,000). Speculators: US$12,000 per contract (US$6,000).
Spread margin	US$200 per spread position (US$200). Various intra-market straddle concessions are also available (please contact the exchange or your broker for full details).
Reuters Monitor (Quote)	SPIE (C_1 SP*).
Telerate page	909.

Swiss franc / US dollar currency futures

Contract size	SFr125,000 traded against the US dollar (US$).
Standard delivery method	Physical delivery of currencies concerned as above.
Trading months	The March, June, September and December cycle.
Trading hours	7.20 a.m. – 2.00 p.m. (trading ceases in the expiring contract at 9.16 a.m. on the last trading day).

Price quotation method	In US dollars (US$) per Swiss franc (SFr).
Minimum price move (value)	US$0.0001 per SFr1.00 (US$12.50 per contract).
Daily price limits	The opening limit between 7.20 a.m. and 7 35 a.m. only is 150 points (US$0.015 per SFr1.00).
Position limits	None.
Last trading day	The second business day before the third Wednesday of the contract month.
Delivery day	The third Wednesday of the contract month.
Initial (Variation) margin	Hedgers: US$1,500 per contract (US$1,500).
	Speculators: US$2,063 per contract (US$1,875).
Spread margin	Zero.
Reuters Monitor (Quote)	SWIE (C₁ SF*).
Telerate page	914.

Three-month Eurodollar time deposit futures

Contract size	US$1,000,000 nominal face value.
Standard delivery method	Cash settlement on the last trading day (there is no facility for physical delivery).
Trading months	The March, June, September and December cycle.
Trading hours	7.20 a.m. – 2.00 p.m. (trading ceases in the expiring contract at 9.30 a.m. on the last trading day).
Price quotation method	In US dollars (US$) per cent of par.
Minimum price move (value)	0.01% per annum of nominal face value (US$25.00 per contract).
Daily price limits	None.
Position limits	None.
Last trading day	The second London business day before the third Wednesday of the contract month.
Delivery day	The business day following the last trading day.
Initial (Variation) margin	Hedgers: US$1,000 per contract (US$1,000).
	Speculators: US$1,400 per contract position (US$1,000).
Spread margin	US$200 per spread position (US$200). Various intra-market straddle concessions are also available (please contact the exchange or your broker for full details).
Reuters Monitor (Quote)	EDIE.
Telerate page	910.

Similar futures contracts are traded in London and Singapore.

Three month Euro-rate differential (US dollar–Deutschmark) futures

Contract size	US$1,000,000 nominal face value.
Standard delivery method	Cash settlement at expiry (there is no facility for physical delivery).
Trading months	The nearby (spot) month plus months from the March, June, September and December cycle.
Trading hours	7.20 a.m. – 2.00 p.m. (trading ceases in the expiring contract at 9.30 a.m. on the last trading day).
Price quotation method	100.00 minus the Eurodollar / Euro-Deutschmark interest-rate differential (100.00 − [E$% − EDM%]).
Minimum price move (value)	0.01% of nominal face value (US$25.00 per contract).
Daily price limits	None.
Position limits	None.
Last trading day	The second London business day prior to the third Wednesday of the contract month.
Delivery day	The business day following the last trading day.
Initial (Variation) margin	Hedgers: US$380 per contract (US$380). Speculators: US$523 per contract (US$475).
Spread margin	Various concessions are available for intra-commodity spreads (against currency futures, Eurodollar futures, etc.).

Reuters Monitor (Quote)		
	Eurodollar deposit rates:	DEPO.
	DM deposit and forward rates:	FWDT.
	LIFFE Euro-mark deposit futures:	LFEA.
	MATIF Euro-mark deposit futures:	EDMF.
	Futures:	DDQE.
Telerate page	Eurodollar rates:	270.
	Euro-mark rates:	272.
	LIFFE Euro-mark futures:	997.

Three-month Euro-rate differential (US dollar–pound sterling) futures

Contract size	US$1,000,000 nominal face value.
Standard delivery method	Cash settlement at expiry (there is no facility for physical delivery).
Trading months	The nearby (spot) month plus months from the March, June, September and December cycle.
Trading hours	7.20 a.m. – 2.00 p.m. (trading ceases in the expiring contract at 9.30 a.m. on the last trading day).
Price quotation method	100.00 minus the Eurodollar / Euro-sterling interest rate differential (100.00 − [E$% − E£%]).
Minimum price move (value)	0.01% of nominal face value (US$25.00 per contract).

Daily price limits	None.
Position limits	None.
Last trading day	The second London business day prior to the third Wednesday of the contract month.
Delivery day	The business day following the last trading day.
Initial (Variation) margin	Hedgers: US$750 per contract (US$750). Speculators: US$1,032 per contract (US$938).
Spread margin	Various concessions are available for intra-commodity spreads (against currency futures, Eurodollar futures, etc.).
Reuters Monitor (Quote)	Eurodollar deposit rates: DEPO. Sterling deposit and forwards: FWDW. LIFFE Euro-sterling deposit futures: LIIA. Futures: DPQE.
Telerate page	Eurodollar rates: 270. Euro-sterling rates: 271.

Three-month Euro-rate differential (US dollar–Japanese yen) futures

Contract size	US$1,000,000 nominal face value.
Standard delivery method	Cash settlement at expiry (there is no facility for physical delivery).
Trading months	The spot month plus months from the March, June, September and December cycle.
Trading hours	7.20 a.m. – 2.00 p.m. (trading ceases in the expiring contract at 9.30 a.m. on the last trading day).
Price quotation method	100.00 minus the Eurodollar / Euro-yen interest rate differential ($100.00 - [E\$\% - EY\%]$).
Minimum price move (value)	0.01% of nominal face value (US$25.00 per contract).
Daily price limits	None.
Position limits	None.
Last trading day	The second London business day prior to the third Wednesday of the contract month.
Delivery day	The business day following the last trading day.
Initial (Variation) margin	Hedgers: US$500 per contract (US$500). Speculators: US$688 per contract (US$625).
Spread margin	Various concessions are available for intra-commodity spreads (against currency futures, Eurodollar futures, etc.).
Reuters Monitor (Quote)	Eurodollar deposit rates: DEPO. Yen deposit and forward rates: FWDU. Futures: DYQE.
Telerate page	Eurodollar Rates: 270. Euro-Yen Rates: 273.

Three-month (90-day) US Government Treasury Bills futures

Contract size	US$1,000,000 nominal face value.
Standard delivery method	Physical delivery of 90-day US Government Treasury Bills.
Trading months	The March, June, September and December cycle.
Trading hours	7.20 a.m. – 2.00 p.m. (trading ceases in the expiring contract at 10.00 a.m. on the last trading day).
Price quotation method	In US dollars (US$) per cent of par.
Minimum price move (value)	0.01% of nominal face value (US$25.00 per contract).
Daily price limits	None.
Position limits	None.
Last trading day	The business day prior to the issue date of 13-week (90-day) US Government Treasury Bills.
Delivery day	Three successive days, beginning on the business day following the last trading day.
Initial (Variation) margin	Hedgers: US$500 per contract (US$500). Speculators: US$675 per spread position (US$500).
Spread margin	US$213 per spread position (US$150). Various intra-market straddle concessions are also available (please contact the exchange or your broker for full details).
Reuters Monitor (Quote)	TIIE (C_3 TB*).
Telerate page	910.

Option on CME Australian dollar / US dollar currency futures

Contract size	One CME Australian dollar / US dollar futures contract (of an underlying contract size of A$100,000 traded against the US dollar (US$)).
Standard delivery method	Delivery of a long or short position in a futures contract at the strike price as above.
Trading months	All consecutive calendar months – for options that expire in months other than the March, June, September and December (MJSD) quarterly cycle, the underlying futures contract is the next in the MJSD quarterly cycle.
Trading hours	7.20 a.m. – 2.00 p.m. (options expire at 5.00 p.m. on the last trading day).
Price quotation method	In US dollars (US$) per Australian dollar (A$).
Minimum price move (value)	US$0.0001 per A$1.00 (US$10.00 per contract).
Daily price limits	The option ceases trading when the underlying futures contract hits its limit.
Position limits	None.
Last trading day	The second Friday prior to the third Wednesday of the contract month.

Delivery day	The business day following the day of exercise or the last trading day.
Initial (Variation) margin	The minimum margin for uncovered short positions is the premium received plus US$400 per contract.
Spread margin	Not stated.
Strike price intervals	At US$0.01 per A$1.00 intervals (e.g. US$0.70, US$0.71, etc.).
Option type	American style (the option may be exercised up to 7.00 p.m. on any business day up to and including the last trading day – there is no automatic exercise of in-the-money options).
Method of introduction of new strike prices	New series are added when the underlying futures price touches within half a strike price interval of either the second highest or second lowest strike price. No new series are normally introduced in the last 20 calendar days before expiry.
Reuters Monitor (Quote)	ADVA – ADVL.
Telerate page	N/a.

Option on CME British pound / US dollar currency futures

Contract size	One CME British pound / US dollar futures contract (of an underlying contract size of £62,500 traded against the US dollar (US$)).
Standard delivery method	Delivery of a long or short position in a futures contract at the strike price as above.
Trading months	All consecutive calendar months – for options that expire in months other than the March, June, September and December (MJSD) quarterly cycle, the underlying futures contract is the next in the MJSD quarterly cycle.
Trading hours	7.20 a.m. – 2.00 p.m. (options expire at 5.00 p.m. on the last trading day).
Price quotation method	In US dollars (US$) per pounds sterling (£).
Minimum price move (value)	US$0.0002 per £1.00 (US$12.50 per contract).
Daily price limits	The option ceases trading when the underlying futures contract hits its limit.
Position limits	None.
Last trading day	The second Friday prior to the third Wednesday of the contract month.
Delivery day	The business day following the day of exercise or the last trading day.
Initial (Variation) margin	The minimum margin for uncovered short positions is the premium received plus US$400 per contract.
Spread margin	Not stated.

Strike price intervals	At US$0.025 per £1.00 intervals (e.g. US$1.4500, US$1.4750, etc.).
Option type	American style (the option may be exercised up to 7.00 p.m. on any business day up to and including the last trading day – there is no automatic exercise of in-the-money options).
Method of introduction of new strike prices	New series are added when the underlying futures price touches within half a strike price interval of either the second highest or second lowest strike price. No new series are normally introduced in the last 20 calendar days before expiry.
Reuters Monitor (Quote)	1STA – 1STZ.
Telerate page	960 – 962.

Option on CME Canadian dollar / US dollar currency futures

Contract size	One CME Canadian dollar / US dollar futures contract (of an underlying contract size of C$100,000 traded against the US dollar (US$)).
Standard delivery method	Delivery of a long or short position in a futures contract at the strike price as above.
Trading months	All consecutive calendar months – for options that expire in months other than the March, June, September and December (MJSD) quarterly cycle, the underlying futures contract is the next in the MJSD quarterly cycle.
Trading hours	7.20 a.m. – 2.00 p.m. (options expire at 5.00 p.m. on the last trading day).
Price quotation method	In US dollars (US$) per Canadian dollar (C$).
Minimum price move (value)	US$0.0001 per C$1.00 (US$10.00 per contract).
Daily price limits	The option ceases trading when the underlying futures contract hits its limit.
Position limits	None.
Last trading day	The second Friday prior to the third Wednesday of the contract month.
Delivery day	The business day following the day of exercise or the last trading day.
Initial (Variation) margin	The minimum margin for uncovered short positions is the premium received plus US$125.
Spread margin	Not stated.
Strike price intervals	At US$0.005 per C$1.00 intervals (e.g. US$0.7000, US$0.7050, etc.).
Option type	American style (the option may be exercised up to 7.00 p.m. on any business day up to and including the last trading day – there is no automatic exercise of in-the-money options).

Method of introduction of new strike prices	New series are added when the underlying futures price touches within half a strike price interval of either the second highest or second lowest strike price. No new series are normally introduced in the last 20 calendar days before expiry.
Reuters Monitor (Quote)	CDIF – CDJK.
Telerate page	N/a.

Option on CME Deutschmark / US dollar currency futures

Contract size	One CME Deutschmark / US dollar futures contract (of an underlying contract size of DM125,000 traded against the US dollar (US$)).
Standard delivery method	Delivery of a long or short position in a futures contract at the strike price as above.
Trading months	All consecutive calendar months – for options that expire in months other than the March, June, September and December (MJSD) quarterly cycle, the underlying futures contract is the next in the MJSD quarterly cycle.
Trading hours	7.20 a.m. – 2.00 p.m. (options expire at 5.00 p.m. on the last trading day).
Price quotation method	In US dollars (US$) per Deutschmark (DM).
Minimum price move (value)	US$0.0001 per DM1.00 (US$12.50 per contract).
Daily price limits	The option ceases trading when the underlying futures contract hits its limit.
Position limits	None.
Last trading day	The second Friday prior to the third Wednesday of the contract month.
Delivery day	The business day following the day of exercise or the last trading day.
Initial (Variation) margin	The minimum margin for uncovered short positions is the premium received plus US$350.
Spread margin	Not stated.
Strike price intervals	At US$0.01 per DM1.00 intervals (eg. US$0.40, US$0.41, etc.).
Option type	American style (the option may be exercised up to 7.00 p.m. on any business day up to and including the last trading day – there is no automatic exercise of in-the-money options).
Method of introduction of new strike prices	New series are added when the underlying futures price touches within half a strike price interval of either the second highest or second lowest strike price. No new series are normally introduced in the last 20 calendar days before expiry.
Reuters Monitor (Quote)	1DMA – 1DMX.
Telerate page	957 – 959.

Option on CME Eurodollar time deposit futures

Contract size	One CME Eurodollar time deposit futures contract (of an underlying contract size of US$1,000,000 nominal face value).
Standard delivery method	Delivery of a long or short position in a futures contract at the strike price as above.
Trading months	The March, June, September and December cycle up to two years forward.
Trading hours	7.20 a.m. – 2.00 p.m. (trading ceases in the expiring contract at 9.30 a.m. on the last trading day).
Price quotation method	In US dollars (US$) and cents per percentage point.
Minimum price move (value)	0.01% per annum of nominal value (US$25.00 per contract).
Daily price limits	None.
Position limits	None.
Last trading day	The second London business day before the third Wednesday of the contract month.
Delivery day	The business day following the last trading day.
Initial (Variation) margin	The minimum margin for uncovered short positions is the premium received plus US$175.
Spread margin	Various spread concessions are available. Please consult the exchange or your broker for full details.
Strike price intervals	At 0.25 point intervals for strike prices over 88-00 (e.g. 88-00, 88-25, etc.) and at 0.50 point intervals below 88-00.
Option type	American style (the option may be exercised up to 7.00 p.m. on any business day up to and including the last trading day).
Method of introduction of new strike prices	New series are added when the underlying futures price touches within half a strike price interval of either the second highest or second lowest strike price. No new series are normally introduced in the last 20 calendar days before expiry.
Reuters Monitor (Quote)	EDYA – EDZZ.
Telerate page	9233 – 9240.

A similar contract is traded on LIFFE.

Option on CME feeder cattle futures

Contract size	One CME feeder cattle futures contract (of an underlying contract size of 44,000 pounds).
Standard delivery method	Delivery of a long or short position in a futures contract at the strike price as above.
Trading months	The January, March, April, May, August, September, October and November cycle.

Trading hours	9.05 a.m. – 1.00 p.m. (trading ceases in the expiring contract at 12.00 noon on the last trading day).
Price quotation method	In US dollars (US$) and cents per 100 pounds.
Minimum price move (value)	2.5 US cents (US$0.025) per 100 pounds (US$11.00 per contract).
Daily price limits	None.
Position limits	None.
Last trading day	The last Thursday of the contract month or the immediately preceding business day if that Thursday is not a business day, subject to special provisions.
Delivery day	The business day following the last trading day.
Initial (Variation) margin	The minimum margin for uncovered short positions is the premium received plus US$150.
Spread margin	Not stated.
Strike price intervals	At US$0.02 (2 US cents) per pound intervals (e.g. US$0.60, US$0.62, etc.).
Option type	American style (the option may be exercised up to 7.00 p.m. on any business day up to and including the last trading day). All in-the-money options are automatically exercised at expiry.
Method of introduction of new strike prices	New series are added when the underlying futures price touches within half a strike price interval of either the second highest or second lowest strike price. No new series are normally introduced in the last 20 calendar days before expiry.
Reuters Monitor (Quote)	FCIG – FCIX.
Telerate page	N/a.

Option on CME frozen pork bellies futures

Contract size	One CME frozen pork bellies futures contract (of an underlying contract size of 40,000 pounds).
Standard delivery method	Delivery of a long or short position in a futures contract at the strike price as above.
Trading months	The February, March, May, July and August cycle.
Trading hours	9.10 a.m. – 1.00 p.m.
Price quotation method	In US dollars (US$) and cents per 100 pounds.
Minimum price move (value)	2.5 US cents (US$0.025) per 100 pounds (US$10.00 per contract).
Daily price limits	None.
Position limits	None.
Last trading day	The last Friday that is more than three business days prior to the first business day of the underlying futures' contract month, or the immediately preceding business day if that Friday is not a business day.
Delivery day	The business day following the last trading day.

Initial (Variation) margin	The minimum margin for uncovered short positions is the premium received plus US$300 per contract.
Spread margin	Not stated.
Strike price intervals	At US$0.02 (2 US cents) per pound intervals (e.g. US$0.60, US$0.62, etc.).
Option type	American style (the option may be exercised up to 7.00 p.m. on any business day up to and including the last trading day).
Method of introduction of new strike prices	New series are added when the underlying futures price touches within half a strike price interval of either the second highest or second lowest strike price. No new series are normally introduced in the last 20 calendar days before expiry.
Reuters Monitor (Quote)	PBIG – PBIH.
Telerate page	N/a.

Option on CME Japanese yen / US dollar currency futures

Contract size	One CME Japanese yen / US dollar futures contract (of an underlying contract size of Y12,500,000 traded against the US dollar (US$)).
Standard delivery method	Delivery of a long or short position in a futures contract at the strike price as above.
Trading months	All consecutive calendar months – for options that expire in months other than the March, June, September and December (MJSD) quarterly cycle, the underlying futures contract is the next in the MJSD quarterly cycle.
Trading hours	7.20 a.m. – 2.00 p.m. (options expire at 5.00 p.m. on the last trading day).
Price quotation method	In US dollars (US$) per Japanese yen (Y).
Minimum price move (value)	US$0.000001 per Y1.00 (US$12.50 per contract).
Daily price limits	The option ceases trading when the underlying futures contract hits its limit.
Position limits	None.
Last trading day	The second Friday prior to the third Wednesday of the contract month.
Delivery day	The business day following the day of exercise or the last trading day.
Initial (Variation) margin	The minimum margin for uncovered short positions is the premium received plus US$400 per contract.
Spread margin	Not stated.
Strike price intervals	At US$0.0001 per Y1.00 intervals (e.g. US$0.0042, US$0.0043, etc.).

Option type	American style (the option may be exercised up to 7.00 p.m. on any business day up to and including the last trading day – there is no automatic exercise of in-the-money options).
Method of introduction of new strike prices	New series are added when the underlying futures price touches within half a strike price interval of either the second highest or second lowest strike price. No new series are normally introduced in the last 20 calendar days before expiry.
Reuters Monitor (Quote)	1JYA – 1JYZ.
Telerate page	9229 – 9231.

Option on CME live cattle futures

Contract size	One CME live cattle futures contract (of an underlying contract size of 40,000 pounds).
Standard delivery method	Delivery of a long or short position in a futures contract at the strike price as above.
Trading months	The February, April, June, August, September, October and December cycle.
Trading hours	9.05 a.m. – 1.00 p.m.
Price quotation method	In US dollars (US$) and cents per 100 pounds.
Minimum price move (value)	2.5 US cents (US$0.025) per 100 pounds (US$10.00 per contract).
Daily price limits	None.
Position limits	None.
Last trading day	The last Friday that is more than three business days prior to the last business day of the contract month or the immediately preceding business day if that Friday is not a business day.
Delivery day	The business day following the last trading day.
Initial (Variation) margin	The minimum margin for uncovered short positions is the premium received plus US$200 per contract.
Spread margin	Not stated.
Strike price intervals	At US$0.02 (2 US cents) per pound intervals (e.g. US$0.60, US$0.62, etc.).
Option type	American style (the option may be exercised up to 7.00 p.m. on any business day up to and including the last trading day).
Method of introduction of new strike prices	New series are added when the underlying futures price touches within half a strike price interval of either the second highest or second lowest strike price. No new series are normally introduced in the last 20 calendar days before expiry.
Reuters Monitor (Quote)	LCIG – LCIX.
Telerate page	N/a.

Option on CME live hogs futures

Contract size	One CME live hogs futures contract (of an underlying contract size of 30,000 pounds).
Standard delivery method	Delivery of a long or short position in a futures contract at the strike price as above.
Trading months	The February, April, June, July, August, October and December cycle.
Trading hours	9.10 a.m. – 1.00 p.m.
Price quotation method	In US dollars (US$) and cents per 100 pounds.
Minimum price move (value)	2.5 US cents (US$0.025) per 100 pounds (US$7.50 per contract).
Daily price limits	None.
Position limits	None.
Last trading day	The last Friday that is more than three business days prior to the last business day of the contract month, or the immediately preceding business day if that Friday is not a business day.
Delivery day	The business day following the last trading day.
Initial (Variation) margin	The minimum margin for uncovered short positions is the premium received plus US$200 per contract.
Spread margin	Not stated.
Strike price intervals	At US$0.02 (2 US cents) per pound intervals (e.g. US$0.60, US$0.62, etc.).
Option type	American style (the option may be exercised up to 7.00 p.m. on any business day up to and including the last trading day).
Method of introduction of new strike prices	New series are added when the underlying futures price touches within half a strike price interval of either the second highest or second lowest strike price. No new series are normally introduced in the last 20 calendar days before expiry.
Reuters Monitor (Quote)	LHIG – LHIX.
Telerate page	N/a.

Option on CME random-length lumber futures

Contract size	One CME random length lumber futures contract (of an underlying contract size of 150,000 board feet).
Standard delivery method	Delivery of a long or short position in a futures contract at the strike price as above.
Trading months	The January, March, May, July, September and November cycle.
Trading hours	9.00 a.m. – 1.05 p.m.

Price quotation method	In US cents per thousand board feet (MBF).
Minimum price move (*value*)	10 US cents (US$0.10) per MBF (US$15.00 per contract).
Daily price limits	None.
Position limits	None.
Last trading day	The last Friday not immediately preceding a holiday in the month prior to the underlying futures' contract month or the immediately preceding day if that Friday is not a business day, subject to special provisions.
Delivery day	The business day following the last trading day.
Initial (Variation) margin	The minimum margin for uncovered short positions is the premium received plus US$125.
Spread margin	Not stated.
Strike price intervals	At US$5.00 per MBF intervals (e.g. US$160, US$165, etc.).
Option type	American style (the option may be exercised up to 7.00 p.m. on any business day up to and including the last trading day).
Method of introduction of new strike prices	New series are added when the underlying futures price touches within half a strike price interval of either the second highest or second lowest strike price. No new series are normally introduced in the last 20 calendar days before expiry.
Reuters Monitor (Quote)	LUIG – LUIH.
Telerate page	N/a.

Option on CME Standard & Poors 500 Stock Index futures

Contract size	One CME S&P 500 Stock Index futures contract (of an underlying contract size of US$500 multiplied by the underlying index).
Standard delivery method	Delivery of a long or short position in a futures contract at the strike price as above.
Trading months	The March, June, September and December cycle, and all other consecutive calendar months – for options that expire in months other than the March, June, September and December (MJSD) quarterly cycle, the underlying futures contract is the next in the MJSD quarterly cycle.
Trading hours	8.30 a.m. – 3.15 p.m.
Price quotation method	In US dollars (US$) and cents per index point.
Minimum price move (*value*)	0.05 index points (US$25.00 per contract).
Daily price limits	As per those series of limits for the underlying futures contract (including shock absorbers and circuit breakers). For full details please consult the CME Special Executive Report #S-2033.

Position limits	None.
Last trading day	For the MJSD quarterly cycle – the business day prior to the third Friday of the contract month. For all other contract months, the third Friday of the contract month.
Delivery day	The business day following the last trading day.
Initial (Variation) margin	The minimum margin for uncovered short positions is the premium received plus US$900 per contract.
Spread margin	Various spread concessions are available. Please consult the exchange or your broker for full details.
Strike price intervals	At 5.0 index point intervals.
Option type	American style (the option may be exercised up to 7.00 p.m. on any business day up to and including the last trading day). For the MJSD quarterly expiry only, all in-the-money options are automatically exercised at expiry.
Method of introduction of new strike prices	New series are added when the underlying futures price touches within half a strike price interval of either the second highest or second lowest strike price. No new series are normally introduced in the last 20 calendar days before expiry.
Reuters Monitor (Quote)	1SYA – 1SYZ.
Telerate page	N/a.

Option on CME Swiss franc / US dollar currency futures

Contract size	One CME Swiss franc / US dollar futures contract (of an underlying contract size of SFr125,000 traded against the US dollar (US$)).
Standard delivery method	Delivery of a long or short position in a futures contract at the strike price as above.
Trading months	All consecutive calendar months – for options that expire in months other than the March, June, September and December (MJSD) quarterly cycle, the underlying futures contract is the next in the MJSD quarterly cycle.
Trading hours	7.20 a.m. – 2.00 p.m. (options expire at 5.00 p.m. on the last trading day).
Price quotation method	In US dollars (US$) per Swiss franc (SFr).
Minimum price move (value)	US$0.0001 per SFr1.00 (US$12.50 per contract).
Daily price limits	The option ceases trading when the underlying futures contract hits its limit.
Position limits	None.
Last trading day	The second Friday prior to the third Wednesday of the contract month.

Delivery day	The business day following the day of exercise or the last trading day.
Initial (Variation) margin	The minimum margin for uncovered short positions is the premium received plus US$400 per contract.
Spread margin	Not stated.
Strike price intervals	At US$0.01 per SFr1.00 intervals (e.g. US$0.45, US$0.46, etc.).
Option type	American style (the option may be exercised up to 7.00 p.m. on any business day up to and including the last trading day – there is no automatic exercise of in-the-money options).
Method of introduction of new strike prices	New series are added when the underlying futures price touches within half a strike price interval of either the second highest or second lowest strike price. No new series are normally introduced in the last 20 calendar days before expiry.
Reuters Monitor (Quote)	1SFA – 1SFZ.
Telerate page	900 – 902.

Option on CME US Treasury Bill futures

Contract size	One CME US Treasury Bill futures contract (of an underlying contract size of US$1,000,000 nominal face value).
Standard delivery method	Delivery of a long or short position in a futures contract at the strike price as above.
Trading months	The March, June, September and December cycle.
Trading hours	7.20 a.m. – 2.00 p.m.
Price quotation method	In US dollars (US$) and cents per point.
Minimum price move (value)	0.01% of nominal face value (US$25.00 per contract).
Daily price limits	None.
Position limits	None.
Last trading day	The last business day of the week which is at least six business days prior to the first business day of the contract month.
Delivery day	The business day following the last trading day.
Initial (Variation) margin	The minimum margin for uncovered short positions is the premium received plus US$175.
Spread margin	Various spread concessions are available. Please consult the exchange or your broker for full details.
Strike price intervals	At 0.25 point intervals for strike prices over 91-00 (e.g. 98-00, 98-25, etc.) and at 0.50 point intervals for lower strike prices.
Option type	American style (the option may be exercised up to 7.00 p.m. on any business day up to and including the last trading day).

Method of introduction of new strike prices	New series are added when the underlying futures price touches within half a strike price interval of either the second highest or second lowest strike price. No new series are normally introduced in the last 20 calendar days before expiry.
Reuters Monitor (Quote)	TIIH – TIJA.
Telerate page	890 – 893.

Mid-American Commodity Exchange (MACE) (Affiliated to the CBOT)

incorporating Chicago Rice & Cotton Exchange (CRCE) (a division of the MACE)

Address:

141 West Jackson Boulevard
Chicago
Illinois 60604
USA

Telephone: (312) 341 3000/3500
Fax: (312) 435 7170
Telex: 210286 CBOT VR / 253223

Exchange personnel

Chairman: Karsten Mahlmann
Vice-Chairman: Patrick Arbor
President & CEO: Thomas R. Donovan
Vice-President, Public
  Relations: Ray Carmichael

Futures contracts available on MACE
British pound / US dollar currency
Canadian dollar / US dollar currency
Corn
Deutschmark / US dollar currency
Japanese yen / US dollar currency
Live cattle
Live hogs
90-day US Government Treasury Bills
NY gold
NY platinum
NY silver
Oats
Soyabeans
Soyabean meal
Swiss franc / US dollar currency
US Government Treasury Bonds
US Government Treasury Notes
Wheat

Futures contracts available on CRCE
CRCE rough rice

Options contracts on futures available on MACE
NY gold futures
Soyabean futures
Wheat futures

Clearing House:

Board of Trade Clearing Corporation.

Method of trading:

Open outcry.

Commenced trading:

MACE – 1860; CRCE – 1871.

Exchange links:

Chicago Board of Trade (CBOT) – all contracts are traded on the floor of the Chicago Board of Trade. Chicago Board Options Exchange (CBOE).

A brief synopsis of the exchange
MACE was founded in the 1860's as the Chicago Open Board of Trade, its present name being adopted in 1972. In March 1986, MACE became affiliated with the Chicago Board of Trade and MACE now trades in the same floor as the CBOT.

The contracts traded on the MACE are generally more suited to the smaller investor than are those on the CBOT, and are typically one-fifth of the size of similar contracts on the CBOT and other US exchanges, and demand a similarly lower rate of dollar margin deposit. MACE has over 1,250 members. The exchange's product range includes livestock, currencies, grains and metals, with the US Government Treasury Bond future being the most active contract.

CRCE became affiliated to the MACE in December 1985. It was originally called the New Orleans Cotton Exchange. The CRCE also trades on the same floor as the CBOT, although there is only one contract traded.

British pound / US dollar currency (XP) futures

Contract size	£12,500 traded against the US dollar (US$).
Standard delivery method	Physical exchange of the currencies concerned.
Trading months	The March, June, September and December cycle.
Trading hours	7.20 a.m. – 2.15 p.m.
Price quotation method	In US dollars (US$) per pounds sterling (£).
Minimum price move (value)	US$0.0002 per £1.00 (US$2.50 per contract).
Daily price limits	None.
Position limits	None.
Last trading day	Not stated. Please consult the exchange for full details.
Delivery day	Not stated. Please consult the exchange for full details.
Initial (Variation) margin	Not stated. Please consult the exchange for full details.
Spread margin	A wide range of intra- and inter-commodity spread margin concessions is available. Please consult the exchange or your broker for full details.
Reuters Monitor (Quote)	BPME, BP53.
Telerate page	N/a.

Canadian dollar / US dollar currency (XD) futures

Contract size	C$50,000 traded against the US dollar (US$).
Standard delivery method	Physical exchange of the currencies concerned.
Trading months	The March, June, September and December cycle.
Trading hours	7.20 a.m. – 2.15 p.m.
Price quotation method	In US dollars (US$) per Canadian dollar (C$).
Minimum price move (value)	US$0.0001 per C$1.00 (US$5.00 per contract).
Daily price limits	None.
Position limits	None.
Last trading day	Not stated. Please consult the exchange for full details.
Delivery day	Not stated. Please consult the exchange for full details.
Initial (Variation) margin	Not stated. Please consult the exchange for full details.
Spread margin	A wide range of intra- and inter-commodity spread margin concessions is available. Please consult the exchange or your broker for full details.
Reuters Monitor (Quote)	N/a.
Telerate page	N/a.

**Mid-American
Commodity
Exchange (MACE)
Futures
Softs and
agricultural**

Corn (XC) futures

Contract size	1,000 bushels of corn.
Standard delivery method	Physical delivery of the above.
Trading months	The March, May, July, September and December cycle.
Trading hours	9.30 a.m. – 1.30 p.m. Trading ceases in the expiring contract at 12.00 noon on the last trading day.
Price quotation method	In US cents per bushel.
Minimum price move (value)	One-eighth (1/8) of a US cent per bushel (US$1.25 per contract).
Daily price limits	10 US cents (US$0.10) per bushel (US$100 per contract) above or below the previous day's closing settlement price. There are no price limits on the spot month.
Position limits	None.
Last trading day	Seven business days before the last business day of the contract month.
Delivery day	The last business day of the contract month.
Initial (Variation) margin	Not stated. Please consult the exchange for full details.
Spread margin	A wide range of intra- and inter-commodity spread margin concessions is available. Please consult the exchange or your broker for full details.
Reuters Monitor (Quote)	MZME.
Telerate page	N/a.

Deutschmark / US dollar currency (XM) futures

Contract size	DM62,500 traded against the US dollar (US$).
Standard delivery method	Physical exchange of the currencies concerned.
Trading months	The March, June, September and December cycle.
Trading hours	7.20 a.m. – 2.15 p.m.
Price quotation method	In US dollars (US$) per Deutschmark (DM).
Minimum price move (value)	US$0.0001 per DM1.00 (US$6.25 per contract).
Daily price limits	None.
Position limits	None.
Last trading day	Not stated. Please consult the exchange for full details.
Delivery day	Not stated. Please consult the exchange for full details.
Initial (Variation) margin	Not stated. Please consult the exchange for full details.
Spread margin	A wide range of intra- and inter-commodity spread margin concessions is available. Please consult the exchange or your broker for full details.
Reuters Monitor (Quote)	DMME, DM53.
Telerate page	N/a.

Mid-American
Commodity
Exchange (MACE)
Futures
Softs and
agricultural

Japanese yen / US dollar currency (XJ) futures

Contract size	Y6,250,000 traded against the US dollar (US$).
Standard delivery method	Physical exchange of the currencies concerned.
Trading months	The March, June, September and December cycle.
Trading hours	7.20 a.m. – 2.15 p.m.
Price quotation method	In US dollars (US$) per Japanese yen (Y).
Minimum price move (value)	US$0.000001 per Y1.00 (US$6.25 per contract).
Daily price limits	None.
Position limits	None.
Last trading day	Not stated. Please consult the exchange for full details.
Delivery day	Not stated. Please consult the exchange for full details.
Initial (Variation) margin	Not stated. Please consult the exchange for full details.
Spread margin	A wide range of intra- and inter-commodity spread margin concessions is available. Please consult the exchange or your broker for full details.
Reuters Monitor (Quote)	JYME, JY53.
Telerate page	N/a.

Live cattle (XL) futures

Contract size	20,000 pounds of live cattle.
Standard delivery method	Physical delivery of the above.
Trading months	The February, April, June, August, October and December cycle.
Trading hours	9.05 a.m. – 1.15 p.m. (trading ceases in the expiring contract at 12.00 noon on the last trading day).
Price quotation method	In US cents per pound.
Minimum price move (value)	0.025 US cents per pound (US$5.00 per contract).
Daily price limits	1.5 US cents (US$0.015) per pound above or below the previous day's closing settlement price (US$300 per contract). There are no price limits on the spot month.
Position limits	None.
Last trading day	Not stated. Please consult the exchange for full details.
Delivery day	Not stated. Please consult the exchange for full details.
Initial (Variation) margin	Not stated. Please consult the exchange for full details.
Spread margin	A wide range of intra- and inter-commodity spread margin concessions is available. Please consult the exchange or your broker for full details.
Reuters Monitor (Quote)	N/a.
Telerate page	N/a.

**Mid-American
Commodity
Exchange (MACE)
Futures
Softs and
agricultural**

Live hogs (XH) futures

Contract size	15,000 pounds of live hogs.
Standard delivery method	Physical delivery of the above.
Trading months	The February, April, June, July, August, October and December cycle.
Trading hours	9.05 a.m. – 1.15 p.m. (trading ceases in the expiring contract at 12.00 noon on the last trading day).
Price quotation method	In terms of US cents per pound.
Minimum price move (value)	0.025 US cents per pound (US$3.75 per contract).
Daily price limits	1.5 US cents (US$0.015) per pound above or below the previous day's closing settlement price (US$225 per contract). There are no price limits on the spot month.
Position limits	None.
Last trading day	Not stated. Please consult the exchange for full details.
Delivery day	Not stated. Please consult the exchange for full details.
Initial (Variation) margin	Not stated. Please consult the exchange for full details.
Spread margin	A wide range of intra- and inter-commodity spread margin concessions is available. Please consult the exchange or your broker for full details.
Reuters Monitor (Quote)	N/a.
Telerate page	N/a.

90-day US Government Treasury Bills (XT) futures

Contract size	US$500,000 nominal face value of notional long term US Government Treasury Bills.
Standard delivery method	Physical delivery of the above.
Trading months	The March, June, September and December cycle.
Trading hours	7.20 a.m. – 2.15 p.m.
Price quotation method	In index terms with a quotation of 100.00 minus the annualised Treasury Bill yield, quoted in US dollars (US$).
Minimum price move (value)	0.01% of nominal face value (US$12.50 per contract).
Daily price limits	None.
Position limits	None.
Last trading day	Seven business days before the last business day of the contract month.
Delivery day	The last business day of the contract month.
Initial (Variation) margin	Not stated. Please consult the exchange for full details.
Spread margin	A wide range of intra- and inter-commodity spread margin concessions is available. Please consult the exchange or your broker for full details.
Reuters Monitor (Quote)	TBMF, TC53.
Telerate page	N/a.

NY gold (XK) futures

Contract size	33.2 fine troy ounces of NY gold bullion.
Standard delivery method	Physical delivery of refined (0.995 fineness) gold bullion.
Trading months	All consecutive calendar months.
Trading hours	7.20 a.m. – 1.40 p.m.
Price quotation method	In US dollars (US$) and cents per troy ounce.
Minimum price move (value)	10 US cents (US$0.10) per troy ounce (US$3.32 per contract).
Daily price limits	None.
Position limits	None.
Last trading day	The fourth business day before the last business day of the contract month.
Delivery day	The delivery process in the contract month is as follows: first business day – seller gives notice of intention to deliver, second business day – buyer is notified, last business day – buyer receives vault receipts and must pay promptly.
Initial (Variation) margin	Not stated. Please consult the exchange for full details.
Spread margin	A wide range of intra- and inter-commodity spread margin concessions is available. Please consult the exchange or your broker for full details.
Reuters Monitor (Quote)	N/a.
Telerate page	N/a.

NY platinum (XU) futures

Contract size	25 troy ounces of NY platinum.
Standard delivery method	Physical delivery of the above.
Trading months	All consecutive calendar months.
Trading hours	7.20 a.m. – 1.40 p.m.
Price quotation method	In US cents per troy ounce.
Minimum price move (value)	10 US cents (US$0.10) per troy ounce (US$2.50 per contract).
Daily price limits	US$25.00 per troy ounce (US$625 per contract) above or below the previous day's closing settlement price. There are no price limits in the spot month.
Position limits	None.
Last trading day	The fourth to last business day of the contract month.
Delivery day	The delivery process in the contract month is as follows: first business day – seller gives notice of intention to deliver, second business day – buyer is notified; last business day – buyer receives vault receipts and must pay promptly.
Initial (Variation) margin	Not stated. Please consult the exchange for full details.

Spread margin	A wide range of intra- and inter-commodity spread margin concessions is available. Please consult the exchange or your broker for full details.
Reuters Monitor (Quote)	N/a.
Telerate page	N/a.

NY silver (XY) futures

Contract size	1,000 troy ounces of NY silver bullion.
Standard delivery method	Physical delivery of refined (999 fineness) silver bullion.
Trading months	All consecutive calendar months.
Trading hours	7.25 a.m. – 1.40 p.m.
Price quotation method	In US cents per troy ounce.
Minimum price move (value)	0.1 US cents (US$0.001) per troy ounce (US$1.00 per contract).
Daily price limits	None.
Position limits	None.
Last trading day	The fourth to last business day of the contract month.
Delivery day	The delivery process in the contract month is as follows: first business day – seller gives notice of intention to deliver, second business day – buyer is notified; last business day – buyer receives vault receipts and must pay promptly.
Initial (Variation) margin	Not stated. Please consult the exchange for full details.
Spread margin	A wide range of intra- and inter-commodity spread margin concessions is available. Please consult the exchange or your broker for full details.
Reuters Monitor (Quote)	N/a.
Telerate page	N/a.

Oats (XO) futures

Contract size	1,000 bushels of oats.
Standard delivery method	Physical delivery of the above.
Trading months	The March, May, July, September and December cycle.
Trading hours	9.30 a.m. – 1.30 pm. (trading ceases in the expiring contract at 12.00 noon on the last trading day).
Price quotation method	In US cents per bushel.
Minimum price move (value)	One-eighth (1/8) of a US cent per bushel (US$1.25 per contract).
Daily price limits	10 US cents (US$0.10) per bushel (US$10.00 per contract) above or below the previous day's closing settlement price. There are no price limits on the spot month.

Mid-American
Commodity
Exchange (MACE)
Futures
Softs and
agricultural

Position limits	None.
Last trading day	Seven business days before the last business day of the contract month.
Delivery day	The business day following the last trading day.
Initial (Variation) margin	Not stated. Please consult the exchange for full details.
Spread margin	A wide range of intra- and inter-commodity spread margin concessions is available. Please consult the exchange or your broker for full details.
Reuters Monitor (Quote)	N/a.
Telerate page	N/a.

Soyabean (XS) futures

Contract size	1,000 bushels of soyabeans.
Standard delivery method	Physical delivery of the above.
Trading months	The January, March, May, July, August, September and November cycle.
Trading hours	9.30 a.m. – 1.30 pm. (trading ceases in the expiring contract at 12.00 noon on the last trading day).
Price quotation method	In US cents per bushel.
Minimum price move (value)	One-eighth (1/8) of a US cent per bushel (US$1.25 per contract).
Daily price limits	30 US cents (US$0.30) per bushel (US$300 per contract) above or below the previous day's closing settlement price. There are no price limits on the spot month.
Position limits	None.
Last trading day	Seven business days before the last business day of the contract month.
Delivery day	The business day following the last trading day.
Initial (Variation) margin	Not stated. Please consult the exchange for full details.
Spread margin	A wide range of intra- and inter-commodity spread margin concessions is available. Please consult the exchange or your broker for full details.
Reuters Monitor (Quote)	N/a.
Telerate page	N/a.

Soyabean meal (XE) futures

Contract size	20 tons (2,000 pounds per ton) of soyabean meal.
Standard delivery method	Physical delivery of the above.
Trading months	The January, March, May, July, August, September, October and December cycle.
Trading hours	9.30 a.m. – 1.30 p.m. (trading ceases in the expiring contract at 12.00 noon on the last trading day).

**Mid-American
Commodity
Exchange (MACE)
Futures
Softs and
agricultural**

Price quotation method	In US dollars (US$) and cents per ton.
Minimum price move (value)	US$0.10 (10 US cents) per ton (US$2.00 per contract).
Daily price limits	US$10.00 per ton (US$200 per contract) above or below the previous day's closing settlement price. There are no price limits in the spot month.
Position limits	None.
Last trading day	Seven business days before the last business day of the contract month.
Delivery day	The business day following the last trading day.
Initial (Variation) margin	Not stated. Please consult the exchange for full details.
Spread margin	A wide range of intra- and inter-commodity spread margin concessions is available. Please consult the exchange or your broker for full details.
Reuters Monitor (Quote)	N/a.
Telerate page	N/a.

Swiss franc / US dollar currency (XF) futures

Contract size	SFr62,500 traded against the US dollar (US$).
Standard delivery method	Physical exchange of the currencies concerned.
Trading months	The March, June, September and December cycle.
Trading hours	7.20 a.m. – 2.15 p.m.
Price quotation method	In US dollars (US$) per Swiss franc (SFr).
Minimum price move (value)	US$0.0001 per SFr1.00 (US$6.25 per contract).
Daily price limits	None.
Position limits	None.
Last trading day	Not stated. Please consult the exchange for full details.
Delivery day	Not stated. Please consult the exchange for full details.
Initial (Variation) margin	Not stated. Please consult the exchange for full details.
Spread margin	A wide range of intra- and inter-commodity spread margin concessions is available. Please consult the exchange or your broker for full details.
Reuters Monitor (Quote)	SSME, SF53.
Telerate page	N/a.

US Government Treasury Bond (XB) futures

Contract size	US$50,000 nominal face value of a notional long-term US Government Treasury Bond.
Standard delivery method	Physical delivery of the above bonds maturing at least 15 years from the first day of the contract month, with a notional coupon rate of 8%.

Trading months	The March, June, September and December cycle.
Trading hours	7.20 a.m. – 3.15 p.m.
Price quotation method	In percentage of par in increments of one thirty-second (1/32), quoted in US dollars (US$).
Minimum price move (value)	One thirty-second (1/32) of one point (US$15.625 per contract).
Daily price limits	96/32 (three points) above or below the previous day's closing price (US$1,500 per contract).
Position limits	None.
Last trading day	Seven business days prior to the last business day of the contract month.
Delivery day	The last business day of the contract month. Delivery may take place on any business day during the contract month.
Initial (Variation) margin	Not stated. Please consult the exchange for full details.
Spread margin	A wide range of intra- and inter-commodity spread margin concessions is available. Please consult the exchange or your broker for full details.
Reuters Monitor (Quote)	TBMD – TBME, TB53 – TB54.
Telerate page	N/a.

US Government Treasury Notes (XN) futures

Contract size	US$500,000 nominal face value of notional long-term US Government Treasury Notes.
Standard delivery method	Physical delivery of the above notes, maturing in at least 6.5 years, but not more than 10 years from the first day of the contract month, with a nominal coupon rate of 8%.
Trading months	The March, June, September and December cycle.
Trading hours	7.20 a.m. – 3.15 p.m.
Price quotation method	In percentage of par in increments of one thirty-second (1/32), quoted in US dollars (US$).
Minimum price move (value)	One thirty-second (1/32) of one point (US$15.625 per contract).
Daily price limits	96/32 (three points) above or below the previous day's closing price (US$1,500 per contract).
Position limits	None.
Last trading day	Seven business days prior to the last business day of the contract month.
Delivery day	The last business day of the contract month.
Initial (Variation) margin	Not stated. Please consult the exchange for full details.
Spread margin	A wide range of intra- and inter-commodity spread margin concessions is available. Please consult the exchange or your broker for full details.
Reuters Monitor (Quote)	N/a.
Telerate page	N/a.

Mid-American
Commodity
Exchange (MACE)
Futures
Softs and
agricultural

Wheat (XW) Futures

Contract size	1,000 bushels of wheat.
Standard delivery method	Physical delivery of the above.
Trading months	The March, May, July, August, September and December cycle.
Trading hours	9.30 a.m. – 1.30 p.m. (trading ceases in the expiring contract at 12.00 noon on the last trading day).
Price quotation method	In US cents per bushel.
Minimum price move (value)	One-eighth (1/8) of a US cent per bushel (US$1.25 per contract).
Daily price limits	20 US cents (US$0.20) per bushel (US$200 per contract) above or below the previous day's closing settlement price. There are no price limits on the spot month.
Position limits	None.
Last trading day	Seven business days before the last business day of the contract month.
Delivery day	The business day following the last trading day.
Initial (Variation) margin	Not stated. Please consult the exchange for full details.
Spread margin	A wide range of intra- and inter-commodity spread margin concessions is available. Please consult the exchange or your broker for full details.
Reuters Monitor (Quote)	N/a.
Telerate page	N/a.

CRCE rough rice futures

Contract size	2,000 hundredweight (200,000 pounds) of US No. 2 or better long grain rough rice.
Standard delivery method	Physical delivery of the above through a warehouse receipt issued by an exchange-approved warehouse.
Trading months	The January, March, May, September and November cycle.
Trading hours	9.15 a.m. – 1.30 p.m. Trading ceases in the expiring contract at 12.00 noon on the last trading day.
Price quotation method	In US dollars (US$) and cents per hundredweight.
Minimum price move (value)	US$0.005 per hundredweight (US$10.00 per contract).
Daily price limits	30 US cents (US$0.30) per hundredweight (US$600 per contract) above or below the previous day's settlement price. This limit does not apply to the spot month on or after the second business day prior to the first day of the current month. Expanded limits of 50% may be introduced if on two successive business days, three contracts close on a limit, for three business days.

Position limits	500 contracts of combined months (or 250 contracts of one month).
Last trading day	The eighth to last business day of the contract month.
Delivery day	Throughout the contract month (a three-day process), being the day after the first notice day. The first notice day is the business day before the first business day of the contract month.
Initial (Variation) margin	Margins increase by 50% when expanded price limits are in force.
Spread margin	Not stated.
Reuters Monitor (Quote)	RICE.
Telerate page	N/a.

Option on MACE NY gold (XK) futures

Contract size	One MACE NY gold futures contract (of an underlying contract size of 33.2 ounces of gold bullion).
Standard delivery method	Delivery of a long or short position in a futures contract at the strike price as above.
Trading months	The February, April, June, August, October and December cycle.
Trading hours	7.20 a.m. – 1.40 p.m.
Price quotation method	In US cents per troy ounce.
Minimum price move (value)	10 US cents (US$0.10) per troy ounce (US$3.32 per contract).
Daily price limits	None.
Position limits	None.
Last trading day	The last Friday before the first notice day of the underlying futures contract by at least five business days. The option expires at 10.00 a.m. on the first Saturday following the last trading day.
Delivery day	The business day following the last trading day.
Initial (Variation) margin	Uncovered short positions require a margin deposit equal to the premium received plus the greater of: (a) the current initial margin for the underlying futures contract less half the amount by which the option is out-of-the-money; or (b) half the current initial margin of the underlying futures contract.
Spread margin	A wide range of intra- and inter-commodity spread margin concessions is available. Please consult the exchange or your broker for full details.
Strike price intervals	Not stated. Please consult the exchange for full details.
Option type	American style (the option may be exercised on any business day up to and including the last trading day).
Method of introduction of new strike prices	Not stated. Please consult the exchange for full details.
Reuters Monitor (Quote)	N/a.
Telerate page	N/a.

**Mid-American
Commodity
Exchange (MACE)
Options on futures
Softs and
agricultural**

Option on MACE soyabean (XE) futures

Contract size	One MACE soyabean futures contract (of an underlying contract size of 1,000 bushels).
Standard delivery method	Delivery of a long or short position in a futures contract at the strike price as above.
Trading months	The January, March, May, July, August, September and November cycle.
Trading hours	9.30 a.m. – 1.30 p.m. (trading ceases in the expiring contract at 12.00 noon on the last trading day).
Price quotation method	In US cents per bushel.
Minimum price move (value)	One-eighth (1/8) of a US cent per bushel (US$1.25 per contract).
Daily price limits	30 US cents (US$0.30) per bushel above or below the previous day's settlement premium.
Position limits	None.
Last trading day	The last Friday before the first notice day of the underlying futures contract by at least five business days.
Delivery day	The business day following the last trading day.
Initial (Variation) margin	Uncovered short positions require a margin deposit equal to the premium received plus the greater of: (a) the current initial margin for the underlying futures contract less half the amount by which the option is out-of-the-money; or (b) half the current initial margin of the underlying futures contract.
Spread margin	A wide range of intra- and inter-commodity spread margin concessions is available. Please consult the exchange or your broker for full details.
Strike price intervals	At 25 US cents (US$0.25) per bushel intervals.
Option type	American style (the option may be exercised on any business day up to and including the last trading day).
Method of introduction of new strike prices	There are generally 11 initial strike prices available. New strike prices are introduced when the underlying futures contract trades at least halfway above (below) the current highest (lowest) available strike price and the next strike price due to be introduced. No new strike prices are normally added during the month in which the option expires.
Reuters Monitor (Quote)	N/a.
Telerate page	N/a.

Option on MACE wheat (XW) futures

Contract size	One MACE wheat futures contract (of an underlying contract size of 1,000 bushels).
Standard delivery method	Delivery of a long or short position in a futures contract at the strike price as above.

Mid-American
Commodity
Exchange (MACE)
Options on futures
Softs and
agricultural

Trading months	The March, May, July, September and December cycle.
Trading hours	9.30 a.m. – 1.30 p.m. (trading ceases in the expiring contract at 12.00 noon on the last trading day).
Price quotation method	In US cents per bushel.
Minimum price move (value)	One-eighth (1/8) of a US cent per bushel (US$1.25 per contract).
Daily price limits	20 US cents (US$0.20) per bushel above or below the previous day's settlement premium.
Position limits	None.
Last trading day	The last Friday preceding the first notice day of the underlying futures contract by at least five business days.
Delivery day	The business day following the last trading day.
Initial (Variation) margin	Uncovered short positions require a margin deposit equal to the premium received plus the greater of: (a) the current initial margin for the underlying futures contract less half the amount by which the option is out-of-the-money; or (b) half the current initial margin of the underlying futures contract.
Spread margin	A wide range of intra- and inter-commodity spread margin concessions is available. Please consult the exchange or your broker for full details.
Strike price intervals	At 10 US cents (US$0.10) per bushel intervals.
Option type	American style (the option may be exercised on any business day up to and including the last trading day).
Method of introduction of new strike prices	Not stated. Please consult the exchange for full details.
Reuters Monitor (Quote)	N/a.
Telerate page	N/a.

American Stock Exchange (AMEX)

Address:	86 Trinity Place New York New York 10006 USA
Telephone:	(212) 306 1000
Fax:	(212) 306 1802
Telex:	129297

Exchange personnel

Chairman:	Arthur Levitt Jr
President:	Kenneth Liebler
Senior VP, Options:	Howard A Baker
Information Officer:	Frank Magnani

London Representative Office:

Address:	St Alphage House 18th Floor 2 Fore Street London EC2H 5BA United Kingdom
Telephone:	(01) 588 2966
Fax:	N/a.
Telex:	N/a.
Contact:	David Helson

Futures contracts available
None

Options contracts on physical/cash available
Computer Technology Stock Index
Institutional Stock Index
International Market (ADR) Stock Index
Major Market Stock Index
Oil Stock Index

Also available are traded options on over 170 US equities. The contract size in each case is 100 shares of the underlying issue, and the tick size is one-sixteenth (1/16) of a point per contract. There is physical delivery only of

*the underlying shares, and the trading hours are from
9.30 a.m. – 4.10 p.m. The expiry cycle is the nearest
three consecutive calendar months.*

Clearing House:	Options Clearing Corporation (OCC).
Method of trading:	Open outcry.
Commenced trading:	1975 for options.
Exchange links:	Optiebeurs NV (EOE) Amsterdam.

A brief synopsis of the exchange
The options programme at AMEX began in 1975 with
individual equity options and was soon followed by
debt instruments in the form of US Government
Treasury Notes and US Government Treasury Bills.
The most successful contract is the Major Market
Stock Index option.

Gold options (introduced in 1985) are traded on the
AMEX subsidiary, the AMEX Commodities
Corporation.

There are nearly 700 Regular Exchange Members
and over 200 Option Principal Members.

Option on Computer Technology Stock Index (XCI)

Contract size	US$100 multiplied by the Computer Technology Stock Index (XCI)*.
Standard delivery method	Cash settlement at expiry. There is no facility for physical delivery of the constituent stocks in the index.
Trading months	The nearest three consecutive calendar months plus the next two in the January, April, July and October cycle.
Trading hours	9.30 a.m. – 4.10 p.m.
Price quotation method	In US dollars (US$) and cents per index point.
Minimum price move (value)	One-sixteenth (1/16) of an index point (US$6.25 per contract) for premiums up to US$3.00 and one-eighth (1/8) of an index point (US$12.50 per contract) for all higher premiums.
Daily price limits	None.
Position limits	8,000 contracts on the same side of the market.
Last trading day	The third Friday of the contract month.
Delivery day	The business day following the last trading day. The option expires on the Saturday following the third Friday of the contract month.
Initial (Variation) margin	For uncovered short positions, 20% of the aggregate index value, less any out-of-the-money element, subject to a minimum of 10% of the aggregate index value.
Spread margin	Not stated.
Strike price intervals	At 5.0 index point intervals.
Option type	American style (the option may be exercised on any business day up to and including the last trading day).
Method of introduction of new strike prices	There are normally at least six strike prices available for trading. New series are introduced when the index touches the highest or lowest currently available strike price.
Reuters Monitor (Quote)	N/a.
Telerate page	N/a.

* The Computer Technology Stock Index (XCI) is designed to represent a cross-section of widely held US corporations involved in various phases of the computer industry. There are 30 issues and the index is based on the aggregate market value of those stocks.

Option on Institutional Stock Index (XII)

Contract size	US$100 multiplied by the Institutional Stock Index (XII).*
Standard delivery method	Cash settlement based on the final index level at the close of trading on the last trading day. There is no facility for the physical delivery of the constituent stocks in the index.
Trading months	The nearest three consecutive calendar months plus the March, June, September and December cycle. In addition two- and three-year long-term December expiry month options will be available.

Trading hours	9.30 a.m. – 4.15 p.m.
Price quotation method	In US dollars (US$) and cents per index point.
Minimum price move (value)	One-sixteenth (1/16) of an index point (US$6.25 per contract) for premiums up to US$3.00 and one-eighth (1/8) of an index point (US$12.50 per contract) for all higher premiums.
Daily price limits	None.
Position limits	25,000 contracts of which no more than 18,000 contracts may be held in the spot month. Bona fide hedgers may hold up to 75,000 contracts open with the prior approval of the exchange.
Last trading day	The third Friday of the contract month.
Delivery day	The business day following the last trading day. The option expires on the Saturday following the third Friday of the contract month.
Initial (Variation) margin	For uncovered short positions, 15% of the aggregate index value, less any out-of-the-money element, subject to a minimum of 10% of the aggregate index value.
Spread margin	Not stated.
Strike price intervals	At 5.0 index point intervals.
Option type	European style (the option may only be exercised on the last trading day and not at other times during its life).
Method of introduction of new strike prices	There are normally at least six strike prices available for trading. New series are introduced when the index touches the highest or lowest currently available strike price.
Reuters Monitor (Quote)	Reuters 2000: XII*.a <CHAIN>
Telerate page	N/a.

* The Institutional Stock Index (XII) is based on 75 constituent stocks held in the highest US dollar amounts in institutional portfolios that have a market value of more than US$100,000,000 in investment funds.

Option on International Market (ADR) Stock Index

Contract size	US$100 multiplied by the International Market (ADR) Stock Index.*
Standard delivery method	Cash settlement based on the index level on the morning of the last business day prior to expiration. There is no facility for the physical delivery of the constituent stocks in the index.
Trading months	The nearest three consecutive calendar months plus the next two months from the January, April, July and October cycle.
Trading hours	9.30 a.m. – 4.15 p.m.
Price quotation method	In US dollars (US$) and cents per index point.

Minimum price move (value)	One-sixteenth (1/16) of an index point (US$6.25 per contract) for premiums up to US$3.00 and one-eighth (1/8) of an index point (US$12.50 per contract) for all higher premiums.
Daily price limits	None.
Position limits	25,000 contracts on the same side of the market, with no more than 15,000 contracts held open in the spot month.
Last trading day	The second to last business day prior to expiration in the contract month (normally a Thursday).
Delivery day	The business day following the last trading day. The option expires on the Saturday following the third Friday of the contract month.
Initial (Variation) margin	For uncovered short positions, 15% of the aggregate index value, less any out-of-the-money element, subject to a minimum of 10% of the aggregate index value.
Spread margin	Not stated.
Strike price intervals	At 5.0 index point intervals.
Option type	European style (the option may only be exercised at expiry and not at other times during its life).
Method of introduction of new strike prices	There are normally at least six strike prices available for trading. New series are introduced when the index touches the highest or lowest currently available strike price.
Reuters Monitor (Quote)	N/a.
Telerate page	N/a.

* The International Market (ADR) Stock Index is a capitalisation-weighted index of 50 foreign securities actively traded on the NYSE, AMEX or NASDAQ (National Association of Securities Dealers Automated Quotations) in the form of American Depository Receipts (ADRs), foreign or New York shares. Countries covered in the index include those from the European Economic Community (EEC), Australia, Hong Kong and Japan.

Futures contracts on the ADR Index are traded at the Coffee, Sugar & Cocoa Exchange (CSCE) in New York.

Option on Major Market Stock Index (XMI)

Contract size	US$100 multiplied by the Major Market Stock Index (XMI).*
Standard delivery method	Cash settlement at expiry. There is no facility for physical delivery of the constituent stocks in the index.
Trading months	The nearest three consecutive calendar months plus the March, June, September and December cycle.
Trading hours	10.00 a.m. – 4.15 p.m.
Price quotation method	In US dollars (US$) and cents per index point.

Minimum price move (value)	One-sixteenth (1/16) of an index point (US$6.25 per contract) for premiums up to US$3.00 and one-eighth (1/8) of an index point (US$12.50 per contract) for all higher premiums.
Daily price limits	None.
Position limits	17,000 contracts of which no more than 10,000 contracts may be held in the spot month.
Last trading day	The third Friday of the contract month.
Delivery day	The business day following the last trading day. The option expires on the Saturday following the third Friday of the contract month.
Initial (Variation) margin	For uncovered short positions, 15% of the aggregate index value, less the out-of-the-money element, subject to a minimum of 10% of the aggregate index value.
Spread margin	Not stated.
Strike price intervals	At 5.0 index point intervals.
Option type	American style (the option may be exercised on any business day up to and including the last trading day).
Method of introduction of new strike prices	There are normally at least six strike prices available for trading. New series are introduced when the index touches the highest or lowest currently available strike price.
Reuters Monitor (Quote)	XMIA – XMIP, MJNA – MJOH.
Telerate page	N/a.

* This contract is fungible with the XMI futures traded on Optiebeurs (EOE) Amsterdam. The contract specifications are therefore the same.

The Major Market Index (XMI) is a price-weighted index based on weighting factors equal to each of the 20 constituents. The current constituents are as follows:

American Express	AT&T	Chevron
Coca-Cola	Dow Chemical	Du Pont
Eastman Kodak	Exxon	General Electric
General Motors	IBM	International Paper
Johnson & Johnson	Merck & Co.	Minnesota Mining & Mfg
Mobil	Philip Morris	Procter & Gamble
Sears, Roebuck	USX	

Option on Oil Stock Index (XOI)

Contract size	US$100 multiplied by the Oil Stock Index.
Standard delivery method	Cash settlement at expiry. There is no facility for the physical delivery of the constituent stocks in the index.
Trading months	The nearest three consecutive calendar months plus the January, April, July and October cycle.
Trading hours	9.30 a.m. – 4.10 p.m.
Price quotation method	In US dollars (US$) and cents per index point.

Minimum price move (*value*)	One-sixteenth (1/16) of an index point (US$6.25 per contract) for premiums up to US$3.00 and one-eighth (1/8) of an index point (US$12.50 per contract) for all higher premiums.
Daily price limits	None.
Position limits	8,000 contracts on the same side of the market.
Last trading day	The third Friday of the contract month.
Delivery day	The business day following the last trading day. The option expires on the Saturday following the third Friday of the contract month.
Initial (*Variation*) margin	For uncovered short positions, 20% of the aggregate index value, less any out-of-the-money element, subject to a minimum of 10% of the aggregate index value.
Spread margin	Not stated.
Strike price intervals	At 5.0 index point intervals.
Option type	American style (the option may be exercised on any business day up to and including the last trading day).
Method of introduction of new strike prices	There are normally at least six strike prices available for trading. New series are introduced when the index touches the highest or lowest currently available strike price.
Reuters Monitor (*Quote*)	PPAO – PPAT.
Telerate page	N/a.

Coffee, Sugar & Cocoa Exchange (CSCE)

Address:

4 World Trade Center
New York
New York 10048
USA

Telephone: (212) 938 2800
Fax: (212) 524 9363
Telex: 127066

Exchange personnel

President: Bennett J. Corn
Chairman: Charles P. Nastro
First Vice-Chairman: Clifford S. Evans
Marketing Assistant: Elsie Wolters
Information Officer: Janet Troy

Futures contracts available
Cocoa
Coffee 'C'
International Market (ADR) Stock Index
Sugar No. 11 (world)
Sugar No. 14 (domestic)
World white sugar

Options contracts on futures available
Cocoa futures
Coffee 'C' futures
Sugar No. 11 (world) futures

Clearing House: CSC Clearing Corporation.

Method of trading: Open outcry.

Commenced trading: 1882.

Exchange links: Joint venture with COMEX, NYMEX and the NYFE including a shared trading arena.

A brief synopsis of the exchange

The Coffee, Sugar & Cocoa Exchange was founded in 1882 as the Coffee Exchange of New York. The trading of sugar was added in 1914, and the exchange was finally merged with the New York Cocoa Exchange in 1979. Options were introduced in 1982 on sugar, the first US exchange to list such a product. The CSCE is the world's leading market-place for these types of agricultural products.

In 1988, the International Market (ADR) Stock Index was added to the list of products, maintaining the exchange's development. There are over 770 full and associate members.

Coffee, Sugar &
Cocoa Exchange
(CSCE)
Futures
Softs and
agricultural

Cocoa futures

Contract size	10 metric tons (22,046 pounds) of deliverable cocoa.
Standard delivery method	Physical delivery of the above at the seller's choice at licensed warehouses in the Port of New York District, Delaware River Port District or Port of Hampton Roads.
Trading months	The March, May, July, September and December cycle.
Trading hours	9.30 a.m. – 2.15 p.m.
Price quotation method	In US dollars (US$) and cents per metric ton.
Minimum price move (*value*)	US$1.00 per metric ton (US$10.00 per contract).
Daily price limits	US$88.00 per metric ton above or below the previous day's settlement price (expandable by 50% to US$132.00 per metric ton under certain conditions). There are no price limits in the two nearby contract months.
Position limits	500 contracts for any month for which delivery notices may have been issued; 1,000 contracts net position in any one month, other than during the delivery notice period; 2,000 contracts net total position.
Last trading day	The 11th business day prior to the last business day of the contract month.
Delivery day	The business day following the last trading day.
Initial (Variation) margin	US$750 per contract (US$562.50).
Spread margin	US$300 per spread position (US$225). In the spot month: US$450 per spread position (US$337.50).
Reuters Monitor (Quote)	COKA.
Telerate page	929.

Coffee 'C' futures

Contract size	37,500 pounds of coffee Grade 'C' in approximately 250 bags.
Standard delivery method	Physical delivery of washed arabica coffee produced in several Central and South American, Asian and African countries, by grading Certificates of Exchange at licensed warehouses.
Trading months	The March, May, July, September and December cycle.
Trading hours	9.15 a.m. – 1.58 p.m. (at 2.00 p.m. the closing call commences).
Price quotation method	In US cents per pound.
Minimum price move (*value*)	0.05 US cents per pound (US$18.75 per contract).

Coffee, Sugar &
Cocoa Exchange
(CSCE)
Futures
Softs and
agricultural

Daily price limits	US$0.06 (6 US cents) is a variable limit that comes into effect under certain conditions. No price limits are introduced on the nearest two contract months on or after the first business day immediately succeeding the last trading day of the current contract month.
Position limits	200 contracts for any month for which delivery notices may have been issued, with a total net position of 750 contracts in any one month other than during the delivery notice period; 1,000 contracts net long or short total position.
Last trading day	The business day that is one day before seven business days prior to the last business day of the contract month.
Delivery day	The business day following the last trading day.
Initial (Variation) margin	US$2,000 per contract (US$1,500).
Spread margin	US$250 per spread position (US$187.50). In the spot month: US$1,250 per spread position (US$937.50).
Reuters Monitor (Quote)	COFA.
Telerate page	929.

International Market (ADR) Stock Index (IMI) futures

Contract size	US$250 multiplied by the International Market Stock Index (IMI).*
Standard delivery method	Cash settlement based on the opening value of the IMI on the business day following the last trading day.
Trading months	The spot month, the next two consecutive calendar months and then the March, June, September and December cycle up to 15 months forward.
Trading hours	9.30 a.m. – 4.15 p.m.
Price quotation method	In US dollars (US$) and cents per index point.
Minimum price move (value)	0.05 of one IMI index point (US$12.50 per contract).
Daily price limits	There is an initial daily price limit of 30 index points below the previous day's settlement price. There is a 30-minute trading halt if the Dow Jones Industrial Average (DJIA) falls by 250 points. The maximum daily movement in the IMI will be 50 points. There will be a two-hour trading halt if the DJIA falls by 400 points.
Position limits	Speculative limit of 5,000 contracts in all months combined.
Last trading day	The business day prior to the third Friday of the contract month, or the preceding day if this is not an exchange business day.
Delivery day	The business day following the last trading day.

Coffee, Sugar &
Cocoa Exchange
(CSCE)
Futures
Softs and
agricultural

Initial (Variation) margin	Not stated. Please consult the exchange for the current margin requirements.
Spread margin	Not stated. Please consult the exchange.
Reuters Monitor (Quote)	N/a.
Telerate page	N/a.

* The International Market Stock Index (IMI) is a capitalisation-weighted stock index comprising 50 leading international companies whose shares trade either directly or in ADR form in the US markets. These stocks come from the Far East, Europe and Australia and cover 20 industry groups.

The corresponding options contract is traded on the AMEX.

Sugar No. 11 (world) futures

Contract size	50 long tons (112,000 pounds) of No 11 (world) sugar (raw centrifugal cane sugar based on 96 degrees average polarisation).
Standard delivery method	Physical delivery of the above at a port in the country of origin, or a port of export, FOB and stored in bulk.
Trading months	The January, March, May, July and October cycle (no new January contracts will be listed after 1990).
Trading hours	10.00 a.m. – 1.43 p.m. (at 1.45 p.m. the closing call commences).
Price quotation method	In US cents per pound.
Minimum price move (value)	0.01 US cents per pound (US$11.20 per contract).
Daily price limits	US$0.005 (0.5 US cents) is a variable limit that comes into effect under certain conditions. No price limits are introduced on the nearest two contract months on or after the first business day immediately succeeding the last trading day of the current contract month.
Position limits	4,000 contracts net in any single month; 6,000 contracts net in total.
Last trading day	The last business day of the month preceding the contract month.
Delivery day	The business day following the last trading day.
Initial (Variation) margin	US$750 per contract (US$562.50).
Spread margin	US$250 per spread position (US$187.50). In the spot month: US$500 per spread position (US$375).
Reuters Monitor (Quote)	SUGA.
Telerate page	929.

Sugar No. 14 (domestic) futures

Contract size	50 long tons (112,000 pounds) of No. 14 (domestic) sugar (raw centrifugal cane sugar based on 96 degrees average polarisation).

Coffee, Sugar &
Cocoa Exchange
(CSCE)
Futures
Softs and
agricultural

Standard delivery method	Physical delivery of the above in New York, Baltimore, Galveston, New Orleans or Savannah.
Trading months	The January, March, May, July and November cycle.
Trading hours	9.40 a.m. – 1.43 p.m. plus a closing call at the completion of the CSCE world white sugar futures call.
Price quotation method	In US cents per pound.
Minimum price move (value)	0.01 US cents per pound (US$11.20 per contract).
Daily price limits	US$0.005 (0.5 US cents) is a variable limit that comes into effect under certain conditions. No price limits are introduced on the nearest two contract months on or after the first business day immediately succeeding the last trading day of the current contract month.
Position limits	1,000 contracts in any single month. 1,000 contracts net total.
Last trading day	The eighth calendar day of the month preceding the contract month; or the next business day, if the eighth is not an exchange business day.
Delivery day	The business day following the last trading day.
Initial (Variation) margin	US$600 per contract (US$450).
Spread margin	US$250 per spread position (US$187.50). In the spot month: US$500 per spread position (US$375).
Reuters Monitor (Quote)	SUNF.
Telerate page	929.

World white sugar futures

Contract size	50 metric tons of white refined crystal beet or cane sugar, in new jute bags of 50 kilograms net weight, based on a minimum of 99.8 degrees polarisation.
Standard delivery method	Physical delivery of the above at par, at the seller's option at a selection of worldwide ports (please consult the exchange for full details).
Trading months	The January, March, May, July and October cycle up to 18 months forward.
Trading hours	9.45 a.m. – 1.43 p.m. plus a closing call that commences after the completion of the CSCE No.11 sugar futures call.
Price quotation method	In US cents per ton.
Minimum price move (value)	20 US cents (US$0.20) per ton (US$10.00 per contract).
Daily price limits	US$10.00 per metric ton is a variable limit that comes into effect under certain conditions. No price limits are introduced on the nearest two contract months on or after the first business day immediately succeeding the last trading day of the current contract month.

Coffee, Sugar &
Cocoa Exchange
(CSCE)
Options on futures
Softs and
agricultural

Position limits	2,000 contracts in any single month; 2,000 contracts net total.
Last trading day	The 15th calendar day of the month preceding the contract month, or the next business day, if the 15th is not an exchange business day.
Delivery day	The business day following the last trading day.
Initial (Variation) margin	US$750 per contract (US$562.50).
Spread margin	US$250 per spread position (US$187.50). In the spot month: US$500 per spread position (US$375).
Reuters Monitor (Quote)	SQNE.
Telerate page	929.

Option on CSCE cocoa futures

Contract size	One CSCE cocoa futures contract (of an underlying contract size of 10 metric tons).
Standard delivery method	Delivery of a long or short position in a futures contract at the strike price as above.
Trading months	The March, May, July, September and December cycle.
Trading hours	9.30 a.m. – 2.15 p.m.
Price quotation method	In US dollars (US$) and cents per metric ton.
Minimum price move (value)	US$1.00 per metric ton (US$10.00 per contract).
Daily price limits	None.
Position limits	2,000 contracts of long calls, short calls, long puts or short puts, provided that no more than 1,000 contracts are in any one single contract month.
Last trading day	The first Friday of the month preceding the contract month of the underlying futures contract. The option expires at 9.00 p.m. on the last trading day.
Delivery day	Notification of the intent of the holder of an option to exercise it must be made by 4.00 p.m. on any business day, for execution on the next business day.
Initial (Variation) margin	Not stated. Please consult the exchange for the current margin requirements.
Spread margin	Not stated. Please consult the exchange.
Strike price intervals	Futures price under US$3,600: US$100 intervals. Futures price over US$3,600: US$200 intervals.
Option type	American style (the option may be exercised on any business day up to and including the last trading day).
Method of introduction of new strike prices	Not stated.
Reuters Monitor (Quote)	CKME – CKMP.
Telerate page	N/a.

**Coffee, Sugar &
Cocoa Exchange
(CSCE)
Options on futures
Softs and
agricultural**

Option on CSCE coffee 'C' futures

Contract size	One CSCE coffee 'C' futures contract (of an underlying contract size of 37,500 pounds).
Standard delivery method	Delivery of a long or short position in a futures contract at the strike price as above.
Trading months	The March, May, July, September and December cycle.
Trading hours	9.15 a.m. – 2.23 p.m. (the closing call commences at 2.25 p.m.).
Price quotation method	In US cents per pound.
Minimum price move (value)	0.05 US cents per pound (US$18.75 per contract).
Daily price limits	None.
Position limits	1,000 contracts of long calls, short calls, long puts or short puts, provided that no more than 750 contracts are in any one single contract month.
Last trading day	The first Friday of the month preceding the contract month of the underlying futures contract. The option expires at 9.00 p.m. on the last trading day.
Delivery day	Notification of the intent of the holder of an option to exercise it must be made by 4.00 p.m. on any business day, for execution on the next business day.
Initial (Variation) margin	Not stated. Please consult the exchange for the current margin requirements.
Spread margin	Not stated. Please consult the exchange.
Strike price intervals	Futures price under US$2.00: at US$0.05 intervals. Futures price over US$2.00: at US$0.10 intervals.
Option type	American style (the option may be exercised on any business day up to and including the last trading day).
Method of introduction of new strike prices	Not stated.
Reuters Monitor (Quote)	KFME – KFMT.
Telerate page	N/a.

Option on CSCE sugar No. 11 (world) futures

Contract size	One CSCE sugar No. 11 (world) futures contract (of an underlying contract size of 112,000 pounds).
Standard delivery method	Delivery of a long or short position in a futures contract at the strike price as above.
Trading months	The nearest five months from the March, May, July and October cycle plus an option expiring in December and calls for the delivery of the March futures.
Trading hours	10.00 a.m. – 1.48 p.m. (the closing call commences at 1.50 p.m.).

**Coffee, Sugar &
Cocoa Exchange
(CSCE)
Options on futures
Softs and
agricultural**

Price quotation method	In US cents per pound.
Minimum price move (value)	0.01 US cents per pound (US$11.20 per contract).
Daily price limits	None.
Position limits	These are considered in conjunction with positions in the underlying futures contract.
Last trading day	The second Friday of the month preceding the contract month of the underlying futures contract, or the second Friday of December for the December option. The option expires at 9.00 p.m. on the last trading day.
Delivery day	Notification of the intent of the holder of an option to exercise it must be made by 3.00 p.m. on any business day, for execution on the next business day.
Initial (Variation) margin	Not stated. Please consult the exchange for the current margin requirements.
Spread margin	Not stated. Please consult the exchange.
Strike price intervals	Futures price under 10 US cents: 0.5 US cents. Futures price from 10 to 40 US cents: 1.0 US cents. Futures price over 40 US cents: 2.0 US cents. In each case, these intervals relate to the two nearby months. For all other months, the interval is double that shown with the exception that for strike prices between 10 and 16 US cents, the interval remains at 1.0 US cents.
Option type	American style (the option may be exercised on any business day up to and including the last trading day).
Method of introduction of new strike prices	Not stated.
Reuters Monitor (Quote)	SUGG – SUGV.
Telerate page	N/a.

Commodity Exchange Inc. (COMEX)

Address:
4 World Trade Center
New York
New York 10048
USA

Telephone: (212) 938 2900
Fax: (212) 432 1154
Telex: 127066

Exchange personnel
Chairman: Robert Fink
President & CEO: Arnold F. Staloff
Marketing Department: Gina Greer

Futures contracts available
Aluminium
Gold
High-grade copper (*Grade 2 copper was delisted in December 1989*)
Moody's Corporate Bond Index
Silver

Options contracts on futures available
Gold futures
High-grade copper futures
Silver futures

Clearing House: COMEX Clearing Association.

Method of trading: Open outcry.

Commenced trading: 1933.

Exchange links: Sydney Futures Exchange (SFE).
Joint venture with CSCE, NYMEX and NYFE including a shared trading arena.

A brief synopsis of the exchange
COMEX is a non-profit organisation that opened in 1933 as a merger of four older exchanges, and is currently the world's most active metals market-place, and a major force in the world gold market. Its history

may be traced back to the New York Metal Exchange that opened in 1883, the National Metal Exchange, the Rubber Exchange of New York and the National Raw Silk Exchange. Contracts with a value of over US$700 million were trading by 1933. Trading was halted during the Second World War, but resumed again in 1947.

There are nearly 800 exchange seats held by firms and individuals, whose business is cleared by one of the 70-plus clearing members. Trading is conducted in a 22,000-square-foot trading floor, shared by three other New York futures exchanges.

COMEX is the third largest futures exchange in the USA and is regulated by the CTFC (Commodities and Futures Trading Commission). Options were first introduced in 1982. Future plans include the introduction of the world's first diamond futures contract.

Aluminium futures

Contract size	44,000 pounds of New York primary aluminium of a minimum 99.7% purity.
Standard delivery method	Physical delivery of the above. Alternative grades may be substituted at the seller's option. Exchange for physicals (EFPs) are also allowed at the agreement of both the buyer and seller.
Trading months	The nearby three consecutive calendar months plus months from the January, March, May, July, September and December cycle up to 23 months forward.
Trading hours	9.30 a.m. – 2.10 p.m.
Price quotation method	In US dollars (US$) and cents per pound.
Minimum price move (value)	0.05 US cents per pound (US$22.00 per contract).
Daily price limits	None.
Position limits	None.
Last trading day	The third to last business day of the contract month.
Delivery day	The notice period runs from the last business day of the month preceding the contract month to the second last business day of the contract month.
Initial (Variation) margin	US$2,500 per contract.
Spread margin	Not stated.
Reuters Monitor (Quote)	ALXE – ALXF.
Telerate page	921.

Gold futures

Contract size	100 troy ounces of refined gold bullion of not less than 995 fineness.
Standard delivery method	Physical delivery of the above. A cash settlement alternative is also available.
Trading months	The current (spot) month, the next two consecutive calendar months then months from the February, April, June, August, October and December cycle up to 23 months forward.
Trading hours	8.20 a.m. – 2.30 p.m.
Price quotation method	In US dollars (US$) and cents per troy ounce.
Minimum price move (value)	US$0.10 per troy ounce (US$10.00 per contract).
Daily price limits	None.

Position limits	Speculators only: 6,000 contracts (3,000 contracts in the spot month).
Last trading day	The third to last business day of the contract month.
Delivery day	The notice period runs from the last business day of the month preceding the contract month to the second to last business day of the contract month.
Initial (Variation) margin	Hedgers: US$1,300 per contract (US$975). Speculators: US$1,300 per contract (US$1,000).
Spread margin	Not stated.
Reuters Monitor (Quote)	GDXE – GDXF, GDQE – GDQF.
Telerate page	920.

High-grade copper (HG) futures

Contract size	25,000 pounds of high-grade (Grade 1) electrolytic cathode copper.
Standard delivery method	Physical delivery of Grade 1 electrolytic copper (per ASTM specifications) only. For a complete list of exchange-approved brands and markings, warehouses, assayers and weightmasters, please contact the exchange. A cash settlement alternative is also available.
Trading months	The current (spot) month, the next 11 consecutive calendar months and then months from the January, March, May, July, September and December cycle up to 23 months forward.
Trading hours	9.25 a.m. – 2.00 p.m.
Price quotation method	In US dollars (US$) and cents per pound.
Minimum price move (value)	Five-hundredths (5/100) of a US cent (US$0.0005) per pound (US$12.50 per contract).
Daily price limits	None.
Position limits	None.
Last trading day	The third to last business day of the contract month.
Delivery day	The notice period runs from the last business day of the month preceding the contract month to the second to last business day of the contract month.
Initial (Variation) margin	Not stated. Please consult the exchange for the current margin requirements.
Spread margin	Not stated.
Reuters Monitor (Quote)	CWQE – CWQF.
Telerate page	933.

Moody's Corporate Bond Index futures

Contract size	US$500 multiplied by the Moody's Investment Grade Corporate Bond ('Moody's Index') Index.*
Standard delivery method	Cash settlement at the closing value of the Moody's Index on the last trading day.
Trading months	The March, June, September and December cycle, up to 23 months forward from the current month.
Trading hours	8.20 a.m. – 3.00 p.m.
Price quotation method	In US dollars (US$) per Moody's Index point.
Minimum price move (value)	0.05 of one Moody's Index point (US$25.00 per contract).
Daily price limits	None.
Position limits	None.
Last trading day	The first business day of the contract month when COMEX and NYSE are both open for trading.
Delivery day	The business day following the last trading day.
Initial (Variation) margin	Not stated. Please consult the exchange for the current margin requirements.
Spread margin	Not stated.
Reuters Monitor (Quote)	N/a.
Telerate page	15200 (Spot Index).

* The Moody's Index is a price-weighted, total-return index of 80 investment grade eligible corporate bonds, rated Baa or greater, non-convertible, non-taxable, with more than five years to maturity and with fixed coupons. All are issued by domestic corporations, and a minimum of 40 separate issuers are represented in the Index. The base value for the index is 31 December 1979. The index is adjusted quarterly, and bonds are removed if they are downgraded below grade Baa. The index is quoted officially at 3.00 p.m. daily.

Silver (SI) futures

Contract size	5,000 troy ounces of refined silver of not less than 0.999 fineness.
Standard delivery method	Physical delivery of the above, 6% more or less in cast bars. A cash settlement alternative is also available.
Trading months	The current (spot) month, the next two consecutive calendar months then months from the January, March, May, July, September and December cycle up to 23 months forward.
Trading hours	9.05 a.m. – 2.25 p.m.
Price quotation method	In US dollars (US$) and cents per troy ounce.
Minimum price move (value)	0.1 US cents (US$0.001) per troy ounce (US$5.00 per contract).
Daily price limits	50 US cents (US$0.50) per troy ounce above or below the previous day's settlement price. Limits are expanded after two successive limit up or limit-down days. There are no limits in the spot month.

Position limits	None.
Last trading day	The third to last business day of the contract month.
Delivery day	The notice period runs from the last business day of the month preceding the contract month to the second to last business day of the contract month.
Initial (Variation) margin	Hedgers: US$975 per contract (US$975) – or approximately 6% of the underlying contract value.
	Speculators: US$1,300 per contract (US$975).
Spread margin	Not stated.
Reuters Monitor (Quote)	SIQE – SIQF, SIXE – SIXF.
Telerate page	922.

Option on COMEX gold futures

Contract size	One COMEX gold futures contract (of an underlying contract size of 100 troy ounces).
Standard delivery method	Delivery of a long or short position in a futures contract at the strike price as above.
Trading months	The nearest four months of the February, April, June, August, October and December cycle.
Trading hours	8.20 a.m. – 2.30 p.m.
Price quotation method	In US dollars (US$) and cents per troy ounce.
Minimum price move (value)	10 US cents (US$0.10) per troy ounce (US$10.00 per contract).
Daily price limits	None.
Position limits	None.
Last trading day	The second Friday of the month preceding the contract month of the underlying futures contract.
Delivery day	The business day following the last trading day.
Initial (Variation) margin	For uncovered short option positions, margin is calculated as the premium received plus the greater of: (a) the initial futures margin minus half the amount (if any) by which the option is out-of-the-money; or (b) half the initial futures margin.
Spread margin	Various spread concessions are available for different strategies.
Strike price intervals	Futures price under US$500: US$10.00.
	Futures price from US$500 to US$1,000: US$20.00.
	Futures price over US$1,000: US$50.00.
Option type	American style (the options may be exercised up to 3.00 p.m. on any business day up to and including the last trading day and up to 4.00 p.m. on the last trading day). Options are automatically exercised at expiry if they are in-the-money by at least US$300 per contract in total value.

Method of introduction of new strike prices	There are nine strike prices listed initially. New strikes are introduced so as to allow there to be at least four series both in-the-money and out-of-the-money. No new strike prices are normally introduced after the fourth day before the second Friday of the month preceding the contract month.
Reuters Monitor (Quote)	GDYE – GDYR, 1AUA – 1AUN.
Telerate page	8490-8497.

Option on COMEX high-grade copper (HX) futures

Contract size	One COMEX high-grade copper futures contract (of an underlying contract size of 25,000 pounds).
Standard delivery method	Delivery of a long or short position in a futures contract at the strike price as above.
Trading months	The nearest four months of the March, May, July, September and December cycle.
Trading hours	9.25 a.m. – 2.00 p.m.
Price quotation method	In US dollars (US$) and cents per pound.
Minimum price move (value)	US$0.0005 per pound (US$12.50 per contract).
Daily price limits	None.
Position limits	None.
Last trading day	The second Friday of the month preceding the contract month of the underlying futures contract.
Delivery day	The option may be exercised until 3.00 p.m. on any business day up to the last trading day and up to 4.00 p.m. on the last trading day.
Initial (Variation) margin	For uncovered short option positions, margin is calculated as the premium received plus the greater of: (a) the initial futures margin minus half the amount (if any) by which the option is out-of-the-money; or (b) half the initial futures margin.
Spread margin	Various spread concessions are available for different strategies.
Strike price intervals	Strike price under US$0.40: 1 US cent. Strike price between US$0.40 and US$1.00: 2 US cents. Strike price over US$1.00: 5 US cents.
Option type	American style (the option may be exercised up to 3.00 p.m. on any business day up to and including the last trading day). Options are automatically exercised at expiry if they are in-the-money by at least US$300 per contract in total value.

Method of introduction of new strike prices	Nine strikes are available initially. New strike prices are added based on movements in the underlying futures contract price. No new strike prices are added after the fourth day before the second Friday on the month preceding the contract month.
Reuters Monitor (Quote)	CPXA – CPXX, CWQH – CWRA.
Telerate page	934 – 937, 895 – 898.

Option on COMEX silver (SI) futures

Contract size	One COMEX silver futures contract (of an underlying contract size of 5,000 troy ounces).
Standard delivery method	Delivery of a long or short position in a futures contract at the strike price as above.
Trading months	The nearest four months of the March, May, July, September and December cycle.
Trading hours	8.25 a.m. – 2.25 p.m.
Price quotation method	In US dollars (US$) and cents per troy ounce.
Minimum price move (value)	0.1 US cents (US$0.001) per troy ounce (US$5.00 per contract).
Daily price limits	None.
Position limits	None.
Last trading day	The second Friday of the month preceding the contract month of the underlying futures contract.
Delivery day	The business day following the last trading day.
Initial (Variation) margin	For uncovered short option positions, margin is calculated as the premium received plus the greater of: (a) the initial futures margin minus half the amount (if any) by which the option is out-of-the-money; or (b) half the initial futures margin.
Spread margin	Various spread concessions are available for different strategies.
Strike price intervals	Futures price under US$8.00: US$0.25. Futures price between US$8.00 and US$15.00: US$0.50. Futures price over US$15.00: US$1.00.
Option type	American style (the options may be exercised up to 3.00 p.m. on any business day up to and including the last trading day and up to 4.00 p.m. on the last trading day). Options are automatically exercised at expiry if they are in-the-money by at least US$300 per contract in total value.
Method of introduction of new strike prices	There are nine strike prices listed initially. New strike prices are introduced so as to allow there to be at least four series both in-the-money and out-of-the-money. No new strike prices are normally introduced after the fourth day before the second Friday of the month preceding the contract month.
Reuters Monitor (Quote)	SIIA – SIIV, 1AGA – 1AGV.
Telerate page	963 – 970.

New York Cotton Exchange, Inc (NYCE)

Citrus Associates of the New York Cotton
Exchange (CA)
(an affiliate of the NYCE)
Financial Instrument Exchange (FINEX)
(a division of the NYCE)

Address:	4 World Trade Center New York New York 10048 USA
Telephone:	(212) 938 2650 – NYCE (212) 938 2607 – CA (212) 938 2652 – FINEX
Fax:	(212) 839 8061
Telex:	961312

Exchange personnel

Chairman:	Donald Conlin
President:	Joseph O'Neill
Director of Marketing:	Ann Bruch
Information Officer:	Andrea B. Liebelt

Futures contracts available at NYCE
Cotton

Futures contracts available at CA
Frozen concentrated orange juice

Futures contracts available at FINEX
European Currency Unit (ECU) / US dollar currency
Five-year US Government Treasury Notes
30-year Benchmark US Government Treasury Bonds
(*traded at NYFE*)
Two-year US Government Treasury Notes
US Dollar Index

Options contracts on futures available at NYCE
Cotton futures

Options contracts on futures available at CA
Frozen concentrated orange juice futures

Options contracts on futures available at FINEX
Five-year US Government Treasury Note futures
US Dollar Index futures

Clearing House: Commodity Clearing Corporation (CCC).

Method of trading: Open outcry.

Commenced trading: NYCE: 1870.
                           CA: 1966.
                           FINEX: 1985.

Exchange links: The New York Futures Exchange (NYFE) is now an
                           affiliate of the NYCE.

A brief synopsis of the exchange
The New York Cotton Exchange is the oldest
commodity exchange in New York, and has been an
integral part of the cotton industry for over a century.
In 1966, agricultural futures and options were
introduced via an affiliate, the Citrus Associates of the
NYCE, while in 1985 the Financial Instrument
Exchange (FINEX) was created to expand into the
area of financial futures and options.

In 1988, the New York Futures Exchange (NYFE)
became an affiliate of NYCE and the trading floor is
shared by other New York futures exchanges
(COMEX, NYFE and NYMEX). The exchange has
around 450 seat memberships but when the other
exchanges on the same floor are included there can be
over 1,500 traders in the World Trade Center.

Cotton futures

Contract size	50,000 pounds net weight of cotton (approximately 100 bales).
Standard delivery method	Physical delivery of the above in Galveston, Houston, New Orleans, Memphis or Greenville.
Trading months	The current (spot) month plus the next 17 consecutive calendar months (the most active trading months are March, May, July, October and December).
Trading hours	10.30 a.m. – 3.00 p.m.
Price quotation method	In US cents and one-hundredths (1/100) of a US cent per pound net weight.
Minimum price move (value)	One-hundredth (1/100) of a US cent per pound (US$5.00 per contract).
Daily price limits	Two US cents (US$0.02) above or below the previous day's settlement price. There are no limits for the spot month after the first notice day.
Position limits	1,200 contracts (single month position – 450 contracts, spot month limit – 300 contracts).
Last trading day	17 business days from the end of the contract month.
Delivery/notice days	The delivery period runs from the first business day of the contract month to five business days after the last notice day. The first notice day is five business days from the end of the month preceding the contract month. The final notice day is five business days after the last trading day.
Initial (Variation) margin	Hedgers: US$750 per contract (US$750). Speculators: US$1,500 per contract (US$1,125).
Spread margin	Hedgers: US$100 per spread position (US$100). Speculators: US$200 per spread position (US$150).
Reuters Monitor (Quote)	CNNE.
Telerate page	930.

Frozen concentrated orange juice (FCOJ) futures

Contract size	15,000 pounds of orange solids (3% more or less).
Standard delivery method	Physical delivery of the above in Florida warehouses in drums or tanks, at the seller's choice.
Trading months	The January, March, May, July, September and November cycle.
Trading hours	10.15 a.m. – 2.45 p.m.
Price quotation method	In US cents and one-hundredths (1/100) of a US cent per pound.
Minimum price move (value)	0.05 of a US cent per pound (US$7.50 per contract).

Daily price limits	Five US cents (US$0.05) per pound (US$750 per contract). with the exception of the spot month – 10 US cents (US$0.10) per pound (US$1,500 per contract).
Position limits	None.
Last trading day	The ninth business day prior to the last delivery day.
Delivery/notice days	The delivery period runs from five business days after the first notice day through to the last business day of the contract month. The first notice day is the first business day of the contract month. The final notice day is five business days prior to the last delivery day of the contract month.

Initial (Variation) margin	Hedgers:	US$750 per contract (US$563).
	Speculators:	US$1,500 per contract (US$1,125).
Spread margin	Hedgers:	US$500 per spread position (US$375).
	Speculators:	US$500 per spread position (US$375).
Reuters Monitor (Quote)	ORNE.	
Telerate page	930.	

European Currency Unit (ECU) / US dollar currency futures

Contract size	ECU100,000 traded against the US dollar (US$).
Standard delivery method	Physical delivery of the ECU* against the US dollar (US$) at expiry.
Trading months	The March, June, September and December cycle.
Trading hours	8.20 a.m. – 3.00 p.m.
Price quotation method	In US cents and one-hundredths (1/100) of a US cent per ECU (each US cent represents US$1,000 per futures contract).
Minimum price move (value)	0.01 of a US cent (US$0.0001) per ECU1.00 (US$10.00 per contract).
Daily price limits	Two US cents (US$0.02) per ECU1.00 above or below the previous night's settlement price. Trading ccases for 15 minutes, then a further two US cents (US$0.02) per ECU1.00 limit is set.
Position limits	None.
Last trading day	Two business days prior to the third Wednesday of the contract month.
Delivery day	The business day following the last trading day.

Initial (Variation) margin	Hedgers:	US$1,250 per contract (US$937.50).
	Speculators:	US$2,500 per contract (US$1,875).
Spread margin	Hedgers:	US$200 per spread position (US$150).
	Speculators:	US$200 per spread position (US$150).

Reuters Monitor (Quote)	ECNE, EC61.
Telerate page	907

* The ECU is defined as the sum of the following amount of each currency and was last revised on 21 September 1989:

Currency	Amount	Currency	Amount
West German Deutschmark	0.6242	French franc	1.332
British pound	0.08784	Italian lira	151.80
Dutch guilder	0.2198	Belgian/Luxembourg franc	3.431
Spanish peseta	6.885	Danish krone	0.1976
Greek drachma	1.440	Irish punt	0.008552
Portuguese escudo	1.393		

Five-year US Government Treasury Note (FYTR) futures

Contract size	US Government Treasury Notes with a nominal face value at maturity of US$100,000 and a notional coupon rate of 8%.
Standard delivery method	Physical delivery of the above Treasury Notes, adjusted by conversion factors to account for coupon rates different to 8%.
Trading months	The March, June, September and December cycle.
Trading hours	8.20 a.m. – 4.15 p.m. Trading ceases in the expiring contract at 1.00 p.m. on the last trading day.
Price quotation method	In US dollars (US$) and cents per cent of par.
Minimum price move (value)	Increments of one-half (1/2) of one thirty-second (1/32) of 1% (US$15.625 per contract).
Daily price limits	None.
Position limits	None.
Last trading day	The eighth to last business day of the contract month.
Delivery day	The delivery period is from the first business day of the contract month through to the last business day of the contract month.
Initial (Variation) margin	Hedgers: US$500 per contract (US$375). Speculators: US$1,000 per contract (US$750).
Spread margin	Hedgers: US$200 per spread position (US$150). Speculators: US$200 per spread position (US$150).
Reuters Monitor (Quote)	TONE.
Telerate page	906.

Two-year US Government Treasury Notes (2YTN) futures

Contract size	US Government Treasury Notes with a nominal face value at maturity of US$200,000 and a notional coupon rate of 8%.
Standard delivery method	Physical delivery of the above Treasury Notes, adjusted by conversion factors to account for coupon rates different to 8%.

Trading months	Each consecutive calendar month.
Trading hours	8.20 a.m. – 4.15 p.m. Trading ceases in the expiring contract at 1.00 p.m. on the last trading day.
Price quotation method	In US dollars (US$) and cents per cent of par.
Minimum price move (value)	Increments of one-quarter (1/4) of one thirty-second (1/32) of 1% (US$15.625 per contract).
Daily price limits	None.
Position limits	None.
Last trading day	The eighth to last business day of the contract month.
Delivery day	The delivery period runs from the first business day of the contract month through to the latter of either the last business day of the contract month or the business day on which there is an auction of a two-year Treasury Note during the contract month.
Initial (Variation) margin	Hedgers: US$500 per contract (US$375). Speculators: US$1,000 per contract (US$750).
Spread margin	Hedgers: US$200 per spread position (US$150). Speculators: US$200 per spread position (US$150).
Reuters Monitor (Quote)	TNNE.
Telerate page	919.

US Dollar Index (USDX) futures

Contract size	US$500 multiplied by the US Dollar Index (the index is a trade-weighted geometric average of the 10 currencies listed below).*
Standard delivery method	Cash settlement based on the final settlement value of the US Dollar Index at 10.00 a.m. of the last trading day of the contract.
Trading months	The March, June, September and December cycle.
Trading hours	8.20 a.m. – 3.00 p.m.
Price quotation method	The US Dollar Index is quoted as a percentage of its value as of March 1973, calculated to two decimal places (for example, 101.57), in US dollars (US$).
Minimum price move (value)	0.01% (US$5.00 per contract).
Daily price limits	Two index points above or below the previous night's settlement price. Trading ceases for 15 minutes, then a further limit of two index points is set.
Position limits	None.
Last trading day	The third Wednesday of the contract month.
Delivery day	The business day following the last trading day.
Initial (Variation) margin	Hedgers: US$500 per contract (US$375). Speculators: US$1,000 per contract (US$750).

Spread margin	Hedgers: US$200 per spread position (US$150).
	Speculators: US$200 per spread position (US$150).
Reuters Monitor (Quote)	DLRN (USDX for the underlying index).
Telerate page	907.

* The constituent currencies of the US Dollar Index (USDX) are as follows:

West German Deutschmark (DM)	Japanese yen (Y)
French franc (FFr)	British pound (£)
Canadian dollar (C$)	Italian lira (L)
Dutch guilder (Dfl)	Belgian franc (BFr)
Swedish krona (SKr)	Swiss franc (SFr)

Option on NYCE cotton futures

Contract size	One NYCE cotton futures contract (of an underlying contract size of 50,000 pounds).
Standard delivery method	Delivery of a long or short position in a futures contract at the strike price as above.
Trading months	The March, May, July, October and December cycle with the nearest seven contract months available for trading.
Trading hours	10.30 a.m. – 3.00 p.m. The option is exercisable up to 3.00 p.m. on any business day or up to 4.00 p.m. on the last trading day.
Price quotation method	In US cents and one-hundredths (1/100) of a US cent per pound net weight.
Minimum price move (value)	One-hundredth (1/100) of a US cent per pound (US$5.00 per contract).
Daily price limits	None.
Position limits	1,200 contracts (single month position – 450 contracts, spot month limit – 300 contracts).
Last trading day	The first Friday of the month preceding the contract month.
Delivery day	The business day following the last trading day.
Initial (Variation) margin	Not stated. Please consult the exchange or your broker for the current details.
Spread margin	Not stated. Please consult the exchange or your broker for the current details.
Strike price intervals	For the nearest three contract months: at one US cent (US$0.01) intervals up to 74 US cents (US$0.74), thereafter at two US cent (US$0.02) intervals.
	For the distant four contract months: at two US cent (US$0.02) intervals.
Option type	American style (the option may be exercised on any business day up to and including the last trading day).
Method of introduction of new strike prices	Not stated.
Reuters Monitor (Quote)	CNNF – CNOU.
Telerate page	N/a.

**Citrus Associates
of the NYCE (CA)
Options on futures
Softs and
agricultural**

Option on CA frozen concentrated orange juice (FCOJ) futures

Contract size	One CA frozen concentrated orange juice (FCOJ) futures contract (of an underlying contract size of 15,000 pounds).
Standard delivery method	Delivery of a long or short position in a futures contract at the strike price as above.
Trading months	The January, March, May, July, September and November cycle (the nearest six contract months are available for trading at all times).
Trading hours	10.15 a.m. – 2.45 p.m. The option may be exercised until 2.45 p.m. on any business day or up to 4.00 p.m. on the last trading day.
Price quotation method	In US cents and one-hundredths (1/100) of a US cent per pound.
Minimum price move (value)	0.05 of a US cent per pound (US$7.50 per contract).
Daily price limits	None.
Position limits	None.
Last trading day	The first Friday of the month preceding the underlying futures contract month.
Delivery day	The business day following the last trading day.
Initial (Variation) margin	Not stated. Please consult the exchange or your broker for the current details.
Spread margin	Not stated. Please consult the exchange or your broker for the current details.
Strike price intervals	At 2.50 US cents (US$0.025) intervals for all contract months.
Option type	American style (the option may be exercised on any business day up to and including the last trading day).
Method of introduction of new strike prices	Not stated.
Reuters Monitor (Quote)	N/a.
Telerate page	N/a.

Option on FINEX five-year US Government Treasury Note (FYTR) futures

Contract size	One FINEX five-year Treasury Note (FYTR) futures contract (of an underlying contract size of US$100,000 nominal face value).
Standard delivery method	Delivery of a long or short position in a futures contract at the strike price as above.
Trading months	The March, June, September and December cycle.
Trading hours	8.20 a.m. – 4.15 p.m. The option may be exercised until 5.00 p.m. on the last trading day.

Price quotation method	In points and sixty-fourths (1/64) of 1%, quoted in US dollars (US$).
Minimum price move (value)	One sixty-fourth (1/64) of 1% (US$15.625 per contract).
Daily price limits	None.
Position limits	None.
Last trading day	The first Friday that is at least five business days prior to the first business day of the contract month.
Delivery day	The business day following the last trading day.
Initial (Variation) margin	Not stated. Please consult the exchange or your broker for the current details.
Spread margin	Not stated. Please consult the exchange or your broker for the current details.
Strike price intervals	At 0.5 FYTR futures contract point intervals.
Option type	American style (the option may be exercised on any business day up to and including the last trading day).
Method of introduction of new strike prices	Not stated.
Reuters Monitor (Quote)	N/a.
Telerate page	8482 – 8484.

Option on FINEX US Dollar Index (USDX) futures

Contract size	One FINEX US Dollar Index futures contract (of an underlying contract size of US$500 multiplied by the USDX index).
Standard delivery method	Delivery of a long or short position in a futures contract at the strike price as above.
Trading months	The March, June, September and December cycle.
Trading hours	8.20 a.m. – 3.00 p.m.
Price quotation method	In US Dollar Index points and one-hundredths (1/100) of a point quoted in US dollars (US$).
Minimum price move (value)	0.01 of a US dollar Index point (US$5.00 per contract).
Daily price limits	Two index points above or below the previous night's settlement price. Trading ceases for 15 minutes, then a further limit of two index points is set.
Position limits	None.
Last trading day	Two Fridays before the third Wednesday of the contract month.
Delivery day	The business day following the last trading day.
Initial (Variation) margin	Not stated. Please consult the exchange or your broker for the current details.
Spread margin	Not stated. Please consult the exchange or your broker for the current details.

Strike price intervals	At intervals of two US dollar Index points (200 basis points).
Option type	American style (the option may be exercised on any business day up to and including the last trading day).
Method of introduction of new strike prices	Not stated.
Reuters Monitor (Quote)	N/a.
Telerate page	8476 – 8583.

New York Mercantile Exchange (NYMEX)

Address:

4 World Trade Center
New York
New York 10048
USA

Telephone: (212) 938 2200
Fax: (212) 938 2985
Telex: N/a.

Exchange personnel

Chairman: Z. Lou Guttman
President: R. Patrick Thompson
SVP, Marketing: Jan B. Kay
Consultant: Rosemary McFadden

UK Representative Office

Address:

NYMEX London Information Bureau
c/o Trimedia
16 John Adam Street
London WC2N 6LU
United Kingdom

Telephone: (01) 930 1900
Fax: (01) 839 3579
Telex: 8812128 TRIMED G
Contact: Katy Glaister

Futures contracts available
Crude oil
Natural gas (*proposed*)
No.2 heating oil
Palladium
Platinum
Propane
Residual heavy fuel oil
Unleaded gasoline

Option contracts on futures available
Crude oil futures
No.2 heating oil futures
Platinum futures
Unleaded gasoline futures

Clearing House:	NYMEX Clearing House.
Method of trading:	Open outcry.
Commenced trading:	1872.
Exchange links:	Joint venture with COMEX, CSCE and the NYFE including a shared trading floor.

A brief synopsis of the exchange

The exchange was founded in 1872 as the Butter and Cheese Exchange of New York, the switch to strategic commodities beginning in 1956 with the introduction of platinum futures. Platinum futures was the first precious metals futures contract to be traded in the world.

In 1978, NYMEX pioneered energy futures trading with the heating oil contract. NYMEX is the largest energy exchange worldwide.

Crude oil futures

Contract size	1,000 US barrels (42,000 gallons) of par West Texas intermediate crude oil.
Standard delivery method	Physical delivery of the above, FOB seller's facility, Cushing, Oklahoma at any pipeline or storage facility with pipeline access to Arco or Texaco, by in-tank transfer, in-line transfer, book-out or inter-facility transfer. Other deliverable crude oil grades are Mid-continent sweet, Low sweet mix, New Mexican sweet, Oklahoma sweet, South Texas sweet, Brent blend, Bonny light and Oseberg.
Trading months	The 18 nearest consecutive calendar months commencing with the current (spot) calendar month.
Trading hours	9.45 a.m. – 3.10 p.m.
Price quotation method	In US dollars (US$) and cents per barrel.
Minimum price move (value)	US$0.01 (one US cent) per barrel (US$10.00 per contract).
Daily price limits	US$1.00 per barrel above or below the previous day's settlement price. There are no limits during the month preceding the contract month.
Position limits	None.
Last trading day	The third business day prior to the 25th calendar day of the month preceding the contract month.
Delivery day	All deliveries must be initiated after the first calendar day and completed before the last calendar day of the contract month.
Initial (Variation) margin	US$2,500 per contract.
Spread margin	US$200 (inter-market), US$750 (intra-market), per spread position.
Reuters Monitor (Quote)	PPNI – PPNJ.
Telerate page	8810 – 8811, Composite page: 8805.

Natural gas futures (*proposed*)

Contract size	10,000 MMBtu (million British thermal units) of natural gas.
Standard delivery method	Physical delivery of the above to pipeline specifications in force at the time of delivery through the Sabine Pipe Line Company's Henry Hub in Louisiana. There are alternative delivery procedures (AVPs) and exchange for physicals (AFPs) procedures also available.
Trading months	Not yet determined.
Trading hours	Not yet determined.
Price quotation method	In US dollars (US$) and cents per MMBtu.

Minimum price move (value)	US$0.001 per MMBtu (US$10.00 per contract).
Daily price limits	10 US cents (US$0.10) per MMBtu (US$1,000 per contract) above or below the previous day's settlement price. There are no limits during the month in which the futures expire.
Position limits	None.
Last trading day	Nine business days prior to the first calendar day of the contract month.
Delivery day	Delivery takes place from the first calendar day of the contract month through to the last calendar day of the contract month. Payment is to be made by Fed Funds wire transfer by 12.00 noon on the 20th calendar day of the month following the contract month.
Initial (Variation) margin	Not yet announced.
Spread margin	Not yet announced.
Reuters Monitor (Quote)	LGNG – LGNH, UG65 – UG66.
Telerate page	Composite page: 8805.

No.2 heating oil futures

Contract size	42,000 US gallons (1,000 barrels) of industry standard fungible No.2 heating oil.
Standard delivery method	Physical delivery of the above, FOB seller's facility, New York Harbour ex-shore. Delivery may also take place by pipeline, tanker, book transfer or inter- or intra-facility transfer.
Trading months	The 15 nearest consecutive calendar months commencing with the current (spot) calendar month.
Trading hours	9.50 a.m. – 3.10 p.m.
Price quotation method	In US dollars (US$) and cents per gallon.
Minimum price move (value)	0.01 US cents per gallon (US$4.20 per contract).
Daily price limits	Two US cents (US$0.02) per gallon above or below the previous day's settlement price. There are no price limits during the month preceding the contract month.
Position limits	None.
Last trading day	The last business day of the month preceding the contract month.
Delivery day	All deliveries must be initiated after the fifth business day and be completed before the last business day of the contract month.
Initial (Variation) margin	US$2,500 per contract.
Spread margin	US$200 (inter-market), US$750 (intra-market), per spread position.
Reuters Monitor (Quote)	PPNE – PPNF, HO65 – HO66.
Telerate page	8806, Composite page: 8805.

Palladium futures

Contract size	100 troy ounces of minimum 99.9% content palladium.
Standard delivery method	Physical delivery of the above, or 99.8% palladium at a US$6.00 per troy ounce discount.
Trading months	The 15 months beginning with the current (spot) month and the next two consecutive calendar months plus months from the March, June, September and December cycle.
Trading hours	8.10 a.m. – 2.20 p.m.
Price quotation method	In US dollars (US$) and cents per troy ounce.
Minimum price move (value)	US$0.05 per troy ounce (US$5.00 per contract).
Daily price limits	US$6.00 per troy ounce above or below the previous day's settlement price. There are no limits during the current contract month and the preceding three business days.
Position limits	None.
Last trading day	The fourth business day prior to the end of the contract month.
Delivery day	From the last business day in the month preceding the contract month up to and including the third business day prior to the end of the contract month.
Initial (Variation) margin	US$1,000 per contract.
Spread margin	US$500 (inter-market) per spread position.
Reuters Monitor (Quote)	PANE, PAQE.
Telerate page	924, Composite page: 8805.

Platinum futures

Contract size	50 troy ounces of minimum 99.99% content platinum.
Standard delivery method	Physical delivery of the above, or 99.5% platinum discounted by US$7.50 per troy ounce.
Trading months	The 15 months beginning with the current (spot) month and the next two consecutive months plus months from the January, April, July and October cycle.
Trading hours	8.20 a.m. – 2.30 p.m.
Price quotation method	In US dollars (US$) and cents per troy ounce.
Minimum price move (value)	US$0.10 per troy ounce (US$5.00 per contract).
Daily price limits	US$25.00 per troy ounce above or below the previous day's settlement price. There are no limits during the current contract month and the three business days preceding it.
Position limits	None.
Last trading day	The fourth business day prior to the end of the contract month.

Delivery day	From the last business day in the month preceding the contract month up to and including the third business day prior to the end of the contract month.
Initial (Variation) margin	US$2,000 per contract.
Spread margin	US$300 (inter-market) per spread position.
Reuters Monitor (Quote)	PLQE, PLNE.
Telerate page	924, Composite page: 8805.

Propane futures

Contract size	42,000 US gallons (1,000 barrels) of liquidified propane gas as determined by the Gas Processors Association (GPA-HD5).
Standard delivery method	Physical delivery of the above, FOB seller's pipeline, storage or fractionation facility in Mont Belvieu, Texas with direct pipeline access to the Texas Eastern Transmission Pipeline in Mont Belvieu, Texas. Delivery may also be made in-line, in-well, inter-facility transfer, pump-over or book transfer.
Trading months	The nearest 15 consecutive calendar months commencing with the current (spot) calendar month.
Trading hours	9.50 a.m. – 3.10 p.m.
Price quotation method	In US dollars (US$) and cents per gallon.
Minimum price move (value)	US$0.01 (one US cent) per gallon (US$4.20 per contract).
Daily price limits	Two US cents (US$0.02) per gallon above or below the previous day's settlement price. There are no limits during the month preceding the delivery month.
Position limits	5,000 contracts net long or short speculative limit in all months combined (1,000 in the spot month).
Last trading day	The last business day of the month preceding the contract month.
Delivery day	All deliveries must be initiated after the ninth business day and completed before the second to last business day of the contract month.
Initial (Variation) margin	US$1,250 per contract.
Spread margin	US$200 (inter-market), US$1,000 (intra-market), per spread position.
Reuters Monitor (Quote)	PRNE – PRNF, PR65 – PR66.
Telerate page	8812 – 8813, Composite page: 8805.

Residual heavy fuel oil futures

Contract size	1,000 US barrels (42,000 gallons) of 1% low-pour residual heavy fuel oil, conforming to industry standards.

Standard delivery method	Physical delivery of the above, FOB seller's facility, Houston Ship Canal ex-shore. Delivery may also be taken by tanker, barge, stock transfer or pump-over.
Trading months	The nearest 15 consecutive calendar months commencing with the current (spot) calendar month.
Trading hours	9.45 a.m. – 3.10 p.m.
Price quotation method	In US dollars (US$) and cents per barrel.
Minimum price move (value)	US$0.01 (one US cent) per barrel (US$10.00 per contract).
Daily price limits	US$1.00 per barrel (US$1,000 per contract) above or below the previous day's settlement price. There are no price limits in the month preceding the contract month.
Position limits	None.
Last trading day	The last business day of the month preceding the contract month.
Delivery day	All deliveries must be initiated after the fifth business day and be completed before the last business day of the contract month.
Initial (Variation) margin	Not stated. Please consult the exchange or your broker for the current margin requirements.
Spread margin	Not stated. Please consult the exchange or your broker for the current spread concessions.
Reuters Monitor (Quote)	N/a.
Telerate page	Composite page: 8805.

Unleaded gasoline futures

Contract size	42,000 US gallons (1,000 barrels) of fungible northern grades 47 and 48 unleaded gasoline.
Standard delivery method	Physical delivery of the above, FOB seller's shore facility, New York Harbour ex-shore, capable of delivery into trucks or barges at the buyer's option. Delivery may also be completed by tanker, pipeline, book transfer or inter- or intra-facility transfer.
Trading months	The 15 nearest consecutive calendar months commencing with the current (spot) calendar month.
Trading hours	9.50 a.m. – 3.10 p.m.
Price quotation method	In US dollars (US$) and cents per gallon.
Minimum price move (value)	0.01 US cents per gallon (US$4.20 per contract).
Daily price limits	US$0.02 per gallon above or below the previous day's settlement price. There are no limits during the month preceding the delivery month.
Position limits	None.
Last trading day	The last business day of the month preceding the contract month.

Delivery day	All deliveries must be initiated after the fifth business day and before the last business day of the contract month.
Initial (Variation) margin	US$2,500 per contract.
Spread margin	US$300 (intra-market), US$750 (inter-market), per spread position.
Reuters Monitor (Quote)	LGNG.
Telerate page	8807.

Option on NYMEX crude oil futures

Contract size	One NYMEX crude oil futures contract (of an underlying contract size of 1,000 barrels).
Standard delivery method	Delivery of a long or short position in a futures contract at the strike price as above.
Trading months	The six nearby consecutive calendar months.
Trading hours	9.45 a.m. – 3.10 p.m.
Price quotation method	In US dollars (US$) and cents per barrel.
Minimum price move (value)	US$0.01 (one US cent) per barrel (US$10.00 per contract).
Daily price limits	None.
Position limits	None.
Last trading day	The second Friday of the month prior to the underlying futures contract month, provided there are at least five days remaining to trade in the underlying futures contract.
Delivery day	The business day following the last trading day.
Initial (Variation) margin	For uncovered short positions, the premium received plus an additional risk premium.
Spread margin	Not stated. Please consult the exchange or your broker for the current spread concessions.
Strike price intervals	At US$1.00 per gallon intervals.
Option type	American style (the option may be exercised on any business day up to 4.30 p.m. up to and including the last trading day).
Method of introduction of new strike prices	There are always at least seven strike prices available. The middle strike price is closest to the previous day's close of the underlying futures contract.
Reuters Monitor (Quote)	CRNE – CRNR, 1CRA – 1CRN.
Telerate page	8460 – 8466, 8470 – 8474, Composite page: 8805.

Option on NYMEX No.2 heating oil futures

Contract size	One NYMEX No.2 heating oil futures contract (of an underlying contract size of 42,000 gallons).
Standard delivery method	Delivery of a long or short position in a futures contract at the strike price as above.

Trading months	The six nearest consecutive calendar months.
Trading hours	9.50 a.m. – 3.10 p.m.
Price quotation method	In US dollars (US$) and cents per gallon.
Minimum price move (value)	0.1 US cents per gallon (US$4.20 per contract).
Daily price limits	None.
Position limits	None.
Last trading day	The second Friday of the month prior to the underlying futures' contract month.
Delivery day	The business day following the last trading day.
Initial (Variation) margin	For uncovered short positions, the premium received plus an additional risk premium.
Spread margin	Not stated. Please consult the exchange or your broker for the current spread concessions.
Strike price intervals	At US$0.02 (two US cents) per gallon intervals.
Option type	American style (the option may be exercised on any business day up to 4.30 p.m. up to and including the last trading day).
Method of introduction of new strike prices	There are always at least seven strike prices available. The middle strike price is closest to the previous day's close of the underlying futures contract.
Reuters Monitor (Quote)	HOQA – HOQN, 1HOA – 1HON.
Telerate page	8469 – 8474, Composite page: 8805.

Option on NYMEX platinum futures

Contract size	One NYMEX platinum futures contract (of an underlying contract size of 50 troy ounces).
Standard delivery method	Delivery of a long or short position in a futures contract at the strike price as above.
Trading months	All consecutive calendar months are available for trading, and are exercisable into underlying quarterly futures contracts as follows:
	November, December and January: January
	February, March and April: April
	May, June and July: July
	August, September and October: October.
Trading hours	8.20 a.m. – 2.30 p.m.
Price quotation method	In US dollars (US$) and cents per troy ounce.
Minimum price move (value)	10 US cents (US$0.10) per troy ounce (US$5.00 per contract).
Daily price limits	None.
Position limits	None.
Last trading day	The second Friday of the month preceding the contract month of the option.
Delivery day	The business day following exercise or the last trading day.

Initial (Variation) margin	For uncovered short positions, the premium received plus an additional risk premium.
Spread margin	Not stated. Please consult the exchange or your broker for the current spread concessions.
Strike price intervals	At US$20.00 per troy ounce intervals.
Option type	American style (the option may be exercised on any business day up to 4.00 p.m. up to and including the last trading day).
Method of introduction of new strike prices	There are seven strike prices listed initially. New series are introduced in line with movements in the underlying futures contract, retaining the middle strike price close to the previous day's close of the underlying futures contract.
Reuters Monitor (Quote)	N/a.
Telerate page	N/a.

Option on NYMEX unleaded gasoline futures

Contract size	One NYMEX unleaded gasoline futures contract (of an underlying contract size of 42,000 US gallons).
Standard delivery method	Delivery of a long or short position in a futures contract at the strike price as above.
Trading months	The six nearest consecutive calendar months.
Trading hours	9.50 a.m. – 3.10 p.m.
Price quotation method	In US dollars (US$) and cents per gallon.
Minimum price move (value)	0.1 US cents per gallon (US$4.20 per contract).
Daily price limits	None.
Position limits	None.
Last trading day	The second Friday of the month prior to the underlying futures contract month.
Delivery day	The business day following the last trading day.
Initial (Variation) margin	For uncovered short positions, the premium received plus an additional risk premium.
Spread margin	Not stated. Please consult the exchange or your broker for the current spread concessions.
Strike price intervals	At US$0.02 (two US cents) per gallon intervals.
Option type	American style (the option may be exercised on any business day up to 4.30 p.m. up to and including the last trading day).
Method of introduction of new strike prices	There are always at least seven strike prices available. The middle strike price is closest to the previous day's close of the underlying futures contract.
Reuters Monitor (Quote)	GOQE – GOQV.
Telerate page	Composite page: 8805.

New York Stock Exchange (NYSE)

New York Futures Exchange (NYFE)
(a subsidiary of the NYSE)

New York Stock Exchange

Address:	11 Wall Street
	New York
	New York 10005
	USA
Telephone:	(212) 656 8533
Fax:	(212) 656 2925
Telex:	710 581 5464

Exchange personnel

Chairman:	John Phelan
President:	Richard Grasso
Executive VP, Derivative Products:	Lewis Horowitz
VP, Options/Index Products:	David Krell
Managing Director:	Joseph Mimms
Information Officer:	Sharon Gamsin

New York Futures Exchange

Address:	20 Broad Street
	New York
	New York 10005
	USA
Telephone:	(212) 656 4949
Fax:	(212) 656 2925
Telex:	Twix 7105815464

Exchange personnel

Chairman & President:	Lewis Horowitz
Senior Vice-President:	Richard Edgar
Managing Director:	Charles Epstein
Information Officer:	Sharon Gamsin

Futures contracts available on NYFE
Commodity Research Bureau (CRB) Index
NYSE Composite Stock Index
30-year Benchmark US Government Treasury Bonds
(*traded with FINEX*)

*Options contracts on cash/physical available on
NYSE*
NYSE Composite Stock Index

Options contracts on futures available on NYFE
Commodity Research Bureau (CRB) Index futures
NYSE Composite Stock Index futures

*The NYSE also trades options on over 40 US equities, the
contract size of these equity options being 100 shares
underlying each option. Options trade the nearby two
months plus the next two months in their quarterly
expiration cycle.*

Clearing House:

Options Clearing Corporation (NYSE options).
Intermarket Clearing Corporation (NYFE).

Method of trading:

Open outcry (at NYFE).
Specialists plus competitive option traders (for NYSE
options).

Commenced trading:

1980 (at NYFE).
1983 (at NYSE options).

Exchange links:

NYFE is an affiliate of the New York Cotton
Exchange (NYCE). Joint venture with COMEX,
CSCE and NYMEX including a shared trading arena.

A brief synopsis of the exchange
NYFE, as a wholly owned futures trading subsidiary
of the NYSE, is one of the newest futures exchanges in
the USA, and specialises in stock and other index
products for institutional users.
US Government Treasury Bonds are traded as an
affiliate of the NYCE.

Commodity Research Bureau (CRB) Index futures

Contract size	US$250 multiplied by the Commodity Research Bureau (CRB) Futures Price Index.*
Standard delivery method	Cash settlement at the contract maturity. There is no facility for physical delivery available.
Trading months	The nearest four months of the March, May, July, September and December cycle.
Trading hours	9.00 a.m. – 3.15 p.m.
Price quotation method	In US dollars (US$) and cents per index point.
Minimum price move (value)	0.05 index points (US$12.50 per contract).
Daily price limits	None.
Position limits	10,000 contracts net long or short.
Last trading day	The third business day of the contract month.
Delivery day	The business day following the last trading day.
Initial (Variation) margin	Hedgers: US$1,500 per contract (US$1,250). Speculators: US$2,000 per contract (US$1,500).
Spread margin	Intra-contract: US$200 per spread (US$100). CRB vs components: US$1,200 per spread (US$800).
Reuters Monitor (Quote)	NFIE.
Telerate page	N/a.

* The Commodity Research Bureau (CRB) Index is a geometrically weighted price index of 27 commodity futures markets' simple price average of all contracts trading up to 11 months forward, converted to a percentage of base year value (1967 = 100). The contracts listed in the index are as follows:

Grains:	barley, corn, oats, rye, soyabean meal, CBOT wheat, MGE wheat.
Livestock:	cattle, hogs, pork bellies.
Precious metals:	gold, platinum, silver.
Industrials:	cotton, copper, crude oil, lumber, silver, platinum.
Oilseeds:	flaxseed, soyabean, rapeseed.
Softs:	coffee, sugar, cocoa.
Energy:	heating oil, crude oil.
Miscellaneous:	orange juice, potatoes, soyabean oil.

NYSE Composite Stock Index futures

Contract size	US$500 multiplied by the NYSE Composite Stock Index.
Standard delivery method	Cash settlement at the maturity of the contract based on a special calculation of the opening prices of the index constituents on the third Friday of the contract month, to the nearest 0.01 index points. There is no facility for physical delivery of the stocks to the index.
Trading months	The nearest four months from the March, June, September and December cycle.

Trading hours	9.30 a.m. – 4.15 p.m.
Price quotation method	In US dollars (US$) and cents per index point.
Minimum price move (value)	0.05 index points (US$25.00 per contract).
Daily price limits	None.
Position limits	10,000 contracts on the same side of the market.
Last trading day	The Thursday preceding the third Friday of the contract month, or the preceding business day if this day is not both a NYFE and NYSE working day.
Delivery day	The business day following the last trading day. Final settlement is based on a special calculation of the third Friday's opening prices of all stocks listed in the NYSE Composite Index.
Initial (Variation) margin	Hedgers: US$1,750 per contract (US$1,500). Speculators: US$3,500 per contract (US$1,750).
Spread margin	Intra-contract: US$200 per spread (US$100). Intra-exchange: US$400 per spread (US$300).
Reuters Monitor (Quote)	NSNE (C_1 YX*).
Telerate page	N/a.

30-year Benchmark US Government Treasury Bond futures

Contract size	US$100,000 nominal face value of US Government Treasury Bonds with at least 15 years to maturity and, if callable, with 15-year call protection, adjusted to an 8% coupon rate.
Standard delivery method	Physical delivery of the above bonds through the Federal Reserve Book entry wire transfer system.
Trading months	The March, June, September and December cycle.
Trading hours	8.20 a.m. – 4.15 p.m.
Price quotation method	In US dollars (US$) and cents per cent of par.
Minimum price move (value)	One half of one thirty-second (1/32) of 1% (US$15.625 per contract).
Daily price limits	96/32 (three full points) above or below the previous day's settlement price.
Position limits	None.
Last trading day	The eighth to last business day of the contract month. Trading ceases at 11.00 a.m. in the expiring contract on the last trading day.
Delivery day	Any business day through the contract delivery month. The first notice day is two business days preceding the first business day of the contract month.
Initial (Variation) margin	Not stated.
Spread margin	Reduced margin deposits are available between this contract and the FINEX five-year Treasury Notes futures and two-year Treasury Notes futures contracts.

Reuters Monitor (Quote)
Telerate page

New York Stock
Exchange (NYSE)
Options on
cash/physical
Stock indices

NFTB.
N/a.

This contract is traded in conjunction with The Financial
Instrument Exchange (FINEX) at the NYFE.

Option on the NYSE Composite Stock Index

Contract size	US$100 multiplied by the NYSE Composite Stock Index.
Standard delivery method	Cash settlement based on the difference between the strike price and the settlement index level on the day of exercise or the last trading day. There is no facility for physical delivery of the stocks underlying the index.
Trading months	The three nearby consecutive calendar months.
Trading hours	9.30 a.m. – 4.15 p.m.
Price quotation method	Premiums are expressed in index points and fractions of a point, and quoted in US dollars (US$).
Minimum price move (value)	One-sixteenth (1/16) of an index point (US$6.25 per contract) for premiums up to US$3.00, and one-eighth (1/8) of an index point (US$12.50 per contract) for higher premiums.
Daily price limits	None.
Position limits	Options with not more than an underlying value of US$300 million. Positions are reportable at 200 contracts of any class on the same side of the market.
Last trading day	The business day before the third Friday of the contract month. Options exercised at this time are based on the opening index on the business day prior to the expiration Saturday (the Saturday after the third Friday of the contract month).
Delivery day	The business day following the last trading day. The options expire on the Saturday following the third Friday of the contract month.
Initial (Variation) margin	For uncovered short positions, the dollar amount of the current option premium plus 15% of the market value of the underlying index (multiplied by US$100), less any out-of-the-money amount, subject to a minimum of 10% of the underlying value.
Spread margin	Not stated.
Strike price intervals	At 5.0 index point intervals, with selective 2.5 point intervals in the nearest two expiry months.
Option type	American style (options may be exercised on any business day up to and including the last trading day). All in-the-money options at expiry are automatically exercised.

Method of introduction of new strike prices	Not stated.
Reuters Monitor (Quote)	NFNE – NFNN, MJNE, NSQA – NSQN.
Telerate page	N/a.

Option on NYFE Commodity Research Bureau (CRB) Index futures

Contract size	One NYFE Commodity Research Bureau (CRB) Index* futures contract (of an underlying contract size of US$250 multiplied by the index level).
Standard delivery method	Delivery of a long or short position in a futures contract at the strike price as above.
Trading months	The nearest three months from the March, May, July, September and December cycle.
Trading hours	9.00 a.m. – 3.15 p.m.
Price quotation method	In US dollars (US$) and cents per index point.
Minimum price move (value)	0.05 index points (US$12.50 per contract).
Daily price limits	None.
Position limits	None.
Last trading day	The third business day of the contract month.
Delivery day	The business day following the last trading day.
Initial (Variation) margin	Not stated. Please consult the exchange for the current margin requirements.
Spread margin	Not stated.
Strike price intervals	At 5.00 index point intervals for strike prices under 300 index points. Thereafter at 10.00 index point intervals. There is a minimum of five strike prices available at any one time.
Option type	American style (the option may be exercised on any NYFE business day up to and including the last trading day, up to 6.00 p.m. on these days). All in-the-money options are automatically exercised at expiry.
Method of introduction of new strike prices	Not stated. Please consult the exchange.
Reuters Monitor (Quote)	NFIF – NFIM.
Telerate page	N/a.

* The Commodity Research Bureau (CRB) Index is a geometrically weighted price index of 27 commodity futures markets' simple price average of all contracts trading up to 11 months forward, converted to a percentage of base year value (1967 = 100). The contracts listed in the index are as follows:

Grains:	barley, corn, oats, rye, soyabean meal, CBOT wheat, MGE wheat.
Livestock:	cattle, hogs, pork bellies.
Precious metals:	gold, platinum, silver.
Industrials:	cotton, copper, crude oil, lumber, silver, platinum.
Oilseeds:	flaxseed, soyabean, rapeseed.
Softs:	coffee, sugar, cocoa.
Energy:	heating oil, crude oil.
Miscellaneous:	orange juice, potatoes, soyabean oil.

Option on NYFE NYSE Composite Stock Index futures

Contract size	One NYFE NYSE Composite Stock Index futures contract (of an underlying contract size of US$500 multiplied by the index level).
Standard delivery method	Delivery of a long or short position in a futures contract at the strike price as above.
Trading months	The current (spot) month, the next two consecutive calendar months plus the next month from the March, June, September and December cycle. The futures contract that underlies the non-quarterly cycle months is the next futures contract following the option's expiry.
Trading hours	9.30 a.m. – 4.15 p.m.
Price quotation method	In US dollars (US$) and cents per index point.
Minimum price move (value)	0.05 index points (US$25.00 per contract).
Daily price limits	None.
Position limits	None.
Last trading day	For the calendar quarterly cycle months, the business day preceding the third Friday of the contract month. For other months, the third Friday of the contract month. In both cases if that day is a non-trading day, the business day immediately preceding that day will be taken as the last trading day.
Delivery day	The business day following the last trading day. For quarterly expiry cycle options, final settlement is based on a special calculation of the third Friday's opening prices of all stocks listed in the NYSE Composite Index. For non-calendar quarterly months, final settlement is taken as the settlement price of the underlying futures contract on the option's last trading day.
Initial (Variation) margin	For uncovered short positions, the daily settlement premium plus the underlying futures contract margin less the amount by which the option is out-of-the-money, subject to a minimum of US$750 per contract.
Spread margin	There are various spread concessions for option spreads and option/future combinations. Please consult the exchange or your broker for full details.
Strike price intervals	Integers divisible by two (e.g. 142.00, 144.00, 146.00 etc.), with a minimum of nine strike prices always available.
Option type	American style (the option may be exercised on any NYFE business day, up to and including the last trading day up to 6.00 p.m. on these days). All in-the-money options are automatically exercised at expiry (but in the case of non-calendar quarterly cycle months, only if they are in-the-money by US$300 per contract).

Method of introduction of new strike prices	Not stated.
Reuters Monitor (Quote)	NFNE – NFNN, NSQA – NSQN.
Telerate page	N/a.

Philadelphia Stock Exchange (PHLX)

Philadelphia Board of Trade (PBOT)
(a subsidiary of the PHLX)

Address:	Stock Exchange Building 1900 Market Street Philadelphia PA 19103 USA
Telephone:	(215) 496 5000/5357 (496 5367 for PBOT)
Fax:	(215) 496 5653
Telex:	476 1031 PHLX

Exchange personnel

Chairman:	John J. Wallace
President:	Nicholas A. Giordano
President (PBOT):	Joseph S. Rizello
Public Relations Officer:	Nancy B. Tague

European Representative Office

Address:	39 King Street London EC2V 8DQ United Kingdom
Telephone:	(01) 606 2348
Fax:	(01) 606 3548
Telex:	892735 PHLXUK G
Managing Director:	Gary Delaney
Administrative Assistant:	Jane Barclay

Far Eastern Representative Office

Address:	Kyobashi Tokiwa Building 11 4th Floor 8–5 Kyobashi 2 Chrome Chou-Ku Tokyo 104 Japan

Telephone: (3) 561 2851
Fax: (3) 561 2850
Telex: 532 384

Managing Director: Douglas Augustine

Futures contracts available on PBOT
Australian dollar / US dollar currency
British pound / US dollar currency
Canadian dollar / US dollar currency
Deutschmark / US dollar currency
ECU / US dollar currency
French franc / US dollar currency
Japanese yen / US dollar currency
National OTC Stock Index
Swiss franc / US dollar currency

Options contracts on physical/cash available on PHLX
Australian dollar / US dollar currency
British pound / US dollar currency
Canadian dollar / US dollar currency
Deutschmark / US dollar currency
ECU / US dollar currency
French franc / US dollar currency
Gold/Silver Stock Index
Japanese yen / US dollar currency
National OTC Stock Index
PHLX Utility Stock Index
Swiss franc / US dollar currency
Value Line Composite Stock Index

The Philadelphia Stock Exchange also trades options on over 130 US stocks, each contract representing 100 shares of the underlying issue. The trading hours for each class are 9.30 a.m. – 4.10 p.m. with expiry months being the nearby three consecutive months.

Clearing House: Options Clearing Corporation (PHLX).
Intermarket Clearing Corporation (PBOT).

Method of trading: Open outcry.

Commenced trading: 1790 (options in 1982).

Exchange links: None.

A brief synopsis of the exchange
Philadelphia is the oldest stock exchange in the US, established initially in 1790 as the Philadelphia Board of Brokers. Equity options were introduced in 1975 and foreign currency options were introduced in 1982

(starting with the British pound). The PHLX is now the world's largest market-place for exchange-traded currency options. AUTOM (the Automated Options Market) was developed to handle option orders involving up to five contracts. There are over 500 exchange members.

The PBOT was established in 1985 and began trading in 1986 as the futures subsidiary of the PHLX. However, there are not cross-margining facilities between the PBOT currency futures and the PHLX currency options, and this has proved to be a barrier to PBOT volumes.

In 1987 the Chicago Board Options Exchange (CBOE) transferred all of its European-style currency options to the PHLX. The PHLX now trades both American-style and European-style currency options side by side. Cash Index Participations (CIPs) were introduced in 1987, but were subsequently delisted due to regulatory problems.

Night trading hours and morning trading sessions were introduced in 1987 to extend the trading scope to allow the participation of the Asian markets. The market-place in Philadelphia is now open from 4.30 a.m. to 2.30 p.m. (Monday to Friday) and 7.00 p.m. to 11.00 p.m. (Sunday to Thursday), with the exchange awaiting approval to extend these hours even further so trading will be available at all times with the exception of 2.30 p.m. – 6.00 p.m.

Australian dollar / US dollar currency (ZA) futures

Contract size	A$100,000 traded against the US dollar (US$).
Standard delivery method	Physical exchange of the currencies concerned.
Trading months	The March, June, September and December cycle.
Trading hours	Morning session: 4.30 a.m. – 2.30 p.m. (Monday to Friday). Evening session: 7.00 p.m. – 11.00 p.m. (Sunday to Thursday).
Price quotation method	In terms of US cents per Australian dollar (A$).
Minimum price move (value)	0.01 US cents (US$0.0001) per A$1.00 (US$10.00 per contract).
Daily price limits	None.
Position limits	6,000 contracts on the same side of the market.
Last trading day	The Friday before the third Wednesday of the contract month.
Delivery day	The third Wednesday of the contract month.
Initial (Variation) margin	Not stated. Please consult the exchange or your broker for the current details.
Spread margin	Not stated.
Reuters Monitor (Quote)	N/a.
Telerate page	N/a.

British pound / US dollar currency (ZB) futures

Contract size	£62,500 traded against the US dollar (US$).
Standard delivery method	Physical exchange of the currencies concerned.
Trading months	The March, June, September and December cycle.
Trading hours	Morning session: 4.30 a.m. – 2.30 p.m. (Monday to Friday). Evening session: 7.00 p.m. – 11.00 p.m. (Sunday to Thursday).
Price quotation method	In terms of US cents per pounds sterling (£).
Minimum price move (value)	0.01 US cents (US$0.0001) per £1.00 (US$6.25 per contract).
Daily price limits	None.
Position limits	6,000 contracts on the same side of the market.
Last trading day	The Friday before the third Wednesday of the contract month.
Delivery day	The third Wednesday of the contract month.
Initial (Variation) margin	Not stated. Please consult the exchange or your broker for the current details.
Spread margin	Not stated.
Reuters Monitor (Quote)	N/a.
Telerate page	N/a.

Canadian dollar / US dollar currency (ZC) futures

Contract size	C$100,000 traded against the US dollar (US$).
Standard delivery method	Physical exchange of the currencies concerned.
Trading months	The March, June, September and December cycle.
Trading hours	Morning session only: 4.30 a.m. – 2.30 p.m. (Monday to Friday).
Price quotation method	In terms of US cents per Canadian dollar (C$).
Minimum price move (value)	0.01 US cents (US$0.0001) per C$1.00 (US$10.00 per contract).
Daily price limits	None.
Position limits	6,000 contracts on the same side of the market.
Last trading day	The Friday before the third Wednesday of the contract month.
Delivery day	The third Wednesday of the contract month.
Initial (Variation) margin	Not stated. Please consult the exchange or your broker for the current details.
Spread margin	Not stated.
Reuters Monitor (Quote)	N/a.
Telerate page	N/a.

Deutschmark / US dollar currency (ZD) futures

Contract size	DM125,000 traded against the US dollar (US$).
Standard delivery method	Physical exchange of the currencies concerned.
Trading months	The March, June, September and December cycle.
Trading hours	Morning session: 4.30 a.m. – 2.30 p.m. (Monday to Friday). Evening session: 7.00 p.m. – 11.00 p.m. (Sunday to Thursday).
Price quotation method	In terms of US cents per Deutschmark (DM).
Minimum price move (value)	0.01 US cents (US$0.0001) per DM1.00 (US$12.50 per contract).
Daily price limits	None.
Position limits	6,000 contracts on the same side of the market.
Last trading day	The Friday before the third Wednesday of the contract month.
Delivery day	The third Wednesday of the contract month.
Initial (Variation) margin	Not stated. Please consult the exchange or your broker for the current details.
Spread margin	Not stated.
Reuters Monitor (Quote)	N/a.
Telerate page	N/a.

ECU (European Currency Unit) / US dollar currency (ZE) futures

Contract size	ECU125,000 traded against the US dollar (US$).
Standard delivery method	Physical exchange of the currencies concerned.
Trading months	The March, June, September and December cycle.
Trading hours	Morning session only: 4.30 a.m. – 2.30 p.m. (Monday to Friday).
Price quotation method	In terms of US cents per European Currency Unit (ECU).*
Minimum price move (value)	0.01 US cents (US$0.0001) per ECU1.00 (US$12.50 per contract).
Daily price limits	None.
Position limits	4,000 contracts on the same side of the market (during the last five days in the spot month).
Last trading day	The Friday before the third Wednesday of the contract month.
Delivery day	The third Wednesday of the contract month.
Initial (Variation) margin	Not stated. Please consult the exchange or your broker for the current details.
Spread margin	Not stated.
Reuters Monitor (Quote)	N/a.
Telerate page	N/a.

* The European Currency Unit (ECU) is defined as the sum of the following amount of each currency, as last updated on 21 September 1989:

Currency	Amount	Currency	Amount
West German Deutschmark	0.6242	French franc	1.332
British pound	0.08784	Italian lira	151.8
Dutch guilder	0.2198	Belgian/Luxembourg franc	3.431
Danish krone	0.1976	Greek drachma	1.44
Irish punt	0.008552	Spanish peseta	6.885
Portuguese escudo	1.393		

French franc / US dollar currency (ZF) futures

Contract size	FFr500,000 traded against the US dollar (US$).
Standard delivery method	Physical exchange of the currencies concerned.
Trading months	The March, June, September and December cycle.
Trading hours	Morning session only: 4.30 a.m. – 2.30 p.m. (Monday to Friday).
Price quotation method	In terms of US cents per French franc (FFr).
Minimum price move (value)	0.002 US cents (US$0.00002) per FFr1.00 (US$10.00 per contract).
Daily price limits	None.
Position limits	6,000 contracts on the same side of the market.

Last trading day	The Friday before the third Wednesday of the contract month.
Delivery day	The third Wednesday of the contract month.
Initial (Variation) margin	Not stated. Please consult the exchange or your broker for the current details.
Spread margin	Not stated.
Reuters Monitor (Quote)	N/a.
Telerate page	N/a.

Japanese yen / US dollar currency (ZJ) futures

Contract size	Y12,500,000 traded against the US dollar (US$).
Standard delivery method	Physical exchange of the currencies concerned.
Trading months	The March, June, September and December cycle.
Trading hours	Morning session: 4.30 a.m. – 2.30 p.m. (Monday to Friday). Evening session: 7.00 p.m. – 11.00 p.m. (Sunday to Thursday).
Price quotation method	In terms of US cents per Japanese yen (Y).
Minimum price move (value)	0.0001 US cents (US$0.000001) per Y1.00 (US$12.50 per contract).
Daily price limits	None.
Position limits	6,000 contracts on the same side of the market.
Last trading day	The Friday before the third Wednesday of the contract month.
Delivery day	The third Wednesday of the contract month.
Initial (Variation) margin	Not stated. Please consult the exchange or your broker for the current details.
Spread margin	Not stated.
Reuters Monitor (Quote)	N/a.
Telerate page	N/a.

National OTC Stock Index (XOC) futures

Contract size	US$500 multiplied by the National Over-the-Counter (OTC) Stock Index.*
Standard delivery method	Cash settlement at expiry based on the National OTC Index at 4.00 p.m. on the last trading day. There is no facility for physical delivery of the stocks underlying the index.

Trading months	The two nearby consecutive calendar months plus months from the March, June, September and December cycle.
Trading hours	9.30 a.m. – 4.15 p.m. The expiring contract ceases trading at 4.00 p.m. on the last trading day.
Price quotation method	In US dollars (US$) per index point.
Minimum price move (value)	One half of one index point (US$25.00 per contract).
Daily price limits	None.
Position limits	None.
Last trading day	The third Friday of the contract month.
Delivery day	The first business day following the last trading day.
Initial (Variation) margin	Not stated. Please consult the exchange or your broker for the current details.
Spread margin	Not stated.
Reuters Monitor (Quote)	N/a.
Telerate page	N/a.

* The National Over-the-Counter (OTC) Stock Index is based on the common stocks of the 100 largest domestic corporations based on market value. Only tier 1 stocks of the National Market System (NMS) are eligible. The index is continuously updated throughout the day.

Swiss franc / US dollar currency (ZS) futures

Contract size	SFr125,000 traded against the US dollar (US$).
Standard delivery method	Physical exchange of the currencies concerned.
Trading months	The March, June, September and December cycle.
Trading hours	Morning session: 4.30 a.m. – 2.30 p.m. (Monday to Friday). Evening session: 7.00 p.m. – 11.00 p.m. (Sunday to Thursday).
Price quotation method	In terms of US cents per Swiss franc (SFr).
Minimum price move (value)	0.01 US cents (US$0.0001) per SFr1.00 (US$12.50 per contract).
Daily price limits	None.
Position limits	6,000 contracts on the same side of the market.
Last trading day	The Friday before the third Wednesday of the contract month.
Delivery day	The third Wednesday of the contract month.
Initial (Variation) margin	Not stated. Please consult the exchange or your broker for the current details.
Spread margin	Not stated.
Reuters Monitor (Quote)	N/a.
Telerate page	N/a.

Option on Australian dollar / US dollar currency (XAD)

Contract size	A$50,000 traded against the US dollar (US$).
Standard delivery method	Physical exchange of the currencies concerned at the strike price. A delivery versus payment (DVP) method of delivery is also acceptable.
Trading months	The two nearby consecutive calendar months plus months from the March, June, September and December cycle (one, two, three, six, nine and 12 months forward).
Trading hours	Morning session: 4.30 a.m. – 2.30 p.m. (Monday to Friday). Evening session: 7.00 p.m. – 11.00 p.m. (Sunday to Thursday).
Price quotation method	In terms of US cents per Australian dollar (A$).
Minimum price move (value)	0.01 US cents (US$0.0001) per A$1.00 (US$5.00 per contract).
Daily price limits	None.
Position limits	100,000 contracts on the same side of the market (this limit also applies to exercising).
Last trading day	The Friday before the third Wednesday of the contract month.
Delivery day	The business day following the last trading day. The options expire on the Saturday before the third Wednesday of the contract month.
Initial (Variation) margin	For uncovered short positions: the premium received plus 4% of the underlying contract value less the out-of-the-money element (if any), subject to a minimum of 0.75% of the underlying contract value, paid in US dollars, and marked to market daily. Margin may be deposited in the form of cash, authorised securities or letters of credit.
Spread margin	Various spread margin concessions are available. Please contact the exchange or your broker for full details.
Strike price intervals	At one US cent (US$0.01) per A$1.00 intervals.
Option type	This option class may be traded with either American-style or European-style exercise procedures. See below for explanation.*
Method of introduction of new strike prices	Not stated.
Reuters Monitor (Quote)	American style: PIAD, European style: ADQF.
Telerate page	American style: 15020, European style: 16075.

* The Chicago Board Options Exchange (CBOE) recently transferred their European style foreign currency options contracts to the PHLX. As a result, all foreign currency options are now available at the PHLX with both American-style (the option may be exercised on any business day up to and including the last trading day) and European-style (the option may only be exercised on the last trading day) exercise procedures. All other contract specifications are identical.

Option on British pound / US dollar currency (XBP)

Contract size	£31,250 traded against the US dollar (US$).
Standard delivery method	Physical exchange of the currencies concerned at the strike price. A delivery versus payment (DVP) method of delivery is also acceptable.
Trading months	The two nearby consecutive calendar months plus months from the March, June, September and December cycle (one, two, three, six, nine and 12 months forward).
Trading hours	Morning session: 4.30 a.m. – 2.30 p.m. (Monday to Friday). Evening session: 7.00 p.m. – 11.00 p.m. (Sunday to Thursday).
Price quotation method	In terms of US cents per pounds sterling (£).
Minimum price move (value)	0.01 US cents (US$0.0001) per £1.00 (US$3.125 per contract).
Daily price limits	None.
Position limits	100,000 contracts on the same side of the market (this limit also applies to exercising).
Last trading day	The Friday before the third Wednesday of the contract month.
Delivery day	The business day following the last trading day. The options expire on the Saturday before the third Wednesday of the contract month.
Initial (Variation) margin	For uncovered short positions: the premium received plus 4% of the underlying contract value less the out-of-the-money element (if any), subject to a minimum of 0.75% of the underlying contract value, paid in US dollars, and marked to market daily. Margin may be deposited in the form of cash, authorised securities or letters of credit.
Spread margin	Various spread margin concessions are available. Please contact the exchange or your broker for full details.
Strike price intervals	At 2.5 US cents (US$0.025) per £1.00 intervals.
Option type	This option class may be traded with either American-style or European-style exercise procedures. See below for explanation.*
Method of introduction of new strike prices	Not stated.
Reuters Monitor (Quote)	American style: PHBP, European style: BPRA.
Telerate page	American style: 15035, European style: 16020.

* The Chicago Board Options Exchange (CBOE) recently transferred their European-style foreign currency options contracts to the PHLX. As a result, all foreign currency options are now available at the PHLX with both American-style (the option may be exercised on any business day up to and including the last trading day) and European-style (the option may only be exercised on the last trading day) exercise procedures. All other contract specifications are identical.

Option on Canadian dollar / US dollar currency (XCD)

Contract size	C$50,000 traded against the US dollar (US$).
Standard delivery method	Physical exchange of the currencies concerned at the strike price. A delivery versus payment (DVP) method of delivery is also acceptable.
Trading months	The two nearby consecutive calendar months plus months from the March, June, September and December cycle (one, two, three, six, nine and 12 months forward).
Trading hours	Morning session only: 4.30 a.m. – 2.30 p.m. (Monday to Friday).
Price quotation method	In terms of US cents per Canadian dollar (C$).
Minimum price move (value)	0.01 US cents (US$0.0001) per C$1.00 (US$5.00 per contract).
Daily price limits	None.
Position limits	100,000 contracts on the same side of the market (this limit also applies to exercising).
Last trading day	The Friday before the third Wednesday of the contract month.
Delivery day	The business day following the last trading day. The options expire on the Saturday before the third Wednesday of the contract month.
Initial (Variation) margin	For uncovered short positions: the premium received plus 4% of the underlying contract value less the out-of-the-money element (if any), subject to a minimum of 0.75% of the underlying contract value, paid in US dollars, and marked to market daily. Margin may be deposited in the form of cash, authorised securities or letters of credit.
Spread margin	Various spread margin concessions are available. Please contact the exchange or your broker for full details.
Strike price intervals	At 0.1 US cents (US$0.001) per C$1.00 intervals.
Option type	This option class may be traded with either American style or European-style exercise procedures. See below for explanation.*
Method of introduction of new strike prices	Not stated.
Reuters Monitor (Quote)	American style: PHQD, European style: CDHF.
Telerate page	American style: 15090, European style: 16055.

* The Chicago Board Options Exchange (CBOE) recently transferred their European-style foreign currency options contracts to the PHLX. As a result, all foreign currency options are now available at the PHLX with both American-style (the option may be exercised on any business day up to and including the last trading day) and European-style (the option may only be exercised on the last trading day) exercise procedures. All other contract specifications are identical.

Option on Deutschmark / US dollar currency (XDM)

Contract size	DM62,500 traded against the US dollar (US$).
Standard delivery method	Physical exchange of the currencies concerned at the strike price. A delivery versus payment (DVP) method of delivery is also acceptable.
Trading months	The two nearby consecutive calendar months plus months from the March, June, September and December cycle (one, two, three, six, nine and 12 months forward).
Trading hours	Morning session: 4.30 a.m. – 2.30 p.m. (Monday to Friday). Evening session: 7.00 p.m. – 11.00 p.m. (Sunday to Thursday).
Price quotation method	In terms of US cents per Deutschmark (DM).
Minimum price move (value)	0.01 US cents (US$0.0001) per DM1.00 (US$6.25 per contract).
Daily price limits	None.
Position limits	100,000 contracts on the same side of the market (this limit also applies to exercising).
Last trading day	The Friday before the third Wednesday of the contract month.
Delivery day	The business day following the last trading day. The options expire on the Saturday before the third Wednesday of the contract month.
Initial (Variation) margin	For uncovered short positions: the premium received plus 4% of the underlying contract value less the out-of-the-money element (if any), subject to a minimum of 0.75% of the underlying contract value, paid in US dollars, and marked to market daily. Margin may be deposited in the form of cash, authorised securities or letters of credit.
Spread margin	Various spread margin concessions are available. Please contact the exchange or your broker for full details.
Strike price intervals	At one US cent (US$0.01) per DM1.00 intervals.
Option type	This option class may be traded with either American-style or European-style exercise procedures. See below for explanation.*
Method of introduction of new strike prices	Not stated.
Reuters Monitor (Quote)	American style: PHDI, European style: DMCB.
Telerate page	American style: 15060, European style: 16025.

* The Chicago Board Options Exchange (CBOE) recently transferred their European-style foreign currency options contracts to the PHLX. As a result, all foreign currency options are now available at the PHLX with both American-style (the option may be exercised on any business day up to and including the last trading day) and European-style (the option may only be exercised on the last trading day) exercise procedures. All other contract specifications are identical.

Option on ECU (European Currency Unit) / US dollar currency (ECU)

Contract size	ECU62,500 traded against the US dollar (US$).
Standard delivery method	Physical exchange of the currencies concerned at the strike price. A delivery versus payment (DVP) method of delivery is also acceptable.
Trading months	The two nearby consecutive calendar months plus months from the March, June, September and December cycle (one, two, three, six, nine and 12 months forward).
Trading hours	Morning session only: 4.30 a.m. – 2.30 p.m. (Monday to Friday).
Price quotation method	In terms of US cents per European Currency Unit (ECU).*
Minimum price move (value)	0.01 US cents (US$0.0001) per ECU1.00 (US$6.25 per contract).
Daily price limits	None.
Position limits	100,000 contracts on the same side of the market (this limit also applies to exercising).
Last trading day	The Friday before the third Wednesday of the contract month.
Delivery day	The business day following the last trading day. The options expire on the Saturday before the third Wednesday of the contract month.
Initial (Variation) margin	For uncovered short positions: the premium received plus 4% of the underlying contract value less the out-of-the-money element (if any), subject to a minimum of 0.75% of the underlying contract value, paid in US dollars, and marked to market daily. Margin may be deposited in the form of cash, authorised securities or letters of credit.
Spread margin	Various spread margin concessions are available. Please contact the exchange or your broker for full details.
Strike price intervals	At two US cents (US$0.02) per ECU1.00 intervals.
Option type	American style (the option may be exercised on any business day up to and including the last trading day).
Method of introduction of new strike prices	Not stated.
Reuters Monitor (Quote)	PLEC – PLEX.
Telerate page	15080.

* The European Currency Unit (ECU) is defined as the sum of the following amount of each currency, as was last updated on 21st September 1989:

Currency	Amount	Currency	Amount
West German Deutschmark	0.6242	French franc	1.332
British pound	0.08784	Italian lira	151.8
Dutch guilder	0.2198	Belgian/Luxembourg franc	3.431
Danish krone	0.1976	Greek drachma	1.44
Irish punt	0.008552	Spanish peseta	6.885
Portugese escudo	1.393		

Option on French franc / US dollar currency (XFF)

Contract size	FFr125,000 traded against the US dollar (US$).
Standard delivery method	Physical exchange of the currencies concerned at the strike price. A delivery versus payment (DVP) method of delivery is also acceptable.
Trading months	The two nearby consecutive calendar months plus months from the March, June, September and December cycle (one, two, three, six, nine and 12 months forward).
Trading hours	Morning session only: 4.30 a.m. – 2.30 p.m. (Monday to Friday).
Price quotation method	In terms of US cents per French franc (FFr).
Minimum price move (value)	0.005 US cents (US$0.00005) per FFr1.00 (US$6.25 per contract).
Daily price limits	None.
Position limits	100,000 contracts on the same side of the market (this limit also applies to exercising).
Last trading day	The Friday before the third Wednesday of the contract month.
Delivery day	The business day following the last trading day. The options expire on the Saturday before the third Wednesday of the contract month.
Initial (Variation) margin	For uncovered short positions: the premium received plus 4% of the underlying contract value less the out-of-the-money element (if any), subject to a minimum of 0.75% of the underlying contract value, paid in US dollars, and marked to market daily. Margin may be deposited in the form of cash, authorised securities or letters of credit.
Spread margin	Various spread margin concessions are available. Please contact the exchange or your broker for full details.
Strike price intervals	At 0.50 US cents (US$0.005) per FFr1.00 intervals.
Option type	This option class may be traded with either American-style or European-style exercise procedures. See below for explanation.*
Method of introduction of new strike prices	Not stated.
Reuters Monitor (Quote)	American style: PHFR, European style: FFCF.
Telerate page	American style: 15070, European style: 16065.

* The Chicago Board Options Exchange (CBOE) recently transferred their European-style foreign currency options contracts to the PHLX. As a result, all foreign currency options are now available at the PHLX with both American-style (the option may be exercised on any business day up to and including the last trading day) and European-style (the option may only be exercised on the last trading day) exercise procedures. All other contract specifications are identical.

Option on Gold / Silver Stock Index

Contract size	US$100 multiplied by the Gold/Silver Stock (cash) Index.*
Standard delivery method	Cash settlement at expiry. There is no facility for physical delivery of the shares underlying the index.
Trading months	The two nearby consecutive calendar months plus months from the March, June, September and December cycle.
Trading hours	9.30 a.m. – 4.10 p.m.
Price quotation method	In US dollars (US$) and cents per index point.
Minimum price move (value)	One-sixteenth (1/16) of an index point for premiums under US$3.00 (US$6.25 per contract) and one-eighth (1/8) of an index point for all higher premiums (US$12.50 per contract).
Daily price limits	None.
Position limits	6,000 contracts on the same side of the market.
Last trading day	The third Friday of the contract month.
Delivery day	The business day following the third Friday of the contract month. The options expire on the Saturday following the third Friday of the contract month.
Initial (Variation) margin	Not stated. Please consult the exchange or your broker for the current details.
Spread margin	Not stated.
Strike price intervals	At five index point intervals.
Option type	American style (the option may be exercised on any business day up to and including the last trading day, and the exercise value will be based on the closing value of the index on that day).
Method of introduction of new strike prices	Not stated.
Reuters Monitor (Quote)	INND – INNS.
Telerate page	N/a.

* The capitalisation-weighted Gold/Silver Index comprises the following stock issues:

ASA Ltd	Battle Mountain Gold Co.	Echo Bay Mines Ltd
Hecla Mines Ltd	Homestake Mining Co.	Newmont Mining Corp.
Placer Dome Inc.		

Option on Japanese yen / US dollar currency (XJY)

Contract size	Y6,250,000 traded against the US dollar (US$).
Standard delivery method	Physical exchange of the currencies concerned at the strike price. A delivery versus payment (DVP) method of delivery is also acceptable.
Trading months	The two nearby consecutive calendar months plus months from the March, June, September and December cycle (one, two, three, six, nine and 12 months forward).

Trading hours	Morning session: 4.30 a.m. – 2.30 p.m. (Monday to Friday). Evening session: 7.00 p.m. – 11.00 p.m. (Sunday to Thursday).
Price quotation method	In terms of US cents per Japanese yen (Y).
Minimum price move (value)	0.0001 US cents (US$0.000001) per Y1.00 (US$6.25 per contract).
Daily price limits	None.
Position limits	100,000 contracts on the same side of the market (this limit also applies to exercising).
Last trading day	The Friday before the third Wednesday of the contract month.
Delivery day	The business day following the last trading day. The options expire on the Saturday before the third Wednesday of the contract month.
Initial (Variation) margin	For uncovered short positions: the premium received plus 4% of the underlying contract value less the out-of-the-money element (if any), subject to a minimum of 0.75% of the underlying contract value, paid in US dollars, and marked to market daily. Margin may be deposited in the form of cash, authorised securities or letters of credit.
Spread margin	Various spread margin concessions are available. Please contact the exchange or your broker for full details.
Strike price intervals	At 0.01 US cents (US$0.0001) per Y1.00 intervals.
Option type	This option class may be traded with either American-style or European-style exercise procedures. See below for explanation.*
Method of introduction of new strike prices	Not stated.
Reuters Monitor (Quote)	American style: PHJY, European style: JYCF.
Telerate page	American style: 15040, European style: 16035.

* The Chicago Board Options Exchange (CBOE) recently transferred their European-style foreign currency options contracts to the PHLX. As a result, all foreign currency options are now available at the PHLX with both American-style (the option may be exercised on any business day up to and including the last trading day) and European-style (the option may only be exercised on the last trading day) exercise procedures. All other contract specifications are identical.

Option on National OTC Stock Index (XOC)

Contract size	US$100 multiplied by the National Over-the-Counter (OTC) Stock Index.*
Standard delivery method	Cash settlement. There is no facility for physical delivery of the shares underlying the index.

Trading months	The two nearby consecutive calendar months plus months from the March, June, September and December cycle.
Trading hours	9.30 a.m. – 4.15 p.m.
Price quotation method	In US dollars (US$) and cents per index point.
Minimum price move (value)	One-sixteenth (1/16) of an index point for premiums under US$3.00 (US$6.25 per contract) and one-eighth (1/8) of an index point for all higher premiums (US$12.50 per contract).
Daily price limits	None.
Position limits	Option positions with a total underlying value of US$300 million on the same side of the market.
Last trading day	The third Friday of the contract month. Notices of intention of exercise must be submitted by 4.10 p.m. on any business day except the last trading day.
Delivery day	The business day following the last trading day. The option expires on the Saturday following the third Friday of the contract month.
Initial (Variation) margin	For uncovered short positions, the current market value of the option premium plus 10% of the closing option index value, less the amount by which the option is out-of-the-money (if any), subject to a minimum of 2% of the closing index value.
Spread margin	Not stated.
Strike price intervals	At five index point intervals.
Option type	American style (the option may be exercised on any business day up to and including the last trading day).
Method of introduction of new strike prices	Additional strike prices are added when the index touches the next highest or lowest existing strike price.
Reuters Monitor (Quote)	N/a.
Telerate page	N/a.

* The National Over-the-Counter (OTC) Stock Index is based on the common stocks of the 100 largest domestic corporations based on market value. Only tier 1 stocks of the National Market System (NMS) stocks are eligible. The index is continuously updated throughout the day.

Option on PHLX Utility Stock Index (UTY)

Contract size	US$100 multiplied by the PHLX Utility Stock Index.
Standard delivery method	Cash settlement at expiry. There is no facility for physical delivery of the shares underlying the index.
Trading months	The two nearby consecutive calendar months plus the next three expiry months from the March, June, September and December cycle.
Trading hours	9.30 a.m. – 4.10 p.m.

Price quotation method	In US dollars (US$) and cents per index point.
Minimum price move (value)	One-sixteenth (1/16) of an index point for premiums under US$3.00 (US$6.25 per contract) and one-eighth (1/8) of an index point for all higher premiums (US$12.50 per contract).
Daily price limits	None.
Position limits	8,000 contracts on the same side of the market.
Last trading day	The third Friday of the contract month.
Delivery day	The business day following the last trading day. The option expires on the Saturday following the third Friday of the contract month.
Initial (Variation) margin	Not stated. Please consult the exchange or your broker for the current details.
Spread margin	Not stated.
Strike price intervals	At five index point intervals.
Option type	American style (the option may be exercised on any business day up to and including the last trading day).
Method of introduction of new strike prices	Not stated.
Reuters Monitor (Quote)	N/a.
Telerate page	N/a.

Option on Swiss franc / US dollar currency (XSF)

Contract size	SFr62,500 traded against the US dollar (US$).
Standard delivery method	Physical exchange of the currencies concerned at the strike price. A delivery versus payment (DVP) method of delivery is also acceptable.
Trading months	The two nearby consecutive calendar months plus months from the March, June, September and December cycle (one, two, three, six, nine and 12 months forward).
Trading hours	Morning session: 4.30 a.m. – 2.30 p.m. (Monday to Friday). Evening session: 7.00 p.m. – 11.00 p.m. (Sunday to Thursday).
Price quotation method	In terms of US cents per Swiss franc (SFr).
Minimum price move (value)	0.01 US cents (US$0.0001) per SFr1.00 (US$6.25 per contract).
Daily price limits	None.
Position limits	100,000 contracts on the same side of the market (this limit also applies to exercising).
Last trading day	The Friday before the third Wednesday of the contract month.
Delivery day	The business day following the last trading day. The options expire on the Saturday before the third Wednesday of the contract month.

Initial (Variation) margin	For uncovered short positions: the premium received plus 4% of the underlying contract value less the out-of-the-money element (if any), subject to a minimum of 0.75% of the underlying contract value, paid in US dollars, and marked to market daily. Margin may be deposited in the form of cash, authorised securities or letters of credit.
Spread margin	Various spread margin concessions are available. Please contact the exchange or your broker for full details.
Strike price intervals	At one US cent (US$0.01) per SFr1.00 intervals.
Option type	This option class may be traded with either American-style or European-style exercise procedures. See below for explanation.*
Method of introduction of new strike prices	Not stated.
Reuters Monitor (Quote)	American style: PHSB, European style: SQSA.
Telerate page	American style: 15050, European style: 16045.

* The Chicago Board Options Exchange (CBOE) recently transferred their European-style foreign currency options contracts to the PHLX. As a result, all foreign currency options are now available at the PHLX with both American-style (the option may be exercised on any business day up to and including the last trading day) and European-style (the option may only be exercised on the last trading day) exercise procedures. All other contract specifications are identical.

Option on Value Line Composite Stock Index (VLE)

Contract size	US$100 multiplied by the Value Line Composite Stock Index.*
Standard delivery method	Cash settlement at expiry. There is no facility for physical delivery of the shares underlying the index.
Trading months	The two nearby consecutive calendar months plus months from the March, June, September and December cycle.
Trading hours	9.30 a.m. – 4.15 p.m.
Price quotation method	In US dollars (US$) and cents per index point.
Minimum price move (value)	One-sixteenth (1/16) of an index point for premiums under US$3.00 (US$6.25 per contract) and one-eighth (1/8) of an index point for all higher premiums (US$12.50 per contract).
Daily price limits	None.
Position limits	Options with a total underlying value of US$300 million on the same side of the market.
Last trading day	The third Friday of the contract month.

Delivery day	The business day following the last trading day. The option expires on the Saturday following the third Friday of the contract month.
Initial (Variation) margin	For uncovered short positions, the current market value of the option premium plus 10% of the closing option index value, less the amount by which the option is out-of-the-money (if any), subject to a minimum of 2% of the closing index value.
Spread margin	Not stated.
Strike price intervals	At five index point intervals.
Option type	European style (the option may only be exercised on the last trading day and not at other times during its life).
Method of introduction of new strike prices	Additional strike prices are added when the index touches the next highest or lowest existing strike price.
Reuters Monitor (Quote)	VLNE – VLNP.
Telerate page	N/a.

* The Value Line Composite Stock Index (VL) comprises over 1,650 second-tier stock issues and is calculated on an unweighted geometric basis, and as such it more closely reflects the direction of the stock market in the long term. Stock index futures on the Value Line Composite Stock Index are available on the Kansas City Board of Trade (KBOT).

These options have replaced the American style options on the Value Line Composite Stock Index (XVL).

Kansas City Board of Trade (KBOT)

Address:

Suite 303
4800 Main Street
Kansas City
MO 64112
USA

Telephone: (816) 753 7500
Fax: (816) 753 3944
Telex: N/a.

Exchange personnel

Chairman: Roger B. Stover
President: Michael Braude
Information: Melissa Cordonier

Futures contracts available
Grain sorghum
Hard red winter wheat
Maxi Value Line Stock Index
Mini Value Line Stock Index

Options contracts on futures available
Hard red winter wheat future

Clearing House: KBOT Clearing Corporation.

Method of trading: Open outcry.

Commenced trading: 1856.

Exchange links: None.

A brief synopsis of the exchange
Although the KBOT was founded in 1856, wheat futures did not start trading until 1876, and this is the longest surviving contract with Kansas being the primary world marketplace in wheat.

The exchange has over 200 full trading members and around 70 others with access to the Value Line Index futures only. The 1,700-share Value Line Composite Index was the first stock index futures contract introduced worldwide in 1982 and the KBOT's first financially based product. A special membership (Class B) exists for traders in this contract.

Grain sorghum futures

Contract size	5,000 bushels of grain sorghum.
Standard delivery method	Physical delivery of the above.
Trading months	The March, May, July, September and December cycle.
Trading hours	9.30 a.m. – 1.15 p.m.
Price quotation method	In US cents and quarter cents per bushel.
Minimum price move (value)	0.25 US cents per bushel (US$12.50 per contract).
Daily price limits	None.
Position limits	None.
Last trading day	The eighth business day preceding the penultimate business day of the contract month.
Delivery day	Delivery may take place on any business day during the contract month. The notice period is from the last business day in the month preceding the delivery month to the penultimate business day of the contract month.
Initial (Variation) margin	Not stated. Please consult the exchange or your broker for the current margin requirements.
Spread margin	Not stated.
Reuters Monitor (Quote)	SGKE.
Telerate page	N/a.

Hard red winter wheat (KW) futures

Contract size	5,000 bushels of No.2 hard red winter wheat.
Standard delivery method	Physical delivery of the above by exchange-registered warehouse receipts, or of No.1 wheat or No.3 wheat at differentials established by the exchange, at Kansas City.
Trading months	The March, May, July, September and December cycle.
Trading hours	9.30 a.m. – 1.15 p.m.
Price quotation method	In US cents and quarter cents per bushel.
Minimum price move (value)	0.25 US cents per bushel (US$12.50 per contract).
Daily price limits	25 US cents (US$0.25) per bushel above or below the previous day's settlement level (US$1,250 per contract).
Position limits	None.
Last trading day	The eighth business day preceding the penultimate business day of the contract month.
Delivery day	Delivery may take place on any business day during the contract month. The notice period is from the last business day in the month preceding the delivery month to the penultimate business day of the contract month.

Initial (Variation) margin	Hedgers: US$600 per contract (US$600).
	Speculators: US$750 per contract (US$600).
Spread margin	Inter-market: US$250 per spread position.
	Intra-market: US$100 per spread position.
Reuters Monitor (Quote)	WHKE.
Telerate page	N/a.

Maxi Value Line Stock Index futures

Contract size	US$500 multiplied by the Kansas City Board of Trade (KBOT) Value Line Composite Stock Index (VL).*
Standard delivery method	Cash settlement based on the Value Line Composite Index at the close of futures on the last trading day (there is no facility available for physical delivery of the stocks underlying the index).
Trading months	The March, June, September and December cycle.
Trading hours	8.30 a.m. – 3.15 p.m.
Price quotation method	In US dollars (US$) and cents per index point.
Minimum price move (value)	0.05 index points (US$25.00 per contract).
Daily price limits	None.
Position limits	5,000 contracts on the same side of the market.
Last trading day	The third Friday of the contract month.
Delivery day	The business day following the last trading day.
Initial (Variation) margin	Hedgers: US$2,500 per contract (US$1,500), or approximately 5% of the underlying value of the contract.
	Speculators: US$6,500 per contract (US$2,000).
Spread margin	Inter-market: US$400 per spread position (US$200).
	Intra-market spread concessions are also available.
Reuters Monitor (Quote)	VLKE (C_1 KV*).
Telerate page	N/a.

* The Value Line Index (VL) is a broadly based stock index covering around 1,650 issues and represents around 96% of the dollar trading volume in the United States. The index is equally geometrically weighted to each stock irrespective of price or number of shares outstanding.

Mini Value Line Stock Index futures

Contract size	US$100 multiplied by the Kansas City Board of Trade (KBOT) Value Line Composite Stock Index (VL).*
Standard delivery method	Cash settlement based on the Value Line Composite Index at the close of futures on the last trading day (there is no facility available for physical delivery of the stocks underlying the index).

Trading months	The March, June, September and December cycle.
Trading hours	8.30 a.m. – 3.15 p.m.
Price quotation method	In US dollars (US$) and cents per index point.
Minimum price move (value)	0.05 index points (US$5.00 per contract).
Daily price limits	None.
Position limits	None.
Last trading day	The third Friday of the contract month.
Delivery day	The business day following the last trading day.
Initial (Variation) margin	Hedgers: US$500 per contract (US$300), or approximately 5% of the underlying value of the contract.
	Speculators: US$1,800 per contract (US$400).
Spread margin	Inter-market: US$80.00 per spread position (US$40.00).
	Intra-market spread concessions are also available.
Reuters Monitor (Quote)	VLKF.
Telerate page	N/a.

* The Value Line Index (VL) is a broadly based stock index covering around 1,650 issues and represents around 96% of the dollar trading volume in the United States. The index is equally geometrically weighted to each stock irrespective of price or number of shares outstanding.

Option on KBOT hard red winter wheat futures

Contract size	One KBOT hard red winter wheat futures contract (of an underlying contract size of 5,000 bushels).
Standard delivery method	Delivery of a long or short position in a futures contract at the strike price as above.
Trading months	The March, May, July, September and December cycle.
Trading hours	9.30 a.m. – 1.15 p.m.
Price quotation method	In US cents and one-eighths (1/8) of a US cent per bushel.
Minimum price move (value)	One-eighth (1/8) of a US cent per bushel (US$6.25 per contract).
Daily price limits	25 US cents (US$0.25) per bushel above or below the previous day's settlement level (US$1,250 per contract).
Position limits	600 contracts net long or short, reportable at 25 contracts.
Last trading day	The Friday that is at least five business days prior to the first notice day (the last business day of the month preceding the contract month). Trading ceases in the expiring contract at 1.00 p.m. on the last trading day.

Delivery day	The business day following the last trading day. The option expires at 10.00 a.m. on the Saturday following the last trading day.
Initial (Variation) margin	For uncovered short positions, the same margin as that for the underlying futures contract plus the premium received from the option sale, revalued daily.
Spread margin	Not stated.
Strike price intervals	Intervals of 10 US cents (US$0.10) per bushel (e.g. US$2.40, US$2.50, US$2.60, etc).
Option type	American style (the option may be exercised on any business day up to and including the last trading day). There is no automatic exercise at expiry of in-the-money options.
Method of introduction of new strike prices	Not stated.
Reuters Monitor (Quote)	N/a.
Telerate page	N/a.

Minneapolis Grain Exchange (MGE)

Address:

150 Grain Exchange Building
Minneapolis
Minnesota 55415
USA

Telephone: (612) 338 6212
Fax: (612) 339 1155
Telex: N/a.

Exchange personnel
Chairman: Donald Brummer
President: James H. Lindau
Information Officer: John Wood

Futures contracts available
Hard red spring wheat
High-fructose corn syrup
Oats
White wheat

Options contracts on futures available
Hard red spring wheat futures

In addition to the above, cash market grains and oilseeds are actively traded on the exchange floor.

Clearing House: MGE Clearing House.

Method of trading: Open outcry.

Commenced trading: 1881.

Exchange links: None.

A brief synopsis of the exchange
The exchange was founded in 1881 as the Minneapolis Chamber of Commerce, and now has over 400 members. It has been the central US market-place for grains and oilseeds in the Upper Midwest, and is also the world's largest cash grain market.

Hard red spring wheat (MW) futures

Contract size	5,000 bushels of hard red spring wheat, or 5 job lots of 1,000 bushels.
Standard delivery method	Physical delivery of No.2 or better Northern spring wheat with a protein content of 13.5% or higher, with 13% protein also deliverable at a discount, at exchange-designated elevator points in Minneapolis/St Paul and Duluth/Superior.
Trading months	The March, May, July, September and December cycle.
Trading hours	9.30 a.m. – 1.15 p.m.
Price quotation method	In US dollars (US$) and cents per bushel.
Minimum price move (value)	One-eighth (1/8) of a US cent per bushel (US$6.25 per contract).
Daily price limits	20 US cents (US$0.20) per bushel above or below the previous day's settlement price.
Position limits	Speculative limits exist of 6,000,000 bushels (1,200 contracts) in all months combined and 3,000,000 bushels (600 contracts) in any single month including the spot month.
Last trading day	No trading may take place during the last seven business days of the contract month.
Delivery day	The first delivery day is the first business day of the contract month. The notice period runs from the last business day of the month preceding the contract month to the second to last business day of the contract month.
Initial (Variation) margin	Not stated. Please consult the exchange or your broker for the current details.
Spread margin	Not stated. Please consult the exchange or your broker for the current details.
Reuters Monitor (Quote)	WHKG.
Telerate page	N/a.

High-fructose corn syrup (HF) futures

Contract size	37,000 pounds of dry or one tank truck high-fructose corn syrup.
Standard delivery method	Physical delivery of second-generation high-fructose corn syrup 55 conforming to quality standards to Chicago, Illinois.
Trading months	The first seven expiry months from the March, May, July, September and December cycle.
Trading hours	9.00 a.m. – 1.25 p.m.
Price quotation method	In US dollars (US$) and cents per hundredweight.

Minimum price move (*value*)	0.02 US cents per hundredweight (US$7.40 per contract).
Daily price limits	US$1.00 per hundredweight above or below the previous day's settlement price.
Position limits	600 contracts in all months combined and 450 contracts in any single month and 300 contracts in the spot month from the third business day prior to the first business day of the contract month.
Last trading day	No trading may take place during the last seven business days of the contract month.
Delivery day	The first delivery day is the first business day of the contract month. The notice period runs from the last business day of the month preceding the contract month to the second to last business day of the contract month.
Initial (*Variation*) margin	Not stated. Please consult the exchange or your broker for the current details.
Spread margin	Not stated. Please consult the exchange or your broker for the current details.
Reuters Monitor (*Quote*)	CSME.
Telerate page	N/a.

Oats (OM) futures

Contract size	5,000 bushels of No.1 or No.2 heavy oats.
Standard delivery method	Physical delivery of the above, or other deliverable grades at a premium or discount to the contract price, in regular warehouses within the Minneapolis or St Paul switching districts.
Trading months	March, May, July, September and December cycle.
Trading hours	9.30 a.m. – 1.15 p.m.
Price quotation method	In US dollars (US$) and cents per bushel.
Minimum price move (*value*)	0.25 US cents per bushel (US$12.50 per contract).
Daily price limits	10 US cents (US$0.10) per bushel above or below the previous day's settlement price.
Position limits	2,000,000 bushels (400 contracts) for all months combined and 2,000,000 bushels (400 contracts) in any single month including the spot month.
Last trading day	No trading may take place during the last seven business days of the contract month.
Delivery day	The first delivery day is the first business day of the contract month. The notice period runs from the last business day of the month preceding the contract month to the second to last business day of the contract month.

Initial (Variation) margin	Not stated. Please consult the exchange or your broker for the current details.
Spread margin	Not stated. Please consult the exchange or your broker for the current details.
Reuters Monitor (Quote)	OAME.
Telerate page	N/a.

White wheat (NW) futures

Contract size	5,000 bushels or 5 job lots of 1,000 bushels of white wheat.
Standard delivery method	Physical delivery of No.1 white wheat, or No.2 white wheat at a US$0.02 discount to the contract price, at exchange-approved regular distributors to the Columbia River District.
Trading months	The March, May, July, September and December cycle.
Trading hours	9.30 a.m. – 1.15 p.m.
Price quotation method	In US dollars (US$) and cents per bushel.
Minimum price move (value)	0.25 US cents per bushel (US$12.50 per contract).
Daily price limits	20 US cents (US$0.20) per bushel above or below the previous day's settlement price.
Position limits	3,000,000 bushels (600 contracts) for all months combined and 3,000,000 bushels (600 contracts) in any single month including the spot month, with the exception of 1,000,000 bushels (200 contracts) in the May expiry month.
Last trading day	No trading may take place during the last seven business days of the contract month.
Delivery day	The first delivery day is the first business day of the contract month. The notice period runs from the last business day of the month preceding the contract month to the second to last business day of the contract month.
Initial (Variation) margin	Not stated. Please consult the exchange or your broker for the current details.
Spread margin	Not stated. Please consult the exchange or your broker for the current details.
Reuters Monitor (Quote)	N/a.
Telerate page	N/a.

Option on MGE hard red spring wheat futures

Contract size	One MGE hard red spring wheat futures contract (with an underlying contract size of 5,000 bushels).

Standard delivery method	Delivery of a long or short position in a futures contract at the strike price as above.
Trading months	The March, May, July, September and December cycle.
Trading hours	9.35 a.m. – 1.25 p.m. (trading ceases in the expiring contract at 1.00 p.m. on the last trading day).
Price quotation method	In US dollars (US$) and cents per bushel.
Minimum price move (value)	One-eighth (1/8) of a US cent per bushel (US$6.25 per contract).
Daily price limits	20 US cents (US$0.20) per bushel above or below the previous day's settlement premium.
Position limits	The speculative position limit is 600 contracts long or short of the same type, or 1,200 contracts where the excess contracts are components of a conversion or reversion strategy.
Last trading day	The last Friday that precedes by at least five business days the first notice day of the underlying futures contract, or the preceding business day if that Friday is not a business day.
Delivery day	The business day following the last trading day. Notices must be delivered by 1.00 p.m. on the last trading day.
Initial (Variation) margin	Not stated. Please consult the exchange or your broker for the current details.
Spread margin	Not stated. Please consult the exchange or your broker for the current details.
Strike price intervals	Not stated. Please consult the exchange or your broker for the current details.
Option type	European style (the option may only be exercised on the last trading day and not at other times during its life). There is no automatic exercise facility for in-the-money series. American-style exercise procedure options are also available (where the option may be exercised on any business day no later than 4.00 p.m. up to and including the last trading day).
Method of introduction of new strike prices	Not stated. Please consult the exchange or your broker for the current details.
Reuters Monitor (Quote)	WHKH – WHKO.
Telerate page	N/a.

Pacific Stock Exchange Ltd (PSE)

Address:	301 Pine Street San Francisco California 94104 USA
Telephone:	(415) 393 4000/4245
Fax:	(415) 393 4202/4227
Telex:	N/a.

Exchange personnel

Chairman:	Maurice Mann
President:	Herbert Kawahara
Options Marketing:	Marie Hirsch
Information:	Dale Carlson

Los Angeles Representative Office

Address	233 South Beaudry Avenue Los Angeles California 90012 USA
Telephone:	(213) 977 4500
Fax:	N/a.
Telex:	N/a.

Futures contracts available
Financial News Network (FNN) Composite Stock Index *(traded on INTEX)*.

Options contracts on cash/physical available
Financial News Network (FNN) Composite Stock Index

The PSE also lists options on around 120 US equities.

Clearing House:	International Commodities Clearing House (ICCH) London.
Method of trading:	Open outcry.
Commenced trading:	1957 (1987 for futures and options).

Pacific Stock Exchange Ltd (PSE)

Exchange links: New York Stock Exchange (joint equity options listings).
International Futures Exchange (Bermuda).

A brief synopsis of the exchange
The Pacific Stock Exchange is one of the seven US securities exchanges registered with the SEC, and the largest after the NYSE. It was formed in 1957 as the amalgamation of the Los Angeles and San Francisco Stock Exchanges, but its history dates back to the 1880s.

There are currently over 550 members of the exchange. In terms of options the PSE is ranked third in the USA after the CBOE and AMEX. Although there are two trading floors, options are only traded in San Francisco. D-RAM (computer chip) futures are awaiting CFTC approval.

FNN Composite Stock Index (FNCI) futures

Contract size	US$100 multiplied by the FNN Composite Stock Index (FNCI).*
Standard delivery method	Cash settlement at the FNCI index level published on the last trading day.
Trading months	The two nearest consecutive calendar months plus the next two months from the March, June, September and December cycle.
Trading hours	6.30 a.m. – 1.15 p.m. (Pacific Standard Time).
Price quotation method	In US dollars (US$) and cents per index point.
Minimum price move (value)	0.05 index points (US$5.00 per contract).
Daily price limits	None.
Position limits	None.
Last trading day	The third Friday of the contract month.
Delivery day	The business day following the last trading day.
Initial (Variation) margin	Not stated. Please consult the exchange or your broker for the current details.
Spread margin	Not stated. Please consult the exchange or your broker for the current details.
Reuters Monitor (Quote)	N/a.
Telerate page	N/a.

* The Financial News Network (FNN) Composite Stock Index (FNCI) is a price-weighted index of 30 highly capitalised publicly listed NYSE stocks. The index is calculated continuously (every 15 seconds) throughout the day, and displayed every 15 minutes on the FNN TV channel.

This contract is traded on the computerised INTEX exchange in Bermuda. The corresponding options contract is traded on the Pacific Stock Exchange (PSE) in San Francisco.

Option on FNN Composite Stock Index (FNCI)

Contract size	US$100 multiplied by the FNN Composite Stock Index (FNCI).*
Standard delivery method	Cash settlement based on the difference between the strike price and the spot FNCI index level on the last trading day.
Trading months	The two nearest consecutive calendar months plus the next two months from the March, June, September and December cycle.
Trading hours	6.30 a.m. – 1.15 p.m. (Pacific Standard Time).
Price quotation method	In US dollars (US$) and cents per unit of one-tenth (1/10) of the index.

Minimum price move (value)	0.01 index points (US$1.00 per contract).
Daily price limits	None.
Position limits	15,000 contracts on either side of the market.
Last trading day	The third Friday of the contract month.
Delivery day	The business day following the last trading day. The options expire on the Saturday following the third Friday of the contract month.
Initial (Variation) margin	Not stated. Please consult the exchange or your broker for the current details.
Spread margin	Not stated. Please consult the exchange or your broker for the current details.
Strike price intervals	At five index point intervals for index levels up to 200 and at 10 point intervals thereafter, except in the case of the spot month or where the index is quoted below 25, when the intervals are at 2.5 index points.
Option type	European style (the option may only be exercised on the last trading day and not continuously during its life).
Method of introduction of new strike prices	New strike prices are introduced two days after the index trades through the last previously available highest or lowest strike price.
Reuters Monitor (Quote)	QOZA – QOZF.
Telerate page	N/a.

* The Financial News Network (FNN) Composite Stock Index (FNCI) is a price-weighted index of 30 highly capitalised publicly listed NYSE stocks, many of which are also constituents of the Dow Jones Industrial Average (DJIA). The index is calculated continuously (every 15 seconds) throughout the day, and displayed every 15 minutes on the FNN TV channel.

The corresponding FNCI futures contract is traded on the computerised INTEX exchange in Bermuda.

Twin Cities Board of Trade (TCBOT)

Address:

310 South Fourth Avenue
Suite 924
Minneapolis
MN 55415
USA

Telephone: (612) 333 6742
Fax: (612) 333 1711
Telex: N/a.

Exchange personnel
Vice-President: Jeffrey R. Hohertz

Futures contracts available
British pound / Deutschmark currency
Dynamic random access memory (DRAM) chips

Options contracts available
None

Clearing House: Cleared by the exchange itself.

Method of trading: Open outcry, although computerised trading is planned.

Commenced trading: 1988.

Exchange links: None.

A brief synopsis of the exchange
'The Twin Cities' describes the area in the USA of Minneapolis and St. Paul, which has experienced substantial growth in computer and high-technology industries in recent years.
Clearing members of the exchange must own at least two memberships.
The British pound / Deutschmark currency cross-rate is the only such available futures contract worldwide. Excalibur is the TCBOT's real-time electronic cash commodities market. It will be PC compatible, and will be used for order-entry, position reconciliation and monitoring, etc.

British pound / Deutschmark currency futures

Contract size	£50,000 traded against the Deutschmark (DM).
Standard delivery method	Cash settlement in US dollars (US$) determined at 9.00 a.m. on the final trading day of the contract month.
Trading months	The March, June, September and December cycle.
Trading hours	7.00 a.m. – 2.00 p.m.
Price quotation method	In Deutschmarks (DM) per British pound sterling (£).
Minimum price move (value)	DM0.0005 per £1.00 (DM25.00 per contract).
Daily price limits	None.
Position limits	There are no limits for bona fide hedgers. There is a speculative limit of 5,000 contracts net long or short.
Last trading day	Two business days prior to the third Wednesday of the contract month.
Delivery day	The third Wednesday of the contract month.
Initial (Variation) margin	All positions are margined in US dollars. Please consult the exchange or your broker for the current details.
Spread margin	Not stated. Please consult the exchange or your broker for the current details.
Reuters Monitor (Quote)	N/a.
Telerate page	N/a.

Dynamic random access memory (DRAM) chip futures

Contract size	One 'lot', representing 1,000 pieces of dynamic random access memory (DRAM) chips.
Standard delivery method	Cash settlement daily.
Trading months	Daily trading for the cash settlement market.
Trading hours	7.00 a.m. – 3.00 p.m. on the Excalibur electronic system.
Price quotation method	In US dollars (US$) and cents per piece.
Minimum price move (value)	1 US cent (US$0.01) per piece (US$10.00 per contract).
Daily price limits	None.
Position limits	Determined by pre-qualification. Please consult the exchange.
Last trading day	Daily.
Delivery day	Daily, by insured overnight mail. Payment must be made within 24 hours of the closing of the purchase day market.

Initial (Variation) margin	Not stated. Please consult the exchange or your broker for the current details.
Spread margin	Not stated. Please consult the exchange or your broker for the current details.
Reuters Monitor (Quote)	N/a.
Telerate page	N/a.

Part III Europe

Contents

13 Denmark

Contents

Copenhagen Stock Exchange (CSE) (Garantifonden for Danske Optioner og Futures) (Guarantee Fund for Danish Futures and Options)

Copenhagen Stock Exchange

Address:
Nikolaj Plads 6
Box 1040
DK-1007 Kobenhavn (Copenhagen) K
Denmark

Telephone: (45 33) 93 33 66
Fax: (45 33) 12 86 13
Telex: 16496 costex dk

Exchange personnel

Chairman: Sven Caspersen
President: Bent Mebus

Guarantee Fund for Danish Futures and Options

Address:
Kompagnistraede 13
Box 2017
DK-1208 Kobenhavn (Copenhagen) K
Denmark

Telephone: (1) 93 33 11
Fax: (1) 93 49 80
Telex: N/a.

Fund personnel

Chairman: Jens Otto Velle
Chief Executive: Tyge Vorstrup Ramussen
Information Officers: Peter Belling & Lis Jorgensen

Futures contracts available
Danish Treasury Bond basket
KFX Stock Index (*planned*)
Long Danish (FUTOP) Bond Index
9% 2006 annuity Mortgage Credit Bond

Options contracts on cash/physical available
9% 2006 annuity Mortgage Credit Bond

Options contracts on futures available
Danish Treasury Bond basket futures
KFX Stock Index futures
Long Danish (FUTOP) Bond Index futures

Clearing House: Guarantee Fund for Danish Futures and Options.

Method of trading: Electronic (screen) trading system.

Commenced trading: 1987.

Exchange links: None.

A brief synopsis of the exchange
Options and futures were until 1989 quoted through an open outcry method, but are now traded through a decentralised electronic trading system. Trading may still, however, be conducted outside the electronic system, but these trades must be reported to the registration system without delay.

All options and futures contracts are officially listed instruments on the Copenhagen Stock Exchange.

Danish Treasury Bond basket futures

Contract size	DKr1,000,000 of a Treasury Bond basket comprising between one and four Danish Treasury Bond issues, each having the same weight in the basket, the price of the basket being the simple arithmetic average of the four bond prices.
Standard delivery method	Cash settlement on the last trading day. There is no facility for physical delivery of the bonds underlying the basket.
Trading months	The nearest three months of the January, April, July and October cycle.
Trading hours	9.00 a.m. – 3.30 p.m.
Price quotation method	In Danish kroner (DKr) per DKr100 nominal.
Minimum price move (value)	0.05% per DKr100 of nominal face value (DKr500 per contract).
Daily price limits	None.
Position limits	None.
Last trading day	The first calendar day of the contract month or the first subsequent trading day if the first is not a business day.
Delivery day	The business day following the last trading day.
Initial (Variation) margin	4% of the underlying value of the contract. All positions are marked to market daily for variation margin purposes.
Spread margin	There are no specific spread margin concessions; instead the clearing house adopts some general offsetting rules.
Reuters Monitor (Quote)	DKOA – DKOB.
Telerate page	N/a.

KFX Stock Index futures (*planned*)

Contract size	DKr 100,000 multiplied by the KFX (Copenhagen Stock Exchange) Stock Index, comprising 25 stocks. The index is revised every three months.
Standard delivery method	Cash settlement on the last trading day (there is no facility for physical delivery of the underlying stocks to the index).
Trading months	The nearest three months from the March, June, September and December cycle.
Trading hours	9.00 a.m. – 3.30 p.m.
Price quotation method	In Danish kroner (DKr) per index point.
Minimum price move (value)	0.05 index points (DKr50.00 per contract).

Daily price limits	None.
Position limits	None.
Last trading day	The first calendar day of the contract month, or the first subsequent trading day if the first is not a business day.
Delivery day	The business day following the last trading day.
Initial (Variation) margin	12% of the underlying value of the contract. All positions are marked to market daily for variation margin purposes.
Spread margin	There are no specific spread margin concessions; instead the clearing house adopts some general offsetting rules.
Reuters Monitor (Quote)	DKOA – DKOB.
Telerate page	N/a.

Long Danish (FUTOP) Bond Index futures

Contract size	DKr1,000,000 multiplied by the FUTOP Bond Index.*
Standard delivery method	Cash settlement on the last trading day. There is no facility for physical delivery of the underlying bond issues.
Trading months	The nearest three months of the January, April, July and October expiry cycle.
Trading hours	9.00 a.m. – 3.30 p.m.
Price quotation method	In Danish kroner (DKr) per DKr100 nominal.
Minimum price move (value)	0.05 index points (DKr500 per contract).
Daily price limits	None.
Position limits	None.
Last trading day	The first calendar day of the contract month or the first subsequent trading day if the first is not a business day.
Delivery day	The business day following the last trading day.
Initial (Variation) margin	4% of the underlying value of the contract. All positions are marked to market daily for variation margin purposes.
Spread margin	There are no specific spread margin concessions; instead the clearing house adopts some general offsetting rules.
Reuters Monitor (Quote)	DKOA – DKOB.
Telerate page	N/a.

*The FUTOP Bond Index is based on 20 selected bonds and constructed as a 20 year synthetic annuity bond. The selection of bonds is reviewed every three months.

9% 2006 Annuity Mortgage Credit Bond futures

Contract size	DKr1,000,000 of the Danish 9% coupon, 2006 maturity Mortgage Credit Bond, comprising the following three issues:
	9% 2006 Byggeriets Realkreditfond
	9% 2006 Kreditforeningen Danmark
	9% 2006 Nykredit.
Standard delivery method	Cash settlement on the last trading day. There is no facility for physical delivery of the individual bond issues.
Trading months	The nearest three months of the January, April, July and October cycle.
Trading hours	9.00 a.m. – 3.30 p.m.
Price quotation method	In Danish kroner (DKr) per DKr100 of nominal face value.
Minimum price move (value)	0.05% per DKr100 of nominal face value (DKr500 per contract).
Daily price limits	None.
Position limits	None.
Last trading day	The first calendar day of the contract month or the first subsequent trading day if the first is not a business day.
Delivery day	The business day following the last trading day.
Initial (Variation) margin	4% of the underlying value of the contract. All positions are marked to market daily for variation margin purposes.
Spread margin	There are no specific spread margin concessions; instead the clearing house adopt some general offsetting rules.
Reuters Monitor (Quote)	DKOA – DKOB, DKMM.
Telerate page	N/a.

Option on 9% 2006 annuity Mortgage Credit Bond

Contract size	DKr1,000,000 of the Danish 9% coupon, 2006 maturity Mortgage Credit Bond, comprising the following three issues:
	9% 2006 Byggeriets Realkreditfond
	9% 2006 Kreditforeningen Danmark
	9% 2006 Nykredit.
Standard delivery method	Cash settlement at the strike price on the last trading day. There is no facility for physical delivery of the underlying bond issues.
Trading months	The nearest three months of the January, April, July and October cycle.
Trading hours	9.00 a.m. – 3.30 p.m.

Price quotation method	In Danish kroner (DKr) per DKr100 of nominal face value.
Minimum price move (value)	0.05% per DKr100 of nominal face value (DKr500 per contract).
Daily price limits	None.
Position limits	None.
Last trading day	The first calendar day of the contract month or the first subsequent trading day if the first is not a business day.
Delivery day	The business day following the last trading day.
Initial (Variation) margin	4% of the underlying value of the contract. All positions are marked to market daily for variation margin purposes, which is based on a margin premium and the intrinsic value.
Spread margin	There are no specific spread margin concessions; instead the clearing house adopts some general offsetting rules.
Strike price intervals	At two point (2.00%) intervals.
Option type	European style (the option may only be exercised at expiry and not at other times during its life). All options with an intrinsic value at expiry are automatically exercised.
Method of introduction of new strike prices	Not stated.
Reuters Monitor (Quote)	DKOA – DKOB, DAMM.
Telerate page	N/a.

Option on Danish Treasury Bond basket futures

Contract size	One Copenhagen Stock Exchange (CSE) Danish Treasury Bond futures contract (of an underlying contract size of DKr1,000,000 nominal face value).
Standard delivery method	Cash settlement only (there is no actual delivery of a futures contract).
Trading months	The nearest three months of the January, April, July and October cycle.
Trading hours	9.00 a.m. – 3.30 p.m.
Price quotation method	In Danish kroner (DKr) per DKr100 of nominal face value.
Minimum price move (value)	0.05% per DKr100 of nominal face value (DKr500 per contract).
Daily price limits	None.
Position limits	None.
Last trading day	The first calendar day of the contract month or the first subsequent trading day if the first is not a business day.
Delivery day	The business day following the last trading day.

Initial (Variation) margin	4% of the underlying value of the contract. All positions are marked to market daily for variation margin purposes, which is based on a margin premium and the intrinsic value.
Spread margin	There are no specific spread margin concessions; instead the clearing house adopts some general offsetting rules.
Strike price intervals	At two point (2.00%) intervals.
Option type	European style (the option may only be exercised at expiry). All options with an intrinsic value at expiry are automatically exercised.
Method of introduction of new strike prices	Not stated.
Reuters Monitor (Quote)	DKOA – DKOB.
Telerate page	N/a.

Option on KFX Stock Index futures (*planned*)

Contract size	One Copenhagen Stock Exchange KFX Stock Index futures contract (of an underlying contract size of DKr100,000 multiplied by the KFX Stock Index).
Standard delivery method	Cash settlement only on the last trading day (there is no actual delivery of a futures contract).
Trading months	The nearest three months from the March, June, September and December cycle.
Trading hours	9.00 a.m. – 3.30 p.m.
Price quotation method	In Danish kroner (DKr) per index point.
Minimum price move (value)	0.05 index points (DKr50.00 per contract).
Daily price limits	None.
Position limits	None.
Last trading day	The first calendar day of the contract month or the first subsequent trading day if the first is not a business day.
Delivery day	The business day following the last trading day.
Initial (Variation) margin	12% of the underlying value of the contract. All positions are marked to market daily for variation margin purposes, which is based on a margin premium and the intrinsic value.
Spread margin	There are no specific spread margin concessions; instead the clearing house adopts some general offsetting rules.
Strike price intervals	At five index point intervals.
Option type	European style (the option may only be exercised at expiry and not at other times during its life). All options with an intrinsic value at expiry are automatically exercised.

Method of introduction of new strike prices	Not stated.
Reuters Monitor (Quote)	DKOA – DKOB.
Telerate page	N/a.

Option on long Danish (FUTOP) Bond Index futures

Contract size	One Copenhagen Stock Exchange (CSE) FUTOP Bond Index* futures contract (of an underlying contract size of DKr1,000,000 nominal).
Standard delivery method	Cash settlement only (there is no actual delivery of a futures contract).
Trading months	The nearest three months of the January, April, July and October cycle.
Trading hours	9.00 a.m. – 3.30 p.m.
Price quotation method	In Danish kroner (DKr) per DKr100 of nominal face value.
Minimum price move (value)	0.05 index points (DKr500 per contract).
Daily price limits	None.
Position limits	None.
Last trading day	The first calendar day of the contract month or the first subsequent trading day if the first is not a business day.
Delivery day	The business day following the last trading day.
Initial (Variation) margin	4% of the underlying value of the contract. All positions are marked to market daily for variation margin purposes, which is based on a margin premium and the intrinsic value.
Spread margin	There are no specific spread margin concessions; instead the clearing house adopts some general offsetting rules.
Strike price intervals	At two index point (2.00%) intervals.
Option type	European style (the option may only be exercised at expiry and not at other times during its life). All options with an intrinsic value at expiry are automatically exercised.
Method of introduction of new strike prices	Not stated.
Reuters Monitor (Quote)	DKOA – DKOB.
Telerate page	N/a.

*The FUTOP Bond Index is based on 20 selected bonds and constructed as a 20-year synthetic annuity bond. The selection of bonds is reviewed every three months.

14 Eire

Contents

Irish Futures & Options Exchange (IFOX)

Address:	Segrave House Earlsfort Terrace Dublin 2 Eire
Telephone:	(01) 767413
Fax:	(01) 614645
Telex:	N/a.

Exchange personnel

Chairman:	Dermot Desmond
Chief Executive:	Diarmiund Bradley
Financial Controller:	Patricia Morris
Options Director:	Kieran Luddy

Futures contracts available
Irish punt / US dollar currency
Long-term (20-year) Irish Government Bonds
Three-month DIBOR (Dublin Interbank Offered Rate)
interest rate

Options contracts available
None

Clearing House:	Cleared by the exchange itself.
Method of trading:	Automated.
Commenced trading:	1989.
Exchange links:	None.

A brief synopsis of the exchange
This relatively new exchange opened in May 1989 and
has 24 members drawn from the Irish investment
community. There is no central exchange floor. The
longer-term plans of the exchange are to list a full
range of fixed-interest, currency, equity and equity
index futures and options.

IFOX is a self-regulatory body under the formal
supervision of the Central Bank of Ireland.

Irish punt / US dollar currency futures

Contract size	US$50,000 traded against the Irish punt (I£).
Standard delivery method	Cash settlement at expiry. There is no facility for physical delivery of the two currencies.
Trading months	The March, June, September and December cycle.
Trading hours	8.30 a.m. – 4.15 p.m.
Price quotation method	In Irish punts (I£) per US dollar (US$).
Minimum price move (value)	I£0.0001 per US$1.00 (I£5.00 per contract).
Daily price limits	2% of the underlying contract value above or below the previous day's settlement price.
Position limits	These are set at individual member level.
Last trading day	Two business days before the third Wednesday of the contract month. Trading ceases in the expiring contract at 3.00 p.m. on the last trading day.
Delivery day	The third Wednesday of the contract month.
Initial (Variation) margin	I£1,250 per contract. Variation margin is based on a daily mark to market.
Spread margin	I£300 per spread position.
Reuters Monitor (Quote)	IPPA.
Telerate page	N/a.

Long-term (20-year) Irish Government Bond futures

Contract size	I£50,000 nominal face value of a notional 8% coupon, 20-year Irish Government Bond.
Standard delivery method	Physical delivery of any 'deliverable' Irish Government security with 15–25 years to maturity, at the seller's discretion.
Trading months	The March, June, September and December cycle.
Trading hours	8.30 a.m. – 4.15 p.m.
Price quotation method	In Irish punts (I£) per I£100 of nominal face value.
Minimum price move (value)	I£0.01 of nominal face value (I£5.00 per contract).
Daily price limits	2% of the nominal face value of the contract above or below the previous day's settlement price. Trading halts for 90 minutes after which time new limits will be set.
Position limits	These are set at individual member level.
Last trading day	Two business days before the third Wednesday of the contract month. Trading ceases in the expiring contract at 11.00 a.m. on the last trading day.
Delivery day	The third Wednesday of the contract month.

Initial (*Variation*) margin	5% of the nominal face value of the contract (currently I£2,500 per contract). Variation margin is based on a daily mark to market.
Spread margin	I£500 per spread position.
Reuters Monitor (*Quote*)	IFOY.
Telerate page	N/a.

Three-month DIBOR (Dublin Interbank Offered Rate) interest rate futures

Contract size	I£100,000 nominal value of a deposit on the three-month Dublin Interbank Offered Rate (DIBOR).
Standard delivery method	Cash settlement on the last trading day.
Trading months	The March, June, September and December cycle.
Trading hours	8.30 a.m. – 4.15 p.m.
Price quotation method	100.00 minus the annualised rate of interest (calculated to two decimal places), quoted in Irish punts (I£).
Minimum price move (*value*)	0.01% annualised rate of interest (I£2.50 per contract).
Daily price limits	1.20% of the underlying contract value above or below the previous day's settlement price (120 basis points).
Position limits	These are set at individual member level.
Last trading day	Two business days before the third Wednesday of the contract month. Trading ceases in the expiring contract at 11.00 a.m. on the last trading day.
Delivery day	The third Wednesday of the contract month.
Initial (*Variation*) margin	I£300 per contract. Variation margin is based on a daily mark to market.
Spread margin	I£90.00 per spread position.
Reuters Monitor (*Quote*)	DIBO, IFOZ.
Telerate page	N/a.

15 Finland

Contents

Finnish Options Brokers Ltd (FOB)
(Suomen Optiomeklarit OY)

Address:	Keskuskatu 7 3rd Floor SF 00100 Helsinki Finland
Telephone:	(358) 0 13 12 11
Fax:	(358) 0 13 12 12 11

Exchange personnel

Chairman:	Gunnar Korhornen
Managing Director:	Asko Schrey
Marketing Manager:	Matti Byman
Marketing Assistant:	Elisabet Forsblom

Futures contracts available
Finnish Stock Options Index (FOX)

Options contracts on physical/cash available
Finnish Stock Options Index (FOX)

Also available are American-style traded options on the following individual Finnish equities:
Kymmene Ltd (400 shares)
Union Bank of Finland (1,000 shares)
Kansallis Osake Pankki (1,000 shares)
Kesko Oy (1,000 shares).

Both puts and calls are available on the nearest two months of the January, March, May, July, September and November expiry cycle.

Clearing House:	Finnish Options Brokers Ltd.
Method of trading:	Automated (screen-based) trading.
Commenced trading:	1988.
Exchange links:	The other exchanges in the OM family are as follows: OM France (OM-F) OM Iberica (OM-I) OM London (OM-L) OM Norway (NOM) OM Sweden (OM-S).

Reuters Composite pages: FOMA onwards.

A brief synopsis of the exchange
This exchange is the first Finnish market-place for standardised options and futures with an integrated clearing function. Currently there are options and futures available only on equity and equity-related products.

Finnish Stock Options Index (FOX) futures

Contract size	FIM100 multiplied by the Finnish Stock Options Index (FOX).*
Standard delivery method	Cash settlement on the last trading day. There is no facility for physical delivery of the stocks underlying the index.
Trading months	The nearest two months from the February, April, June, August, October and December cycle.
Trading hours	9.30 a.m. – 3.00 p.m.
Price quotation method	In Finnish marks (FIM) per index point, calculated to 0.01 index points.
Minimum price move (value)	0.5 index points (FIM50.00 per contract).
Daily price limits	None.
Position limits	None.
Last trading day	The fourth Thursday of the contract month.
Delivery day	The business day following the last trading day.
Initial (Variation) margin	Please consult the exchange or your broker for the current margin requirements.
Spread margin	Please consult the exchange or your broker for the current spread concessions.
Reuters Monitor (Quote)	FOMA – FOMM.
Telerate page	20830.

* The Finnish Stock Options Index (FOX) is based on the 25 most actively traded stocks on the Helsinki Stock Exchange.

Option on Finnish Stock Options Index (FOX)

Contract size	FIM100 multiplied by the Finnish Stock Options Index (FOX).*
Standard delivery method	Cash settlement on the last trading day. There is no facility for physical delivery of the stocks underlying the index.
Trading months	The February, April, June, August, October and December cycle.
Trading hours	9.30 a.m. – 3.00 p.m.
Price quotation method	In Finnish marks (FIM) per index point, calculated to 0.01 index points.
Minimum price move (value)	0.05 index points (FIM5.00 per contract).
Daily price limits	None.
Position limits	None.

Last trading day	The fourth Friday of the contract month.
Delivery day	The business day following the last trading day.
Initial (Variation) margin	Please consult the exchange or your broker for the current margin requirements.
Spread margin	Please consult the exchange or your broker for the current spread concessions.
Strike price intervals	Not stated.
Option type	European style (the option may only be exercised at expiry and not at other times during its life).
Method of introduction of new strike prices	Not stated.
Reuters Monitor (Quote)	FOMA – FOMM.
Telerate page	20830.

* The Finnish Stock Options Index (FOX) is based on the 25 most actively traded stocks on the Helsinki Stock Exchange.

16 France

Contents

Marché à Terme International de France (MATIF) (Paris International Futures Exchange)

Address:	176 rue Montmartre 75002 Paris France
Telephone:	(1) 40 28 82 82
Fax:	(1) 40 28 80 01
Telex:	218362

Exchange personnel

Chairman:	Gerard Pfauwadel
Managing Director:	Gilbert Durieux
Information Officer:	Jean Sicard

Futures contracts available
CAC 40 Stock Index
Cocoa beans
Long-term notional French Government Treasury
Bond
Robusta coffee
Three-month Euro-Deutschmark interest rate
Three-month PIBOR (Paris Interbank Offered Rate)
interest rate
White sugar

Options contracts on futures available
Long-term notional French Government Treasury
Bond futures
White sugar futures

Clearing House:	Chambre de Compensation des Instruments Financiers de Paris (CCIFP).
Method of trading:	Open outcry.
Commenced trading:	1986.
Exchange links:	Lille Potato Futures Market (LPM) – a subsidiary. Member of ECOFEX.

A brief synopsis of the exchange

Originally established by Parisian stock brokers in 1986, MATIF allowed foreign financial institutions membership in 1987. Trading began in the French Government Notional Treasury Bond in the same building as the Paris Bourse, and with rapid international expansion MATIF has soon become the third most active futures exchange worldwide. There are around 100 exchange members.

After-hours automated trading was also introduced in 1988, and the exchange remains part of the USA's CME GLOBEX screen trading development project. Commodity futures were recently brought under the MATIF umbrella and are now traded on the same floor. Additionally, the Lille Potato Futures Market is now a subsidiary.

A major competitor of LIFFE in the UK, MATIF already lists a Euro-Deutschmark deposit rate contract and is actively considering currency futures, futures on the ECU interest rate (LIFFE's most recently introduced contract) and futures on gold bullion.

Marché à Terme
International de
France (MATIF)
Futures
Softs and
agricultural

CAC 40 Stock Index (CAC) futures

Contract size	FFr200.00 multiplied by the CAC 40 Stock Index (eg. an underlying value of FFr200,000 per contract when the (spot) index stands at 1,000).
Standard delivery method	Cash settlement at the spot index level at 4.00 p.m. on the last trading day. There is no facility for physical delivery of the stocks underlying the index.
Trading months	The three nearby consecutive calendar months plus the next month from the March, June September and December cycle.
Trading hours	10.00 a.m. – 5.00 p.m.
Price quotation method	In French francs (FFr) per index point calculated to one decimal place.
Minimum price move (value)	0.1 index points (FFr20.00 per contract).
Daily price limits	50 index points above or below the previous day's clearing price, would halt trading for one half-hour. A further 75-point movement halts trading for a further one half-hour.
Position limits	None.
Last trading day	The last business day of the contract month.
Delivery day	The business day following the last trading day.
Initial (Variation) margin	100 index points (FFr20,000 per contract).
Spread margin	Not stated.
Reuters Monitor (Quote)	CACF.
Telerate page	N/a.

Cocoa beans futures

Contract size	10 metric tons of good fermented Ivory Coast cocoa beans, in bags.
Standard delivery method	Physical delivery of the above in authorised warehouses in the ports of Amsterdam or Dunkirk.
Trading months	The March, May, July, October and December cycle.
Trading hours	Two sessions daily: 10.30 a.m. – 1.00 p.m. and 3.00 p.m. – 6.30 p.m.
Price quotation method	In French francs (FFr) per 100 kilograms on a CIF basis.
Minimum price move (value)	FFr0.50 per 100 kilograms (FFr50.00 per contract).
Daily price limits	None.
Position limits	None.
Last trading day	The last business day of the contract month. Trading ceases in the expiring contract at 1.00 p.m. on the last trading day.

**Marché à Terme
International de
France (MATIF)
Futures
Softs and
agricultural**

Delivery day	The business day following the last trading day.
Initial (Variation) margin	FFr15,000 per contract.
Spread margin	Not stated.
Reuters Monitor (Quote)	COKA, CKPE.
Telerate page	N/a.

Long-term notional French Government Treasury Bond (NNN) futures

Contract size	FFr500,000 nominal face value of a notional 10-year French Government Treasury Bond, with a 10% coupon rate.
Standard delivery method	Physical delivery of 7–10-year eligible French Government Treasury Bonds, with a 10% coupon rate, redeemable at maturity.
Trading months	The March, June, September and December cycle.
Trading hours	10.00 a.m. – 4.00 p.m.
Price quotation method	In terms of percent of par, quoted in French francs (FFr).
Minimum price move (value)	0.02% of nominal face value (FFr100.00 per contract).
Daily price limits	200 basis points (2.00%) above or below the previous day's clearing price.
Position limits	None.
Last trading day	Four business days prior to the last business day of the contract month.
Delivery day	Two business days after the last trading day.
Initial (Variation) margin	4.00% of the underlying contract value (FFr20,000 per contract).
Spread margin	Not stated.
Reuters Monitor (Quote)	MATD.
Telerate page	3209.

Robusta coffee futures

Contract size	Five metric tons of Robusta coffee of Ivory Coast origin, in bags.
Standard delivery method	Physical delivery of the above, in authorised warehouses in exchange-approved ports.
Trading months	The January, March, May, July, September and November cycle.
Trading hours	Two sessions daily: 10.15 a.m. – 1.00 p.m. and 3.00 p.m. – 6.30 p.m.
Price quotation method	In French francs (FFr) per 100 kilograms.

Minimum price move (value)	FFr1.00 per 100 kilograms (FFr50.00 per contract).
Daily price limits	None.
Position limits	None.
Last trading day	The last business day of the contract month. Trading ceases in the expiring contract at 12.00 noon on the last trading day.
Delivery day	The business day following the last trading day.
Initial (Variation) margin	FFr10,000 per contract.
Spread margin	Not stated.
Reuters Monitor (Quote)	COFC, KFPE.
Telerate page	N/a.

Three-month Euro-Deutschmark interest rate (EDM) futures

Contract size	DM1,000,000 nominal face value.
Standard delivery method	Cash settlement based on the Exchange Delivery Settlement Price (EDSP)* on the last trading day.
Trading months	March, June, September and December cycle.
Trading hours	9.30 a.m. – 4.00 p.m.
Price quotation method	100.00 minus the annualised rate of interest, quoted in Deutschmarks (DM).
Minimum price move (value)	0.01% per annum of nominal face value (DM25.00 per contract).
Daily price limits	None.
Position limits	None.
Last trading day	Two days prior to the third Wednesday of the contract month.
Delivery day	The business day following the last trading day.
Initial (Variation) margin	0.10% of the face value of the contract (DM1,000 per contract). Additional margin is due upon a 30 basis point (0.30%) adverse movement. Margins may only be deposited in the form of cash, but are interest bearing.
Spread margin	0.05% of the face value of the contract (DM500 per spread position). This spread concession is not available in the last five days of a contract's life.
Reuters Monitor (Quote)	EDMF.
Telerate page	N/a.

* The Exchange Delivery Settlement Price (EDSP) is based on interest-rate quotations for three-month Euro-Deutschmark deposits obtained from 12 reference banks between 9.30 a.m. and 11.00 a.m. (Paris time) on the last trading day, disregarding the two highest and two lowest quotes. The EDSP will be quoted at 100.00 minus the average of the remaining quotations.

Three-month PIBOR (Paris Interbank Offered Rate) interest rate (PIB) futures

Contract size	FFr5,000,000 nominal face value.
Standard delivery method	Cash settlement at expiry based on the three-month PIBOR published by the AFB at 11.00 a.m. on the last trading day.
Trading months	The March, June, September and December cycle.
Trading hours	9.30 a.m. – 4.00 p.m.
Price quotation method	In percentage terms (to two decimal places) – 100.00 minus the annualised yield, quoted in French francs (FFr).
Minimum price move (value)	0.01% of nominal face value (FFr125.00 per contract).
Daily price limits	60 basis points (0.60%) above or below the previous day's clearing price.
Position limits	None.
Last trading day	Two Paris Stock Exchange business days prior to the 11th Thursday of the contract month. Trading ceases in the expiring contract at 11.00 a.m. on the last trading day.
Delivery day	The business day following the last trading day.
Initial (Variation) margin	0.30% of the underlying contract value (FFr15,000 per contract). Additional margin is due upon a 60 basis points (0.60%) adverse movement. Margins may be deposited in the form of cash or Treasury Bills.
Spread margin	Not stated.
Reuters Monitor (Quote)	PIBN.
Telerate page	N/a.

White sugar futures

Contract size	50 metric tons of white sugar.
Standard delivery method	Physical delivery of 50 tons of white crystal sugar or refined sugar in bags of 50 kilograms, FOB in an exchange-approved port.
Trading months	The March, May, August, October and December cycle.
Trading hours	Two sessions daily: 10.45 a.m. – 1.00 p.m. and 3.00 p.m. – 7.00 p.m.
Price quotation method	In French francs (FFr) per metric ton.
Minimum price move (value)	FFr1.00 per metric ton (FFr50.00 per contract).
Daily price limits	There are no price limits on the two nearest contract months within 30 days from the expiry of the nearest contract month.
Position limits	None.

Last trading day	The mid-month trading day (normally the 15th) of the month preceding the contract month, or the preceding business day if the 15th is not a business day.
Delivery day	The business day following the last trading day.
Initial (Variation) margin	FFr7,000 per contract.
Spread margin	Not stated.
Reuters Monitor (Quote)	SUGC, SUGP, CCAP.
Telerate page	N/a.

Option on MATIF long-term notional French Government Treasury Bond futures

Contract size	One MATIF long-term notional French Treasury Bond futures contract (of an underlying contract size of FFr500,000 nominal face value).
Standard delivery method	Delivery of a long or short position in a futures contract at the strike price as above.
Trading months	The March, June, September and December cycle.
Trading hours	10.05 a.m. – 4.00 p.m.
Price quotation method	In terms of percentage of par calculated to two decimal places, quoted in French francs (FFr).
Minimum price move (value)	0.01% of nominal face value (FFr50.00 per contract).
Daily price limits	None.
Position limits	None.
Last trading day	The last Friday of the month prior to the contract month of the underlying futures contract.
Delivery day	The business day following the last trading day.
Initial (Variation) margin	Please consult the exchange or your broker for the current margin requirements.
Spread margin	Please consult the exchange or your broker for the current spread concessions.
Strike price intervals	At even strike prices, i.e. at 2.00% intervals (eg. 88-00, 90-00, 92-00, etc.).
Option type	American style (the option may be exercised on any business day up to and including the last trading day).
Method of introduction of new strike prices	There are at least five strike prices available at all times around the current price of the underlying futures contract.
Reuters Monitor (Quote)	BTQY – BTRW.
Telerate page	N/a.

Marché à Terme
International de
France (MATIF)
Options on futures
Softs and
agricultural

Option on MATIF white sugar futures

Contract size	One MATIF white sugar futures contract (of an underlying contract size of 50 metric tons).
Standard delivery method	Delivery of a long or short position in a futures ' contract at the strike price as above.
Trading months	The March, May, August and October cycle for a total period of 16 months forward including the current month.
Trading hours	Two sessions daily: 10.45 a.m. – 1.00 p.m. and 3.00 p.m. – 7.00 p.m.
Price quotation method	In French francs (FFr) per metric ton.
Minimum price move (value)	FFr1.00 per metric ton (FFr50.00 per contract).
Daily price limits	None.
Position limits	None.
Last trading day	The last business day of the penultimate month to the underlying futures contract month.
Delivery day	The business day following the last trading day.
Initial (Variation) margin	The seller receives the premium but pays the same margin as the holder of a futures position (currently FFr20,000 per contract).
Spread margin	Not stated.
Strike price intervals	At FFr100 per metric ton intervals.
Option type	Not stated.
Method of introduction of new strike prices	There are five strike prices always available. New strike prices are introduced if none of the existing option series are above or below the contract settlement price.
Reuters Monitor (Quote)	SQPE – SQPN.
Telerate page	N/a.

Marché à Terme de la Pomme de Terre de Lille, Rouxbaix, Tourcoing (LPM) (Lille Potato Futures Market) (a subsidiary of MATIF, Paris)

Address:	Bourse de Commerce du Marché à Terme
	Centre d'Affairs Mercure
	445 Boulevard Gambetta
	59200 Tourcoing
	France
Telephone:	20 26 22 13
Fax:	20 36 65 09
Telex:	110 155

Exchange personnel

President:	Luc Lemaire
General Secretary:	Lucien Pinchede

Futures contracts available
No. 1 Potatoes
No. 2 Potatoes

Options contracts available
None

Clearing House:	Banque Centrale de Compensation (BCC).
Method of trading:	Open outcry.
Commenced trading:	1984.
Exchange links:	A subsidiary of MATIF, Paris.

No. 1 potato futures

Contract size
20 tonnes of potatoes (40mm+ calibre).

Standard delivery method
Physical delivery of the above, in 25 kilogram sacks, at a location of the seller's choice.

Trading months
April and November only.

Trading hours
Two sessions daily: 11.00 a.m. – 12.45 p.m. and 3.00 p.m. – 4.30 p.m.

Price quotation method
In French francs (FFr) per 100 kilograms.

Minimum price move (value)
FFr0.25 per 100 kilograms (FFr50.00 per contract).

Daily price limits
FFr15.00 per 100 kilograms above or below the previous day's closing price.

Position limits
None.

Last trading day
The fourth Tuesday of the contract month.

Delivery day
The third business day of the second week following the last trading day.

Initial (Variation) margin
Approximately 15% of the underlying value of the contract.

Spread margin
Not stated.

Reuters Monitor (Quote)
PTRE.

Telerate page
N/a.

No. 2 potato futures

Contract size
20 tonnes of potatoes (50mm+ calibre).

Standard delivery method
Physical delivery of the above, in 25 kilogram sacks, at a location of the seller's choice.

Trading months
The February, April, May and November cycle.

Trading hours
Two sessions daily: 11.00 a.m. – 12.45 p.m. and 3.00 p.m. – 4.30 p.m.

Price quotation method
In French francs (FFr) per 100 kilograms.

Minimum price move (value)
FFr0.25 per 100 kilograms (FFr50.00 per contract).

Daily price limits
FFr15.00 per 100 kilograms above or below the previous day's closing price.

Position limits
None.

Last trading day
The fourth Tuesday of the contract month.

Delivery day
The second business day of the week following the last trading day.

Initial (Variation) margin
Approximately 15% of the underlying value of the contract.

Spread margin
Not stated.

Reuters Monitor (Quote)
PTRE.

Telerate page
N/a.

Marché des Options Négociables de la Bourse de Paris (MONEP) (Paris Traded Options Market)

Address:	15 rue du Faubourg Montmartre 75009 Paris France
Telephone: Fax: Telex:	(1) 45 23 05 04 (1) 42 46 82 08 290402

Exchange personnel

President:	Alain Morice
Managing Director:	Raymond Lucas
Trading Manager:	Louis Grunthal

Futures contracts available
None

Options contracts on cash/physical available
CAC 40 Stock Index

Also available are options on around 20 leading French equities, the contract size being 100 shares of the underlying stock in each case. These trade on the March, June, September and December expiry cycle, expiring on the penultimate business day of the contract month.

Clearing House:	Société de Compensation des Marches Conditionnels, a subsidiary of the Société des Bourses Françaises.
Method of trading:	Open outcry – a public order book handles customer orders of up to 20 contracts.
Commenced trading:	September 1987 (November 1988 for index options).
Exchange links:	None.

A brief synopsis of the exchange
The options traded on MONEP are executed on the floor of the Paris Bourse, stock options being limited to the most active issues traded on the forward market. Only French brokers (45 member firms) are authorised to trade on MONEP. There are 17 registered market-makers.

**Marché des Options
Négociables de la
Bourse de Paris
(MONEP)
Options on
cash/physical
Stock indices**

Option on CAC 40 Stock Index

Contract size	FFr200 multiplied by the CAC 40 Stock Index.
Standard delivery method	Cash settlement on the last trading day. There is no facility for physical delivery of the stocks underlying the index.
Trading months	The three nearby consecutive calendar months and the next month from the March, June, September and December cycle (to a maximum of six months forward).
Trading hours	10.00 a.m. – 5.00 p.m. Trading ceases in the expiring contract at 4.00 p.m. on the last trading day.
Price quotation method	In French francs (FFr) per index point.
Minimum price move (value)	0.01 index points (FFr2.00 per contract).
Daily price limits	Upon a movement in the underlying index of 50 points above or below the previous day's close, trading halts for one half-hour. A further one half-hour trading halt would come into force upon a subsequent 75 point movement in the CAC 40 Index.
Position limits	None.
Last trading day	The last business day of the contract month.
Delivery day	The second business day following the submission of the exercise notice or the last trading day.
Initial (Variation) margin	Uncovered short positions demand a deposit of 20% of the underlying value of the option in cash, Treasury Bills or the underlying equities to the CAC 40 Stock Index.
Spread margin	Not stated.
Strike price intervals	At 25 index point intervals.
Option type	American style (the option may be exercised on any business day up to and including the last trading day).
Method of introduction of new strike prices	There is a minimum of five strike prices always available. No new strike prices are normally added during the last 10 days of an option's life.
Reuters Monitor (Quote)	KQAI – KQAP.
Telerate page	N/a.

OM France (OM-F)

Address:	52 Avenue des Champs Elysées 75008 Paris France
Telephone: Fax: Telex:	(1) 42 25 66 25 (1) 42 25 72 45 650563

Exchange personnel

Chairman:	Jacques Mayoux
Chief Executive Officer:	Evrard Van Hertsen
Senior VP, Trading:	Michel Slupowski
Marketing Manager:	Roger de Brantes

Futures contracts available
Four-year BTAN (Bon à taux annuel normalisé)
French Treasury Notes

Options contracts on futures available
None

Clearing House:	OM France (OM-F).
Method of trading:	Semi-automated screen trading and clearing, matching bids and offers anonymously.
Commenced trading:	1988.

Exchange links:	The other exchanges in the OM family are as follows:
	    OM Finland (FOB)
	    OM Iberica (OM-I)
	    OM London (OM-L)
	    OM Norway (NOM)
	    OM Sweden (OM-S).

Reuters Composite pages:	OXBG onwards.

A brief synopsis of the exchange

The exchange was formed as a private company, with the largest shareholder being OM Sweden with 20%. Major French banks make up the other majority shareholders. Block trading exists for orders greater than 50 contracts. All orders less than 50 contracts are handled by automatic execution, the system being able to handle up to 100 orders per second. Liquidity of the OM-F contracts are rather low in comparison with its main French competitor, MATIF, although it is hoped the BTAN contract will provide an edge for the exchange, following the delisting of the OMF 50 Stock Index futures and options contracts in 1989.

There are over 50 exchange members and seven registered market-makers.

Four-year BTAN (Bon à taux annuel normalisé) French Treasury Note futures

Contract size	FFr1,000,000 nominal face value of a notional French Treasury Note with a coupon rate of 8% and a life to maturity of four years.
Standard delivery method	Physical delivery of securities held in a pool* with a life to maturity of between three and five years at the time of delivery.
Trading months	The March, June, September and December cycle.
Trading hours	9.00 a.m. – 5.00 p.m.
Price quotation method	In French francs (FFr) as a percentage of the nominal value of the underlying security, ex of accrued interest.
Minimum price move (value)	0.02% of nominal face value (FFr200 per contract).
Daily price limits	100 ticks (2.00%) above or below the previous day's settlement price.
Position limits	None.
Last trading day	The third business day preceding the end of the contract month.
Delivery day	The business day following the last trading day. The last delivery day is the last business day of the contract month.
Initial (Variation) margin	5% of the underlying value of the contract. Variation margin is recalculated daily.
Spread margin	2% of the underlying value of the linked straddle.
Reuters Monitor (Quote)	OXBA-G, OXNG.
Telerate page	3214.

* The pool ('*gisement*') consists of fixed-rate BTANs repayable at expiry with remaining maturities of three to five years at the time of the futures contract expiry.

17 Germany

Contents

Deutsche Terminboerse GmbH (DTB) (German Futures Exchange)

Address:	Grueneburgweg 102 D-6000 Frankfurt am Main 1 Bethmannstrasse 50-54 West Germany
Telephone:	(49 69) 12 303-0
Fax:	(49 69) 55 74 92
Telex:	N/a.

Exchange personnel

Chief Executive:	Dr Jorg Franke
Chairman:	Dr Rolf E. Breuer
Information Officer:	Wilhelm Brandt

Futures contracts available
German Stock Index (DAX)
Notional German Government Treasury Bond
(*both planned for summer 1990*).

Options contracts available
None

Also available are American-style traded options on the following German equities. The trading hours are 10.00 a.m. to 4.00 p.m., and each contract represents 50 shares of the underlying issue. Trading months available are the near month plus months two, three and six from the March, June, September and December cycle.

Allianz	*BASF*	*Bayer*
BMW	*Commerzbank*	*Daimler Benz*
Deutsche Bank	*Dresdner Bank*	*Hoechst*
Mannesmann	*Seimens*	*Thyssen*
VEBA	*VW*	

Clearing House:	Cleared by the exchange itself.
Method of trading:	Automated (screen) traded.
Commenced trading:	1989

Deutsche Terminboerse GmbH (DTB)

Exchange links:

None, but computer link in the Federal Republic of Germany is planned from 1993.

A brief synopsis of the exchange
The exchange, following the SOFFEX automated trading system, commenced trading in options in early 1989 on a range of domestic equity options. Major expansion is planned for 1990.

German Stock Index (DAX) futures (*planned*)

Contract size	DM100 multiplied by the DAX German Stock Index.
Standard delivery method	Cash settlement on the business day following the last trading day. The daily settlement price is the last traded futures price within the last 10 minutes of trading. The final settlement price will be the value of the DAX index at 12.30 p.m. on the last trading day. There is no facility for the physical delivery of the stocks underlying the index.
Trading months	The nearest three expiry months from the March, June, September and December cycle.
Trading hours	11.00 a.m. – 2.00 p.m. (opening before and closing 30 minutes after the Frankfurt Exchange).
Price quotation method	In Deutschmarks (DM) per index point to one decimal place.
Minimum price move (*value*)	0.5 index points (DM50.00 per contract).
Daily price limits	None, but the exchange may impose limits in extreme market conditions.
Position limits	None.
Last trading day	The business day before the third Saturday of the contract month. Trading ceases in the expiring contract at 12.30 p.m. on the last trading day.
Delivery day	The business day following the last trading day.
Initial (*Variation*) margin	Not yet announced.
Spread margin	Not yet announced.
Reuters Monitor (*Quote*)	N/a.
Telerate page	N/a.

Notional German Government Treasury Bond futures (*planned*)

Contract size	DM250,000 nominal face value of a notional 8–10 year German Government Treasury Bond with a 6% coupon rate.
Standard delivery method	Physical delivery of the above bonds, through the Frankfurter Kassenverein, with a two day process.
Trading months	The nearest three expiry months from the March, June, September and December cycle.
Trading hours	8.00 a.m. – 4.00 p.m.
Price quotation method	In Deutschmarks (DM) per DM100 nominal, quoted to two decimal points.
Minimum price move (*value*)	0.01% nominal face value of one contract point (DM25.00 per contract).

Daily price limits	None, but the exchange may impose limits in extreme market conditions.
Position limits	None.
Last trading day	Two business days before the delivery day. Trading ceases in the expiring contract at 12.30 p.m. on the last trading day. The final settlement price is based on the greater of the average either of the last minute of trading or of the last five trades.
Delivery day	The 10th calendar day of the contract month.
Initial (Variation) margin	Not yet announced.
Spread margin	There are reduced margin requirements for spread positions.
Reuters Monitor (Quote)	N/a.
Telerate page	N/a.

18 The Netherlands

Contents

Amsterdam Pork & Potato Terminal Market (APPTM)

Address:	Postbus 252 100 AG Amsterdam The Netherlands
Telephone: Fax: Telex:	(20) 550 4390 (20) 23 66 59 16582 NLK NL

Exchange personnel

Managing Director:	M. P. A. de Vries
Assistant Manager:	Kasper Walet

Futures contracts available
Porker (hogs) terminal
Potato terminal

Options contracts available
None

Clearing House:	Amsterdam Futures Clearing House (NLKKAS).
Method of trading:	Open outcry in the 'ring'.
Commenced trading:	1988.
Exchange links:	None.

A brief synopsis of the exchange
The Amsterdam terminal markets were formed in 1988 as the amalgamation of the Potato Terminal Market (established in 1958) and the Porker Terminal Market (established in 1980).

**Amsterdam Pork &
Potato Terminal
Market (APPTM)
Futures
Softs and
agricultural**

Porker (hogs) terminal futures

Contract size	10,000 kilograms net of live porkers (hogs).
Standard delivery method	Physical delivery of live porkers (hogs) as above, each porker (hog) to weigh between 90 and 120 kilograms, at warehouses at the seller's option.
Trading months	All consecutive calendar months plus one expiry month 12 months forward.
Trading hours	Two sessions daily: 10.30 a.m. – 12.00 noon and 1.30 p.m. – 4.15 p.m.
Price quotation method	In Dutch guilders (Dfl), cents and half cents per kilogram.
Minimum price move (value)	Dfl0.005 per kilogram (Dfl50.00 per contract).
Daily price limits	None.
Position limits	None.
Last trading day	During the contract month.
Delivery day	The Thursday after which there remains a minimum of five working days in the contract month.
Initial (Variation) margin	Dfl2,000 per contract.
Spread margin	Dfl47.50 per spread position (for non-associates).
Reuters Monitor (Quote)	PBGE.
Telerate page	N/a.

Potato terminal futures

Contract size	25,000 kilograms of potatoes.
Standard delivery method	Physical delivery of the above at exchange-approved potato warehouses in the Netherlands.
Trading months	The February, March, May, June and November cycle.
Trading hours	Two sessions daily: 10.45 a.m. – 12.45 p.m. and 2.00 p.m. – 4.00 p.m.
Price quotation method	In Dutch guilders (Dfl), and cents per 100 kilograms.
Minimum price move (value)	Dfl0.10 per kilogram (Dfl25.00 per contract).
Daily price limits	None.
Position limits	None.
Last trading day	During the delivery month.
Delivery day	The fourth working day before the beginning of the contract month.
Initial (Variation) margin	Dfl1,200 per contract.
Spread margin	Dfl40.00 per spread position.
Reuters Monitor (Quote)	PTGE.
Telerate page	N/a.

Optiebeurs NV (EOE)
(European Options Exchange NV)

Address:	Rokin 65
	Amsterdam
	1012 KK
	The Netherlands
Telephone:	(020) 550 4550
Fax:	(020) 230 012
Telex:	14596 eoepr nl

Exchange personnel

President:	Tjerk E. Westerterp
Deputy Managing Director:	Ulf Doornbos
Information Officer:	Lex Van Drooge
Commercial Affairs:	Mark Adema

Futures contracts available
None

Options contracts on physical/cash available
British pound / Dutch guilder currency
EOE Dutch Stock Index
FTA Bullet Bond Index
IOCC gold bullion
IOCC silver bullion
Jumbo US dollar / Dutch guilder currency
Major Market Stock Index
Specific Dutch Government Treasury Bonds
US dollar / Dutch guilder currency

American-style traded options are also available on around 24 international equities where the unit of trading is 100 shares of the underlying security, with an initial life of three, six and nine months.

Clearing Houses:	European Stock Options Clearing Corporation (ESCC).
	International Options Clearing Corporation (IOCC).
	Associate Clearing House Amsterdam (ACHA).
Method of trading:	Open outcry.
Commenced trading:	1978.

Exchange links:

IOCC link – Montreal Exchange (ME).
IOCC link – Vancouver Stock Exchange (VSE).
IOCC link – Australian Stock Exchange (Sydney) Ltd (AOM).
American Stock Exchange (AMEX).

A brief synopsis of the exchange

The EOE was Europe's first options exchange in 1978, and has been closely modelled on the Chicago Board Options Exchange (CBOE), the world's largest and oldest options market. Volumes increased by 50 times in the first 10 years of operation. The EOE was the first exchange to introduce gold, bond and currency options.

Round-the-world trade in precious metal options is possible through the IOCC (International Options Clearing Corporation BV) link between the Netherlands, Canada and Australia and this allows trading for nearly 20 hours per day on this fully fungible link that involves an electronic limit order book rotating between the exchanges. There is also fungibility with the Major Market Stock Index on the American Stock Exchange (AMEX) which was the first US index option to trade outside the US itself. This is cleared by the OCC (Options Clearing Corporation).

From the inception of the exchange in 1978, the number of seats has risen from around 140 to nearly 400. The different membership types are Public Order Member, Market-Maker and Clearing Member. There are over 220 member companies and individuals to these 400 registered capacities.

The EOE's 100% futures subsidiary, FTA, started trading in 1987 and the Rotterdam Energy Futures Exchange (a 49% subsidiary) in 1989.

Option on British pound / Dutch guilder currency (DGS)

Contract size	£10,000 traded against the Dutch guilder (Dfl).
Standard delivery method	Physical exchange of the currencies concerned at the strike price.
Trading months	The nearby three consecutive calendar months plus the next three months from the March, June, September and December expiry cycle.
Trading hours	10.00 a.m. – 4.30 p.m.
Price quotation method	In Dutch guilders (Dfl) per British pounds (£).
Minimum price move (value)	Dfl0.05 per £1.00 (Dfl5.00 per contract).
Daily price limits	None.
Position limits	25,000 contracts on the same side of the market.
Last trading day	The third Friday of the contract month. Trading ceases in the expiring contract at 4.00 p.m. on the last trading day.
Delivery day	The business day following the last trading day. Options expire on the Saturday following the third Friday of the contract month.
Initial (Variation) margin	The option premium received plus a percentage of (if any) twice the intrinsic value of the option.
Spread margin	Not stated.
Strike price intervals	At Dfl0.05 per £1.00 intervals.
Option type	European style (the option may only be exercised at expiry, and not at other times during its life).
Method of introduction of new strike prices	Between four and five series are initially available. New series are introduced so as to allow there to be at least one in-the-money and one out-of-the-money series at all times. No new series are normally introduced in the last 10 business days before expiry.
Reuters Monitor (Quote)	YSGA – YSGP.
Telerate page	N/a.

Option on EOE Dutch Stock Index (EOE)

Contract size	Dfl100 multiplied by the EOE Dutch Stock Index.*
Standard delivery method	Cash settlement at expiry at the strike price. There is no facility for physical delivery of the stocks underlying the index.
Trading months	The nearby three consecutive calendar months plus the next three months in the January, April, July and October quarterly cycle. Additionally, one-year and two-year forward options are available, expiring initially in November 1991 and November 1992.
Trading hours	10.30 a.m. – 4.30 p.m.

Price quotation method	In Dutch guilders (Dfl) and cents per index point.
Minimum price move (value)	Dfl0.10 per index point (Dfl1.00 per contract).
Daily price limits	None.
Position limits	8,000 contracts on the same side of the market.
Last trading day	The third Friday of the contract month. Trading ceases in the expiring contract at 4.00 p.m. on the last trading day.
Delivery day	The business day following the last trading day. Options expire on the Saturday following the third Friday of the contract month.
Initial (Variation) margin	The option premium received plus a percentage of (if any) twice the intrinsic value of the option.
Spread margin	Not stated.
Strike price intervals	At 5.0 index point intervals.
Option type	European style (the option may only be exercised at expiry, and not at other times during its life).
Method of introduction of new strike prices	Between four and five series are initially available. New series are introduced so as to allow there to be at least one in-the-money and one out-of-the-money series at all times. No new series are normally introduced in the last five business days before expiry.
Reuters Monitor (Quote)	YIXA – YIXT, YYLA – YYLP.
Telerate page	N/a.

* The EOE Dutch Stock Index comprises 20 issues of Dutch shares, with the index equal to one-hundredth (1/100) of the value of the portfolio made up of these shares. The index is geometrically weighted.

Option on FTA Bullet Bond Index (OBL)

Contract size	Dfl100 multiplied by the FTA Bullet Bond Index.*
Standard delivery method	Cash settlement at the strike price at expiry. There is no facility for physical delivery.
Trading months	The first four months of the February, May, August and November cycle.
Trading hours	9.30 a.m. – 5.00 p.m.
Price quotation method	In Dutch Guilders (Dfl) per index point.
Minimum price move (value)	Dfl0.05 per index point (Dfl5.00 per contract).
Daily price limits	None.
Position limits	20,000 contracts on the same side of the market.
Last trading day	The third Friday of the contract month.
Delivery day	The business day following the last trading day. Options expire on the Saturday following the third Friday of the contract month.
Initial (Variation) margin	The option premium received plus a percentage of (if any) twice the intrinsic value of the option.
Spread margin	Not stated.
Strike price intervals	At Dfl5.00 per index point intervals.

Option type	European style (the option may only be exercised at expiry, and not at other times during its life).
Method of introduction of new strike prices	At least two series are initially available. New series are introduced so as to allow there to be at least one in-the-money and one out-of-the-money series at all times. No new series are normally introduced in the last 20 business days before expiry.
Reuters Monitor (Quote)	YAOA – YAOP.
Telerate page	N/a.

*The FTA Bullet Bond Index comprises the following Dutch Government Bonds:

6% Netherlands 1987 due 1994	6% Netherlands 1988 due 1995
6.25% Netherlands 1988 due 1994	6.25% Netherlands 1987 I due 1995
6.25% Netherlands 1987 III due 1995	6.25% Netherlands 1987 due 1997
6.25% Netherlands 1986 due 1995	6.25% Netherlands 1986 due 1996
6.50% Netherlands 1986 due 1996	7% Netherlands 1987 due 1993

For each bond in the index an average is taken of all prices quoted between 10.30 a.m. and 4.00 p.m. on the last trading day (the third Friday of the contract month). The index is recalculated on the basis of this average, and this forms the basis for the final settlement price.

Option on IOCC gold bullion (GD)

Contract size	10 troy ounces of fine gold bullion of 0.995 fineness acceptable for good London delivery.
Standard delivery method	Physical delivery of the above with one of the five members of the London Gold Market or an institution acting as its delivery depot.
Trading months	The nearest three months of the February, May, August and November cycle.
Trading hours	The local dealing times on the IOCC link exchanges are as follows:
	AOM (Nov – Mar): 11.00 a.m. – 1.00 p.m. and 2.30 p.m. – 4.30 p.m.
	AOM (Apr – Oct): 10.30 a.m. – 12.30 p.m. and 2.00 p.m. – 4.00 p.m.
	EOE: 10.30 a.m. – 4.30 p.m.
	ME: 9.00 a.m. 2.30 p.m.
	VSE: 11.30 a.m. – 4.00 p.m.
Price quotation method	In US dollars (US$) and cents per troy ounce.
Minimum price move (value)	US$0.10 per troy ounce (US$1.00 per contract).
Daily price limits	None.
Position limits	5,000 contracts on the same side of the market.
Last trading day	The third Friday of the contract month. Trading ceases in the expiring contract at 4.00 p.m. (Amsterdam), 2.30 p.m. (Montreal), 4.00 p.m. (Vancouver) or 5.00 p.m. (Sydney) on the last trading day. These are all local times.

Delivery day	The business day following the last trading day. The options expire on the Monday following the third Friday of the contract month, this being the last time for exercise. Settlement is due on the fourth business day following the submission of tender notice.
Initial (Variation) margin	The option premium received plus a percentage of (if any) twice the intrinsic value of the option.
Spread margin	Not stated.
Strike price intervals	Gold price under US$400: US$10.00 intervals Gold price US$400 – US$600: US$20.00 intervals Gold price US$600 – US$900: US$30.00 intervals Gold price greater than US$900: US$40.00 intervals
Option type	American style (the option may be exercised on any business day up to and including the last trading day).
Method of introduction of new strike prices	Between four and five series are initially available. New series are introduced so as to allow there to be at least one in-the-money and one out-of-the-money series at all times. No new series are normally introduced in the last 20 business days before expiry. The other link exchanges take the lead from the EOE Amsterdam on issuing new strike prices.
Reuters Monitor (Quote)	YGDA – YGDP (EOE), MEGA – MEGB (ME), VEGA – VEGB (VSE), GDMB – GDMG.
Telerate page	N/a.

This contract is traded on the IOCC (International Options Clearing Corporation BV) link between the Australian Stock Exchange (Sydney) Ltd (AOM), the Montreal Exchange (ME), Optiebeurs Amsterdam (EOE) and the Vancouver Stock Exchange (VSE), allowing trading for 18.5 hours a day. A limit order book is passed from exchange to exchange. The contracts are fully fungible.

Option on IOCC silver bullion (SIL)

Contract size	1,000 troy ounces 999 parts to 1,000 parts of good London delivery silver bullion.
Standard delivery method	Physical delivery of the above with one of the five members of the London Silver Market.
Trading months	The nearby three months of the March, June, September and December cycle.
Trading hours	The following are the local trading times for the IOCC link exchanges: EOE: 10.30 a.m. – 4.30 p.m. VSE: 7.30 a.m. – 4.00 p.m. AOM (Nov – Mar): 11.00 a.m. – 1.00 p.m. and 2.30 p.m. – 4.30 p.m. AOM (Apr – Oct): 10.30 a.m. – 12.30 p.m. and 2.00 p.m. – 4.00 p.m.

Price quotation method	In US dollars (US$) and cents per troy ounce.
Minimum price move (value)	One US cent (US$0.01) per troy ounce (US$10.00 per contract).
Daily price limits	None.
Position limits	10,000 contracts on the same side of the market.
Last trading day	The third Friday of the contract month. Trading ceases in the expiring contract at 4.00 p.m. (Amsterdam and Vancouver) or 5.00 p.m. (Sydney), on the last trading day. These times are local times.
Delivery day	The business day following the last trading day. Options expire on the Monday following the third Friday of the contract month, which is the latest time for exercise.
Initial (Variation) margin	The option premium received plus a percentage of (if any) twice the intrinsic value of the option.
Spread margin	Not stated.

Strike price intervals		
	Silver price under US$5.00:	US$0.25 intervals
	Silver price US$5.00 – US$15.00:	US$0.50 intervals
	Silver price over US$15.00:	US$1.00 intervals

Option type	American style (the option may be exercised on any business day up to and including the last trading day).
Method of introduction of new strike prices	Between four and five series are initially available. New series are introduced so as to allow there to be at least one in-the-money and one out-of-the-money series at all times. No new series are normally introduced in the last 20 business days before expiry. The other link exchanges take the lead from the EOE Amsterdam on issuing new strike prices.
Reuters Monitor (Quote)	YAQA – YAQP (EOE).
Telerate page	N/a.

This contract is traded on the IOCC (International Options Clearing Corporation BV) link between the Australian Stock Exchange (Sydney) Ltd (AOM), Optiebeurs Amsterdam (EOE) and the Vancouver Stock Exchange (VSE). Trading therefore takes place for 18.5 hours per day. An order book passes from exchange to exchange. The contracts are fully fungible.

Option on jumbo US dollar / Dutch guilder currency (DXJ)

Contract size	US$100,000 traded against the Dutch guilder (Dfl).
Standard delivery method	Physical exchange of the currencies concerned at the strike price.
Trading months	The nearby three consecutive calendar months plus the next three months from the March, June, September and December expiry cycle.
Trading hours	9.45 a.m. – 4.30 p.m.

Price quotation method	In Dutch guilders (Dfl) per US dollar (US$).
Minimum price move (value)	Dfl0.01 per US$1.00 (Dfl10.00 per contract).
Daily price limits	None.
Position limits	25,000 contracts on the same side of the market.
Last trading day	The third Friday of the contract month. Trading ceases in the expiring contract at 4.00 p.m. on the last trading day.
Delivery day	The business day following the last trading day. Options expire on the Saturday following the third Friday of the contract month.
Initial (Variation) margin	The option premium received plus a percentage of (if any) twice the intrinsic value of the option.
Spread margin	Not stated.
Strike price intervals	At Dfl0.05 per US$1.00 intervals.
Option type	European style (the option may only be exercised at expiry, and not at other times during its life).
Method of introduction of new strike prices	Between four and five series are initially available. New series are introduced so as to allow there to be at least one in-the-money and one out-of-the-money series at all times. No new series are normally introduced in the last 10 business days before expiry.
Reuters Monitor (Quote)	YZXA – YZXZ.
Telerate page	N/a.

Option on Major Market Stock Index (XMI)

Contract size	US$100 multiplied by the Major Market Stock Index (XMI).*
Standard delivery method	Cash settlement at expiry. There is no facility for physical delivery of the stocks underlying the index.
Trading months	The nearby three consecutive calendar months.
Trading hours	12.00 noon – 4.30 p.m. (Amsterdam) and 9.30 a.m. – 4.10 p.m. (New York time on AMEX).
Price quotation method	In US dollars (US$) and cents per index point.
Minimum price move (value)	One-sixteenth (1/16) of an index point (US$6.25 per contract) for premiums lower than US$3.00, or one-eighth (1/8) of an index point (US$12.50 per contract) for all higher premiums.
Daily price limits	None.
Position limits	10,000 contracts on the same side of the market.
Last trading day	The third Friday of the contract month. Trading ceases in the expiring contract at 4.30 p.m. on the last trading day.
Delivery day	The business day following the last trading day. Options expire on the Saturday following the third Friday of the contract month.

Initial (Variation) margin	The option premium received plus a percentage of (if any) twice the intrinsic value of the option.
Spread margin	Not stated.
Strike price intervals	At 5.0 index point intervals.
Option type	European style (the option may only be exercised at expiry, and not at other times during its life).
Method of introduction of new strike prices	Between four and five series are initially available. New series are introduced so as to allow there to be at least one in-the-money and one out-of-the-money series at all times. No new series are normally introduced in the last five business days before expiry.
Reuters Monitor (Quote)	YECA – YECP, YFCA – YFCP, XMIA – XMIP (AMEX).
Telerate page	N/a.

* The Major Market Index (XMI) is price weighted based on weighting factors equal to each of the 20 constituents. The constituents are as follows:

American Express	AT&T	Chevron
Coca-Cola	Dow Chemical	Du Pont
Eastman Kodak	Exxon	General Electric
General Motors	IBM	International Paper
Johnson & Johnson	Merck & Co	Minnesota Mining & Mfg
Mobil	Philip Morris	Procter & Gamble
Sears, Roebuck	USX	

This contract is fungible with the Major Market Stock Index option traded on the American Stock Exchange (AMEX). The contract specifications are therefore the same.

Option on specific Dutch Government Treasury Bonds

Contract size	Dfl10,000 nominal face value of a specific issue of Dutch Government Treasury Bonds as listed below.*
Standard delivery method	Physical (giro) delivery of the above in the form of 10 bonds of Dfl1,000 nominal face value each.
Trading months	The first three months of the February, May, August and November cycle, and for the three funds (NLW, NLY and NLZ), a three year (November) series.
Trading hours	9.30 a.m. – 5.00 p.m.
Price quotation method	In Dutch guilders (Dfl) per nominal stock.
Minimum price move (value)	Dfl0.05 (Dfl5.00 per contract).
Daily price limits	None.
Position limits	Between 2,500 and 8,800 contracts depending on the specific issue of bonds traded.
Last trading day	The third Friday of the contract month. Trading ceases in the expiring contract at 4.00 p.m. on the last trading day.

Delivery day	The business day following the last trading day. Options expire on the Saturday following the third Friday of the contract month.
Initial (Variation) margin	The option premium received plus a percentage of (if any) twice the intrinsic value of the option.
Spread margin	Not stated.
Strike price intervals	At 2.50 percentage point intervals.
Option type	American style (the option may be exercised on any business day up to and including the last trading day).
Method of introduction of new strike prices	At least two series are initially available. New series are introduced so as to allow there to be at least one in-the-money and one out-of-the-money series at all times. No new series are normally introduced in the last 20 business days before expiry.
Reuters Monitor (Quote)	See below.
Telerate page	N/a.

* The following Dutch Government Treasury Bonds are available for trading under the above contract specifications:

Bond issue	*Reuters Page*
NLA 12.75% Netherlands 1986–92/96	YQAA – YQAP
NLB 7.75% Netherlands 1990 due 2000	
NLD 7.5% Netherlands 1989–1999	
NLF 7.5% Netherlands 1989 II due 1999	
NLX 7.5% Netherlands 1989–I–91/95	YVXA – YVXH
NLV 7% Netherlands 1987–1993	YUNA – YUNP
NLP 7% Netherlands 1989–I–II–1999	YATA – YATP
NLW 6.75% Netherlands 1988–1998 (three-year option also traded)	YPLA – YPLP
NLY 6.5% Netherlands 1986–1996 (three-year option also traded)	YEOE – YEOP
NLZ 6.25% Netherlands 1986–1995 (three-year option also traded)	YZLA – YZLP
NLQ 6.25% Netherlands 1988 – 1994	YQMA – YQMP

Option on US dollar / Dutch guilder currency (DGX)

Contract size	US$10,000 traded against the Dutch guilder (Dfl).
Standard delivery method	Physical exchange of the currencies concerned at the strike price.
Trading months	The nearby three consecutive calendar months plus the next three months from the March, June, September and December expiry cycle.
Trading hours	10.00 a.m. – 4.30 p.m.
Price quotation method	In Dutch guilders (Dfl) per US dollar (US$).
Minimum price move (value)	Dfl0.05 per US$1.00 (Dfl5.00 per contract).
Daily price limits	None.
Position limits	25,000 contracts on the same side of the market.

Last trading day	The third Friday of the contract month. Trading ceases in the expiring contract at 4.00 p.m. on the last trading day.
Delivery day	The business day following the last trading day. Options expire on the Saturday following the third Friday of the contract month.
Initial (Variation) margin	The option premium received plus a percentage of (if any) twice the intrinsic value of the option.
Spread margin	Not stated.
Strike price intervals	At Dfl0.05 per US$1.00 intervals.
Option type	American style (the option may be exercised on any business day up to and including the last trading day).
Method of introduction of new strike prices	Between four and five series are initially available. New series are introduced so as to allow there to be at least one in-the-money and one out-of-the-money series at all times. No new series are normally introduced in the last 10 business days before expiry.
Reuters Monitor (Quote)	YDGA – YDGZ.
Telerate page	N/a.

Financiele Termijnmarkt Amsterdam NV (FTA) (Amsterdam Futures Market) (a 100% subsidiary of Optiebeurs NV (EOE))

Address:	Nes 49 1012 KD Amsterdam The Netherlands
Telephone:	(020) 550 4555
Fax:	(020) 236 659
Telex:	N/a.

Exchange personnel

General Manager:	R. F. Sandelowsky

Futures contracts available
Dutch Government Guilder Bond
EOE Dutch Stock Index
FTA Bullet Bond Index

Options contracts available:
None

Clearing House:	European Futures Clearing Corporation (EFCC).
Method of trading:	Open outcry on exchange floor.
Commenced trading:	1987.
Exchange links:	A subsidiary of Optiebeurs NV (EOE) Amsterdam.

A brief synopsis of the exchange
The FTA is a wholly owned subsidiary of the European Options Exchange, created in 1987, solely to trade futures contracts. Membership of the exchange is as follows: Clearing Member, Broker, Off-floor Trader or Market-Maker. Future plans include the introduction of futures contracts on Dutch short-term interest rates and the stock index of Dutch international issues.

Dutch Government Guilder Bond (FTO) futures

Contract size	Dfl250,000 nominal face value of a notional Dutch Government Treasury Bond with a 7% coupon rate.
Standard delivery method	Physical delivery at the seller's choice of Dutch Bullet Bonds with a single redemption date, which, as of the first day of the contract month, have a remaining life of between eight and 10 years to maturity.
Trading months	The March, June, September and December cycle up to one year forward.
Trading hours	9.00 a.m. – 5.00 p.m.
Price quotation method	In Dutch guilders (Dfl) per Dfl100 nominal.
Minimum price move (value)	0.01% of nominal face value (Dfl25.00 per contract).
Daily price limits	None.
Position limits	None.
Last trading day	The seventh calendar day of the contract month, or the following business day if the seventh is a non-business day.
Delivery day	The business day following the last trading day.
Initial (Variation) margin	Please consult the exchange or your broker for the current margin requirements.
Spread margin	Please consult the exchange or your broker for the current spread concessions.
Reuters Monitor (Quote)	FTAC.
Telerate page	N/a.

EOE Dutch Stock Index (FTI) futures

Contract size	Dfl200 multiplied by the EOE Dutch Stock Index.*
Standard delivery method	Cash settlement (there is no facility for physical delivery of the shares underlying the index).
Trading months	The nearby three consecutive calendar months. Also every three months, a 12-month future will be introduced from the January, April, July and October cycle.
Trading hours	10.15 a.m. – 4.30 p.m.
Price quotation method	In Dutch guilders (Dfl) and cents per index point.
Minimum price move (value)	Dfl0.05 per index point (Dfl.10.00 per contract).
Daily price limits	10 index points above or below the previous day's closing price halts trading for 30 minutes. Thereafter there are no further limits for the rest of the day.
Position limits	None.
Last trading day	The third Friday of the contract month. Trading ceases in the expiring contract at 4.00 p.m. on the last trading day.

Delivery day	The business day following the last trading day.
Initial (Variation) margin	Please consult the exchange or your broker for the current margin requirements.
Spread margin	Please consult the exchange or your broker for the current spread concessions.
Reuters Monitor (Quote)	FTAB – FTAE.
Telerate page	N/a.

* The EOE Dutch Stock Index comprises 20 issues of Dutch shares, with the index equal to one-hundredth (1/100) of the value of the portfolio made up of these shares. The index is geometrically weighted.

FTA Bullet Bond Index (FTB) futures

Contract size	Dfl1,000 multiplied by the FTA Bullet Bond Index.*
Standard delivery method	Cash settlement based on the final settlement price of the FTA Bullet Bond Index as described below.
Trading months	The February, May, August and November cycle up to one year forward.
Trading hours	9.00 a.m. – 5.00 p.m.
Price quotation method	In Dutch Guilders (Dfl) and cents per index point.
Minimum price move (value)	0.05 index points (Dfl50.00 per contract).
Daily price limits	1.50 index points above or below the previous day's closing level closes the market for 30 minutes. Thereafter there will be no further limits for the rest of the day.
Position limits	None.
Last trading day	The last business day of the contract month. Trading ceases in the expiring contract at 4.00 p.m. on the last trading day.
Delivery day	The business day following the last trading day.
Initial (Variation) margin	Please consult the exchange or your broker for the current margin requirements.
Spread margin	Please consult the exchange or your broker for the current spread concessions.
Reuters Monitor (Quote)	FTAG.
Telerate page	N/a.

* The EOE-FTA Bullet Bond Index comprises the weighted average of the following Dutch Government Bonds on 30 December 1986:

6% Netherlands 1987 due 1994	6% Netherlands 1988 due 1995
6.25% Netherlands 1988 due 1994	6.25% Netherlands 1987 I due 1995
6.25% Netherlands 1987 III due 1995	6.25% Netherlands 1987 due 1997
6.25% Netherlands 1986 due 1995	6.25% Netherlands 1986 due 1996
6.50% Netherlands 1986 due 1996	7% Netherlands 1987 due 1993

For each bond in the index an average is taken of all prices quoted between 10.30 a.m. and 4.00 p.m. on the last trading day (the third Friday of the contract month). The index is recalculated on the basis of this average, and this forms the basis for the final settlement price.

Rotterdam Energy Futures Exchange (ROEFEX) (a 49% subsidiary of Optiebeurs NV (EOE))

Address:	World Trade Centre
	Beursplein 37
	PO Box 30214
	3001 DE Rotterdam
	The Netherlands
Telephone:	(31) 10 405 2250
Fax:	(31) 10 405 5068
Telex:	N/a.

Exchange personnel

Project Manager:	P. W. H. de Jong
Information Officer:	J. H. L. Muhleim

Futures contracts available
Brent blend crude oil
Gas oil
Heavy fuel oil

Options contracts available
None

Clearing House:	International Petroleum Clearing Corporation.
Method of trading:	Open outcry.
Commenced trading:	1989.
Exchange links:	Optiebeurs NV (EOE) Amsterdam.

A brief synopsis of the exchange
ROEFEX is a 49% subsidiary of the European Options Exchange (EOE), concentrating on energy futures in the European time zone and intending to capitalise on the importance of Rotterdam as a leading world port in this industry.

Brent blend crude oil futures

Contract size	1,000 US barrels of Brent blend crude oil.
Standard delivery method	Physical delivery of the above, or the following alternative crudes: Forties, Ninian, Oseberg, Stastfjord and Bonny light, by in-tank transfer, pump-over, delivery ex-Europak, seagoing vessel or by river barge.
Trading months	The nearest nine consecutive calendar months commencing with the current calendar month.
Trading hours	10.00 a.m. – 6.30 p.m.
Price quotation method	In US dollars (US$) and cents per barrel.
Minimum price move (value)	US$0.01 per barrel (US$10.00 per contract).
Daily price limits	US$1.00 per barrel above or below the previous day's closing price. This limit is expanded by 50% on the day following a limit movement. There are no limits during the month preceding the contract month.
Position limits	None.
Last trading day	The third business day prior to the 25th calendar day of the month preceding the contract month, or the previous day if the 25th is a non-business day.
Delivery day	All deliveries must be initiated after the first business day and completed before the last business day of the contract month. All open contracts at expiry are automatically taken to delivery.
Initial (Variation) margin	Please consult the exchange or your broker for the current margin requirements.
Spread margin	Please consult the exchange or your broker for the current spread concessions.
Reuters Monitor (Quote)	N/a.
Telerate page	N/a.

Gas oil futures

Contract size	100 metric tons (based on volume) of gas oil of merchantable quality.
Standard delivery method	Physical delivery of the above, ex-refinery, in the Antwerp, Flushing, Rotterdam, Europoort range at the seller's option. Loading is by barges, coasters or tankers, or where the seller's facility permits, by pump-over or in-tank transfer.
Trading months	The nearby nine consecutive calendar months commencing with the current calendar month.
Trading hours	10.00 a.m. – 6.30 p.m.
Price quotation method	In US dollars (US$) and cents per metric ton.

Minimum price move (value)	US$0.05 per metric ton (US$5.00 per contract).
Daily price limits	US$6.00 per metric ton above or below the previous day's closing price. This limit is expanded by 50% on the day following a limit movement. There are no limits during the month preceding the contract month.
Position limits	None.
Last trading day	The last business day of the month preceding the contract month.
Delivery day	All deliveries must be initiated after the fifth business day and completed before the last business day of the contract month. All open contracts at expiry are automatically taken to delivery.
Initial (Variation) margin	Please consult the exchange or your broker for the current margin requirements.
Spread margin	Please consult the exchange or your broker for the current spread concessions.
Reuters Monitor (Quote)	N/a.
Telerate page	N/a.

Heavy fuel oil futures

Contract size	100 metric tons (based on volume) of heavy fuel oil of merchantable quality.
Standard delivery method	Physical delivery of the above, FOB storage installation/refinery, in the Antwerp, Flushing, Rotterdam, Europoort range at the seller's option. Loading is by barges, coasters or tankers, or where the seller's facility permits, by pump-over or in-tank transfer.
Trading months	The nearby nine consecutive calendar months commencing with the current calendar month.
Trading hours	10.00 a.m. – 6.30 p.m.
Price quotation method	In US dollars (US$) and cents per metric ton.
Minimum price move (value)	US$0.05 per metric ton (US$5.00 per contract).
Daily price limits	US$6.00 per metric ton above or below the previous day's closing price. This limit is expanded by 50% on the day following a limit movement. There are no limits during the month preceding the contract month.
Position limits	None.
Last trading day	The last business day of the month preceding the contract month.

Delivery day	All deliveries must be initiated after the fifth business day and completed before the last business day of the contract month. All open contracts at expiry are automatically taken to delivery.
Initial (Variation) margin	Please consult the exchange or your broker for the current margin requirements.
Spread margin	Please consult the exchange or your broker for the current spread concessions.
Reuters Monitor (Quote)	N/a.
Telerate page	N/a.

19 Norway

Contents

No contracts yet trading.

Norwegian Options Market (NOM)
(Norsk Opsjonsmarked AS)

Address:	Tordenskjoldsgatan 8–10 Postboks 1494 Vika N–0160 OSLO 1 Norway
Telephone:	(472) 33 15 50
Fax:	(472) 33 27 93
Telex:	N/a.

Exchange personnel

Chairman:	Baard Syrrist
Managing Director:	Dag Holler
Information Officer:	Carl Fredrick Morken

Futures contracts available
None yet trading

Options contracts on physical/cash available
None yet trading

There will also be available traded options on individual Norwegian equities.

Clearing House:	Cleared by the exchange itself.
Method of trading:	Fully automated trading and clearing.
Commenced trading:	Trading is expected to commence early in 1990.
Exchange links:	The OM family of exchanges is as follows:

OM Finland (FOB)
OM France (OM-F)
OM Iberia (OM-I)
OM London (OM-L)
OM Sweden (OM-S).

A brief synopsis of the exchange
The lack of rules and regulations on futures and options trading in Norway is such that no official market-place has yet been authorised for the trading of

these products. However, at the time of writing, the regulations are expected to be agreed upon soon.

NOM is 33% owned by the Stockholm Options Market, the remainder being held by Norwegian banks and brokers.

20 Spain

Contents

Mercado Español de Futuros Financiero (MEFF) (Spanish financial futures exchange)

Address:

Placa Gala Placida
1–3, 13th Floor
Escalada B
Barcelona 08006
Spain

Telephone: (343) 238 3000
Fax: (343) 218 3832
Telex: N/a.

Exchange personnel

Contact: Jose Luiz Oller

Futures contracts available
Mid-term Public Bonds (*planned*)
90-day Public Debt Repos (*planned*)

Clearing House: Not yet announced.

Method of trading: Not yet announced.

Commenced trading: Trading is expected to begin in early 1990.

Exchange links: None.

A brief synopsis of the exchange
The MEFF is a specialist futures subsidiary of the Barcelona Stock Exchange. Until 1990 there was no formalised options and futures trading in Spain, but now MEFF will compete with OM Iberica in Madrid for activity in this area.

OM Iberica (OM-I)

Address:	Torre Picasso Planta 26 Pablo Ruiz Picasso 28020 Madrid Spain
Telephone:	(1) 585 08 00
Fax:	(1) 571 95 42
Telex:	N/a.

Exchange personnel

President:	Pedro Garcia
Project Manager:	Carl Rosencrantz
Marketing Manager:	Francisca Minguella
Information Officer:	Enrique Elosegui

Futures contracts available
None yet

Options contracts on cash/physical available
Short-term Spanish Government Treasury Bond '

Clearing House:	Cleared by the exchange itself.
Method of trading:	Automated (screen based) trading and clearing.
Commenced trading:	1989.
Exchange links:	The OM family of exchanges is as follows:

OM Finland (FOB)
OM France (OM-F)
OM London (OM-L)
OM Norway (NOM)
OM Sweden (OM-S).

Reuters Composite pages:	OIMA onwards.

A brief synopsis of the exchange
Until recently there was no formal futures and options exchange trading activity in Spain. OM Iberica will compete directly with MEFF in Barcelona for Spanish futures and options business. OM Iberica and OM London are the two most recent additions to the OM stable of exchanges.

Option on short-term Spanish Government Treasury Bond

Contract size	Pta20,000,000 nominal face value of a notional Spanish Government Treasury Bond.
Standard delivery method	Physical delivery of the following Spanish Treasury Bond at the strike price: Issue #1120-7 B 12.50/89 Maturity 25/10/92, with two to three years remaining to maturity, through the Bank of Spain public debt book entry system.
Trading months	The two nearest expiry months from the March, June, September and December cycle.
Trading hours	9.30 a.m. – 1.30 p.m.
Price quotation method	In Spanish pesetas (Pta) per cent of nominal face value.
Minimum price move (value)	0.0005% of nominal face value (Pta100 per contract).
Daily price limits	None.
Position limits	None.
Last trading day	The Monday before the third Wednesday of the contract month.
Delivery day	Two business days following the last trading day.
Initial (Variation) margin	Based on the OM collateral system.
Spread margin	Based on the OM collateral system.
Strike price intervals	At 0.50% of nominal face value intervals.
Option type	European style (the option may only be exercised at expiry and not at other times during its life).
Method of introduction of new strike prices	New strike prices are added when the forward price of the Treasury Bond is higher (lower) than the existing second highest (lowest) strike price.
Reuters Monitor (Quote)	OIMA – OIMZ.
Telerate page	N/a.

21 Sweden

Contents

Stockholm Options Market (OM-S)
(Stockholms Optionsmarknad)

Address:

Fondkommission AB
Brunkenbergstorg 2
Box 16305
103 26 Stockholm
Sweden

Telephone: (468) 700 06 00
Fax: (468) 723 10 92
Telex: OPTION S

Exchange personnel

Chairman: Hans Werthen
President: Olof Stenhammer
Marketing Manager: Margareta Montgomerie

Forwards/Futures contracts available
OMX 30 Stock Index (forward)
US dollar / Deutschmark currency
US dollar / Swedish krona currency

*Also available are stock forward contracts of normally
100 shares on the following Swedish issues:*
1. S-E-Banken   *2. Volvo B*
3. Skandia (unrestricted)   *4. Trelleborg B*
*The life of these forwards is three and six months on the
January, April, July and November cycle (stocks 1 and 4)
or the February, May, August and November cycle
(stocks 2 and 3). Forwards expire on the third Friday of
the contract month.*

Options contracts on physical/cash available
OMR2 (Treasury Note) interest rate
OMX 30 Stock Index
US dollar / Deutschmark currency
US dollar / Swedish krona currency

*Also available are options on over 16 individual Swedish
equities, the contract size being 1,000 shares underlying
normally. Some stocks have both puts and calls, whilst
others are limited to calls only. The normal life of these*

*options is three and six months on either the January,
April, July and November cycle, the February, May,
August and November cycle or the March, June,
September and December cycle, expiring on the third
Friday of the contract month.*

Clearing House: Stockholms Optionsmarknad (OM-S).

Method of trading: Semi-automated (screen) trading and clearing.

Commenced trading: 1985.

Exchange links: The OM family of exchanges is as follows:

OM Finland (FOB)
OM France (OM-F)
OM Iberia (OM-I)
OM London (OM-L)
OM Norway (NOM).

Reuters Composite Pages: OMCA onwards.

A brief synopsis of the exchange
OM-S is the market-place and clearing house for
trading in derivative instruments in Sweden and
although originally a private company, went public in
1987, and is now owned by banks and brokers on the
exchange as well as Swedish institutions. Membership
to the exchange is free. It claims to be the only
exchange with an integrated automated trading and
clearing facility.

At present, forwards, futures and options are
available on individual shares, the stock index, a
Swedish Treasury Note and the US dollar currency.
Orders under 10 contracts are placed on the automated
trading system, whilst larger orders (block trades) are
phoned through to a matching desk. The exchange
opened for foreign trading in 1987.

OM-S is considered to be the parent of the family of
European OM exchanges. Already trading are OM
France, OM Finland, OM Iberica and OM London
whilst OM Norway will begin trading soon.

OMX 30 Stock Index forward

Contract size	SKr100 multiplied by the OMX Stock Index, based on 30 stocks (A1 list) with the heaviest volume on the Stockholm Stock Exchange, updated semi-annually.
Standard delivery method	Cash settlement at expiry. There is also the facility for physical delivery of the stocks underlying the OMX Stock Index.
Trading months	All consecutive calendar months, with the nearest one, two and four months available for trading at any one time.
Trading hours	10.00 a.m. – 4.00 p.m.
Price quotation method	Prices are quoted in Swedish krona (SKr) per one-hundredth (1/100) of the OMX index excluding fees.
Minimum price move (value)	SKr0.01 (SKr1.00 multiplied by the OMX index level per contract).
Daily price limits	None.
Position limits	None.
Last trading day	The day prior to the expiration day, which is the fourth Friday of the contract month. The index settlement level is the average index value for the trading day prior to the expiration day.
Delivery day	The fifth day after the expiration day.
Initial (Variation) margin	Based on the OM collateral system (OM-S).
Spread margin	Based on the OM collateral system (OM-S).
Reuters Monitor (Quote)	N/a.
Telerate page	N/a.

US Dollar / Deutschmark currency futures

Contract size	US$50,000 traded against the Deutschmark (DM).
Standard delivery method	Physical delivery of the currencies concerned.
Trading months	The March, June, September and December cycle, with the nearest two expiry months available for trading at any one time.
Trading hours	9.30 a.m. – 4.00 p.m.
Price quotation method	In West German pfennigs per US dollar (US$) calculated to two decimal places.
Minimum price move (value)	0.01 pfennig (DM0.0001) per US$1.00 (US$5.00 per contract).
Daily price limits	None.
Position limits	None.
Last trading day	Two days before the third Wednesday of the contract month.

Delivery day	The third Wednesday of the contract month.
Initial (Variation) margin	Based on the OM collateral system (OM-S).
Spread margin	Based on the OM collateral system (OM-S).
Reuters Monitor (Quote)	N/a.
Telerate page	N/a.

US dollar / Swedish krona currency (SEK) futures

Contract size	US$50,000 traded against the Swedish krona (SKr).
Standard delivery method	Physical exchange of the currencies concerned.
Trading months	The March, June, September and December cycle, with the nearest two expiry months available for trading at any one time.
Trading hours	9.30 a.m. – 4.00 p.m.
Price quotation method	In Swedish krona (SKr) per US dollar (US$), calculated to two decimal places.
Minimum price move (value)	SKr0.0001 per US$1.00 (US$5.00 per contract).
Daily price limits	None.
Position limits	None.
Last trading day	Two days before the third Wednesday of the contract month.
Delivery day	The third Wednesday of the contract month.
Initial (Variation) margin	Based on the OM collateral system (OM-S).
Spread margin	Based on the OM collateral system (OM-S).
Reuters Monitor (Quote)	N/a.
Telerate page	N/a.

Option on OMR2 (Treasury Note) interest rate

Contract size	SKr1,000,000 nominal of a specific Swedish five-year Treasury Note.
Standard delivery method	Cash (or if desired, physical) settlement against a specific Swedish Treasury Note.
Trading months	The March, June, September and December cycle with the nearest two expiry months quoted.
Trading hours	9.30 a.m. – 4.00 p.m. Trading ceases in the expiring option at 12.00 noon on the last trading day.
Price quotation method	Prices are quoted in Swedish krona (SKr) per one-hundredth (1/100) of an option excluding fees.
Minimum price move (value)	SKr0.01 (SKr100 per contract).
Daily price limits	None.

Position limits	None.
Last trading day	Six days before the exercise settlement (or cash settlement) day.
Delivery day	The fifth day after the day of the transaction or expiration.
Exercise/Cash settlement	The third Wednesday of the contract month.
Initial (Variation) margin	Based on the OM collateral system (OM-S), currently approximately 12% of the value of the underlying index.
Spread margin	Based on the OM collateral system (OM-S).
Strike price intervals	At 10 basis points (0.10%) intervals.
Option type	European style (the option may only be exercised at expiry, and not at other times during its life).
Method of introduction of new strike prices	Not stated.
Reuters Monitor (Quote)	N/a.
Telerate page	N/a.

Option on OMX 30 Stock Index

Contract size	SKr100 multiplied by the OMX 30 Stock Index, based on 30 stocks (A1 list) with the heaviest volume on the Stockholm Stock Exchange, updated semi-annually.
Standard delivery method	Cash settlement at expiry. Physical delivery of the underlying stocks to the index is also available.
Trading months	All consecutive calendar months, with the nearest one, two and four months available for trading at any one time.
Trading hours	10.00 a.m. – 4.00 p.m.
Price quotation method	Prices are quoted in Swedish krona (SKr) per one-hundredth (1/100) of an option excluding fees.
Minimum price move (value)	SKr0.01 (SKr1.00 multiplied by the index level per contract).
Daily price limits	None.
Position limits	None.
Last trading day	The day prior to the expiration day, which is the fourth Friday of the contract month. The index settlement level is the average index value for the trading day prior to the expiration day.
Delivery day	The third day after the transaction day.
Exercise/Cash settlement	The fifth day after the expiration day.
Initial (Variation) margin	Based on the OM collateral system (OM-S), currently approximately 15% of the value of the underlying index with a minimum of SKr1,000 per uncovered short position.
Spread margin	Based on the OM collateral system (OM-S).
Strike price intervals	At 20.0 index point intervals.

Option type	European style (the option may only be exercised at expiry, and not at other times during its life).
Method of introduction of new strike prices	Not stated.
Reuters Monitor (Quote)	OMHB.
Telerate page	N/a.

Option on US dollar / Deutschmark currency

Contract size	US$50,000 traded against the Deutschmark (DM).
Standard delivery method	Physical exchange of the currencies concerned at the strike price.
Trading months	The March, June, September and December cycle, with the nearest two expiry months available for trading at any one time.
Trading hours	9.30 a.m. – 4.00 p.m.
Price quotation method	In West German pfennigs per US dollar (US$) calculated to two decimal places.
Minimum price move (value)	0.01 pfennig (DM0.0001) per US$1.00 (US$5.00 per contract).
Daily price limits	None.
Position limits	None.
Last trading day	Two days before the third Wednesday of the contract month.
Delivery day	The third Wednesday of the contract month.
Initial (Variation) margin	Based on the OM collateral system (OM-S).
Spread margin	Based on the OM collateral system (OM-S).
Strike price intervals	At intervals of 2.5 pfennigs (DM0.025) per US$1.00.
Option type	European style (the option may only be exercised at expiry, and not at other times during its life). All in-the-money options are automatically exercised on expiry.
Method of introduction of new strike prices	Not stated.
Reuters Monitor (Quote)	N/a.
Telerate page	N/a.

Option on US dollar / Swedish krona (SEK) currency

Contract size	US$50,000 traded against the Swedish krona (SKr).
Standard delivery method	Physical exchange of the currencies concerned at the strike price.
Trading months	The March, June, September and December cycle, with the nearest two expiry months available for trading at any one time.

Trading hours	9.30 a.m. – 4.00 p.m.
Price quotation method	In Swedish krona (SKr) per US dollar (US$) calculated to two decimal places.
Minimum price move (value)	SKr0.0001 per US$1.00 (US$5.00 per contract).
Daily price limits	None.
Position limits	None.
Last trading day	Two days before the third Wednesday of the contract month.
Delivery day	The third Wednesday of the contract month.
Initial (Variation) margin	Based on the OM collateral system (OM-S).
Spread margin	Based on the OM collateral system (OM-S).
Strike price intervals	At intervals of SKr0.025 per US$1.00.
Option type	European style (the option may only be exercised at expiry, and not at other times during its life). All in-the-money options are automatically exercised at expiry.
Method of introduction of new strike prices	Not stated.
Reuters Monitor (Quote)	OMFE – OMFF.
Telerate page	N/a.

22 Switzerland

Contents

Swiss Options and Financial Futures Exchange AG (SOFFEX)

Address:	Neumattstrasse 7 CH-8953 Dietikon Zurich Switzerland
Telephone:	(01) 740 30 20
Fax:	(01) 740 10 00
Telex:	828392 SOFX CH

Exchange personnel

Chairman:	Ernst Mollet
Chief Executive:	Otto E. Nageli
Marketing Co-ordinator:	Karin Wagner

Futures contracts available

None yet – planned for 1990 on the Swiss Market Index.

Options contracts on physical/cash available

Swiss Market Index (SMI)

Also available are options on the following individual Swiss equities (contracts of five shares):

Ciba Geigy	*CS Holdings*
Roche Holdings	*Jacobs-Suchard*
Nestlé	*Swiss Reinsurance*
Sandoz	*Swiss Bank Corporation*
Union Bank of Switzerland	*Swiss Volksbank*
Zurich Insurance	*BBC Brown Boveri*
Swiss Aluminium	

Trading hours: 9.30 a.m. – 2.30 p.m.

Expiry cycle: January, April, July and October.

Clearing House:	Cleared by exchange itself.
Method of trading:	Computerised (screen) trading and clearing.
Commenced trading:	May 1988.
Exchange links:	None.

A brief synopsis of the exchange
SOFFEX opened in early 1988 with a range of options
on Swiss equities. It is the first since the New Zealand
Futures Exchange and INTEX (Bermuda) to be fully
screen-traded as opposed to open outcry. Its
membership comprises current members of the Swiss
Stock Exchanges and other professional securities
dealers in Switzerland.

Swiss Options and
Financial Futures
Exchange
(SOFFEX)
Options on
cash/physical
Stock indices

Option on Swiss Market Index (SMI)

Contract size	SFr5.00 multiplied by the Swiss Market Index (SMI), a capitalisation-weighted index comprising 24 stocks.
Standard delivery method	Cash settlement at the 11.30 a.m. settlement index level on the last trading day. There is no facility for physical delivery of the stocks underlying the index.
Trading months	The January, April, July and October cycle, with the latest expiry six months forward.
Trading hours	From shortly after the start of permanent trading at the Zurich Stock Exchange to 15 minutes after the end of permanent trading at the Zurich Stock Exchange.
Price quotation method	In Swiss francs (SFr) per index point.
Minimum price move (value)	For premium values over SFr500: SFr1.00 per index point (SFr5.00 per contract).
Daily price limits	None.
Position limits	None.
Last trading day	The third Friday of the contract month, or if this is not a business day, the closest business day available. Trading ceases in the expiring contract at 11.30 a.m. on the last trading day.
Delivery day	The business day following the last trading day.
Initial (Variation) margin	Please consult the exchange or your broker for the current margin requirements.
Spread margin	Please consult the exchange or your broker for the current spread margin concessions.
Strike price intervals	At 50 index point intervals.
Option type	Not stated.
Method of introduction of new strike prices	Not stated.
Reuters Monitor (Quote)	N/a.
Telerate page	N/a.

23 United Kingdom

Contents

London FOX (The London Futures & Options Exchange) (FOX)

London International Financial Futures Exchange Ltd (LIFFE)

London Metal Exchange (LME) 23/49

London Traded Options Market (LTOM) 23/59

OM London (OM-L) 23/63

Baltic Futures Exchange (BFE)

incorporating Baltic International Freight Futures Exchange (BIFFEX),
London Grain Futures Market (LGFM),
London Meat Futures Market (LMFM),
London Potato Futures Market (LPFM),
Soyabean Meal Futures Market (SMFM)

Address:	Baltic Exchange Chambers 24-28 St Mary Axe London EC3A 8EP United Kingdom
Telephone:	(071) 626 7985
Fax:	(071) 623 2917
Telex:	916434 BALFUT G

Exchange personnel

Chairman:	P. Elmer
Secretary General:	S. M. Carter
Director of Futures:	Bill Englebright
Futures Market Manager:	Peter Freeman

Futures contracts available on BIFFEX
Baltic Freight Index

Futures contracts available on LGFM
EEC barley
EEC wheat

Futures contracts available on LMFM
Live cattle
Pigs (live hogs)

Futures contracts available on LPFM
Potatoes (cash)
Potatoes (deliverable)

Futures contracts available on SMFM
Soyabean meal

Options contracts on futures available on LGFM
EEC barley futures
EEC wheat futures

Options contracts on futures available on LPFM
Potatoes (deliverable) futures

Clearing House:
International Commodities Clearing House (ICCH) and the GAFTA Clearing House Co. Ltd.

Method of trading:
Open outcry.

Commenced trading:
Baltic Futures Exchange: 1987.
GAFTA: 1929.
SMFM: 1975.
LPFM: 1980.

Exchange links:
None.

A brief synopsis of the exchange
Trading in grain futures started in 1929 on the Manitoba wheat contract, but volumes decreased in grain contracts as a result of war-time Government controls.

In 1971, the Grain and Feed Trade Association (GAFTA) was formed from the London Corn Trade Association and the London Cattle Feed Trade Association. The Soyabean Meal Futures Association was formed in the early 1970s, and was joined at the Baltic Exchange in 1980 by the London Potato Futures Association, and by the London Meat Futures Exchange in 1984. There are now four agricultural markets and the Freight Index futures market under one roof.

Baltic Freight Index (BFI) futures

Contract size	US$10.00 multiplied by the Baltic Freight Index (BFI).*
Standard delivery method	Cash settlement automatically at expiry.
Trading months	The spot (nearby calendar) month, the following calendar month and then months from the January, April, July and October cycle up to two years forward.
Trading hours	Two sessions daily: 10.15 a.m. – 12.30 p.m. and 2.30 p.m. – 4.30 p.m.
Price quotation method	In US dollars (US$) per full index point.
Minimum price move (value)	0.50 index points (US$5.00 per contract).
Daily price limits	50 index points above or below the previous day's settlement price.
Position limits	None.
Last trading day	The last business day in the contract month.
Delivery day	The first business day after the last trading day, based on the BFI averaged over the last five days of the settlement month.
Initial (Variation) margin	US$500 per contract.
Spread margin	Not stated.
Reuters Monitor (Quote)	Prices: FRLE/OFLE; index: OFLF; page index: TTTB.
Telerate page	939.

* The Baltic Freight Index (BFI) comprises 12 of the most important dry-bulk cargo freight routes being chartered on the international market daily, providing a continuous measure of world freight movements, with the weightings reflecting the relative importance of the voyages included. The components of the index and their weightings are listed below:

Route number	Cargo size (tons)	Voyage	Weight
1	55,000 grain	US Gulf/Northern Europe	20.0%
2	52,000 grain	US Gulf/South Japan	20.0%
3	52,000 grain	US North Pacific/South Japan	15.0%
4	21,000 grain	US Gulf/Venezuela	5.0%
5	35,000 barley	Antwerp/Jeddah/Saudi Arabia	5.0%
6	120,000 coal	USA/South Japan	7.5%
7	65,000 coal	USA/Northern Europe	5.0%
8	110,000 coal	Queensland/Rotterdam	5.0%
9	55,000 coke	Vancouver/San Diego/Rotterdam	5.0%
10	90,000 iron ore	Monrovia/Rotterdam	5.0%
11	15 – 25,000 phosphate	Casablanca/West India	2.5%
12	14,000 phosphate	Aquba/West Coast India	5.0%

EEC barley futures

Contract size	100 metric tonnes of EEC barley subject to certain tests calculated on a weight basis.
Standard delivery method	Physical delivery of the above at a Clearing House registered futures store in mainland Great Britain.

Trading months	The January, March, May, September and November cycle.
Trading hours	Two sessions daily: 11.00 a.m. – 12.30 p.m. and 2.45 p.m. – 4.00 p.m.
Price quotation method	In pounds sterling (£) per metric tonne.
Minimum price move (value)	£0.05 per metric tonne (£5.00 per contract).
Daily price limits	None.
Position limits	None.
Last trading day	The 23rd day of the contract month.
Delivery day	The notice period runs from the seventh day prior to the contract month to the 22nd or 23rd day of the contract month. Cash payment is due seven days from the date of tender.
Initial (Variation) margin	£100 per contract.
Spread margin	Not stated.
Reuters Monitor (Quote)	GNXI, BRLE.
Telerate page	N/a.

EEC wheat futures

Contract size	100 metric tonnes of EEC wheat subject to certain tests calculated on a weight basis.
Standard delivery method	Physical delivery of the above at a Clearing House registered futures store in mainland Great Britain.
Trading months	The January, March, May, July, September and November cycle.
Trading hours	Two sessions daily: 11.00 a.m. – 12.30 p.m. and 2.45 p.m. – 4.00 p.m.
Price quotation method	In pounds sterling (£) per metric tonne.
Minimum price move (value)	£0.05 per metric tonne (£5.00 per contract).
Daily price limits	None.
Position limits	None.
Last trading day	The 23rd day of the contract month.
Delivery day	The notice period runs from the seventh day prior to the contract month to the 22nd or 23rd day of the contract month. Cash payment is due seven days from the date of tender.
Initial (Variation) margin	£100 per contract.
Spread margin	Not stated.
Reuters Monitor (Quote)	WHLE.
Telerate page	N/a.

Live cattle futures

Contract size	5,000 kilograms multiplied by the Meat & Livestock Commission England and Wales All Centres Medium Certified Steers Price (MLC E&WACMCSP).*
Standard delivery method	Cash settlement according to the MLC E&WACMCSP. No physical delivery of live cattle is involved.
Trading months	The January, February, April, June, August, October and November cycle.
Trading hours	Two sessions daily: 10.30 a.m. – 12.00 noon and 2.45 p.m. – 4.30 p.m.
Price quotation method	In UK pence per kilogram.
Minimum price move (value)	0.10 UK pence (£0.001) per kilogram (£5.00 per contract).
Daily price limits	£0.10 per kilogram above or below the previous day's closing price.
Position limits	None.
Last trading day	The last Friday of the contract month. Trading ceases at 12.00 noon on the last trading day.
Delivery day	The first market day after the last trading day.
Initial (Variation) margin	£100 per contract.
Spread margin	Not stated.
Reuters Monitor (Quote)	LCLE – LCLF.
Telerate page	N/a.

* The MLC E&WACMCSP is published on the Monday following the last trading day, for the week ending the Saturday following the last trading day.

Pig (live hogs) futures

Contract size	3,250 kilograms multiplied by the United Kingdom All Pigs Price (UK APP).*
Standard delivery method	Cash settlement at expiry against the United Kingdom All Pigs Price. No physical delivery of pigs takes place.
Trading months	The February, April, June, August, October and November cycle.
Trading hours	Two sessions daily: 10.30 a.m. – 12.00 noon and 2.45 p.m. – 4.30 p.m.
Price quotation method	In UK pence per kilogram.
Minimum price move (value)	0.10 UK pence (£0.001) per kilogram (£3.25 per contract).
Daily price limits	£0.10 per kilogram above or below the previous day's closing price.
Position limits	None.
Last trading day	The last Tuesday of the contract month. Trading ceases in the expiring contract at 12.00 noon on the last trading day.

Delivery day	The first market day after the last trading day.
Initial (Variation) margin	£65.00 per contract.
Spread margin	Not stated.
Reuters Monitor (Quote)	PBLG.
Telerate page	N/a.

* The United Kingdom All Pigs Price (UK APP) is published by the exchange on the Wednesday following the last trading day, and is calculated by the Meat & Livestock Commission for the week ending on the Saturday before the last trading day.

Potatoes (cash settlement) futures

Contract size	40 tonnes of EEC potatoes.
Standard delivery method	Cash settlement of the above based on the Potato Marketing Board (PMB) weekly average ex-farm price.* There is no facility for physical delivery.
Trading months	The March, July, August and September cycle.
Trading hours	Two sessions daily: 11.00 a.m. – 12.30 p.m. and 2.45 p.m. – 4.00 p.m.
Price quotation method	In pounds sterling (£) per tonne.
Minimum price move (value)	£0.10 per tonne (£4.00 per contract).
Daily price limits	£10.00 per tonne above or below the previous day's closing price.
Position limits	None.
Last trading day	The last Friday of the contract month, or the preceding day if that day is not a business day.
Delivery day	The business day following the last trading day.
Initial (Variation) margin	£400 per contract.
Spread margin	Not stated.
Reuters Monitor (Quote)	GNXJ.
Telerate page	950.

* The Potato Marketing Board weekly average ex-farm price is announced on the Monday following the close of the contract month, or the next day if the Monday is a public holiday.

Potatoes (deliverable) futures

Contract size	40 tonnes of EEC-originated potatoes.
Standard delivery method	Physical delivery of the above in closed 25-kilogram bags from a registered futures store.
Trading months	The February, April, May and November cycle.
Trading hours	Two sessions daily: 11.00 a.m. – 12.30 p.m. and 2.45 p.m. – 4.00 p.m.
Price quotation method	In pounds sterling (£) per tonne.

Minimum price move (value)	£0.10 per tonne (£4.00 per contract).
Daily price limits	£10.00 per tonne above or below the previous day's closing price.
Position limits	None.
Last trading day	The 10th calendar day of the contract month or the next business day, if the 10th is a public holiday.
Delivery day	The first notice day is the first business day of the contract month.
Initial (Variation) margin	£400 per contract.
Spread margin	Not stated.
Reuters Monitor (Quote)	GNXJ, PTLE – PTLF.
Telerate page	950.

Soyabean meal futures

Contract size	20 tonnes of bulk toasted soyabean meal or soyabean pellets (Quality A).
Standard delivery method	Physical delivery of either of the above in Germany, Holland, Belgium or the United Kingdom.
Trading months	The February, April, June, August, October and December cycle up to seven expiry months forward.
Trading hours	Two sessions: 10.30 a.m. – 12.00 noon and 2.45 p.m. – 4.45 p.m.
Price quotation method	In pounds sterling (£) per tonne.
Minimum price move (value)	£0.10 per tonne (£2.00 per contract).
Daily price limits	£5.00 per tonne above or below the previous day's settlement price.
Position limits	None.
Last trading day	The seventh calendar day of the month before the contract month.
Delivery day	The first notice day is the 22nd calendar day of the contract month.
Initial (Variation) margin	£100 per contract (or approximately 10% of the underlying contract value).
Spread margin	Not stated.
Reuters Monitor (Quote)	GNXX, SZLE.
Telerate page	948.

Option on BFE (LGFM) EEC barley futures

| Contract size | One BFE (LGFM) EEC barley futures contract (of an underlying contract size of 100 metric tonnes). |
| Standard delivery method | Delivery of a long or short position in a futures contract at the strike price as above. |

Trading months	The nearby three months of the January, March, May and November cycle.
Trading hours	Two sessions daily: 11.00 a.m. – 12.30 p.m. and 2.45 p.m. – 4.00 p.m.
Price quotation method	In pounds sterling (£) per metric tonne.
Minimum price move (value)	£0.05 per metric tonne (£5.00 per contract).
Daily price limits	None.
Position limits	None.
Last trading day	The second Thursday of the month prior to the contract month of the underlying futures contract. Trading ceases in the expiring contract at 10.30 a.m. on the last trading day.
Delivery day	The business day following the last trading day.
Initial (Variation) margin	For uncovered short positions, £100 per contract.
Spread margin	Not stated.
Strike price intervals	At £1.00 per metric tonne intervals.
Option type	American style (the option may be exercised on any business day up to and including the last trading day). There is automatic exercise of in-the-money options at expiry.
Method of introduction of new strike prices	Not stated.
Reuters Monitor (Quote)	BRLG – BRLL.
Telerate page	N/a.

Option on BFE (LGFM) EEC wheat futures

Contract size	One BFE (LGFM) EEC wheat futures contract (of an underlying contract size of 100 metric tonnes).
Standard delivery method	Delivery of a long or short position in a futures contract at the strike price as above.
Trading months	The nearby three months of the January, March, May and November cycle.
Trading hours	Two sessions daily: 11.00 a.m. – 12.30 p.m. and 2.45 p.m. – 4.00 p.m.
Price quotation method	In pounds sterling (£) per metric tonne.
Minimum price move (value)	£0.05 per metric tonne (£5.00 per contract).
Daily price limits	None.
Position limits	None.
Last trading day	The second Thursday of the month prior to the contract month of the underlying futures contract. Trading ceases in the expiring contract at 10.30 a.m. on the last trading day.
Delivery day	The business day following the last trading day.

Initial (Variation) margin	For uncovered short positions, £100 per contract.
Spread margin	Not stated.
Strike price intervals	At £1.00 per tonne intervals.
Option type	American style (the option may be exercised on any business day up to and including the last trading day). There is automatic exercise of in-the-money options at expiry.
Method of introduction of new strike prices	Not stated.
Reuters Monitor (Quote)	WHLG – WHLL.
Telerate page	N/a.

Option on BFE (LPFM) potatoes (deliverable) futures

Contract size	One BFE (LPFM) potatoes (deliverable) futures contract (of an underlying contract size of 40 tonnes).
Standard delivery method	Delivery of a long or short position in a futures contract at the strike price as above.
Trading months	April only.
Trading hours	Two sessions daily: 11.00 a.m. – 12.30 p.m. and 2.45 p.m. – 4.00 p.m.
Price quotation method	In pounds sterling (£) per tonne.
Minimum price move (value)	£0.10 per tonne (£4.00 per contract).
Daily price limits	None.
Position limits	None.
Last trading day	The second Wednesday of the month prior to the contract month of the underlying futures contract.
Delivery day	The business day following the last trading day.
Initial (Variation) margin	Daily delta (risk-factor) margining operates – consult the exchange or your broker for full details.
Spread margin	As for initial margin.
Strike price intervals	Contract price under £100: at £5.00 intervals. Contract price over £100: at £10.00 intervals.
Option type	American style (the option may be exercised on any business day up to and including the last trading day).
Method of introduction of new strike prices	Not stated.
Reuters Monitor (Quote)	PTOE – PTOJ.
Telerate page	N/a.

International Petroleum Exchange (IPE)

Address:	International House 1 St Katherine's Way London E1 9UU United Kingdom
Telephone:	(071) 481 0643
Fax:	(071) 481 8485
Telex:	927479

Exchange personnel

Chairman:	Derek Whiting
Chief Executive:	Peter Wildblood
Deputy Chief Executive:	Graham Wright
PR/Information:	Stella Fitzgerald

USA Representative Office

Address:	261 Madison Avenue New York NY 10016 USA
Telephone:	(212) 661 8740
Fax:	(212) 661 6311
Telex:	N/a.
Contact:	Ron Sallerson

Japan Representative Office:

Address:	Gavin Anderson (Tokyo) Sunrise Building 2nd Floor 2–11–1 Kanda Surughadai Chiyoda Ku Tokyo 101 Japan
Telephone:	(813) 295 7300
Fax:	(813) 295 7269
Telex:	N/a.
Contact:	Gretchen Booma

Futures contracts available
Brent crude oil
Gas oil
Heavy fuel oil

Options contracts on futures available
Brent crude oil futures
Gas oil futures

Clearing House: International Commodities Clearing House (ICCH).

Method of trading: Open outcry.

Commenced trading: 1981.

Exchange links: London FOX operates a shared trading floor with the IPE.

A brief synopsis of the exchange
The IPE is a specialist exchange for energy futures and options products, and until the recent entry of ROEFEX into this arena, had a monopoly of trading in these products in the European time zone.
There are 35 floor members and two classes of associate members: trading and general associates. An extension of trading hours through the futures contracts now means that the IPE contracts close at around the same time as those on its major US competitor, NYMEX. Plans are also underway to introduce a screen-based trading system.
In 1987, the IPE moved to Commodity Quay, and at the same time introduced local memberships ans soon after traded options contracts. Contract specifications change from time to time as changing demands dictate.

Brent crude oil futures

Contract size	1,000 net barrels (42,000 US gallons) of Brent crude oil.
Standard delivery method	Cash settlement at expiry.* There is the facility for exchange for physical delivery (EFPs) at the agreement of both the buyer and the seller.
Trading months	The six nearby consecutive calendar months including the current calendar month.
Trading hours	9.25 a.m. – 5.30 p.m.
Price quotation method	In US dollars (US$) and cents per barrel.
Minimum price move (value)	US$0.01 per barrel (US$10.00 per contract).
Daily price limits	No limits.
Position limits	None.
Last trading day	The 10th day of the month preceding the contract month or the preceding business day if the 10th is not a business day.
Delivery day	Within 48 hours of the last trading day.
Initial (Variation) margin	US$1,000 per contract.
Spread margin	US$350 per spread position.
Reuters Monitor (Quote)	PPLG, PQLQ, CI33.
Telerate page	940 (Composite pages: 8814 – 8815, 8891).

* The exchange prepares a daily 'Brent Index' based on the average of cash market prices for Brent Blend traded on the previous day, from the start of Tokyo's business day to the close of Houston's business day. The cash settlement price is this index published at 12.00 noon on the last trading day.

Gas oil futures

Contract size	100 metric tonnes of any origin, EEC-qualified gas oil of 'merchantable quality'.
Standard delivery method	Physical delivery of the above for delivery by barge by volume from a customs-bonded refinery or storage installations in Amsterdam, Rotterdam or Antwerp at the seller's choice, FOB delivery. Alternative delivery procedures (e.g. by coaster or inter-tank transfer) are acceptable if agreed upon by the buyer and the seller.
Trading months	The nearby nine consecutive months including the current month.
Trading hours	9.15 a.m. – 5.24 p.m.
Price quotation method	In US dollars (US$) and cents per tonne on an EEC duty paid basis.

Minimum price move (value)	US$0.25 per tonne (US$25.00 per contract).
Daily price limits	US$15.00 per tonne above or below the previous day's closing price.
Position limits	None.
Last trading day	Three business days prior to the 13th calendar day of the contract month. Trading in the expiring contract ceases at 12.00 noon on the last trading day.
Delivery day	The delivery period is between the 15th and the last calendar days of the contract month.
Initial (Variation) margin	US$1,000 per contract.
Spread margin	US$350 per spread position.
Reuters Monitor (Quote)	PPLE, PQLE (Composite pages: PPDA, PPDC).
Telerate page	949 (Composite pages: 8814 – 8815).

Heavy fuel oil futures

Contract size	100 tonnes of any origin, EEC-qualified heavy fuel oil of merchantable quality in bulk.
Standard delivery method	Physical delivery of the above from a Customs-bonded refinery or storage installations in Amsterdam, Rotterdam or Antwerp at the seller's choice. Alternative delivery procedures (ADPs) or exchange for physicals (EFPs) may be agreed upon by the buyer and the seller as alternative delivery options.
Trading months	The nearby nine consecutive calendar months including the current calendar month.
Trading hours	Two sessions daily: 9.30 a.m. – 12.10 p.m. and 2.40 p.m. – 5.05 p.m.
Price quotation method	In US dollars (US$) and cents per tonne.
Minimum price move (value)	US$0.25 per tonne (US$25.00 per contract).
Daily price limits	US$10.00 per tonne above or below the previous day's closing price.
Position limits	None.
Last trading day	At 12.00 noon, three business days prior to the 13th calendar day of the contract month.
Delivery day	The delivery period is between the 15th and the last calendar days of the contract month.
Initial (Variation) margin	US$500 per contract. This is doubled five days prior to tender, and doubled again two days prior to tender.
Spread margin	US$200 per spread position.
Reuters Monitor (Quote)	PPLH, PQLH, HF33 (Composite page: PPDC).
Telerate page	944 (Composite pages: 8814 – 8815).

International
Petroleum
Exchange (IPE)
Options on futures
Energy, oil and gas

Option on IPE Brent crude oil futures

Contract size	One IPE Brent crude oil futures contract (of an underlying contract size of 1,000 net barrels).
Standard delivery method	Delivery of a long or short position in a futures contract at the strike price as above.
Trading months	The three nearest consecutive calendar months, including the current calendar month.
Trading hours	9.25 a.m. – 5.30 p.m.
Price quotation method	In US dollars (US$) and cents per barrel.
Minimum price move (value)	US$0.01 per barrel (US$10.00 per contract).
Daily price limits	None.
Position limits	None.
Last trading day	The third business day preceding the last trading day of the underlying futures contract. Declarations must be at the clearing house no later than one hour after the close of business.
Delivery day	The business day following the last trading day.
Initial (Variation) margin	The premium received plus an additional risk premium.
Spread margin	There are a range of inter- and intra-commodity spread concessions. Please contact the exchange or your broker for full details.
Strike price intervals	At intervals of 50 US cents (US$0.50) per barrel.
Option type	American style (the option may be exercised up to 5.00 p.m. on any business day during the contract's life up to and including expiry). All options that are in-the-money by at least 75 US cents at expiry will automatically be exercised.
Method of introduction of new strike prices	At least seven new strike prices are initially available. Two new series are introduced if there are no longer any in- or out-of-the-money series available.
Reuters Monitor (Quote)	PPCO – PPCZ.
Telerate page	9820 – 9821

Option on IPE gas oil futures

Contract size	One IPE gas oil futures contract (of an underlying contract size of 100 tonnes).
Standard delivery method	Delivery of a long or short position in a futures contract at the strike price as above.
Trading months	The three nearest consecutive calendar months, including the current calendar month, identical to those on the underlying futures contract.
Trading hours	9.15 a.m. – 5.24 p.m. Trading in the options will continue until trading in the underlying futures contract has ceased.

**International
Petroleum
Exchange (IPE)
Options on futures
Energy, oil and gas**

Price quotation method	In US dollars (US$) and cents per tonne.
Minimum price move (value)	US$0.05 per tonne (US$5.00 per contract).
Daily price limits	None.
Position limits	None.
Last trading day	The third Wednesday of the month preceding the contract month. Declarations must be at the clearing house no later than one hour after the close of business.
Delivery day	The business day following the last trading day.
Initial (Variation) margin	The premium received plus an additional risk premium.
Spread margin	There are a range of inter- and intra-commodity spread concessions. Please contact the exchange or your broker for full details.
Strike price intervals	At US$5.00 per tonne intervals.
Option type	American style (the option may be exercised up to 5.00 p.m. on any business day during the contract's life up to and including expiry). All options that are in-the-money at expiry will automatically be exercised.
Method of introduction of new strike prices	At least seven new strike prices are initially available. Two new series are introduced if there are no in- or out-of-the-money series.
Reuters Monitor (Quote)	GQLE – GQLN, 1GOA – 1GOO.
Telerate page	9820 – 9821

London FOX (FOX) (The London Futures & Options Exchange)

Address:

1 Commodity Quay
St Katharine's Dock
London E1 9AX
United Kingdom

Telephone: (071) 481 2080
Fax: (071) 702 9923
Telex: 884370

Exchange personnel

Chairman: Saxon Tate
Chief Executive: Mark Blundell
Executive Director: Antony Rucker
Business Development
 Director: Chris Kennedy
Marketing Manager: Beverly Eatough

Futures contracts available
No.5 white sugar
No.7 cocoa
No.6 raw sugar
Robusta coffee
Rubber (*planned*)

Options contracts on futures available
No.5 white sugar futures
No.7 cocoa futures
No.6 raw sugar futures
Robusta coffee futures

Clearing House: International Commodities Clearing House (ICCH).

Method of trading: Both open outcry and in the case of No.5 white sugar futures and options, automated screen trading.

Commenced trading: 1987.

Exchange links: The International Petroleum Exchange (IPE) with a shared trading floor.

A brief synopsis of the exchange

The London Commodity Exchange (LCE), which brought together after the Second World War the major soft commodity futures market associations, was relaunched in 1987 with a new corporate identity as London FOX and relocated to a purpose-built exchange in the St Katharine's Dock area of London, sharing a trading floor with the IPE. Following the restructuring, local members were allowed entry to the exchange and the traded options market commenced in 1987. Future developments include plans for a rubber futures contract in early 1990.

No.5 white sugar futures

Contract size	50 tonnes of white beet sugar, cane crystal sugar or refined sugar.
Standard delivery method	Physical delivery of the above, FOB stored at designated ports of shipment, from the current crop and subject to certain criteria.
Trading months	The March, May, August, October and December cycle. The nearest seven expiry months are always quoted.
Trading hours	9.45 a.m. – 7.10 p.m.
Price quotation method	In US dollars (US$) and cents per tonne.
Minimum price move (value)	US$0.10 per tonne (US$5.00 per contract).
Daily price limits	None.
Position limits	None.
Last trading day	The close of business on the first business day of the month preceding the contract month.
Delivery day	The business day following the last trading day.
Initial (Variation) margin	Please consult the exchange or your broker for the current margin requirements.
Spread margin	Please consult the exchange or your broker for the current spread concessions.
Reuters Monitor (Quote)	SULG, SU37.
Telerate page	941, 945.

This contract is traded on the Automated Trading System (ATS) developed by the London FOX and the ICCH.

No.7 cocoa futures

Contract size	10 tonnes of No.7 cocoa.
Standard delivery method	Physical delivery of the above from exchange-approved tenderable origins, ex-warehouse UK or in an exchange-approved warehouse in Europe.
Trading months	The March, May, July, September and December cycle.
Trading hours	Two sessions daily: 10.00 a.m. – 12.58 p.m. and 2.30 p.m. – 4.45 p.m.
Price quotation method	In pounds sterling (£) per tonne.
Minimum price move (value)	£1.00 per tonne (£10.00 per contract).
Daily price limits	£40.00 per tonne above or below the previous day's close. When a limit is reached the market closes for 15 minutes, after which time all contracts are limit-free for the rest of that day.
Position limits	None.

Last trading day	The third Wednesday (at the close of business) of the month preceding the contract month.
Delivery day	The business day following the last trading day.
Initial (Variation) margin	Please consult the exchange or your broker for the current margin requirements.
Spread margin	Please consult the exchange or your broker for the current spread concessions.
Reuters Monitor (Quote)	CKLE, COKB.
Telerate page	943.

No.6 raw sugar (FOBS) futures

Contract size	50 tonnes of raw cane sugar, FAQ current crop with a minimum of 96% polarisation at time of shipment.
Standard delivery method	Physical delivery of the above from exchange-approved producing countries, FOBS-designated port.
Trading months	The nearest seven expiry months from the March, May, August, October and December cycle.
Trading hours	Two sessions daily: 10.30 a.m. – 1.30 p.m. and 2.30 p.m. – 7.00 p.m.
Price quotation method	In US dollars (US$) and cents per tonne.
Minimum price move (value)	US$0.20 per tonne (US$10.00 per contract).
Daily price limits	US$40.00 above or below the previous day's 12.30 p.m. call price. When the limit is reached, trading may only continue in the spot month. Other delivery months only become free of the limit if all business at the limit is completed, or at the next 2.30 p.m. call following a limit move.
Position limits	None.
Last trading day	The close of business on the third Wednesday of the month preceding the contract month.
Delivery day	The business day following the last trading day.
Initial (Variation) margin	Please consult the exchange or your broker for the current margin requirements.
Spread margin	Please consult the exchange or your broker for the current spread concessions.
Reuters Monitor (Quote)	SULE/SUGB.
Telerate page	941, 945.

Robusta coffee futures

Contract size	Five tonnes of Robusta coffee.
Standard delivery method	Physical delivery of five tonnes of Robusta coffee from certain exchange-listed tenderable origins, in exchange-approved warehouses in the UK and Europe.

Trading months	The nearest seven expiry months from the January, March, May, July, September and November cycle.
Trading hours	Two sessions daily: 9.45 a.m. – 12.32 p.m. and 2.30 p.m. – 5.00 p.m.
Price quotation method	In pounds sterling (£) per tonne.
Minimum price move (value)	£1.00 per tonne (£5.00 per contract).
Daily price limits	None.
Position limits	None.
Last trading day	The third Wednesday (at the close of business) of the month preceding the contract month.
Delivery day	The business day following the last trading day.
Initial (Variation) margin	Please consult the exchange or your broker for the current margin requirements.
Spread margin	Please consult the exchange or your broker for the current spread concessions.
Reuters Monitor (Quote)	KFLE, COFB.
Telerate page	946.

Option on FOX No.5 white sugar futures

Contract size	One FOX No.5 white sugar futures contract (of an underlying contract size of 50 tonnes).
Standard delivery method	Delivery of a long or short position in a futures contract at the strike price as above.
Trading months	The nearby six expiry months of the March, May, August, October and December cycle of the underlying futures contract.
Trading hours	9.45 a.m. – 7.10 p.m. (trading in the option ceases when trading in the underlying futures contract ceases).
Price quotation method	In US dollars (US$) and cents per tonne.
Minimum price move (value)	US$0.05 per tonne (US$2.50 per contract).
Daily price limits	None.
Position limits	None.
Last trading day	The close of business on the first business day of the month preceding the contract month.
Delivery day	The business day following the last trading day. Declarations of intention to exercise must be received by the clearing house no later than one hour after the close of business.
Initial (Variation) margin	Please consult the exchange or your broker for the current margin requirements.
Spread margin	Please consult the exchange or your broker for the current spread concessions.

Strike price intervals	At US$10.00 per tonne intervals.
Option type	American style (the option may be exercised on any business day up to and including the last trading day).
Method of introduction of new strike prices	Not stated.
Reuters Monitor (Quote)	WQLE – WQLR.
Telerate page	N/a.

This cont. ct is traded on the Automated Trading System (ATS) developed by the London FOX and the ICCH.

Option on FOX No.7 cocoa futures

Contract size	One FOX No.7 cocoa futures contract.
Standard delivery method	Delivery of a long or short position in a futures contract at the strike price as above.
Trading months	The nearest six expiry months of the March, May, July, September and December cycle.
Trading hours	Two sessions daily: 10.00 a.m. – 12.58 p.m. and 2.30 p.m. – 4.45 p.m. (trading in the option ceases when trading in the underlying futures contract ceases).
Price quotation method	In pounds sterling (£) per tonne.
Minimum price move (value)	£1.00 per tonne (£10.00 per contract).
Daily price limits	None.
Position limits	None.
Last trading day	The third Wednesday (at the close of business) of the month preceding the contract month.
Delivery day	The business day following the last trading day. Declaration of intention to exercise must be with the clearing house no later than one hour after the close of business.
Initial (Variation) margin	Please consult the exchange or your broker for the current margin requirements.
Spread margin	Please consult the exchange or your broker for the current spread concessions.
Strike price intervals	At £50.00 per tonne intervals.
Option type	American style (the option may be exercised on any business day up to and including the last trading day).
Method of introduction of new strike prices	Not stated.
Reuters Monitor (Quote)	CKLE – CKLZ, CQLE – CQLR.
Telerate page	N/a.

Option on FOX No.6 raw sugar (FOBS) futures

Contract size	One FOX No.6 raw sugar (FOBS) futures contract (of an underlying contract size of 50 tonnes).
Standard delivery method	Delivery of a long or short position in a futures contract at the strike price as above.
Trading months	The nearby six expiry months from the March, May, August, October and December cycle of the underlying futures contract.
Trading hours	Two sessions daily: 10.30 a.m. – 1.30 p.m. and 2.30 p.m. – 7.00 p.m. (trading in the option ceases when trading in the underlying futures contract ceases).
Price quotation method	In US dollars (US$) and cents per tonne.
Minimum price move (value)	US$0.05 per tonne (US$2.50 per contract).
Daily price limits	None.
Position limits	None.
Last trading day	The close of business on the third Wednesday of the month preceding the contract month.
Delivery day	The business day following the last trading day. Declarations of intention to exercise must be received by the clearing house no later than one hour after the close of business.
Initial (Variation) margin	Please consult the exchange or your broker for the current margin requirements.
Spread margin	Please consult the exchange or your broker for the current spread concessions.
Strike price intervals	At US$10.00 per tonne intervals.
Option type	American style (the option may be exercised on any business day up to and including the last trading day).
Method of introduction of new strike prices	Not stated.
Reuters Monitor (Quote)	SQLE – SQLR.
Telerate page	N/a.

Option on FOX Robusta coffee futures

Contract size	One FOX Robusta coffee futures contract (of an underlying contract size of five tonnes).
Standard delivry method	Delivery of a long or short position in a futures contract at the strike price as above.
Trading months	The nearby six expiry months from the January, March, May, July, September and November cycle.
Trading hours	Two sessions daily: 9.45 a.m. – 12.32 p.m. and 2.30 p.m. – 5.00 p.m. (trading in the option ceases when trading in the underlying futures contract ceases).

Price quotation method	In pounds sterling (£) per tonne.
Minimum price move (value)	£1.00 per tonne (£5.00 per contract).
Daily price limits	None.
Position limits	None.
Last trading day	The third Wednesday (at the close of business) of the month preceding the contract month.
Delivery day	The business day following the last trading day. Declaration of intention to exercise must be with the clearing house no later than one hour after the close of business.
Initial (Variation) margin	Please consult the exchange or your broker for the current margin requirements.
Spread margin	Please consult the exchange or your broker for the current spread concessions.
Strike price intervals	At £50.00 per tonne intervals.
Option type	American style (the option may be exercised on any business day up to and including the last trading day).
Method of introduction of new strike prices	Not stated.
Reuters Monitor (Quote)	KFLY – KFLZ, KQLE – KQLR.
Telerate page	N/a.

London International Financial Futures Exchange Ltd (LIFFE)

Address:

Royal Exchange
London
EC3V 3PJ
United Kingdom

Telephone:
Fax:
Telex:

(071) 623 0444
(071) 588 3624
893893 LIFFE G

Exchange personnel

Chairman:
Chief Executive:
Press Officer:

David Burton
Michael Jenkins
Polly Costley-White

Futures contracts available
Deutschmark / US dollar currency
FT-SE 100 Stock Index
German Government Bond (Bund)
Japanese Government Bond (JGB)
Japanese yen / US dollar currency
Long gilt
Medium gilt
Short gilt
Swiss franc / US dollar currency
Three-month Euro-Deutschmark interest rate
Three-month Eurodollar interest rate
Three-month European Currency Unit (ECU) interest
    rate
Three-month (short) sterling interest rate
US dollar / Deutschmark currency
US dollar / sterling currency
US Government Treasury Bond

Options contracts on futures available
German Government Bond (Bund) futures
Long gilt future
Three-month Euro-Deutschmark interest rate futures
(*planned*)
Three-month Eurodollar interest rate futures

Three-month (short) sterling interest rate futures
US Government Treasury Bond futures

Options contracts on cash/physical available
US dollar / Deutschmark currency
US dollar / sterling currency

Clearing House: International Commodities Clearing House (ICCH).

Method of trading: Open outcry with designated market-makers in certain contracts. Automated Pit Trading (APT) exists for certain contracts outside the pit trading sessions.

Commenced trading: 1982.

Exchange links: Sydney Futures Exchange (SFE).
London Traded Options Market (LTOM).
Member of ECOFEX.

A brief synopsis of the exchange
LIFFE opened in 1982 as the first financial futures and options exchange to be established in the European time zone, and is housed in the Royal Exchange building which dates back to 1566. There are 373 full seats owned by around 200 exchange members representing many sectors of the international financial community holding three different types of dealing seats.

From the early domestic interest rate contracts, LIFFE now boasts a wide range of international interest rate contracts as well as stock index and exchange rate futures, and traded options on these instruments. In fact, it is probably the only truly 'international' futures and options exchange with regard to its product range. After being a 'one-product' exchange for many years with over 50% of the exchange's turnover coming from the long gilt futures contract, there has over the last couple of years been a significant diversification of volume among the other contracts.

In 1986, LIFFE formed a fungible trading link with the Sydney Futures Exchange (SFE) in the US Government Treasury Bond and Eurodollar futures contracts, although little activity takes place on this link. LIFFE's main European competitor is the MATIF where there is a similar Euro-Deutschmark interest rate futures contract, but currently there is no clear winner in the battle. When the Deutsche Terminboerse (DTB) commences trading, perhaps a similar contract on that exchange will change things.

LIFFE has recently developed FORCE and APT (automated pit trading) to cater initially for before- and after-hours trading. The first two contracts to be traded on this system are the Euro-Deutschmark and German Government Bund futures contracts (December 1989).

London
International
Financial Futures
Exchange (LIFFE)
Futures
Currencies

Deutschmark / US dollar currency futures

Contract size	DM125,000 traded against the US dollar (US$).
Standard delivery method	Physical delivery of the currencies involved in the principal financial centres in the country of issue.
Trading months	The March, June, September and December cycle.
Trading hours	8.34 a.m. – 4.04 p.m.
Price quotation method	In US dollars (US$) and cents per Deutschmark (DM).
Minimum price move (value)	0.01 US cents (US$0.0001) per DM1.00 (US$12.50 per contract).
Daily price limits	None.
Position limits	None.
Last trading day	Two business days prior to the delivery day. Trading ceases in the expiring contract at 10.32 a.m. on the last trading day.
Delivery day	The third Wednesday of the contract month.
Initial (Variation) margin	US$1,000 per contract.
Spread margin	US$100 per spread position.
Reuters Monitor (Quote)	LFUA (C$_3$TD*).
Telerate page	992.

FT-SE 100 Stock Index futures

Contract size	£25.00 multiplied by the FT-SE 100 Stock Index, an arithmetically weighted index of the 100 largest UK alpha securities. The index constituents are reviewed quarterly.
Standard delivery method	Cash settlement only (there is no facility for the physical delivery of the underlying stocks to the index). Final settlement is at the Exchange Delivery Settlement Price (EDSP)* on the last trading day.
Trading months	The March, June, September and December cycle. The nearest three exiry months are available for trading.
Trading hours	9.05 a.m. – 4.05 p.m.
Price quotation method	In pounds sterling (£) per index point and half index points.
Minimum price move (value)	0.5 index points (£12.50 per contract).
Daily price limits	None.
Position limits	None.
Last trading day	The last business day of the contract month. Trading ceases in the expiring contract at 11.20 a.m. on the last trading day.
Delivery day	The business day following the last trading day.
Initial (Variation) margin	£2,500 per contract.

London
International
Financial Futures
Exchange (LIFFE)
Futures
Interest rates

Spread margin	£100 per spread position.
Reuters Monitor (Quote)	LIJA (C₃IX*).
Telerate page	996.

*The Exchange Delivery Settlement Price (EDSP) is calculated between 11.10 a.m. and 11.20 a.m. on the last trading day, by averaging the nine middle index quotes during this time, having disregarded the highest and lowest, and rounding to the nearest 0.5 index points.

German Government Bond (Bund) futures

Contract size	DM250,000 nominal face value of a notional German Government Bond with a 6% coupon rate.
Standard delivery method	Delivery of any Bundesanleihe with 8.5–10 years remaining to maturity from the 10th calendar day of the contract month on a free of allowance basis, as listed by the exchange. Delivery takes place through the West German Kassenverein system.
Trading months	The March, June, September and December cycle.
Trading hours	8.05 a.m. – 4.00 p.m. (pit trading) and 4.30 p.m. – 6.00 p.m. (APT).
Price quotation method	Per DM100 nominal face value, quoted in Deutschmarks (DM).
Minimum price move (value)	DM0.01% nominal face value (DM25.00 per contract).
Daily price limits	None.
Position limits	None.
Last trading day	Three Frankfurt working days before the delivery day. Trading ceases in the expiring contract at 11.00 a.m. on the last trading day.
Delivery day	The 10th calendar day of the contract month, or the next business day if the 10th is not a Frankfurt working day.
Initial (Variation) margin	DM1,500 per contract.
Spread margin	DM250 per contract.
Reuters Monitor (Quote)	LFJC (C₃GB*)
Telerate page	994.

This contract is also available for trading outside the stated trading hours from 4.30 p.m. – 6.00 p.m. on the APT (automated pit trading) system developed by LIFFE.

Japanese Government Bond (JGB) futures

| Contract size | Y100,000,000 nominal face value of a notional 'long-term' Japanese Government Bond with a 6% coupon rate. |
| Standard delivery method | Cash settlement at the Exchange Delivery Settlement Price (EDSP) of the Tokyo Stock Exchange's JGB futures contract. |

Trading months	The March, June, September and December cycle.
Trading hours	8.10 a.m. – 4.05 p.m.
Price quotation method	Per Y100 nominal face value, quoted in Japanese yen (Y).
Minimum price move (value)	Y0.01% nominal face value (Y10,000 per contract).
Daily price limits	Y1.00 (Y100,000 per contract) from the closing price of the JGB futures contract at the Tokyo Stock Exchange. If a limit is hit, price limits are removed one hour later for the rest of the day. There are no price limits during the last hour of trading each day.
Position limits	None.
Last trading day	The first business day after the last trading day of the JGB futures contract at the Tokyo Stock Exchange.
Delivery day	One business day after the last trading day of the JGB futures contract at the Tokyo Stock Exchange.
Initial (Variation) margin	Y1,000,000 per contract.
Spread margin	Y250,000 per spread position.
Reuters Monitor (Quote)	LFJB (C$_3$YB*).
Telerate page	996.

A similar contract is traded on the Tokyo Stock Exchange (TSX).

Japanese yen / US dollar currency futures

Contract size	Y12,500,000 traded against the US dollar (US$).
Standard delivery method	Physical delivery of the currencies involved in the principal financial centres in the country of issue.
Trading months	The March, June, September and December cycle.
Trading hours	8.30 a.m. – 4.00 p.m.
Price quotation method	In US dollars (US$) and cents per Japanese yen (Y).
Minimum price move (value)	0.01 US cents (US$0.0001) per Y100 (US$12.50 per contract).
Daily price limits	None.
Position limits	None.
Last trading day	Two business days prior to the delivery day. Trading ceases in the expiring contract at 10.30 a.m. on the last trading day.
Delivery day	The third Wednesday of the contract month.
Initial (Variation) margin	US$1,000 per contract.
Spread margin	US$100 per spread position.
Reuters Monitor (Quote)	LFUC (C$_3$JY*).
Telerate page	993.

London
International
Financial Futures
Exchange (LIFFE)
Futures
Interest rates

Long gilt futures

Contract size	£50,000 nominal face value of a notional 'long-term' gilt with a 9% coupon rate.
Standard delivery method	Delivery of any gilt with a redemption date between 1 January 2003 and 31 December 2009, as listed by the exchange, in multiples of £50,000 nominal face value. Stocks with multiple redemption dates may only be delivered if both the earliest and latest maturities meet these criteria. Stocks are not deliverable within three weeks and one day of their ex-dividend date. Stocks must pay interest half-yearly.
Trading months	The March, June, September and December cycle.
Trading hours	9.00 a.m. – 4.15 p.m.
Price quotation method	Per £100 nominal face value, quoted in pounds sterling (£).
Minimum price move (value)	One thirty-second (1/32) of a point (£15.625 per contract).
Daily price limits	None.
Position limits	None.
Last trading day	Two business days prior to the last business day of the contract month. Trading ceases in the expiring contract at 11.00 a.m. on the last trading day.
Delivery day	Any business day in the contract month, at the seller's choice.
Initial (Variation) margin	£750 per contract.
Spread margin	£150 per spread position (intra-contract spread concessions between the long, medium and short gilt futures contracts of £125 per spread position are also available).
Reuters Monitor (Quote)	LIFK (C$_3$LG*)
Telerate page	994.

Medium gilt futures

Contract size	£50,000 nominal face value of a notional 'medium-term' gilt with a 9% coupon rate.
Standard delivery method	Delivery of any gilt with between seven and 10 years to run and a coupon less than 14%, as listed by the exchange, in multiples of £50,000 nominal face value. Stocks with multiple redemption dates may only be delivered if the earliest maturity is over 10 years or less. Stocks are not deliverable within three weeks and one day of their ex-dividend date. Stocks must pay interest half-yearly.
Trading months	The March, June, September and December cycle.
Trading hours	8.55 a.m. – 4.10 p.m.

London
International
Financial Futures
Exchange (LIFFE)
Futures
Interest rates

Price quotation method	Per £100 nominal face value, quoted in pounds sterling (£).
Minimum price move (value)	One thirty-second (1/32) of a point (£15.625 per contract).
Daily price limits	None.
Position limits	None.
Last trading day	Two business days prior to the last business day of the contract month.
Delivery day	Any business day in the contract month (at the seller's choice).
Initial (Variation) margin	£750 per contract.
Spread margin	£150 per spread position (intra-contract spread concessions between the long, medium and short gilt futures contracts of £125 per spread position are also available).
Reuters Monitor (Quote)	LIFJ (C$_3$MG*)
Telerate page	994.

Short gilt futures

Contract size	£100,000 nominal face value of a notional 'short-term' gilt with a 9% coupon rate.
Standard delivery method	Delivery of any gilt with between three and 4.5 years to maturity, as listed by the exchange, in multiples of £100,000 nominal. Stocks with multiple redemption dates may only be delivered if the earliest maturity is three years or more and the latest 4.5 years or less. Stocks must pay interest half-yearly.
Trading months	The March, June, September and December cycle.
Trading hours	9.05 a.m. – 4.20 p.m.
Price quotation method	Per £100 nominal face value, quoted in pounds sterling (£).
Minimum price move (value)	One sixty-fourth (1/64) of a point (£15.625 per contract).
Daily price limits	None.
Position limits	None.
Last trading day	Two business days prior to the last business day of the contract month.
Delivery day	Any business day in the contract month (at the seller's choice).
Initial (Variation) margin	£750 per contract.
Spread margin	£150 per spread position (intra-contract spread concessions between the long, medium and short gilt futures contracts of £125 per spread position are also available).
Reuters Monitor (Quote)	LIFI (C$_3$TH*).
Telerate page	994.

London
International
Financial Futures
Exchange (LIFFE)
Futures
Interest rates

Swiss franc / US dollar currency futures

Contract size	SFr125,000 traded against the US dollar (US$).
Standard delivery method	Physical delivery of the currencies involved in the principal financial centres in the country of issue.
Trading months	The March, June, September and December cycle.
Trading hours	8.36 a.m. – 4.06 p.m.
Price quotation method	In US dollars (US$) and cents per Swiss franc (SFr).
Minimum price move (value)	0.01 US cents (US$0.0001) per SFr1.00 (US$12.50 per contract).
Daily price limits	None.
Position limits	None.
Last trading day	Two business days prior to the delivery day. Trading ceases in the expiring contract at 10.33 a.m. on the last trading day.
Delivery day	The third Wednesday of the contract month.
Initial (Variation) margin	US$1,000 per contract.
Spread margin	US$100 per spread position.
Reuters Monitor (Quote)	LFUB (C$_3$TF*)
Telerate page	993.

Three-month Euro-Deutschmark interest rate futures

Contract size	DM1,000,000 nominal.
Standard delivery method	Cash settlement based on the Exchange Delivery Settlement Price (EDSP)* on the last trading day.
Trading months	The March, June, September and December cycle.
Trading hours	8.15 a.m. – 4.10 p.m. (pit trading) and 4.30 p.m. – 6.00 p.m. (APT).
Price quotation method	100.00 minus the annualised rate of interest, quoted in Deutschmarks (DM).
Minimum price move (value)	0.01% per annum (DM25.00 per contract).
Daily price limits	None.
Position limits	None.
Last trading day	Two days prior to the third Wednesday of the contract month. Trading ceases in the expiring contract at 11.00 a.m. on the last trading day.
Delivery day	The first business day after the last trading day.
Initial (Variation) margin	DM500 per contract.
Spread margin	DM150 per spread position.
Reuters Monitor (Quote)	LFEA (C$_3$TE*)
Telerate page	997.

* The Exchange Delivery Settlement Price (EDSP) is based on interest rates for three-month Euro-Deutschmark deposits offered to prime banking names between 9.30 a.m. and 11.00 a.m. on the last trading day, selected from a random sample of 16. Disregarding the three highest and three lowest quotes, the EDSP will be 100.00 minus the average of the remaining 10 rates.

London
International
Financial Futures
Exchange (LIFFE)
Futures
Interest rates

Three-month Eurodollar interest rate futures

Contract size	US$1,000,000 nominal.
Standard delivery method	Cash settlement based on the Exchange Delivery Settlement Price (EDSP)* on the last trading day.
Trading months	The March, June, September and December cycle.
Trading hours	8.30 a.m. – 4.00 p.m.
Price quotation method	100.00 minus the annualised rate of interest, quoted in US dollars (US$).
Minimum price move (value)	0.01% nominal (US$25.00 per contract).
Daily price limits	None.
Position limits	None.
Last trading day	Two business days prior to the third Wednesday of the contract month. Trading ceases in the expiring contract at 11.00 a.m. on the last trading day.
Delivery day	The business day following the last trading day.
Initial (Variation) margin	US$750 per contract.
Spread margin	US$200 per spread position.
Reuters Monitor (Quote)	LIGA (C_3IE*)
Telerate page	995.

* The Exchange Delivery Settlement Price (EDSP) is based on interest rates for three-month Eurodollar deposits offered to prime banking names between 9.30 a.m. and 11.00 a.m. on the last trading day, selected from a random sample of 16. Disregarding the three highest and three lowest quotes, the EDSP will be 100.00 minus the average of the remaining 10 rates.

Three-month European Currency Unit (ECU) interest rate futures

Contract size	ECU1,000,000 nominal.*
Standard delivery method	Cash settlement based on the Exchange Delivery Settlement Price (EDSP)** on the last trading day.
Trading months	The March, June, September and December cycle.
Trading hours	8.05 a.m. – 4.05 p.m.
Price quotation method	100.00 minus the annualised rate of interest, quoted in ECUs.
Minimum price move (value)	0.01% per annum nominal (ECU25.00).
Daily price limits	None.
Position limits	None.
Last trading day	Two business days prior to the third Wednesday of the contract month. Trading ceases in the expiring contract at 11.00 a.m. on the last trading day.

London
International
Financial Futures
Exchange (LIFFE)
Futures
Interest rates

Delivery day	The first business day following the last trading day.
Initial (Variation) margin	ECU500 per contract.
Spread margin	ECU150 per spread position.
Reuters Monitor (Quote)	LFCA.
Telerate page	997.

* The European Currency Unit is classified as the sum of each of the following component currencies. It was last recomposed on 21 September 1989.

Currency	Composition	Currency	Composition
Deutschmark	0.6242	French franc	1.332
British pound	0.08784	Italian lira	151.8
Dutch guilder	0.2198	Belgian/Luxembourg franc	3.431
Spanish peseta	6.885	Danish krone	0.1976
Irish punt	0.008552	Portuguese escudo	1.393
Greek drachma	1.440		

** The Exchange Delivery Settlement Price (EDSP) is based on the British Bankers Association Interest Settlement Rate for three-month ECU deposits at 11.00 a.m. on the last trading day, and is quoted as 100.00 minus that rate.

Three-month (short) sterling interest rate futures

Contract size	£500,000 nominal.
Standard delivery method	Cash settlement based on the Exchange Delivery Settlement Price (EDSP)* on the last trading day.
Trading months	The March, June, September and December cycle.
Trading hours	8.20 a.m. – 4.02 p.m.
Price quotation method	100.00 minus the annualised rate of interest, quoted in pounds sterling (£).
Minimum price move (value)	0.01% per annum nominal (£12.50 per contract).
Daily price limits	None.
Position limits	None.
Last trading day	The third Wednesday of the delivery month. Trading ceases in the expiring contract at 11.00 a.m. on the last trading day.
Delivery day	The first business day after the last trading day.
Initial (Variation) margin	£750 per contract.
Spread margin	£150 per spread position.
Reuters Monitor (Quote)	LIIA (C_3IL*)
Telerate page	995.

* The Exchange Delivery Settlement Price (EDSP) is based on interest rates for three-month sterling deposits offered to prime banking names between 9.30 a.m. and 11.00 a.m. on the last trading day, selected from a random sample of 16. Disregarding the three highest and three lowest quotes, the EDSP will be 100.00 minus the average of the remaining 10 rates.

London
International
Financial Futures
Exchange (LIFFE)
Futures
Currencies

US dollar / Deutschmark currency futures

Contract size	US$50,000 traded against the Deutschmark (DM).
Standard delivery method	Physical delivery of the currencies involved in the principal financial centres in the country of issue.
Trading months	The March, June, September and December cycle.
Trading hours	8.34 a.m. – 4.04 p.m.
Price quotation method	In Deutschmarks (DM) and pfennigs per US dollar (US$).
Minimum price move (value)	DM0.0001 per US$1.00 (DM5.00 per contract).
Daily price limits	None.
Position limits	None.
Last trading day	Two business days prior to the delivery day. Trading ceases in the expiring contract at 11.00 a.m. on the last trading day.
Delivery day	The third Wednesday of the contract month.
Initial (Variation) margin	DM1,250 per contract.
Spread margin	DM100 per spread position. The intra-month spread concession between LIFFE dollar–mark futures and dollar–mark options is DM100 per spread position.
Reuters Monitor (Quote)	LFTA (C_3TD*)
Telerate page	997.

US dollar / sterling currency futures

Contract size	£25,000 traded against the US dollar (US$).
Standard delivery method	Physical delivery of the currencies involved in the principal financial centres in the country of issue.
Trading months	The March, June, September and December cycle.
Trading hours	8.32 a.m. – 14.02 p.m.
Price quotation method	In US dollars (US$) and cents per pounds sterling (£).
Minimum price move (value)	0.01 US cents (US$0.0001) per £1.00 (US$2.50 per contract).
Daily price limits	None.
Position limits	None.
Last trading day	Two business days prior to the delivery day. Trading ceases in the expiring contract at 10.31 a.m. on the last trading day.
Delivery day	The third Wednesday of the contract month.
Initial (Variation) margin	US$1,500 per contract.
Spread margin	US$200 per spread position.
Reuters Monitor (Quote)	LFSG (C_3TP*).
Telerate page	992.

London
International
Financial Futures
Exchange (LIFFE)
Options on futures
Interest rates

US Government Treasury Bond futures

Contract size	US$100,000 nominal face value of a notional US Government Treasury Bond with an 8% coupon rate.
Standard delivery method	Delivery of any US Government Treasury Bond maturing at least 15 years from the first day of the contract month (if callable), else the earliest call date must be at least 15 years from the first day of the contract month. Stocks must be delivered in multiples of US$100,000 nominal and must pay interest half-yearly.
Trading months	The March, June, September and December cycle.
Trading hours	8.15 a.m. – 4.10 p.m.
Price quotation method	Per US$100 nominal face value, quoted in US dollars (US$).
Minimum price move (value)	One thirty-second (1/32) of a point (US$31.25 per contract).
Daily price limits	None.
Position limits	None.
Last trading day	Seven Chicago Board of Trade (CBOT) working days prior to the last business day of the contract month. This is set to coincide with the last trading day of US Government Treasury Bond futures at the CBOT.
Delivery day	Any business day in the contract month (at the seller's choice).
Initial (Variation) margin	US$1,250 per contract.
Spread margin	US$125 per spread position.
Reuters Monitor (Quote)	LFDA (C_3TB*)
Telerate page	996.

Option on LIFFE German Government Bond (Bund) futures

Contract size	One LIFFE German Government Bond (Bund) futures contract (of an underlying contract size of DM250,000 nominal face value).
Standard delivery method	Delivery of a long or short position in a futures contract at the strike price as above.
Trading months	The March, June, September and December cycle.
Trading hours	8.07 a.m. – 4.00 p.m.
Price quotation method	Per DM100 nominal face value, quoted in Deutschmarks (DM).
Minimum price move (value)	DM0.01% per annum (DM25.00 per contract).
Daily price limits	None.
Position limits	None.

London
International
Financial Futures
Exchange (LIFFE)
Options on futures
Interest rates

Last trading day	Six business days prior to the first day of the contract month. The option may be exercised up to 5.00 p.m. on any business day (6.00 p.m. on the last trading day).
Delivery day	The first business day following the day of exercise. The option expires at 6.00 p.m. on the last trading day.
Initial (Variation) margin	Initial margin is charged on both long and short option positions with reference to daily published risk factors and the level of initial margin for the underlying futures contract, which it may not exceed. This is revalued daily.
Spread margin	Margin is reduced for all options and option and future combinations with reference to daily published risk factors.
Strike price intervals	At DM0.50 intervals (e.g. 94.00, 94.50, etc).
Option type	American style (the option may be exercised on any business day up to and including the last trading day).
Method of introduction of new strike prices	Initially nine strike prices are available. New strikes are introduced on the business day after the underlying futures contract settlement price is within DM0.25 of the fourth highest or lowest existing strike price.
Reuters Monitor (Quote)	LFJD – LFJK.
Telerate page	15980 – 15984.

Option on LIFFE long gilt futures

Contract size	One LIFFE long gilt futures contract (of an underlying contract size of £50,000 nominal face value).
Standard delivery method	Delivery of a long or short position in a futures contract at the strike price as above.
Trading months	The March, June, September and December cycle.
Trading hours	9.02 a.m. – 4.15 p.m.
Price quotation method	In multiples of sixty-fourths (1/64) per £100 nominal, quoted in pounds sterling (£).
Minimum price move (value)	One sixty-fourth (1/64) of a point (£7.8125 per contract).
Daily price limits	None.
Position limits	None.
Last trading day	Six business days prior to the first day of the contract month. The option may be exercised up to 5.00 p.m. on any business day (6.00 p.m. on the last trading day).
Delivery day	The business day following the day of exercise. The option expires at 6.00 p.m. on the last trading day.
Initial (Variation) margin	Initial margin is charged on both long and short option positions with reference to daily published risk factors and the level of initial margin for the underlying futures contract, which it may not exceed. This is revalued daily.

London
International
Financial Futures
Exchange (LIFFE)
Options on futures
Interest rates

Spread margin	Margin is reduced for all options and option and future combinations with reference to daily published risk factors.
Strike price intervals	At £1.00% intervals (e.g. £96·00, £97·00, etc.).
Option type	American style (the option may be exercised on any business day during its life up to and including the last trading day).
Method of introduction of new strike prices	Initially 13 strike prices are available. New strikes are introduced on the business day after the underlying futures contract settlement price is within 16/32 of the sixth highest or lowest existing strike price.
Reuters Monitor (Quote)	LIFL – LIFS.
Telerate page	15990 – 15991.

Option on LIFFE three-month Eurodollar interest rate futures

Contract size	One LIFFE three-month Eurodollar interest rate futures contract (of an underlying contract size of US$1,000,000 nominal).
Standard delivery method	Delivery of a long or short position in a futures contract at the strike price as above.
Trading months	The March, June, September and December cycle.
Trading hours	8.32 a.m. – 4.00 p.m.
Price quotation method	In multiples of 0.01% nominal, quoted in US dollars (US$).
Minimum price move (value)	0.01% per annum (US$25.00 per contract).
Daily price limits	None.
Position limits	None.
Last trading day	The last trading day of the underlying LIFFE three-month Eurodollar interest rate futures contract (which is two business days prior to the third Wednesday of the contract month). The option may be exercised up to 5.00 p.m. on any business day.
Delivery day	The first business day following the day of exercise. The option expires at 5.00 p.m. on the last trading day.
Initial (Variation) margin	Initial margin is charged on both long and short option positions with reference to daily published risk factors and the level of initial margin for the underlying futures contract, which it may not exceed. This is revalued daily.
Spread margin	Margin is reduced for all options and option and future combinations with reference to daily published risk factors.
Strike price intervals	At 0.25% intervals (e.g. 89.50, 89.25, etc.).

London
International
Financial Futures
Exchange (LIFFE)
Options on futures
Interest rates

Option type	American style (the option may be exercised on any business day during its life up to and including the last trading day). All in-the-money options are automatically exercised at expiry.
Method of introduction of new strike prices	Initially 13 strike prices are available. New strikes are introduced on the business day after the underlying futures contract settlement price is within 0.12% of the third highest or lowest existing strike price.
Reuters Monitor (Quote)	LIGB – LIGW.
Telerate page	980 – 983.

Option on LIFFE three-month (short) sterling interest rate futures

Contract size	One LIFFE three-month (short) sterling interest rate futures contract (of an underlying contract size of £500,000 nominal).
Standard delivery method	Delivery of a long or short position in a futures contract at the strike price as above.
Trading months	The March, June, September and December cycle.
Trading hours	8.22 a.m. – 4.02 p.m.
Price quotation method	In multiples of 0.01%, quoted in pounds sterling (£).
Minimum price move (value)	0.01% per annum nominal (£25.00 per contract).
Daily price limits	None.
Position limits	None.
Last trading day	The last trading day of the underlying LIFFE three-month (short) sterling interest rate futures contract (which is the third Wednesday of the contract month at 11.00 a.m.). The option may be exercised up to 5.00 p.m. on any business day.
Delivery day	The first business day following the day of exercise. The option expires at 5.00 p.m. on the last trading day.
Initial (Variation) margin	Initial margin is charged on both long and short option positions with reference to daily published risk factors and the level of initial margin for the underlying futures contract, which it may not exceed. This is revalued daily.
Spread margin	Margin is reduced for all options and option and future combinations with reference to daily published risk factors.
Strike price intervals	At 0.25% intervals (e.g. 90.50, 90.75, etc.).
Option type	American style (the option may be exercised on any business day during its life up to and including the last trading day). All in-the-money options are automatically exercised at expiry.

London
International
Financial Futures
Exchange (LIFFE)
Options on futures
Interest rates

Method of introduction of new strike prices	Initially 13 strike prices are available. New strikes are introduced on the business day after the underlying futures contract settlement price is within 0.12% of the sixth highest or lowest existing strike price.
Reuters Monitor (Quote)	LIIB – LIII.
Telerate page	N/a.

Option on LIFFE US Government Treasury Bond futures

Contract size	One LIFFE US Government Treasury Bond futures contract (of an underlying contract size of US$100,000 nominal face value).
Standard delivery method	Delivery of a long or short position in a futures contract at the strike price as above.
Trading months	The March, June, September and December cycle.
Trading hours	8.17 a.m. – 4.10 p.m.
Price quotation method	In multiples of one sixty-fourths (1/64) per US$100 nominal, quoted in US dollars (US$).
Minimum price move (value)	One sixty-fourth (1/64) of a point (US$15.625 per contract).
Daily price limits	None.
Position limits	None.
Last trading day	The first Friday preceding by at least six Chicago Board of Trade (CBOT) working days the first delivery day of the underlying US Government Treasury Bond futures contract. The option may be exercised up to 5.00 p.m. on any business day (8.30 p.m. on the last trading day).
Delivery day	The first business day following the day of exercise. The option expires at 8.30 p.m. on the last trading day.
Initial (Variation) margin	Initial margin is charged on both long and short option positions with reference to daily published risk factors and the level of initial margin for the underlying futures contract, which it may not exceed. This is revalued daily.
Spread margin	Margin is reduced for all options and option and future combinations with reference to daily published risk factors.
Strike price intervals	At US$2.00% intervals (e.g. US$98-00, US$100-00, etc.).
Option type	American style (the option may be exercised on any business day during its life up to and including the last trading day).
Method of introduction of new strike prices	Initially 13 strike prices are available. New strikes are introduced on the business day after the underlying

**London
International
Financial Futures
Exchange (LIFFE)
Options on futures
Interest rates**

	futures contract settlement price is within US$1.00 of the sixth highest or lowest existing strike price.
Reuters Monitor (Quote)	LFDB – LFDM.
Telerate page	15996 – 15997.

Option on US dollar / Deutschmark currency

Contract size	US$50,000 traded against the Deutschmark (DM).
Standard delivery method	Delivery of the currencies concerned at the strike price.
Trading months	The March, June, September and December cycle, plus the three nearest consecutive months.
Trading hours	8.36 a.m. – 4.04 p.m.
Price quotation method	In Deutschmarks (DM) and pfennigs per US dollar (US$).
Minimum price move (value)	0.01 pfennigs (DM0.0001) per US$1.00 (DM5.00 per contract).
Daily price limits	None.
Position limits	None.
Last trading day	Three business days before the third Wednesday of the contract month. The option may be exercised up to 5.00 p.m. on any business day up to the last trading day and up to 10.00 a.m. on the last trading day.
Delivery day	The third business day after the exercise day, except for options that are exercised on the last trading day, when delivery is the second business day after exercise. (The option expires at 10.00 a.m., two business days before the third Wednesday of the contract month.)
Initial (Variation) margin	Initial margin is charged on both long and short option positions with reference to daily published risk factors. This is revalued daily.
Spread margin	Margin is reduced for all options combinations with reference to daily published risk factors.
Strike price intervals	At five pfennigs (DM0.05) per US$1.00 intervals (e.g. DM2.45, DM2.50, etc.).
Option type	American style (the option may be exercised on any business day during its life up to and including the last trading day).
Method of introduction of new strike prices	Initially at least five strike prices are available. New strikes are introduced on the business day after the underlying futures contract settlement price, spot US$/DM exchange rate or forward US$/DM exchange rate is within 2.5 pfennigs (DM0.025) of the second highest or lowest existing strike price.
Reuters Monitor (Quote)	LFTB – LFTM.
Telerate page	15985 – 15989.

Option on US dollar / sterling currency

London
International
Financial Futures
Exchange (LIFFE)
Options on
cash/physical
Currencies

Contract size	£25,000 traded against the US dollar (US$).
Standard delivery method	Delivery of the currencies concerned at the strike price.
Trading months	The March, June, September and December cycle, plus the three nearest consecutive months.
Trading hours	8.34 a.m. – 4.02 p.m.
Price quotation method	In US dollars (US$) and cents per pounds sterling (£).
Minimum price move (value)	0.01 US cents (US$0.0001) per £1.00 (US$2.50 per contract).
Daily price limits	None.
Position limits	None.
Last trading day	Three business days before the third Wednesday of the contract month. The option may be exercised up to 5.00 p.m. on any business day until expiry.
Delivery day	The third business day after the exercise day. The option expires at 5.00 p.m. on the last trading day.
Initial (Variation) margin	Initial margin is charged on both long and short option positions with reference to daily published risk factors. This is revalued daily.
Spread margin	Margin is reduced for all options combinations with reference to daily published risk factors.
Strike price intervals	At five US cents (US$0.05) per £1.00 intervals (e.g. US$1.45, US$1.50, etc.).
Option type	American style (the option may be exercised on any business day during its life up to and including the last trading day).
Method of introduction of new strike prices	Initially at least five strike prices are available. New strikes are introduced on the business day after the underlying futures contract settlement price or spot US$/£ exchange rate is within 2.5 US cents (US$0.025) of the second highest or lowest existing strike price.
Reuters Monitor (Quote)	LFSH – LFSO.
Telerate page	984 – 988.

London Metal Exchange (LME)

Address:

Section E
Plantation House
3rd Floor
Fenchurch Street
London EC3M 3AP
United Kingdom

Telephone: (071) 626 3311
Fax: (071) 626 1703
Telex: 8951367

Exchange personnel

President: Jacques K. Lion
Chairman: David E. King
Deputy Chairman: John Wolff
Information Officer: M. Gerard Buckley
Public Relations: Brian Reidy Associates

Telephone: (01) 626 1828

Futures contracts available
Copper Grade A
High-grade (99.7%) aluminium
High-grade (99.95%) zinc
Nickel
Special high-grade (99.995%) zinc
Tin (99.85%)

Options contracts on futures available
Copper Grade A futures
High-grade (99.7%) aluminium futures
High-grade (99.95%) zinc futures
Nickel futures
Special high-grade (99.995%) zinc futures

All options contracts are denominated in both US dollars and pounds sterling and are traded inter-office between the exchange members.

Clearing House: The London Clearing House Division of the International Commodities Clearing House (ICCH).

Method of trading: Open outcry in 'Ring' and also inter-office (for options).

London Metal Exchange (LME)

Commenced trading:　　　1877.

Exchange links:　　　None.

A brief synopsis of the exchange

The exchange dates back to 1877 when Britain was the world's largest producer of tin and copper. At that time, the LME dealt chiefly in Chile copper, Straits tin and pig iron, when dealing took place in the coffee houses surrounding the Royal Exchange. The LME has subsequently grown to be the world's major base metal exchange, recently moving to new premises after nearly 100 years in Whittington Avenue.

Since 1987, the exchange has taken on major restructuring and centralisation, with dual currency listings in many contracts (US dollars and pounds sterling) and the latest move being to relist the tin contract that was suspended following an international default in 1985.

Copper Grade A futures

Contract size	25 tonnes of Grade A (electrolytic) copper in the form of cathodes or wire bars, at the seller's option.
Standard delivery method	Physical delivery of the above at an exchange-registered warehouse in the UK, Europe, the Far East or Japan, at the seller's option.
Trading months	Daily for three months forward and then each consecutive calendar month for the next 12 months.
Trading hours	Rings: 12.00 noon – 12.05 p.m., 12.30 p.m. – 12.35 p.m., 3.30 p.m. – 3.35 p.m., 4.15 p.m. – 4.20 p.m. Kerb: 1.15 p.m. – 1.30 p.m., 4.40 p.m. – 5.05 p.m.
Price quotation method	In pounds sterling (£) per tonne. LME copper futures contracts may also be denominated in US dollars (US$).
Minimum price move (value)	£0.50 per tonne (£12.50 per contract).
Daily price limits	None.
Position limits	None.
Last trading day	Daily for first three months, then the third Wednesday of the contract month for the next 12 months.
Delivery day	Daily for first three months, then the third Wednesday of the contract month for the next 12 months.
Initial (Variation) margin	Approximately 10% of the underlying value of the contract.
Spread margin	Not stated.
Reuters Monitor (Quote)	CWLE – CWLH, Composite page: RING.
Telerate page	N/a.

High-grade (99.7%) aluminium futures

Contract size	25 tonnes of high-grade primary aluminium of minimum 99.7% purity in the form of ingots, T-bars or sows.
Standard delivery method	Physical delivery of the above at an exchange-registered warehouse in the UK, Europe, the Far East or Japan, at the seller's choice.
Trading months	Daily for three months forward and then each consecutive calendar month for the next 12 months.
Trading hours	Rings: 12.00 noon – 12.05 p.m., 12.30 p.m. – 12.35 p.m., 3.30 p.m. – 3.35 p.m., 4.15 p.m. – 4.20 p.m. Kerb: 1.15 p.m. – 1.30 p.m., 4.40 p.m. – 5.05 p.m.
Price quotation method	In US dollars (US$) per tonne. LME aluminium futures contracts may also be denominated in pounds sterling (£).

Minimum price move (value)	US$1.00 per tonne (US$25.00 per contract).
Daily price limits	None.
Position limits	None.
Last trading day	Daily for first three months, then the third Wednesday of the contract month for the next 12 months.
Delivery day	Daily for first three months, then the third Wednesday of the contract month for the next 12 months.
Initial (Variation) margin	Approximately 10% of the underlying value of the contract.
Spread margin	Not stated.
Reuters Monitor (Quote)	ALLI – ALLL, Composite page: RING.
Telerate page	N/a.

High-grade (99.95%) zinc futures

Contract size	25 tonnes of high-grade zinc of minimum 99.95% purity in the form of slabs, plates or ingots.
Standard delivery method	Physical delivery of the above at an exchange-listed warehouse in the UK, the Far East, Europe or Japan, at the seller's choice.
Trading months	Daily for three months forward and then each consecutive calendar month for the next 12 months.
Trading hours	Rings: 12.10 p.m. – 12.15 p.m., 12.45 p.m. – 12.50 p.m., 3.25 p.m. – 3.30 p.m., 4.05 p.m. – 4.10 p.m. Kerb: 1.15 p.m. – 1.30 p.m., 4.40 p.m. – 5.05 p.m.
Price quotation method	In US dollars (US$) per tonne. LME zinc futures contracts may also be denominated in pounds sterling (£).
Minimum price move (value)	US$0.50 per tonne (US$12.50 per contract).
Daily price limits	None.
Position limits	None.
Last trading day	Daily for first three months, then the third Wednesday of the contract month for the next 12 months.
Delivery day	Daily for first three months, then the third Wednesday of the contract month for the next 12 months.
Initial (Variation) margin	Approximately 10% of the underlying value of the contract.
Spread margin	Not stated.
Reuters Monitor (Quote)	SILE – SILH, Composite page: RING.
Telerate page	N/a.

Nickel futures

Contract size	Six tonnes of primary nickel of minimum 99.8% purity in the form of cathodes, pellets or briquettes.
Standard delivery method	Physical delivery of the above at an exchange-listed warehouse in the UK, the Far East, Europe or Japan, at the seller's choice.
Trading months	Daily for three months forward and then each consecutive calendar month for the next 12 months.
Trading hours	Rings: 12.15 p.m. – 12.20 p.m., 1.05 p.m. – 1.10 p.m., 3.45 p.m. – 3.50 p.m., 4.30 p.m. – 4.35 p.m.
	Kerb: 1.15 p.m. – 1.30 p.m., 4.40 p.m. – 5.05 p.m.
Price quotation method	In US dollars (US$) per tonne. LME nickel futures contracts may also be traded in pounds sterling (£).
Minimum price move (value)	US$1.00 per tonne (US$6.00 per contract).
Daily price limits	None.
Position limits	None.
Last trading day	Daily for first three months, then the third Wednesday of the contract month for the next 12 months.
Delivery day	Daily for first three months, then the third Wednesday of the contract month for the next 12 months.
Initial (Variation) margin	Approximately 10% of the underlying value of the contract.
Spread margin	Not stated.
Reuters Monitor (Quote)	NILE – NILH, Composite page: RING.
Telerate page	N/a.

Special high-grade (99.995%) zinc futures

Contract size	25 tonnes of special high-grade zinc of minimum 99.995% purity in the form of slabs, plates or ingots.
Standard delivery method	Physical delivery of the above at an exchange-listed warehouse in the UK, the Far East, Europe or Japan, at the seller's option.
Trading months	Daily for three months forward and then each consecutive calendar month for the next 12 months.
Trading hours	Rings: 12.10 p.m. – 12.15 p.m., 12.50 p.m. – 12.55 p.m., 3.25 p.m. – 3.30 p.m., 4.10 p.m. – 4.15 p.m.
	Kerb: 1.15 p.m. – 1.30 p.m., 4.40 p.m. – 5.05 p.m.
Price quotation method	In US dollars (US$) per tonne. LME zinc futures contracts may also be denominated in pounds sterling (£).
Minimum price move (value)	US$0.50 per tonne (US$12.50 per contract).
Daily price limits	None.
Position limits	None.

Last trading day	Daily for first three months, then the third Wednesday of the contract month for the next 12 months.
Delivery day	Daily for first three months, then the third Wednesday of the contract month for the next 12 months.
Initial (Variation) margin	Approximately 10% of the underlying value of the contract.
Spread margin	Not stated.
Reuters Monitor (Quote)	Composite page: RING.
Telerate page	N/a.

Tin (99.85%) futures

Contract size	25 tonnes of tin of 99.85% purity.
Standard delivery method	Physical delivery of the above at an exchange-listed warehouse in the UK, the Far East, Europe or Japan, at the seller's choice.
Trading months	Daily for three months forward and then each consecutive calendar month for the next 12 months.
Trading hours	Rings: 11.50 a.m. – 11.55 a.m., 12.35 p.m. – 12.40 p.m., 3.40 p.m. – 3.45 p.m., 4.25 p.m. – 4.30 p.m.
	Kerb: 1.15 p.m. – 1.30 p.m., 4.40 p.m. – 5.05 p.m.
Price quotation method	In US dollars (US$) per tonne. LME tin futures contracts may also be denominated in pounds sterling (£).
Minimum price move (value)	US$0.50 per tonne (US$12.50 per contract).
Daily price limits	None.
Position limits	None.
Last trading day	Daily for first three months, then the third Wednesday of the contract month for the next 12 months.
Delivery day	Daily for first three months, then the third Wednesday of the contract month for the next 12 months.
Initial (Variation) margin	Approximately 10% of the underlying value of the contract.
Spread margin	Not stated.
Reuters Monitor (Quote)	THLE – THLH, Composite page: RING.
Telerate page	N/a.

Option on LME copper Grade A futures

Contract size	One LME copper Grade A futures contract (of an underlying contract size of 25 tonnes).
Standard delivery method	Delivery of a long or short position in a futures contract at the strike price as above.

Trading months	The January, March, May, July, September and November cycle (the nearest six months may be traded in US dollars (US$) and the nearest three months in pounds sterling (£)).
Trading hours	Trading is conducted inter-office between exchange members.
Price quotation method	In either pounds sterling (£) or US dollars (US$) per tonne.
Minimum price move (value)	£0.50 per tonne (£12.50 per contract) or US$1.00 per tonne (US$25.00 per contract).
Daily price limits	None.
Position limits	None.
Last trading day	The first Wednesday of the contract month.
Delivery day	The third Wednesday of the contract month (two weeks after the last trading day).
Initial (Variation) margin	Please consult the exchange or your broker for the latest margin requirements.
Spread margin	Not stated.
Strike price intervals	At £25.00 and/or US$50.00 per tonne intervals up to strike prices of US$3,000 per tonne, thereafter at £50.00 and/or US$100 per tonne intervals.
Option type	American style (the option may be exercised on any business day up to and including the last trading day).
Method of introduction of new strike prices	Not stated.
Reuters Monitor (Quote)	LMEO – LMEP.
Telerate page	N/a.

Option on LME high-grade (99.7%) aluminium futures

Contract size	One LME high-grade (99.7%) aluminium futures contract (of an underlying contract size of 25 tonnes).
Standard delivery method	Delivery of a long or short position in a futures contract at the strike price as above.
Trading months	The January, March, May, July, September and November cycle (the nearest six months may be traded in US dollars (US$) and the nearest three months in pounds sterling (£)).
Trading hours	Trading is conducted inter-office between exchange members.
Price quotation method	In pounds sterling (£) or US dollars (US$) per tonne.
Minimum price move (value)	£0.50 per tonne (£12.50 per contract) or US$1.00 per tonne (US$25.00 per contract).
Daily price limits	None.
Position limits	None.
Last trading day	The first Wednesday of the contract month.

Delivery day	The third Wednesday of the contract month (two weeks after the last trading day).
Initial (Variation) margin	Please consult the exchange or your broker for the current margin requirements.
Spread margin	Not stated.
Strike price intervals	At £25.00 and/or US$50.00 per tonne intervals up to strike prices of US$3,000 per tonne, thereafter at £50.00 and/or US$100 per tonne intervals.
Option type	American style (the option may be exercised on any business day up to and including the last trading day).
Method of introduction of new strike prices	Not stated.
Reuters Monitor (Quote)	LMEO – LMEP.
Telerate page	N/a.

Option on LME high-grade (99.95%) zinc futures

Contract size	One LME high-grade (99.95%) zinc futures contract (of an underlying contract size of 25 tonnes).
Standard delivery method	Delivery of a long or short position in a futures contract at the strike price as above.
Trading months	The February, April, June, August, October and December cycle (the nearby two months only are tradable in either US dollars (US$) or pounds sterling (£)).
Trading hours	Trading is conducted inter-office between exchange members.
Price quotation method	In pounds sterling (£) or US dollars (US$) per tonne.
Minimum price move (value)	£0.25 per tonne (£6.25 per contract) or US$0.50 per tonne (US$12.50 per contract).
Daily price limits	None.
Position limits	None.
Last trading day	The first Wednesday of the contract month.
Delivery day	The third Wednesday of the contract month (two weeks after the last trading day).
Initial (Variation) margin	Please consult the exchange or your broker for the current margin requirements.
Spread margin	Not stated.
Strike price intervals	At £20.00 and/or US$20.00 per tonne intervals up to strike prices of US$3,000 per tonne.
Option type	American style (the option may be exercised on any business day up to and including the last trading day).
Method of introduction of new strike prices	Not stated.
Reuters Monitor (Quote)	LMEO – LMEP.
Telerate page	N/a.

Option on LME nickel futures

Contract size	One LME nickel futures contract (of an underlying contract size of six tonnes).
Standard delivery method	Delivery of a long or short position in a futures contract at the strike price as above.
Trading months	The February, April, June, August, October and December cycle (the nearest three months are tradable in US dollars (US$) and the nearest two months in pounds sterling (£)).
Trading hours	Trading is conducted inter-office between exchange members.
Price quotation method	In pounds sterling (£) or US dollars (US$) per tonne.
Minimum price move (value)	£0.50 per tonne (£3.00 per contract) or US$1.00 per tonne (US$6.00 per contract).
Daily price limits	None.
Position limits	None.
Last trading day	The first Wednesday of the contract month.
Delivery day	The third Wednesday of the contract month (two weeks after the last trading day).
Initial (Variation) margin	Please consult the exchange or your broker for the current margin requirements.
Spread margin	Not stated.
Strike price intervals	At £50.00 and/or US$100 per tonne intervals up to strike prices of US$3,000 per tonne.
Option type	American style (the option may be exercised on any business day up to and including the last trading day).
Method of introduction of new strike prices	Not stated.
Reuters Monitor (Quote)	LMEO – LMEP.
Telerate page	N/a.

Option on LME special high-grade (99.995%) zinc futures

Contract size	One LME special high grade (99.995%) zinc futures contract (of an underlying contract size of 25 tonnes).
Standard delivery method	Delivery of a long or short position in a futures contract at the strike price as above.
Trading months	The February, April, June, August, October and December cycle (the nearby two months only are tradable in either US dollars (US$) or pounds sterling (£)).
Trading hours	Trading is conducted inter-office between exchange members.
Price quotation method	In pounds sterling (£) or US dollars (US$) per tonne.

Minimum price move (value)	£0.25 per tonne (£6.25 per contract) or US$0.50 per tonne (US$12.50 per contract).
Daily price limits	None.
Position limits	None.
Last trading day	The first Wednesday of the contract month.
Delivery day	The third Wednesday of the contract month (two weeks after the last trading day).
Initial (Variation) margin	Please consult the exchange or your broker for the current margin requirements.
Spread margin	Not stated.
Strike price intervals	At £20.00 and/or US$20.00 per tonne intervals up to strike prices of US$3,000 per tonne.
Option type	American style (the option may be exercised on any business day up to and including the last trading day).
Method of introduction of new strike prices	Not stated.
Reuters Monitor (Quote)	LMEO – LMEP.
Telerate page	N/a.

London Traded Options Market (LTOM)

Address:	International Stock Exchange Old Broad Street London EC2N 1HP United Kingdom
Telephone:	(071) 588 2355 and (071) 628 1054
Fax:	(071) 374 0451
Telex:	886557

Exchange personnel

Chairman:	Geoffrey H. Chamberlain
Chief Executive:	Anthony de Guingand
Information Officer:	Chris Royal
Marketing Administrator:	Cheryl Meaden

Futures contracts available
None

Options contracts on physical/cash available
FT-SE 100 Stock Index (both American and European style).

The London Traded Options Market also trades options on over 60 listed UK equities, on three different expiry cycles:
A: January, April, July and October
B: February, May, August and November
C: March, June, September and December.
In addition there are restricted life options (RLOs) available from time to time with a two-, four- and six-month life.
The contract size for individual stock options is normally 1,000 shares underlying and the trading hours are 8.35 a.m. – 4.10 p.m.

Clearing House:	London Options Clearing House (LOCH).
Method of trading:	Open outcry.
Commenced trading:	1978.

London Traded Options Market (LTOM)

Exchange links:

London International Financial Futures Exchange (LIFFE).
Member of ECOFEX.

A brief synopsis of the exchange

The London Traded Options Market was established in 1978 and is one of the four divisions of the much older London Stock Exchange (now renamed the International Stock Exchange). Initially only calls were available on a handful of individual stocks, but this soon expanded to cover both puts on individual stocks, and options on a stock index as well as currencies.

Currency contracts were available but rarely traded and eventually were delisted in late 1989.

London Traded
Options Market
(LTOM)
Options on
cash/physical
Stock indices

Option on FT-SE 100 Stock Index
(American style)

Contract size	£10.00 multiplied by the FT-SE 100 Index exercise price.
Standard delivery method	Cash settlement at the Exchange Delivery Settlement Price (EDSP)* on the last trading day.
Trading months	The nearest four consecutive calendar months plus a long-dated expiry month (with a remaining life initially of between six and 12 months).
Trading hours	8.35 a.m. – 4.10 p.m.
Price quotation method	In pence per unit of £10.00 (in pounds sterling (£) per index point).
Minimum price move (value)	0.5 index points (£5.00 per contract).
Daily price limits	None.
Position limits	50,000 contracts net in any one class.
Last trading day	The last business day of the contract month. The option expires at the Exchange Delivery Settlement Price (EDSP)* at 11.20 a.m. on that day.
Delivery day	The business day following the last trading day.
Initial (Variation) margin	12.5% of the value of the underlying index plus or minus the amount by which the option is in-the-money or out-of-the-money, subject to a mimimum of 3% of the underlying value of the index.
Spread margin	Various concessions are available, but in general, margin is payable only on the written option that commands the higher level of margin.
Strike price intervals	At 50 index point intervals (100 point intervals for the long-dated option), – e.g. 2200, 2250, 2300, etc.
Option type	American style (the option may be exercised on any business day up to 4.30 p.m. up to and including the last trading day). All in-the-money options are exercised automatically at expiry.
Method of introduction of new strike prices	New series are introduced when the index rises (or falls) above (below) the current highest (lowest) available strike price. No new series are generally introduced in the last 10 days of an option's life.
Reuters Monitor (Quote)	LKEK, LKRW – LKSG.
Telerate page	N/a.

* The Exchange Delivery Settlement Price (EDSP) is calculated as the average of the nine middle quotations of the FT-SE 100 Index taken each minute between 11.10 a.m. and 11.20 a.m. (ignoring the highest and lowest) on the last trading day. The EDSP is calculated in the same manner for final settlement of the expiring FT-SE 100 Index futures contract on LIFFE.

London Traded
Options Market
(LTOM)
Options on
cash/physical
Stock indices

Option on FT-SE 100 Stock Index (European style)

Contract size	£10.00 multiplied by the FT-SE 100 Index exercise price.
Standard delivery method	Cash settlement at the Exchange Delivery Settlement Price (EDSP)* on the last trading day.
Trading months	The nearest four expiry months from the March, June, September and December cycle.
Trading hours	8.35 a.m. – 4.10 p.m.
Price quotation method	In pence per unit of £10.00 (in pounds sterling (£) per index point).
Minimum price move (value)	0.5 index points (£5.00 per contract).
Daily price limits	None.
Position limits	50,000 contracts net in any one class.
Last trading day	The last business day of the contract month. The option expires at the Exchange Delivery Settlement Price (EDSP)* at 11.20 a.m. on that day.
Delivery day	The business day following the last trading day.
Initial (Variation) margin	12.5% of the value of the underlying index plus or minus the amount by which the option is in-the-money or out-of-the-money, subject to a minimum of 3% of the underlying value of the index.
Spread margin	Various concessions are available, but in general, margin is payable only on the written option that commands the higher level of margin.
Strike price intervals	At 100 index point intervals for the six-, nine- and twelve-month options and at 50 index point intervals for the near month series (e.g. 2225, 2275, 2325, etc, to avoid confusion with the American style FT-SE 100 Index options).
Option type	European style (the option may only be exercised on expiry on the last trading day). There is automatic exercise of all in-the-money options at expiry.
Method of introduction of new strike prices	New series are introduced when the index rises (or falls) above (below) the current highest (lowest) available strike price, or at the request of two-thirds of the registered market-makers. No new series are generally introduced in the last 10 days of an option's life.
Reuters Monitor (Quote)	N/a.
Telerate page	N/a.

* The Exchange Delivery Settlement Price (EDSP) is calculated as the average of the nine middle quotations of the FT-SE 100 Index taken each minute between 11.10 a.m. and 11.20 a.m. (ignoring the highest and lowest) on the last trading day. The EDSP is calculated in the same manner for final settlement of the expiring FT-SE 100 Index futures contract on LIFFE.

OM London Ltd (OM-L)

Address:

6th Floor
Milestone House
107 Cannon Street
London
EC4N 5AD
United Kingdom

Telephone: (071) 283 0678
Fax: (071) 283 0504
Telex: N/a.

Exchange personnel

Managing Director: Peter Jorgensen
Financial Director: Peter Powell
Marketing Director: Karin Forseke
Market-place Manager: Jan Jungstedt

Futures contracts available
OMX 30 Stock Index forward

Options contracts on cash/physical available
OMX 30 Stock Index

Clearing House: Cleared by the exchange itself.

Method of trading: Automated (screen) trading and clearing.

Commenced trading: 1989.

Exchange links: The OM family of exchanges is as follows:
   OM Finland (FOB)
   OM France (OM-F)
   OM Iberica (OM-I)
   OM Norway (NOM)
   OM Sweden (OM-S)

A brief synopsis of the exchange:
OM London is a wholly owned subsidiary of OM
Stockholm AB and is an integrated market-place for
trading and clearing in Swedish stock options and
index products in the United Kingdom. OM London
will be regulated by the SIB in the UK. Orders will be
handled by telephone by OM-L order officials, ranked

according to price and sequence received. Block orders (10 contracts or more) are handled by the block order desk.

The ability to avoid Swedish turnover taxation by trading overseas may help the exchange to succeed.

Reuters Pages: OMCA onwards.

OMX 30 Stock Index forwards

Contract size	SKr100 multiplied by the OMX 30 Stock Index.*
Standard delivery method	Cash settlement on the last trading day, based on the average index on the preceding day. There is no facility for physical delivery of the stocks underlying the index.
Trading months	All consecutive calendar months, with the nearest three available for trading at any one time.
Trading hours	9.00 a.m. – 3.00 p.m.
Price quotation method	In Swedish kronor (SKr) per hundredth (1/100) of the OMX Stock Index.
Minimum price move (value)	SKr0.01 per index point (SKr1.00 per contract).
Daily price limits	None.
Position limits	None.
Last trading day	The day prior to the expiration day.
Delivery day	The fifth day after the expiration day, which is the fourth Friday of the contract month.
Initial (Variation) margin	Based on the OM collateral system. Please consult the exchange for full details.
Spread margin	Based on the OM collateral system. Please consult the exchange for full details.
Reuters Monitor (Quote)	OMCA.
Telerate page	N/a.

* The OMX 30 Stock Index is based on the 30 heaviest traded stocks on the Stockholm Stock Exchange, capitalisation weighted and updated semi-annually.

Option on OMX 30 Stock Index

Contract size	SKr100 multiplied by the OMX 30 Stock Index.*
Standard delivery method	Cash settlement on the last trading day, based on the average index on the preceding day. There is no facility for physical delivery of the stocks underlying the index.
Trading months	All consecutive calendar months, with the nearest three available for trading at any one time.
Trading hours	9.00 a.m. – 3.00 p.m.
Price quotation method	In Swedish kronor (SKr) per hundredth (1/100) of the OMX Stock Index.
Minimum price move (value)	SKr0.01 per index point (SKr1.00 per contract).
Daily price limits	None.
Position limits	None.
Last trading day	The day prior to the expiration (exercise) day.

Delivery day	The fifth day after the expiration (exercise) day, which is the fourth Friday of the contract month. Settlement is to be made on the third day following the day of the transaction.
Initial (Variation) margin	Based on the OM collateral system. Please consult the exchange for full details.
Spread margin	Based on the OM collateral system. Please consult the exchange for full details.
Strike price intervals	At 20 index point intervals.
Option type	European style (the option may only be exercised at expiry and not at other times during its life).
Method of introduction of new strike prices	New series are introduced on the business day following the expiry of an existing class.
Reuters Monitor (Quote)	OMCA.
Telerate page	N/a.

* The OMX 30 Stock Index is based on the 30 heaviest traded stocks on the Stockholm Stock Exchange, capitalisation weighted and updated semi-annually.

Appendices, Glossary and Indexes

Appendix A
Tabular analysis of the exchanges and their products

Exchange	Futures							Options						
	IR	SI	FX	PM	BM	SA	OG	IR	SI	FX	PM	BM	SA	OG
AMEX	No	No	No	No	No	No	No	No	Yes	No	No	No	No	No
AOM	No	No	No	No	No	No	No	No	C/P	No	C/P	No	No	No
APPTM	No	No	No	No	No	Yes	No	No	No	No	No	No	No	No
ASX	No	Yes	No	No	No	No	No	No	No	No	No	No	No	No
BIFFEX	No	Mis	No	No	No	No	No	No	No	No	No	No	No	No
BM&F	Yes	Yes	Yes	Yes	No	Yes	No	No	No	C/P	C/P	No	No	No
BMSP	Yes	Yes	Yes	Yes	No	Yes	No	No	No	Fut	C/P	No	Fut	No
CBOE	No	No	No	No	No	No	No	C/P	C/P	No	No	No	No	No
CBOT	Yes	Yes	No	Yes	No	Yes	No	Fut	No	No	Fut	No	Fut	No
CME	No	No	No	No	No	Yes	No	No	No	No	No	No	No	No
CME(IOM)	No	Yes	No	No	No	No	No	Fut	Fut	Fut	No	No	Fut	No
CME(IMM)	Yes	No	Yes	No	No	No	No	No	No	No	No	No	No	No
COMEX	Yes	No	No	Yes	Yes	No	No	No	No	No	No	No	No	No
CRCE	No	No	No	No	No	Yes	No	No	No	No	No	No	No	No
CSCE	No	Yes	No	No	No	Yes	No	No	Fut	No	No	No	No	No
CSE	Yes	Yes	No	No	No	No	No	C/P	C/P	No	No	No	No	No
DTB	Yes	Yes	No	No	No	No	No	No	No	No	No	No	No	No
EOE	No	No	No	No	No	No	No	C/P	C/P	C/P	C/P	No	No	No
FINEX	Yes	No	Yes	No	No	No	No	Fut	No	Fut	No	No	No	No
FOB	No	Yes	No	No	No	No	No	No	C/P	No	No	No	No	No
FOX	No	No	No	No	No	Yes	No	No	No	No	No	No	Fut	No
FTA	Yes	Yes	No	No	No	No	No	No	No	No	No	No	No	No
HGE	No	No	No	No	No	Yes	No	No	No	No	No	No	No	No
HKFE	No	Yes	No	Yes	No	Yes	No	No	No	No	No	No	No	No
ICEB	No	No	No	No	No	Yes	No	No	No	No	No	No	No	No
IFOX	Yes	No	Yes	No	No	No	No	No	No	No	No	No	No	No
INTEX	No	Yes	No	No	No	No	No	No	No	No	No	No	No	No
IPE	No	No	No	No	No	No	Yes	No	No	No	No	No	No	Fut
KBOT	No	Yes	No	No	No	Yes	No	No	No	No	No	No	Fut	No
KCE	No	No	No	No	No	Yes	No	No	No	No	No	No	No	No
KGE	No	No	No	No	No	Yes	No	No	No	No	No	No	No	No
KLCE	No	No	No	No	Yes	Yes	No	No	No	No	No	No	No	No
KRE	No	No	No	No	No	Yes	No	No	No	No	No	No	No	No
KRSE	No	No	No	No	No	Yes	No	No	No	No	No	No	No	No
LGFM	No	No	No	No	No	Yes	No	No	No	No	No	No	Fut	No
LIFFE	Yes	Yes	Yes	No	No	No	No	Fut	No	C/P	No	No	No	No
LME	No	No	No	No	Yes	No	No	No	No	No	No	Fut	No	No
LMFM	No	No	No	No	No	Yes	No	No	No	No	No	No	No	No
LPFM	No	No	No	No	No	Yes	No	No	No	No	No	No	Fut	No
LPM	No	No	No	No	No	Yes	No	No	No	No	No	No	No	No
LTOM	No	No	No	No	No	No	No	No	C/P	No	No	No	No	No

Exchange	Futures							Options						
	IR	SI	FX	PM	BM	SA	OG	IR	SI	FX	PM	BM	SA	OG
MACE	Yes	No	Yes	Yes	No	Yes	No	No	No	No	Fut	No	Fut	No
MATIF	Yes	Yes	No	No	No	Yes	No	Fut	No	No	No	No	Fut	No
MDCE	No	No	No	No	No	Yes	No	No	No	No	No	No	No	No
ME	Yes	No	No	No	No	No	No	Fut	No	No	C/P	No	No	No
MEFF	Yes	No	No	No	No	No	No	No	No	No	No	No	No	No
MGE	No	No	No	No	No	Yes	No	No	No	No	No	No	Fut	No
MIFEX	No	No	No	No	No	Yes	No	No	No	No	No	No	No	No
MONEP	No	No	No	No	No	No	No	No	C/P	No	No	No	No	No
NGSE	No	No	No	No	No	Yes	No	No	No	No	No	No	No	No
NOM	******Not yet open ******							****** Not yet open ******						
NSX	No	No	No	No	No	No	No	No	C/P	No	No	No	No	No
NTE	No	No	No	No	No	Yes	No	No	No	No	No	No	No	No
NYCE	No	No	No	No	No	Yes	No	No	No	No	No	No	Fut	No
NYCE(CA)	No	No	No	No	No	Yes	No	No	No	No	No	No	Yes	No
NYFE	Yes	Yes	No	No	No	No	No	No	Fut	No	No	No	No	No
NYMEX	No	No	No	Yes	No	No	Yes	No	No	No	Fut	No	No	Fut
NYSE	No	No	No	No	No	No	No	No	C/P	No	No	No	No	No
NZFE	Yes	Yes	Yes	No	No	No	No	Fut	Fut	Fut	No	No	No	No
OGE	No	No	No	No	No	Yes	No	No	No	No	No	No	No	No
OM-F	Yes	No	No	No	No	No	No	No	No	No	No	No	No	No
OM-I	No	No	No	No	No	No	No	C/P	No	No	No	No	No	No
OM-L	No	Yes	No	No	No	No	No	No	C/P	No	No	No	No	No
OM-S	No	Yes	Yes	No	No	No	No	No	C/P	C/P	No	No	No	No
OSE	No	No	No	No	No	Yes	No	No	No	No	No	No	No	No
OSX	No	Yes	No	No	No	No	No	No	C/P	No	No	No	No	No
OTE	No	No	No	No	No	Yes	No	No	No	No	No	No	No	No
PBOT	No	C/P	C/P	No	No	No	No	No	No	No	No	No	No	No
PHLX	No	No	No	No	No	No	No	No	C/P	C/P	No	No	No	No
PSE	No	No	No	No	No	No	No	No	C/P	No	No	No	No	No
ROEFEX	No	No	No	No	No	No	Yes	No	No	No	No	No	No	No
SFE	Yes	Yes	Yes	No	No	Yes	No	Fut	Fut	Fut	No	No	No	No
SIMEX	Yes	Yes	Yes	Yes	No	No	No	Fut	Fut	Fut	No	No	No	No
SMFM	No	No	No	No	No	Yes	No	No	No	No	No	No	No	No
SOFFEX	No	No	No	No	No	No	No	No	C/P	No	No	No	No	No
TCBOT	No	No	Yes	No	No	No	No	No	No	No	No	No	No	No
TDCE	No	No	No	No	No	Yes	No	No	No	No	No	No	No	No
TFE	Yes	Yes	No	No	No	No	No	C/P	No	No	C/P	No	No	No
TGE	No	No	No	No	No	Yes	No	No	No	No	No	No	No	No
TIFFE	Yes	No	Yes	No	No	No	No	No	No	No	No	No	No	No
TOCOM	No	No	No	Yes	No	Yes	No	No	No	No	No	No	No	No
TSE	No	No	No	No	No	No	No	No	C/P	No	No	No	No	No
TSUG	No	No	No	No	No	Yes	No	No	No	No	No	No	No	No
TSX	Yes	Yes	No	No	No	No	No	No	C/P	No	No	No	No	No
VSE	No	No	No	No	No	No	No	No	No	No	C/P	No	No	No
WCE	No	No	No	No	No	Yes	No	No	No	No	No	No	No	No
YRSE	No	No	No	No	No	Yes	No	No	No	No	No	No	No	No

Product key: IR Interest rates BM Base metals
SI Stock indices SA Softs and agricultural
FX Currencies OG Energy, oil and gas
PM Precious metals

Opt-C/P: Options resulting in cash or physical delivery
Opt-Fut: Options resulting in delivery of a futures position

Appendix B
Inter-exchange links

Exchanges involved	Description of the link
CME & SIMEX	There is a fungible trading link in currency futures contracts.
LIFFE & LTOM	These exchanges are involved in merger discussions regarding a shared trading floor at LTOM.
SFE & SIMEX	There is a fungible trading link in the Eurodollar and US Treasury Bond futures contracts.
COMEX & NYFE & NYCE & CSCE & NYMEX	These exchanges have a shared trading floor and allow access of each other's traders to all trading pits.
AOM & VSE & ME & EOE	Members of the IOCC (International Options Clearing Corporation) fungible 20-hour trading link in precious metals (gold, silver and platinum) options and also Canadian dollar options (ME & VSE only).
EOE & AMEX	There is a fungible trading link on the Major Market Stock Index (XMI) option contract.
FOX & IPE	These exchanges share a trading floor.
OSE & OTE	These exchanges share a trading floor.
BIFFEX & LGFM & LMFM & SMFM & LPFM	These exchanges form the Baltic Futures Exchange and share a trading floor.
NYCE & NYSE	The NYSE trades the NYCE US Treasury Bond futures contract.
OM-S & NOM & OM-F & FOB	These exchanges form the OM stable and adopt similar trading formats and exchange software. Plans exist to commence trading in OM-I (OM Iberica) and OM-L (OM London) soon.
TSE & TFE	The TFE is the futures subsidiary of the TSE.
EOE & FTA & ROEFEX	Both ROEFEX and FTA are specialised futures trading subsidiaries of the EOE.

ASX & AOM	ASX and AOM are the futures and options subsidiaries respectively of the Australian Stock Exchange (Sydney) Ltd.
CBOT & MACE & CRCE & CBOE	MACE is an affiliate of the CBOT whilst the CRCE is a subsidiary of MACE. They operate on a shared trading floor. The CBOE, although now independent, was formed by the CBOT and the two are now engaged in mutual product discussions.
CME & CME(IOM) & CME(IMM)	The CME(IMM) and CME(IOM) are the specialist financial products and index and options products divisions of the CME.
NYCE & FINEX & NYCE(CA)	FINEX and NYCE(CA) are the specialist subsidiaries of the NYCE.
PHLX & PBOT	The PBOT is the specialist futures subsidiary of the PHLX.
NYSE & NYFE	NYFE is the specialist futures trading subsidiary of the NYSE.
MATIF & LPM	The LPM is now a subsidiary of the MATIF.

Appendix C
Clearing Houses and their functions

The Clearing House of an exchange is appointed to clear all exchange-traded contracts and to guarantee good delivery. The Clearing House may or may not be wholly independent of the exchange itself.

It has three major functions:

1. To provide a central clearing facility, ensuring all exchange members fulfil their obligations. The advantage here is largely the elimination of any form of credit risk between the counterparties to a trade.
2. To act as a central banker to all exchange members by matching all trades transacted on the exchange floor and by handling movements in margin requirements between these parties.
3. To undertake responsibility for the good delivery of all exchange-traded contracts (i.e. it is the guarantor of all trades).

The Clearing House protects itself against default by demanding margin payments on opening transactions as an initial measure of good faith, and in most cases operates a system of daily margin variations to account for inter-day movements in contract prices. Exchange members will in turn require margin flow from their underlying clients to a contract. In the event of sharp price movements an intra-day margin call may be made. Some exchanges mark to market daily on price movements and demand daily variation margin, whilst others operate a system of initial and maintenance margins.

Only exchange Clearing Members may deal directly with the Clearing House. Non-Clearing Members will have a clearing agreement with a Clearing Member, who will deal with the Clearing House on their behalf. Some exchanges will have a range of different forms of membership, and where possible this is shown in the text relating to the individual exchanges. Strict financial disciplines are placed on exchange members wishing to clear exchange business.

The following are some of the major Clearing Houses servicing the exchanges covered in this directory.

Amsterdam Futures Clearing House (NLKKAS)

Address: Postbus 252
            1000 AG Amsterdam
            Netherlands

Telephone: (20) 550 4390

Board of Trade Clearing Corporation

Address: 141 West Jackson Boulevard
            Suite 1460
            Chicago
            Illinois 60604
            USA

Telephone: (312) 786 5700

President & CEO: Roger D. Rutz
Chairman: Ralph Goldenberg
Executive VP: Delbert Heath

Domestic branch office

Address: Suite 7246
            4 World Trade Center
            New York
            NY 10048
            USA

Telephone: (212) 524 9185
Fax: (212) 912 1125
Telex: 244663

Clearing House for: Chicago Board of Trade

Chambre de Compensation des Instruments Financiers de Paris (CCIFP)

Address: 15 rue de la Banque
            Paris 75002
            France

Telephone: (331) 42 96 53 65
Fax: (331) 42 96 83 16
Telex: 218362

General Director: Gilbert Durieux
Clearing House for: MATIF

Chicago Mercantile Exchange Clearing House

Address: 30 South Wacker Drive
            Chicago
            Illinois 60606
            USA

Telephone:	(312) 930 3170
Vice President:	John Davidson
Clearing House for:	Chicago Mercantile Exchange

COMEX Clearing Association Inc.

Address:	4 World Trade Center New York New York 10048 USA
Telephone:	(212) 775 1480
President:	Vernon Pherson
Clearing House for:	COMEX

Commodity Clearing Corporation

Address:	4 World Trade Center New York New York 10048 USA
Telephone:	(212) 775 0190
President:	Phil Saponara
Clearing House for:	New York Cotton Exchange (NYCE) FINEX Citrus Associates of the NYCE

CSC Clearing Corporation

Address:	4 World Trade Center New York New York 10048 USA
Telephone:	(212) 775 0090
President:	Harry Furey
Clearing House for:	Coffee Sugar & Cocoa Exchange (CSCE)

European Stock Options Clearing Corporation (ESCC)

Address:	Nes 49 1012 KD Amsterdam Netherlands
Telephone:	(20) 550 4550
Managing Directors:	G. Okkema and A. Payman

Clearing House for:
European Options Exchange (EOE)
Financiele Termijnmarkt (through the subsidiary:
European Futures Clearing Corporation)

International Commodities Clearing House (ICCH)

Address:
Roman Wall House
1–2 Crutched Friars
London EC3N 2AN
United Kingdom

Telephone: (071) 488 3200
Fax: (071) 481 3462
Telex: 887234

Chairman: R. R. StJ. Barkshire
Marketing Director: J. M. Eades

Clearing House for:
LIFFE and other London exchanges
Hong Kong Futures Exchange (HKFE)
Sydney Futures Exchange (SFE)
New Zealand Futures Exchange (NZFE)

Overseas branch offices

Address:
1st Floor
105 Symonds Street
Auckland
New Zealand

Telephone: (9) 39 6281

Address:
1211 New World Tower
16–18 Queens Road
Central
Hong Kong

Telephone: (5) 868 0338

Address:
Level 9
Grosvenor Place
225 George Street
Sydney
New South Wales 2000
Australia

Telephone: (2) 258 8000

Address:
35 rue des Jeuneurs
75002 Paris
France

Telephone: (1) 42 36 27 69

International Options Clearing Corporation (IOCC)

Contact via the European Options Exchange or The Montreal Exchange

Managing Directors:	G. Okkema, A. Payman, B. Donoghoe, J. Forbes, and R. Schweitzer

Clearing House for and
jointly owned by:

3/7	Optiebeurs Amsterdam (EOE)
2/7	The Montreal Exchange (ME)
1/7	Vancouver Stock Exchange (VSE)
1/7	Australian Stock Exchange (Sydney) Ltd (AOM)

The network passes a trading book between each exchange. This is the longest continuous trading day for precious metal options at nearly 20 hours.

KCBT Clearing Corporation

Address:	4800 Main Street Kansas City MO 64112 USA
Telephone:	(816) 931 8964
President:	A. S. Polonyi
Clearing House for:	Kansas City Board of Trade (KBOT)

Minneapolis Grain Exchange Clearing House

Address:	400 South Forth Room 150 Minneapolis MN 55415 USA
Telephone:	(612) 333 1623
Assistant Vice-President:	Kris Nelson
Clearing House for:	Minneapolis Grain Exchange (MGE)

NYMEX Clearing House

Address:	4 World Trade Center New York New York 10048 USA

Telephone:	(212) 938 2222
Vice-President:	Charles Bebel
Clearing House for:	New York Mercantile Exchange (NYMEX)

**Options Clearing Corporation (OCC)
(subsidiary – Intermarket Clearing Corporation
(ICC))**

Address:	200 South Wacker Drive
Suite 2700
Chicago
Illinois 60606
USA
Telephone:	(312) 322 2060
Fax:	(312) 322 2593
Telex:	9102212616
Chairman:	Wayne Luthringhausen
Information Officer:	R. E. Pfaff
Clearing House for:	
OCC:	Chicago Board Options Exchange (CBOE)
American Stock Exchange (AMEX)
New York Stock Exchange (NYSE)
Philadelphia Stock Exchange (PHLX)
ICC:	Philadelphia Board of Trade (PBOT)
New York Futures Exchange (NYFE)

Domestic and international branch offices

Address:	40 Broad Street
New York
NY 10004
USA
Telephone:	(212) 422 5050
Fax:	(212) 422 5072
Contact:	K. Erickson
Address:	Suite 762
1900 Market Street
Philadelphia
PA 19103
USA
Telephone:	(215) 564 4955
Fax:	(215) 564 1441
Contact:	G. Rzeszutko

Address:	Suite 1060
	The Mills Building
	220 Bush Street
	San Francisco
	CA 94104
	USA

Telephone: (415) 421 9884
Fax: (415) 421 3961

Contact: A. Cooper

Options Clearing House

Address: 21 Bond Street
              Sydney
              New South Wales 2000
              Australia

Telephone: (2) 225 6600

Trans Canada Options Corporation

Address: The Exchange Tower
              First Canadian Place
              Toronto
              Ontario M5X 1B1
              Canada

Telephone: (416) 367 2466

Contact: Anna Bisalwo

Clearing House for: All Canadian exchanges for equity options.

Winnipeg Commodity Clearing

Address: 480 360 Main Street
              Winnipeg
              Manitoba
              Canada R3C 3Z3

Telephone: (604) 689 3334
Fax: (604) 688 9658
Telex: 0455480

Clearing House for: Winnipeg Commodity Exchange (WCE)

Appendix D
Industry organisations and regulatory authorities

In this section we list names, addresses, etc. of some of the more important industry organisations to which the exchanges belong and the authorities in different countries that regulate the exchanges and their members in the conduct of their business.

Association of Futures Brokers & Dealers (AFBD)

Address:

B Section, 5th Floor
Plantation House
5 Mincing Lane
London EC3M 3DX
United Kingdom

Telephone:

(071) 626 9763

Chairman:
Deputy Chairman:
Chief Executive:

The Hon. Christopher Sharples
Sir Alan Neale
Philip Thorpe

Incorporated in 1984 as the self-regulatory body of the futures industry in the UK. This is the British equivalent of the National Futures Association.

Association for Futures Investment (AFI)

Address:

Sugar Quay
Lower Thames Street
London EC3R 6DU
United Kingdom

Telephone:

(071) 626 8788

Chairman:

David Anderson

Association of International Bond Dealers (AIBD)

Address:

Registrasse 60
CH-8033 Zurich
Switzerland

Telephone:	(1) 363 4222
Fax:	(1) 363 7772
Telex:	815812
Secretary General:	Hans Frick

Commodity Futures Trading Commission (CFTC)

Address:	2033 K Street NW Washington DC 20581 USA
Telephone:	(202) 254 6387
Fax:	(202) 254 6265
Chairman:	Wendy Gramm
Markets Trading Director:	Andrea Corcoran
Regional offices in:	Chicago, IL Kansas City, MO New York, NY Minneapolis, MN Los Angeles, CA

Federation of Commodity Associations (FCA)

Address:	1 Commodity Quay St Katherine's Dock London E1 9AX United Kingdom
Telephone:	(071) 481 2080
Fax:	(071) 702 9923

Financial Intermediaries, Managers and Brokers Regulatory Association (FIMBRA)

Address:	Hertsmere House Marsh Wall London E14 9RW United Kingdom
Telephone:	(071) 538 8860
Fax:	(071) 895 8579
Chairman:	Lord Elton
Press Officer:	John Pinniger

Futures Industry Association (FIA)

Address:

1825 Eye Street NW
Suite 1040
Washington
DC 20006
USA

Telephone:
Fax:

(202) 466 5460
(202) 296 3184

President:
General Counsel & VP:
Education:

John M. Damgard
Mary Schapiro
Judith A. Balent

This is the national trade association for futures brokers.

Joint Exchange Committee

Address:

c/o LIFFE
Royal Exchange
London EC3V 3PJ
United Kingdom

Telephone:
Fax:

(071) 623 0444
(071) 588 3624

General Counsel:

Anthony Belchambers

National Association of Securities Dealers (NASD)

Address:

1735 K Street NW
Washington
DC 20006
USA

Telephone:

(202) 728 8233

Senior VP:

John Pinto, Jr

This is the self-regulatory agency for the US securities industry.

National Futures Association

Address:

200 West Madison Avenue
Suite 1600
Chicago
Illinois 60606
USA

Telephone:	(312) 781 1300
Fax:	(312) 781 1467
President:	Robert Wilmouth
General Counsel:	Dan Roth

This is a self-regulatory body for the US futures industry.

The Securities Association (TSA)

Address:	Old Broad Street
	London EC2N 1HP
	United Kingdom
Telephone:	(071) 588 2355
Fax:	(071) 628 1052
Chairman:	Stanislas Yassukovich
Information:	Brian Whitbread

Securities Dealers Association of Japan (SDAJ) (Nihon Shokengyo Kyokai)

Address:	1-5-8 Kayaba-cho
	Nihombashi
	Chou-ku
	Tokyo 103
	Japan
Telephone:	(813) 667 8451

Securities and Exchange Commission (SEC)

Address:	450 Fifth Street NW
	Washington
	DC 20549
	USA
Telephone:	(202) 272 3100
Chairman:	Richard Breeden
Information:	Mary Hill

Securities Industry Association (SIA)

Address:	35th Floor
	120 Broadway
	New York
	NY 10271
	USA
Telephone:	(212) 608 1500
Fax:	(212) 608 1604

President: Edward O'Brian
Public Relations: Art Samansky

Securities and Investments Board (SIB)

Address: 3 Royal Exchange Buildings
London EC3V 3NL
United Kingdom

Telephone: (071) 283 2474
Fax: (071) 929 0433
Telex: 291829

Chairman: David Walker
Deputy Director: Jane Welch
Information Officer: Barbara Conway

Swiss Commodities Futures and Options Association (SCFOA)

Address: 1 Carrefour de Rive
PO Box 260
1211 Geneva 3
Switzerland

Telephone: (22) 786 2188
Fax: (22) 786 8989
Telex: 413562

Chairman: Ferdinand Prisi
Deputy Chairmen: Alfred Meyer and Pobert Pages
General Secretary: Beatrice Brugger

Appendix E
Terminology of futures and options orders

Often, instructions to deal in the futures and options markets are termed differently to those in the underlying markets, and below is an indication of some of the more commonly used terms. Whilst not exhaustive, this section will highlight some of the different uses of market terminology.

At Market

means 'at best', where the order is to be completed at the best currently available price in the pit at the time. Executions may not all be at the level if the order is greater than the size currently being shown in the pit. The term conveys a sense of urgency, but if the order is large, may run the risk of adversely moving the market against the client.

Limit

has the same general meaning as in the cash market. Generally these types of order are given as 'good for the day' unless otherwise specified. A futures limit order impresses greater responsibility to a pit dealer, since a limit should not be allowed to be traded through, even in a single lot. If a limit is missed by a dealer, the underlying client may demand an execution at his limit price, except in certain circumstances, e.g. when a fast market is declared. The advantage of a limit order is that it is less likely to move prices adversely against the client. However, in certain market conditions, a few ticks discretion to the dealer for a large order may be appropriate, to enable the order to be worked gently.

Stop-loss orders

are a useful discipline for short-term traders. The instruction triggers the closing out of a position when a specific price level trades. The order generated may then be either 'at market' or 'limit'. The market order would be termed '*Market if touched*' (*MIT*).

Not held

is a term used to pass discretion to a pit dealer as to whether to execute immediately or to finesse an order in an attempt to improve on the fill for the client. This relies on the dealer's judgement but does not, of course, guarantee a superior performance.

Appendix F
Dealing procedures for futures and options

Trading methods adopted on recognised futures and options exchanges are generally one of two types: open outcry or automated.

Trading takes place during designated trading hours, and in normal circumstances kerb trading outside those hours is prohibited.

1. The open outcry system:

In the case of the open outcry system, trading takes place in a 'pit' on an exchange floor, with bids and offers and, if appropriate, the desired trading size, being called audibly to other market participants in that pit. Hand signals (usually in a form of tic-tac) are also often used. Acceptance of bids and offers by another party must also be clearly heard. Inferior bids or offers to the best currently being shown in the pit may not be made. All trades, bids and offers with running volumes are continuously transmitted to various worldwide quotation systems, ensuring a high degree of public knowledge, in an attempt to create a near 'perfect' market-place.

2. Automated trading systems:

In the case of an automated (or screen-traded) system, there is no market floor as such. Brokers will input through terminals in their offices, bids and offers on behalf of their clients, to a central exchange system, which will in turn transmit the market data to other market participants. Acceptance of bids or offers are also made through the terminals in the brokers' offices, and are normally accepted on a first-come first-served basis.

The flow of an order
On receipt of an order from a client, a broker will pass instructions through to a dealing team on the relevant exchange floor. An order will consist of the client's name, the contract and month, the quantity and price and whether the order is to buy or to sell, together with any special instructions.

The order will then be passed to a pit dealer who will execute the order with a counterparty, principal to principal.

The completed execution is then passed back from the exchange floor to the broker who will in turn report the trade to the underlying client.

Appendix G
Principles of margining of futures and options

Margin is required by most users of futures and holders of short options positions. Margin funds (or collateral in place of margin) are held by the Clearing House as a good faith deposit allowing it to make its guarantees to the counterparties to each trade.

When a transaction is completed both the buyer and seller in the case of futures (and the uncovered writer only in the case of options) are required to deposit margin with the broker with whom they have dealt, to provide a buffer against adverse price movements. Cover in place of margin may also be allowed by certain exchanges, e.g. Treasury Bills, stock, etc. Cover will normally be discounted by an appropriate risk factor when used in place of margin in the form of cash.

The exchange sets a minimum level for initial margin which is often at different levels for speculators and hedgers. Initial margin is set at such a level to reflect volatility in the underlying instrument, and is subject to change with market conditions.

As prices fluctuate on a daily basis, the value of each gain or loss is added to or subtracted from the margin account – called *variation margin*. Some exchanges will require variation margin in lump sums on larger adverse movements, e.g. when initial margin falls by 25%, a further 25% is required.

Delta margining

Some exchanges, e.g. LIFFE, adopt a different form of margining system for option positions, called *risk factor* (or *delta*) *margining*. Initial and variation margins are demanded from both buyers and sellers of the option according to daily published risk factors which are based on the deltas of each option series. Therefore, a position in a deeply in-the-money option with a delta approaching unity, will demand almost 100% margin, whilst an out-of-the-money option with a small delta will require a lower level of margin. These risk factors will change on a daily basis, and consequently there will be a daily margin flow. For example, if the full futures margin were £5,000 and the published risk factor on the day of opening a short position were 0.365, the initial margin due by both the long and the short would be £1,825 (£5,000 x 0.365).

At many exchanges, opposite positions in different delivery months for a single client are matched together to generate a spread transaction and often a reduced margin requirement based on the lower level of inherent risk in this type of transaction. There also exist concessions between futures and options on futures on the same product or across similar products on different exchanges (referred to as intra-commodity spreads).

Advantages of dealing on margin

1. The insurance of no default from the counterparty to a trade.
2. An immediate (daily) realisation of profits and losses resulting from daily mark to market and variation margin flow.
3. Gearing – large profits (and losses) are possible from a small initial margin outlay.

Appendix H
Options and futures codes for quotation equipment

Shown below are the most commonly used code letters adopted by both the exchanges themselves and the quote vendor networks for classifying and displaying contract price information. For example, the September LIFFE FT-SE 100 Stock Index futures contract traded on LIFFE would be classified by the exchange as XU (X representing the contract code and U representing the contract month). Reuters would display the quotation on split mode as C_3IXU.

Month	Futures	Calls	Puts
January	F	A	M
February	G	B	N
March	H	C	O
April	J	D	P
May	K	E	Q
June	M	F	R
July	N	G	S
August	Q	H	T
September	U	I	U
October	V	J	V
November	X	K	W
December	Z	L	X

Option strike price codes (US exchanges)

Shown below are the code letters used by the exchanges and the quote vendor networks to signify the strike price relating to a specific option series. These quotes are used in conjunction with the contract code and the contract month code. In general, these code letters relate to the US stock exchanges, but in many cases apply to other overseas exchanges.

A	5,	105,	205,	etc.	M	65,	165,	265,	etc.
B	10,	110,	210,	etc.	N	70,	170,	270,	etc.
C	15,	115,	215,	etc.	O	75,	175,	275,	etc.
D	20,	120,	220,	etc.	P	80,	180,	280,	etc.
E	25,	125,	225,	etc.	Q	85,	185,	285,	etc.
F	30,	130,	230,	etc.	R	90,	190,	290,	etc.
G	35,	135,	235,	etc.	S	95,	195,	295,	etc.
H	40,	140,	240,	etc.	T	100,	200,	300,	etc.
I	45,	145,	245,	etc.	U	$7\frac{1}{2}$,	etc.		
J	50,	150,	250,	etc.	V	$12\frac{1}{2}$,	etc.		
K	55,	155,	255,	etc.	W	$17\frac{1}{2}$,	etc.		
L	60,	160,	260,	etc.	X	$22\frac{1}{2}$,	etc.		

Option strike price codes – currencies, Eurodollars, etc.

In addition to the strike price letters shown on the previous page, for specific contracts with 'odd' strike prices, the following code letters may be used. These letters increase at 5.75 point intervals.

A	0.25	6.00	11.75	17.50	23.25	....................................Intervals of 5.75				
B	0.50	6.25	12.00	17.75	23.50	....				
C	0.75	6.50	12.25	18.00	23.75	....				
D	1.00	6.75	12.50	18.25	24.00	29.75	35.50	41.25	47.00	52.75
E	1.25	7.00	12.75	18.50	24.25	30.00	35.75	41.50	47.25	53.00
F	1.50	7.25	13.00	18.75	24.50	30.25	36.00	41.75	47.50	53.25
G	1.76	7.50	13.25	19.00	24.75	30.50	36.25	42.00	47.75	53.50
H	2.00	7.75	13.50	19.25	25.00	30.75	36.50	42.25	48.00	53.75
I	2.25	8.00	13.75	19.50	25.25	31.00	36.75	42.50	48.25	54.00
J	2.50	8.25	14.00	19.75	25.50	31.25	37.00	42.75	48.50	54.25
K	2.75	8.50	14.25	20.00	25.75	31.50	37.25	43.00	48.75	54.50
L	3.00	8.75	14.50	20.25	26.00	31.75	37.50	43.25	49.00	54.75
M	3.25	9.00	14.75	20.50	26.25	32.00	37.75	43.50	49.25	55.00
N	3.50	9.25	15.00	20.75	26.50	32.25	38.00	43.75	49.50	55.25
O	3.75	9.50	15.25	21.00	26.75	32.50	38.25	44.00	49.75	55.50
P	4.00	9.75	15.50	21.25	27.00	32.75	38.50	44.25	50.00	55.75
Q	4.25	10.00	15.75	21.50	27.50	33.00	38.75	44.50	50.25	56.00
R	4.50	10.25	16.00	21.75	27.50	33.25	39.00	44.75	50.50	56.25
S	4.75	10.50	16.25	22.00	27.75	33.50	39.25	45.00	50.75	56.50
T	5.00	10.75	16.50	22.25	28.00	33.75	39.50	45.25	51.00	56.75
U	5.25	11.00	16.75	22.50	28.25	34.00	39.75	45.50	51.25	57.00
V	5.50	11.25	17.00	22.75	28.50	34.25	40.00	45.75	51.50	57.25
W	5.75	11.50	17.25	23.00	28.75	34.50	40.25	46.00	51.75	57.50

A	57.75	63.50	69.25	75.00	80.75	....................................Intervals of 5.75				
B	58.00	63.75	69.50	75.25	81.00	....				
C	58.25	64.00	69.75	75.50	81.25	....				
D	58.50	64.25	70.00	75.75	81.50	87.25	93.00	98.75	104.50	110.25
E	58.75	64.50	70.25	76.00	81.75	87.50	93.25	99.00	104.75	110.50
F	59.00	64.75	70.50	76.25	82.00	87.75	93.50	99.25	105.00	110.75
G	59.25	65.00	70.75	76.50	82.25	88.00	93.75	99.50	105.25	111.00
H	59.50	65.25	71.00	76.75	82.50	88.25	94.00	99.75	105.50	111.25
I	59.75	65.50	71.25	77.00	82.75	88.50	94.25	100.00	105.75	111.50
J	60.00	65.75	71.50	77.25	83.00	88.75	94.50	100.25	106.00	111.75
K	60.25	66.00	71.75	77.50	83.25	89.00	94.75	100.50	106.25	112.00
L	60.50	66.25	72.00	77.75	83.50	89.25	95.00	100.75	106.50	112.25
M	60.75	66.50	72.25	78.00	83.75	89.50	95.25	101.00	106.75	112.50
N	61.00	66.75	72.50	78.25	84.00	89.75	95.50	101.25	107.00	112.75
O	61.25	67.00	72.75	78.50	84.25	90.00	95.75	101.50	107.25	113.00
P	61.50	67.25	73.00	78.75	84.50	90.25	96.00	101.75	107.50	113.25
Q	61.75	67.50	73.25	79.00	84.75	90.50	96.25	102.00	107.75	113.50
R	62.00	67.75	73.50	79.25	85.00	90.75	96.50	102.25	108.00	113.75
S	62.25	68.00	73.75	79.50	85.25	91.00	96.75	102.50	108.25	114.00
T	62.50	68.25	74.00	79.75	85.50	91.25	97.00	102.75	108.50	114.25
U	62.75	68.50	74.25	80.00	85.75	91.50	97.25	103.00	108.75	114.50
V	63.00	68.75	74.50	80.25	86.00	91.75	97.50	103.50	109.25	115.00
W	63.25	69.00	74.75	80.50	86.25	92.00	97.75	103.50	109.25	115.00

A	115.25	121.00	126.75	132.50	138.25	....................................Intervals of 5.75				
B	115.50	121.25	127.00	132.75	138.50	....				
C	115.75	121.50	127.25	133.00	138.75	....				
D	116.00	121.75	127.50	133.25	139.00	144.75	150.50	156.25	162.00	167.75
E	116.25	122.00	127.75	133.50	139.25	145.00	150.75	156.50	162.25	168.00
F	116.50	122.25	128.00	133.75	139.50	145.25	151.00	156.75	162.50	168.25

G	116.75	122.50	128.25	134.00	139.75	145.50	151.25	157.00	162.75	168.50
H	117.00	122.75	128.50	134.25	140.00	145.75	151.50	157.25	163.00	168.75
I	117.25	123.00	128.75	134.50	140.25	146.00	151.75	157.50	163.25	169.00
J	117.50	123.25	129.00	134.75	140.50	146.25	152.00	157.75	163.50	169.25
K	117.75	123.50	129.25	135.00	140.75	146.50	152.25	158.00	163.75	169.50
L	118.00	123.75	129.50	135.25	141.00	146.75	152.50	158.25	164.00	169.75
M	118.25	124.00	129.75	135.50	141.25	147.00	152.75	158.50	164.25	170.00
N	118.50	124.25	130.00	135.75	141.50	147.50	153.00	158.75	164.50	170.25
O	118.75	124.50	130.25	136.00	141.75	147.50	153.25	159.00	164.75	170.50
P	119.00	124.75	130.50	136.25	142.00	147.75	153.50	159.25	165.00	170.75
Q	119.25	125.00	130.75	136.50	142.25	148.00	153.75	159.50	165.25	171.00
R	119.50	125.25	131.00	136.75	142.50	148.25	154.00	159.75	165.50	171.25
S	119.75	125.50	131.25	137.00	142.75	148.50	154.25	160.00	165.75	171.50
T	120.00	125.75	131.50	137.25	143.00	148.75	154.50	160.25	166.00	171.75
U	120.25	126.00	131.75	137.50	143.25	149.00	154.75	160.50	166.25	172.00
V	120.50	126.25	132.00	137.75	143.50	149.25	155.00	160.75	166.50	172.25
W	120.75	126.50	132.25	138.00	143.75	149.50	155.25	161.00	166.75	172.50

Glossary of futures and options terminology

American style

An option that may be exercised into its underlying instrument at any time during its life, as opposed to European-style options which may only be exercised upon expiry. Most options available are American style.

Arbitrage

The purchase (or sale) of an instrument in one market-place and the simultaneous taking of an equal and opposite position in an identical instrument in a recognisably different market-place to create a hedged position with a profit element attached.

Assignment

The receipt of an instrument underlying an options contract upon exercise of that option, and notification thereof.

At-the-money

Describes when the strike (or exercise) price of an option is approximately equal to the underlying price of that instrument.

Automatic exercise

Exercise implemented by the exchange at expiry of all options that are in-the-money, unless instructions are received to the contrary.

Backwardation

When the price of a futures contract is lower than the price of the underlying instrument. (See also *Contango*.)

Basis

The difference between the price of a futures contract and the price of the underlying instrument. (See also *Crude basis* and *Fair value basis*.)

Basis point

The smallest incremental move allowable in a specified contract (e.g. in the case of interest rate contracts, this is usually 0.01%).

Bear (market)

One who has negative prospects for the future direction of a market (or a market that is currently in a declining phase).

Bear spread

The simultaneous purchase of an option with a higher strike price and sale of an option from the same expiry month with a lower strike price. This strategy may be undertaken with either puts or calls.

Beta	A statistical measurement of the sensitivity of the movement of a stock's price to movements in the market as a whole. A stock with a beta value of unity would normally be expected to move in line with movements of the market aggregate.
Bid price	The price at which one is prepared to purchase an instrument.
Black & Scholes	Refers to Drs Black and Scholes' 1972 valuation model for traded options based on a normal distribution.
Bond	A long-term Government debt instrument usually characterised by biannual fixed-coupon interest payments and a specified redemption date.
Box spread	Combination of a call spread and a put spread with the same expiry date. Generally used to transfer capital gains from one year to the next.
Bull (market)	One who believes the market is going to move upwards (or a rising market).
Bull spread	Purchase of an option with a lower strike (exercise) price and the simultaneous sale of one with a higher strike (exercise) price.
Butterfly/Condor	A limited-risk option strategy consisting of a bull spread and a bear spread with maximum profit potential achieved at the middle strike price at expiry or between the middle strikes (condor).
Call option	An option that gives the holder the right (not the obligation) to buy a specified quantity of the underlying instrument within a certain time frame. The writer of the option has the obligation to deliver the underlying instrument if 'called'.
CFTC	The Commodities Futures Trading Commission – the US regulatory authority of the options and futures markets.
Class	All listed options of a particular type on a particular instrument, e.g. all FT-SE 100 Index call options traded on LTOM.
Clearing	The process of matching and settling of exchange-traded transactions.
Clearing House	The authority which guarantees good delivery and settlement of exchange-traded bargains in return for margin flow. The Clearing House may or may not be independent of the exchange itself.

Collateral	Stock, debt or other acceptable forms of margin accepted by a clearing house as cover for a short option sale as protection against default by a naked writer.
Combination	A simultaneous trade in an out-of-the-money call and an out-of-the-money put, both in the same direction.
Contango	Where the price of a futures contract is higher than the price of the underlying instrument. (See also *Backwardation*.)
Contract	The unit of trading in futures and options with specifications for delivery, e.g. one contract may be equal to, say, 1,000 shares, 10 tons of wheat, etc.
Contract/Delivery month	The specified month to which trading in a particular options or futures contract relates.
Conversion	The simultaneous purchase of a security, purchase of a put option and sale of a call option with the same strike price and expiry date, to achieve a risk-free arbitrage transaction.
Cost of carry	See *Fair value basis*.
Cover	Stock pledged to a Clearing House as in *Collateral*.
Credit	Generally used to describe an inflow of funds resulting from a particular transaction.
Cross	The simultaneous purchase and sale of the same quantity of the same instrument in the same market-place, usually to satisfy a broker's own buyer and seller, without involving a middleman.
Crowd	A group of floor traders and brokers congregating to form the market-place for a particular class of option.
Crude basis	The simple mathematical difference between the price of a security in the primary market (i.e. cash) and the prevailing futures market price.
Debit	Describes a net outflow of funds resulting from a particular transaction or series of transactions.
Delivery/settlement day	The day on which delivery will take place following exercise or expiry of the relevant contract.
Delivery	The process of satisfying the assignment of an option, or the movement of an instrument from a seller to a buyer on settlement of a futures contract.
Delta	A statistical measurement of an expected change in the price of an option series to movements in the price of the underlying instrument. A deeply in-the-money option will have a delta approaching unity, whilst a deeply out-of-the-money option will have a delta approaching zero. (See also *Hedge Ratio*.)

Derivative	A tradable instrument (in a secondary market) whose price and characteristics are based on price movements of an underlying instrument, e.g. individual stock options, Government debt convertible security, wheat future, etc.
Discount	The amount by which a derivative product is priced below its theoretical or intrinsic value or below the price of the underlying instrument.
Double option	A term in the over-the-counter (OTC) option markets to signify both a put and a call option traded together.
European style	An option that may only be exercised into its underlying instrument on its expiry day. (See also *American style*.)
Exchange	The meeting place for supervised and regulated trading in designated instruments.
Exercise/expiry day	The last day on which the holder of an option may exercise his right to buy or sell the underlying instrument to the writer, after which the option lapses.
Exercise price	The price at which the option may be exercised by the holder, to buy or sell the underlying instrument. Also known as the strike price.
Fair value basis	A theoretically calculated price differential at which there would be no financial arbitrage profit obtainable between trading in the derivative and the underlying instrument with equal and opposite positions. This is an estimate of where an options or futures contract should trade, not where it does trade.
Forward	The anticipated price of an underlying instrument at some time in the future. A futures contract price is a form of forward price, the difference between the two being that a forward contract is a non-standardised over-the-counter instrument, whereas the futures contract is a formalised exchange-regulated contract. Also the over-the-counter (OTC) form of a futures contract.
Fundamental analysis	A method of analysis of securities, etc, using accepted accounting methods. An analysis of value rather than of price. (See also *Technical Analysis*.)
Fungibility	The mutual acceptability and interchangeability of trading, settlement and delivery of a futures or options contract between two or more recognised exchanges, i.e. a position opened on one exchange may be reversed, to close, on another participating exchange, for central settlement (e.g. the IOCC precious metals contracts).

Future	A legally binding agreement on a recognised exchange to make or take delivery of a specified quantity and quality of a specified instrument at a fixed date in the future at a price agreed upon at the time of dealing.
Gamma	A statistical measurement of the rate of change of the delta (or hedge ratio) of an option to changes in the price of the underlying instrument. Also described more formally as the second derivative of the option price with respect to the price of the underlying instrument.
Hedge	A term of risk management. To offset risk via transactions against an initial position, in the opposite direction.
Hedge ratio	The factor based on calculated deltas giving the number of option contracts to create a neutral hedge against a quantity of an underlying instrument. (See also *Delta*.)
Initial margin	The 'part payment' or 'good faith' deposit required by an exchange or Clearing House as protection against default by a counterparty to a futures or options contract, payable when initially entering into such a contract. These sums are subject to frequent changes as market conditions prevail, and may be of different levels to speculators and hedgers.
In-the-money	For call options, where the strike price is below the price of the underlying instrument and for put options, where the strike price is higher than the prevailing price in the underlying instrument.
Intrinsic value	The amount an option is in-the-money, or what it would at least be worth if it were to be exercised at once. An option is made up of intrinsic value and time value, therefore intrinsic value could also be expressed as *option premium − time value*.
Last trading day	The final day for dealing on an exchange in a contract for a particular expiry month.
Leverage (gearing)	The attainment of a greater profit/loss profile for the same monetary investment, e.g. a holder of a call option has a more highly geared position than the holder of the same amount of the underlying instrument to the options contract.
Long	The position of the holder of the call option or opening purchase of a future.
Nearby (spot) month	The closest available contract available for trading or delivery.

Notice (day) period	The day or period in which a holder of a short futures contract may give notice via the exchange to the holder of the long position of his intention to physically deliver, at the allotted time, the instrument underlying the relevant contract.
Offer (Ask) price	The price at which a trader is willing to sell an instrument.
Offset	The liquidation or neutralisation of a futures or options position through the equal and opposite transaction for the same delivery month in the same instrument.
Open interest	The net amount of outstanding positions pertaining to a particular contract. For each long position there is a corresponding short position.
Open outcry	Describes the method of trading where any bids and offers for a particular contract are audibly made to all other members of a crowd or pit.
OTC	Abbreviation for 'over the counter'. A term describing non-exchange-standardised derivative instruments of trading. Often there is no formal secondary market for an OTC product.
Out-of-the-money	For call options, where the strike price of the option is higher than the price of the underlying instrument, and for put options, where the strike price is lower than the prevailing underlying market price.
Parity	Either describing an in-the-money option trading at its intrinsic value (i.e. its time value is zero) or a futures contract trading at its theoretical price (i.e. not at a premium or discount).
Physical	The underlying instrument to an option or futures contract.
Physical delivery	Delivery of the actual instrument underlying the relevant contract, as opposed to cash settlement or delivery of a futures contract.
Pit	A designated area within an exchange where trading in a particular future or options class takes place.
Position limit	The maximum number of net outstanding long or short positions allowable to be held by one party in a specific contract. Often different limits apply to hedgers and speculators.
Premium	In the case of options, the amount payable by the buyer to the seller or writer, for the right to buy or sell the underlying instrument at the strike price over the option's life, made up of time value and intrinsic

value. In the case of futures, the amount by which the price of the futures contract exceeds the price of the underlying security or the excess of the market price to its fair or theoretical value.

Primary market	The normal market for trading in an instrument underlying a futures or options contract.
Put option	The right (but not the obligation) to sell an agreed amount of an underlying instrument within a specific time period or at a specific time at an agreed price. The writer of the contract is obliged to receive and pay for the instrument at the strike price.
Reversion	The simultaneous sale of a security, sale of a put and purchase of a call with the same strike price and expiry date, to achieve a risk-free arbitrage transaction.
Rho	A statistical measure of the sensitivity of the price of an option to movements in market interest rates, generally applied to fixed-interest options and futures contracts.
Rolling-up/-down	Rolling-up is the closing out of an option position at a lower strike and the opening of an option with a higher strike price. The reverse holds true for rolling-down.
Roll-over	The movement of a futures or options position from one expiry month to another; involving the purchase (or sale) of one month and the sale (or purchase) of a further out expiry month.
Round trip	The opening purchase (or sale) of a future or option and the subsequent opposite and closing transaction in the same contract.
SEC	The Securities & Exchange Commission – the regulatory body for the securities and securities option markets in the USA.
Secondary market	The market where instruments may be traded after their initial public issue.
Series	All option contracts on the same instrument with the same delivery (expiry) date, the same strike price and the same unit of trading. Put options and call options with the same strike price and same delivery (strike) date are two different series.
Settlement price	The delivery price of a futures contract upon expiry. In the case of options the settlement price is the strike price.

Short	The writer (or seller) of an options contract or the opening sale of a futures contract.
Sigma	The statistical measure of volatility of the instrument underlying a futures or options contract.
Spread	A combination of both long and short options or futures positions on the same instrument. There are many different alternative spread strategies available through traded options, some of which are discussed further in this glossary. In the futures market, only calendar (horizontal) spreads are available.
Spread margin	Generally a concessionary reduced rate of margin requirement to holders of reduced-risk spread positions in the futures or options markets.
Straddle	A simultaneous trade in the same direction in both the put and call option with the same strike price and the same expiry date.
Strangle	The simultaneous trade in an in-the-money put and an in-the-money call, both in the same direction.
Strap	An option combination consisting of a ratio of two calls to one put, all in the same direction and each with the same strike price and expiry date.
Strike price	See *Exercise price*.
Strip	An option combination consisting of a ratio of two puts to one call, all in the same direction and each with the same strike price and expiry date.
Systematic risk	The risk inherent in a market average, e.g. interest rates, the political environment, etc.
Tail	The adjustment made to the number of contracts used in a hedge transaction to streamline its efficacy, when making allowances for positive and negative margin flow.
Technical analysis	The analytical interpretation of market behaviour and price trends using charting methods.
Theoretical value	The mathematically calculated value of the price of a futures contract or the 'fair value' premium of an option based on recognisable valuation methods, e.g. Black & Scholes, Bird & Henfrey, etc. (See also *Fair value basis*.)
Tick	The smallest incremental move in a futures or option contract, also known as a basis point.
Time spread	See *Vertical spread*.

Time value	The amount of an option's premium that pertains to the remaining life of the option. The longer the life of the option, the higher the time value element of the premium. If the option is out-of-the-money, all the premium will be time value.
Traded option	See *Call option* and *Put option*.
Traditional option	A non-standardised option with regard to contract size and expiry dates (also referred to as an OTC or conventional option). Generally the option may only be exercised or allowed to lapse, rather than trade out during its life.
Uncovered/naked	A writer (seller) of an option that is not covered by an opposite or spread position elsewhere.
Unsystematic risk	The risk associated with individual elements of an index, for example. This will include such factors as a company's profitability, earnings, etc.
Variation margin	The 'top-up' margin required to maintain or boost the initial 'good faith' deposit upon adverse movements in a futures or options position.
Vega	The statistical measure of the change of an option premium to changes in volatility of the underlying instrument.
Vertical spread	The descriptive term of an option spread transaction between different strike prices for the same delivery. This may use either puts or calls to create a bear or bull spread. (See also *Bull spread* and *Bear spread*.)
Volatility	The statistical measurement of the variation of the price of a primary instrument to movements in the wider market over a period. This is statistically better known as the standard deviation.
Warrant	A derivative product with the right attached to subscribe for the underlying instrument at a specified date or within a specified period, at an agreed price and ratio. Generally warrants have a longer life than an option, and upon subscription new shares may be issued to satisfy the warrant holders.
Writer	The seller of an options contract, obliging himself to make delivery in the case of call options (or take delivery in the case of put options) of the underlying instrument upon notification of the buyer (holder) of that option.

Main alphabetical index

This index lists all the products covered in this directory alphabetically and then by exchange and product type.

Product	Exchange	Opt/Fut	Category	Page
Woollen yarn	NTE	Futures	Softs & agricultural	4/50
Woollen yarn	OTE	Futures	Softs & agricultural	4/71
Woollen yarn	TOCOM	Futures	Softs & agricultural	4/78
World white sugar	CSCE	Futures	Softs & agricultural	12/100

Alphabetical index of exchanges

Index according to category and product type

This directory has taken the following sub-types for classification of the 500 futures and options contracts traded on the 80 exchanges surveyed:

Category	Product type
Futures	Base metals
Options on futures	Currencies (exchange rates)
Options on cash/physical	Energy, oil & gas
	Interest rates
	Miscellaneous
	Precious metals
	Softs & agricultural
	Stock indices

This index section shows the breakdown of these product types and categories.

Regional index of exchanges and their products

This index lists all the products covered in this directory initially by time zone:
1. Asia and Australasia
2. The Americas
3. Europe,

and within time zone, by country and exchange.

Product	Opt/Fut	Category	Page
AUSTRALASIA AND ASIA – AUSTRALIA			
ASX Futures Market (ASX)			
Australian Gold Stock Index	Futures	Stock indices	1/5
AOM Twenty Leaders Stock Index	Futures	Stock indices	1/5
Australian Options Market (AOM)			
AOM Twenty Leaders Stock Index	Opt-C/P	Stock indices	1/6
Gold (IOCC gold bullion)	Opt-C/P	Precious metals	1/6
Silver (IOCC silver bullion)	Opt-C/P	Precious metals	1/7
Sydney Futures Exchange (SFX)			
All Ordinaries Share Price Index	Futures	Stock indices	1/12
Australian dollar / US dollar currency	Futures	Currencies	1/12
Five year semi-Government Bond	Futures	Interest rates	1/13
Greasy Wool	Futures	Softs & agricultural	1/14
Live cattle	Futures	Softs & agricultural	1/14
90-day Bank Accepted Bills	Futures	Interest rates	1/15
10-year Commonwealth Treasury Bond	Futures	Interest rates	1/16
Three-year Commonwealth Treasury Bond	Futures	Interest rates	1/16
All Ordinaries Share Price Index future	Opt-Fut	Stock indices	1/17
Australian dollar / US dollar currency future	Opt-Fut	Currencies	1/18
Five-year Semi-Government Treasury Bond future	Opt-Fut	Interest rates	1/19
90-day Bank Accepted Bank Bills future	Opt-Fut	Interest rates	1/20
10-year Commonwealth Treasury Bond future	Opt-Fut	Interest rates	1/20
Three-year Commonwealth Treasury Bond future	Opt-Fut	Interest rates	1/21
AUSTRALASIA AND ASIA – HONG KONG			
Hong Kong Futures Exchange Ltd (HKFE)			
Gold	Futures	Precious metals	2/5
Hang Seng Stock Index	Futures	Stock indices	2/5
Soyabeans	Futures	Softs & agricultural	2/6
Raw sugar	Futures	Softs & agricultural	2/7
AUSTRALASIA AND ASIA – INDONESIA			
Indonesian Commodity Exchange Board (ICEB)			
Coffee (Robusta) – planned	Futures	Softs & agricultural	3/4
Rubber (SIR) – planned	Futures	Softs & agricultural	3/4
Rubber (RSS) – planned	Futures	Softs & agricultural	3/5
AUSTRALASIA & ASIA – JAPAN			
Hokkaido Grain Exchange (HGE)			
Potato starch	Futures	Softs & agricultural	4/7
Red beans	Futures	Softs & agricultural	4/7
Soyabeans (domestic)	Futures	Softs & agricultural	4/8
Soyabeans (imported)	Futures	Softs & agricultural	4/8
White beans	Futures	Softs & agricultural	4/9

Product	Opt/Fut	Category	Page	Regional index of exchanges and their products

Product	Opt/Fut	Category	Page
THE AMERICAS – USA (continued)			
Pacific Stock Exchange (PSE)			
FNN Composite Stock Index	Opt-C/P	Stock indices	12/175
Twin Cities Board of Trade (TCBOT)			
British pound / Deutschmark currency	Futures	Currencies	12/178
Dynamic Randon Access Memory (DRAM) Chips	Futures	Miscellaneous	12/178
EUROPE – DENMARK			
Copenhagen Stock Exchange (CSE)			
Danish Treasury Bond Basket	Futures	Interest rates	13/5
KFX Stock Index (*planned*)	Futures	Stock indices	13/5
Long Danish (FUTOP) Bond Index	Futures	Interest rates	13/6
9% 2006 annuity Mortgage Credit Bond	Futures	Interest rates	13/7
9% 2006 annuity Mortgage Credit Bond	Opt-C/P	Interest rates	13/7
Danish Treasury Bond Basket	Opt-C/P	Interest rates	13/8
KFX Stock Index (*planned*)	Opt-C/P	Stock indices	13/9
Long Danish (FUTOP) Bond Index	Opt-C/P	Interest rates	13/10
EUROPE – EIRE			
Irish Futures & Options Exchange (IFOX)			
Irish punt / US dollar currency	Futures	Currencies	14/4
Long-term (20-year) Irish Government Bonds	Futures	Interest rates	14/4
Three-month DIBOR interest rate	Futures	Interest rates	14/5
EUROPE – FINLAND			
Finnish Options Brokers (FOB)			
Finnish Stock Options Index (FOX)	Futures	Stock indices	15/5
Finnish Stock Options Index (FOX)	Opt-C/P	Stock indices	15/5
EUROPE – FRANCE			
Marché à Terme International de France (MATIF)			
CAC 40 Stock Index	Futures	Stock indices	16/5
Cocoa beans	Futures	Softs & agricultural	16/5
Long-term notional French Government Treasury Bond	Futures	Interest rates	16/6
Robusta coffee	Futures	Softs & agricultural	16/6
Three-month Euro-Deutschmark interest rate	Futures	Interest rates	16/7
Three-month PIBOR interest rate	Futures	Interest rates	16/8
White sugar	Futures	Softs & agricultural	16/8
Long-term notional French Government Treasury Bond future	Opt-Fut	Interest rates	16/9
White sugar future	Opt-Fut	Softs & agricultural	16/10
Marché à Terme de la Pomme de Terre de Lille (LPM)			
Potatoes No. 1	Futures	Softs & agricultural	16/12
Potatoes No. 2	Futures	Softs & agricultural	16/12
Marché des Options Négociables de la Bourse de Paris (MONEP)			
CAC 40 Stock Index	Opt-C/P	Stock indices	16/14
OM France (OM-F)			
Four-year BTAN (French Treasury Notes)	Futures	Interest rates	16/17
EUROPE – GERMANY			
Deutsche Terminboerse GmbH (DTB)			
German Stock Index (DAX) (*planned*)	Futures	Stock indices	17/5
Notional German Government Treasury Bond (*planned*)	Futures	Interest rates	17/5

Product	Opt/Fut	Category	Page

EUROPE – UNITED KINGDOM (continued)

London Meat Futures Market (LMFM)

Product	Opt/Fut	Category	Page
Live cattle	Futures	Softs & agricultural	23/9
Pigs (live hogs)	Futures	Softs & agricultural	23/9

London Potato Futures Market (LPFM)

Product	Opt/Fut	Category	Page
Potatoes (cash)	Futures	Softs & agricultural	23/10
Potatoes (deliverable)	Futures	Softs & agricultural	23/10
Potatoes (deliverable) future	Opt-Fut	Softs & agricultural	23/13

Soyabean Meal Futures Market (SMFM)

Product	Opt/Fut	Category	Page
Soyabean meal	Futures	Softs & agricultural	23/11

International Petroleum Exchange (IPE)

Product	Opt/Fut	Category	Page
Brent crude oil	Futures	Energy, oil & gas	23/17
Gas oil	Futures	Energy, oil & gas	23/17
Heavy fuel oil (*planned*)	Futures	Energy, oil & gas	23/18
Brent crude oil future	Opt-Fut	Energy, oil & gas	23/19
Gas oil future	Opt-Fut	Energy, oil & gas	23/19

London FOX (FOX)

Product	Opt/Fut	Category	Page
No. 5 white sugar	Futures	Softs & agricultural	23/23
No. 7 cocoa	Futures	Softs & agricultural	23/23
No. 6 raw sugar	Futures	Softs & agricultural	23/24
Robusta coffee	Futures	Softs & agricultural	23/24
Rubber (*planned*)	Futures	Softs & agricultural	23/21
No. 5 white sugar future	Opt-Fut	Softs & agricultural	23/25
No. 7 cocoa future	Opt-Fut	Softs & agricultural	23/27
No. 6 raw sugar future	Opt-Fut	Softs & agricultural	23/27
Robusta coffee future	Opt-Fut	Softs & agricultural	23/27

London International Financial Futures Exchange (LIFFE)

Product	Opt/Fut	Category	Page
Deutschmark / US dollar currency	Futures	Currencies	23/32
FT-SE 100 Stock Index	Futures	Stock indices	23/32
German Government (Bund) Bond	Futures	Interest rates	23/33
Japanese Government Bond	Futures	Interest rates	23/33
Japanese yen / US dollar currency	Futures	Currencies	23/34
Long gilt	Futures	Interest rates	23/35
Medium gilt	Futures	Interest rates	23/35
Short gilt	Futures	Interest rates	23/36
Swiss franc / US dollar currency	Futures	Currencies	23/37
Three-month ECU interest rate	Futures	Interest rates	23/38
Three-month Euro-Deutschmark interest rate	Futures	Interest rates	23/37
Three-month Eurodollar interest rate	Futures	Interest rates	23/38
Three-month sterling interest rate	Futures	Interest rates	23/39
US dollar / Deutschmark currency	Futures	Currencies	23/40
US dollar / sterling currency	Futures	Currencies	23/40
US Government Treasury Bond	Futures	Interest rates	23/41
German Government (Bund) Bond future	Opt-Fut	Interest rates	23/41
Long gilt future	Opt-Fut	Interest rates	23/42
Three-month Eurodollar interest rate future	Opt-Fut	Interest rates	23/43
Three-month sterling interest rate future	Opt-Fut	Interest rates	23/44
US Government Treasury Bond future	Opt-Fut	Interest rates	23/45
US dollar / Deutschmark currency	Opt-C/P	Currencies	23/46
US dollar / sterling currency	Opt-C/P	Currencies	23/47

London Metal Exchange (LME)

Product	Opt/Fut	Category	Page
Copper Grade A	Futures	Base metals	23/51
High-grade (99.7%) aluminium	Futures	Base metals	23/51
High-grade (99.95%) zinc	Futures	Base metals	23/52
Nickel	Futures	Base metals	23/53
Special high-grade (99.995%) zinc	Futures	Base metals	23/53